D1084352

SATIRES OF ROME

This book sets out to locate Roman satire's most salient possibilities and effects at the center of every Roman reader's cultural and political self-understanding, by describing the genre's numerous shifts in focus and tone over several centuries (from Lucilius to Juvenal) not as mere "generic adjustments" that reflect the personal preferences of its authors, but as separate chapters in a special, generically encoded story of Rome's lost, and much lionized, Republican identity. Freedom exists in performance in ancient Rome: it is a "spoken" entity. As a result, satire's programmatic shifts, from "open," to "understated," to "cryptic," and so on, can never be purely "literary" and "apolitical" in focus and/or tone. In *Satires of Rome*, Professor Freudenburg reads these shifts as the genre's unique way of staging and agonizing over a crisis in Roman identity. Satire's standard "genre question" in this book becomes a question of the Roman self.

KIRK FREUDENBURG is Professor of Greek and Latin at Ohio State University. He received his doctorate from the University of Wisconsin and has previously taught at Kent State University. He has published widely on Latin literature and is the author of *The Walking Muse: Horace on the Theory of Satire* (Princeton, 1993). He is currently editing *The Cambridge Companion to Roman Satire* and Book II of Horace's *Sermones* for the Cambridge Greek and Latin Classics series.

SATIRES OF ROME

Threatening poses from Lucilius to Juvenal

KIRK FREUDENBURG

Professor of Greek and Latin, Ohio State University

PUBLISHED BY THE PRESS SYNDICATE OF THE UNIVERSITY OF CAMBRIDGE
The Pitt Building, Trumpington Street, Cambridge, United Kingdom

CAMBRIDGE UNIVERSITY PRESS
The Edinburgh Building, Cambridge CB2 2RU, UK
40 West 20th Street, New York NY 10011-4211, USA
10 Stamford Road, Oakleigh, VIC 3166, Australia
Ruiz de Alarcón 13, 28014, Madrid, Spain
Dock House, The Waterfront, Cape Town 8001, South Africa

http://www.cambridge.org

First published 2001

Printed in the United Kingdom at the University Press, Cambridge

Typeset in Baskerville and New Hellenic Greek [AO]

A catalogue record for this book is available from the British Library

Library of Congress Cataloguing in Publication data
Freudenburg, Kirk
Satires of Rome: threatening poses from Lucilius to Juvenal / by Kirk Freudenburg.
p.   cm
Includes bibliographical references and index.
ISBN 0 521 80357 8 (hardback) ISBN 0 521 00621 X (paperback)
1. Verse satire, Latin–History and criticism. 2. Lucilius, Gaius, ca. 180–ca. 102
B.C.–Criticism and interpretation. 3. Persius–Criticism and interpretation.
4. Juvenal–Criticism and interpretation. 5. Horace–Criticism and interpretation.
6. Rome–In literature. I. Title
PA6056 .F74   2001
871'.0109—dc21
2001025772

ISBN 0 521 80357 8 hardback
ISBN 0 521 00621 X paperback

For my parents, Victor and Delores Freudenburg,
with love and appreciation

Contents

Acknowledgments   *Page* ix
Key dates for the study of Roman verse satire   xii
Glossary of key names and technical terms   xv

Introduction   1

1 Horace   15
   The diatribe satires (*Sermones* 1.1–1.3): "You're no Lucilius"   15
   Sermones book 1 and the problem of genre   23
   Remembered voices: satire made new in *Sermones* 1.1   27
   The social poetics of Horatian *libertas*: since when is "enough" a
     "feast"?   44
   Hitting satire's *finis*: along for the ride in *Sermones* 1.5   51
   Dogged by ambition: *Sermones* 1.6–10   58
   Book 2 and the totalitarian squeeze: new rules for a New Age   71
   Panegyric bluster and Ennius' *Scipio* in Horace, *Sermones* 2.1 82
   Coming to terms with Scipio: the new look of post-Actian satire   93
   Big friends and bravado in *Sermones* 2.1   100
   Book 2 and the hissings of compliance   108
   Nasidienus' dinner-party: too much of not enough   117

2 Persius   125
   Of narrative and cosmogony: Persius and the invention of Nero   125
   The Prologue: top-down aesthetics and the making of oneself   134
   Faking it in Nero's orgasmatron: Persius 1 and the death of
     criticism   151
   The satirist-physician and his out-of-joint world   173
   Satire's lean feast: finding a lost "pile" in P. 2   183
   Teaching and tail-wagging, critique as crutch: P. 4   189
   Left for broke: satire as legacy in P. 6   195

3 Juvenal   209
   A lost voice found: Juvenal and the poetics of too much, too late 209

vii

Remembered monsters: time warp and martyr tales in Trajan's
  Rome   215
Ghost-assault in Juv. 1   234
The poor man's Lucilius   242
Life on the edge: from exaggeration to self-defeat   248
Beating a dead fish: the emperor-satirist of Juv. 4   258
Satires 3 and 5: the poor man's lunch of Umbricius and Trebius 264

List of works cited   278
General index   285

Acknowledgments

Thanks are many for a project so long in the tooth. The first urges to write this book were stirred at the Institute for Research in the Humanities at the University of Wisconsin, Madison. There I had been commissioned to write something altogether different (a commentary, still in the works) as one of two inaugural Solmsen Fellows for the academic year 1994–5. But the old lunch crowd there, egged on especially by my fellow Solmsen, Christopher Rowe (taking no sugar whatsoever in his cappuccino), challenged me to think bigger thoughts than I had been thinking. And so I undertook to write this book instead.

Many have read the book in draft. Others have been subjected to its basic notions in lecture form. Horace had the decency to save his "take a look at my high-powered friends" list for the last lines of his first book (and I'll bore you with that in chapter 1). But convention dictates that I pre-impress you right here with mine – and make no mistake, these acknowledgments are always about the business of getting you properly impressed. I am especially grateful to audiences at the University of Basel, UCLA, Baylor University, the University of Bristol, the Cambridge Greek and Latin Seminar, and Durham University for their helpful responses to my Juvenal chapter when it was in bud. Tony Woodman, *qui cogere posset*, opened my eyes to many matters of crucial importance during my days "in the tower" at Durham castle, and he has followed up his conversations with helpful written advice. Denis Feeney changed entirely the way I think about Horace with a few deft strokes in my margins. Michael Putnam pushed hard for a better intertextual reckoning of Virgil in my analysis of Horace's early works. I am most grateful for his insights. Charles Martindale provided comments from start to finish that helped "balance" the book into its several parts. The final product is much better for his hard work. Alessandro Barchiesi provided scores of incisive comments, besides a number of bibliographical suggestions that proved invaluable, saving me much embarrassment. His enthusiasm for the book (because it is *his*) has been most heartening. Andrea Cucchiarelli did me the great favour of both commenting on my manuscript, and allowing me to read his own forthcoming work, thus doubling my debt to him. Tom McGinn kept me from legal trouble in chapter 1, and Emily Gowers carefully read the book in one of its last revisions, leaving me to revise what I could one last time. She is thus to be thanked not only for writing her stellar *The Loaded Table*, but for giving me the benefit of her proven expertise on satire. Also to be thanked for generous insights are the book's anonymous readers for Cambridge University Press. They know who they are. And I think I do, too.

Now to my most indefatigable readers, those who subjected themselves to a second reading of the entire work. When Daniel Hooley first got a hold of this book he caught me spelling Persius with an "e" (Perseus). That will give you some measure of just how far he had to lead me along my journey's yellow brick road, and how patient he has been with me from the start. I hope to have repaid him, my Scarecrow, in some small measure, by letting you know in the course of this book just how brainy his soft-spoken work on Pers-i-us really is. John Henderson, the Wizard himself, needs no stamp of approval from me, and I certainly know better than to try to thank him publicly, and in such a respectable venue as this. He would be the first to tell you to pay no attention to that man behind the curtain, and to insist that such thanks can never be as much about him as they have to be about me. And he's right. That said, I leave it to my readers to judge just how much his diagnostic wizardry has electrified my thinking and (it is hoped) this book's every page.

Penultimate thanks go to my home Department of Greek and Latin at the Ohio State University for taking a chance on me, and encouraging me to be myself, when no other university dared, and to Ohio State's very fine Humanities College for always supporting my research in full. In the end, this book is much better for its having been penned at Ohio State, among colleagues both encouraging and smart.

Pauline Hire encouraged this project at an early stage. Now freshly retired, she deserves not just my heartfelt thanks for what she has done for me, but something much more (a conference in her honor, in Kathmandu) for playing the leading role in promoting "New Latin" studies at Cambridge University Press for the past twenty years. Michael Sharp has taken over from her in a manner that suggests the Press will be well served for many years to come. I thank him for his continued encouragement, his attention to detail, and, especially, for his letting me get away with what you are about to read.

Key dates for the study of Roman verse satire

ca. 440 – ca. 405 BCE   The floruit of Greek Old Comedy (Eupolis, Cratinus, Aristophanes)

ca. 404 – ca. 321   Period of Greek Middle Comedy

ca. 320 – ca. 250   Period of Greek New Comedy (esp. Menander)

ca. 315   Bion of Borysthenes arrives in Athens; active as lecturer until ca. 245

ca. 205–184   Plautus writes Greek-style comedies (*fabulae palliatae*) for the Roman stage

204–169   Quintus Ennius active in Rome as playwright, writer of panegyric epic, and *Saturae*

166–159   Terence writes Greek-style comedies for the Roman stage

134–133   Lucilius serves under P. Cornelius Scipio Aemilianus at the siege of Numantia; thereafter writes 30 books of *Saturae* in Rome ca. 129 – ca. 101

81–67   M. Terentius Varro writes 150 books of satires in the manner of Menippus of Gadara (early third century)

65   Horace born on 8 December in Venusia

42   Horace serves as military tribune under Brutus at the Battle of Philippi

37   Pact of Tarentum renews détente between Octavian and Antony

35   Horace publishes book 1 of his *Sermones*

31   Battle of Actium (2 September). Antony defeated

30   Horace publishes book 2 of his *Sermones*

27   Octavian named "Augustus" by the Roman Senate

23 Horace publishes books 1–3 of his *Carmina*

19 Horace publishes book 1 of his *Epistles*

8 Horace dies on 27 November

14 CE Death of Augustus, succession of Tiberius

14–37 Reign of Tiberius

34 Persius (Aules Persius Flaccus) born to rich, Etruscan parents

37–41 Reign of Gaius (Caligula)

41–54 Reign of Claudius

54 Accession of Nero. The deification of Claudius satirized in Seneca's *Apocolocyntosis*

59 Death of Agrippina. Nero performs on stage at the *Juvenalia*

ca. 60–2 Persius active as a writer of *Satires*. The collection is edited and published after his death, late in 62

68 Suicide of Nero

69 Civil wars. Year of the Four Emperors

69–81 Flavian period commences: reigns of Vespasian and Titus

81–96 Reign of Domitian. Floruit of Statius and Martial

85 Domitian named *censor perpetuus*

93 Death of Agricola. Domitian pursues "Stoic opposition": the Younger Helvidius, Aurulenus Rusticus, and Herennius Senecio executed

96 Domitian murdered in a palace coup, 18 September. Accession of Nerva

97 Tacitus suffect consul. Pliny attacks Certus, prosecutor of Helvidius

98 Death of Nerva. Accession of Trajan (January). Tacitus publishes his *Agricola*. Pliny and Tacitus prosecute Marius Priscus

100 Pliny takes up consulship for September and October; writes his *Panegyricus*

ca. 99–109 Pliny publishes books 1–9 of his *Letters*

ca. 100 – ca. 130 Juvenal writes satires in five books

ca. 105–106 Tacitus collecting material for his *Histories*

ca. 116 Tacitus publishes first book(s) of the *Annales*

117 Death of Trajan. Accession of Hadrian

late second century Helenius Acro writes commentary on Horace

early third century Pomponius Porphyrio writes commentary on Horace

Glossary of key names and technical terms

Actium a bay in northwest Greece where Octavian defeated Antony in 31 BCE

adsentator "flatterer"

Bion Cynic street-preacher (a proto-"satirist") of the late fourth/early third century BCE

Bona Dea lit. "Good Goddess," an Italian deity whose annual rites in Rome were presided over exclusively by women

Callimachean exhibiting the "refined" and "scholarly" tastes of Callimachus, Alexandrian poet of the third century BCE

carmen maledicum "hostile song"

cena a formal, evening dinner-party in Rome

censor an elected Roman magistrate in charge of public morals, the keeping of citizen-lists, and regulating membership of the Senate

choliambic the "limping iambic" meter of Hipponax (late sixth century BCE)

Chrysippus third-century-BCE head of the Stoa and ardent shaper and defender of Stoic orthodoxy

consul the title of Rome's chief civil and military magistrates during the Republic. Two consuls were elected annually

conuiua "dinner-guest"

crux (**pl.** *cruces*) a difficult, "tortured" passage (lit. a "cross") that defies interpretation

Cynic an aggressively anti-social, primitivist (lit. "dog-like") beggar-philosopher in the tradition of Diogenes (fourth century BCE)

deductum carmen a "finely-spun song" in the manner of Callimachus

descriptio a highly contrived "scene-painting" in words, designed to arouse pity and/or indignation

diatribe an informal "street-sermon" in the manner of Bion (above)

eques "horseman," a member of the "equestrian order," the status group immediately below the "senatorial order"

farrago "horse-feed," Juvenal's metaphor for (his own) low-grade satire

fautores Lucili "fans/patrons of Lucilius," critics of Horace in book i of his *Sermones*

finis "end/limit," a watchword of Epicurean moderation

genus a term meaning literary "genre" as well as social "class"

hexameter the six-foot (monostichic) metrical scheme of epic and formal verse satire

homoioteleuton ending consecutive words with similar "rhyming" sounds

iambic the basic short–long meter (in numerous schemes) of Greek and Roman iambic poetry (e.g. Archilochus, Lucilius), tragedy, and comedy

incessus the formal, parade-like "entrance" of a Roman aristocrat into the city

indignatio rage that stems from a lack of due honor (a sense of being "undeservedly" abused)

iunctura a figurative expression that derives from the "joining" of mismatched words and/or ideas

katabasis an epic hero's "descent" into the underworld

lanx satura a "plate stuffed full" to overflowing, satire's most prominent symbol in the ancient world

libertas "freedom / freedom of speech"

Lucilianus modus the "Lucilian manner" of acerbic and uncompromised free speech

Maecenas from the early 30s to 23 BCE he was Octavian's right-hand man in Rome, famous for his generous patronage of Virgil, Horace, and Propertius

modus "limit/measure," a favorite watchword of Horace's political and stylistic discretion

neoteric in the manner of Rome's "new poets" (especially Calvus and Catullus)

nota the censor's "mark" branding bad morals and removing one from the Senate

Octavian adopted son of Julius Caesar, later named Augustus by the Roman Senate

Old Comedy the openly political, fantastical comedies of Aristophanes, Eupolis, and Cratinus (Athens, fifth century BCE)

Palatine Rome's augural hill, site of a temple to Apollo and the emperor's private homes (whence English "palace")

parabasis in an Old Comic play, an interlude where the play's lead actors "step aside," allowing the chorus to address the audience on matters of topical (often literary-critical) import

parasite in Greek and Roman New Comedy, a hungry, bankrupt nobleman who wheedles and connives to satisfy his high-class tastes

Parnassus Apollo's holy mountain in north-central Greece, famous for the shrine of Delphi on its south slope

patella "small plate," a symbol of satire opposed to the larger *lanx* (above)

praescriptio a written "preface" defining the scope of a lawsuit

praeteritio a rhetorical device that touches on certain persons and/or topics by promising to leave them unmentioned

praetor one of several Roman magistrates in charge of the city's legal and financial affairs and the administration of the courts

princeps senatus a leading figure (lit. "first man") in the Roman Senate

recusatio a poet's stylized "refusal" to sing of a great man's (especially military) achievements in epic song

sapiens the ideal "wise man" of the Stoics

satis adverb meaning "enough," attached to "satire" by a false etymology

satur the root word (lit. "stuffed full," cf. *lanx* above) behind most ancient etymologies of "satire"

scholiasts ancient grammarians, both Greek and Latin, who wrote commentaries (often in the margins of texts) on the works of "classical" authors

Second Triumvirate the coalition of "three men" (Octavian, Antony, Lepidus) that ruled Rome from 43 to 36 BCE, subsequently giving way to a temporary détente between Antony and Octavian (36–31 BCE)

semipaganus "half-rustic," a key term in Persius' self-description

sermo "talk." Horace uses the pl. *sermones* ("talks") of his satires

soros the Stoic "grain-pile" paradox that poses the puzzle: "When does a pile become a pile?"

subscriptio the formal, written specification of crimes in an indictment

telos "end/goal" (pl. *tele*)

triuium a bustling intersection of three roads in downtown Rome

ubertas stylistic "richness"

umbra lit. "shadow," an uninvited tag-along guest at a Roman banquet

Vestal Virgin one of six virgin priestesses of Vesta, goddess of the Roman hearth, in charge of tending the goddess's "undying fire" in the Roman Forum

Vita a poet's biography attached as a preface to ancient commentaries

Introduction

The central question put to Roman satire has always been "What is it?" Since antiquity scholars have struggled to identify that solid "something" beneath the shifting surfaces of Ennius, Lucilius, Horace, Persius, and Juvenal (works not of Roman satire generally, but of "verse satire," and with the most prolific of these, Lucilius, now only a smattering of fragments, and the first, Ennius, much slighter still) that would allow us to contain the stunning variety of their works by means of a single, streamlined generic formula.[1] But their best attempts to control the mess have managed only to tell us that the genre's failure to hold together *is* its zero-grade, and its best way of constituting itself as a genre. Their many metaphors for satire, whether of "stuffing," "mish-mash," "heaps," or "overloaded plates," all manage to tell us only that this is a hybrid, blow-out feast, an "anti-genre," where anything goes, so we had better be prepared to "open wide." Their favorite metaphor, that of a "stuffed plate" (*lanx satura*) heaped high with a variety of foodstuffs, spilling over its edges, is less a description of the genre's salient qualities than it is an admission of defeat, and an expression of the scholar's own frustration in trying to contain satire inside the narrow confines of a too-specific generic formula. Failing to plumb the works of Roman verse satire down to that rock-hard, streamlined core (because "it" is not there), scholars have been forced simply to heap these works *en masse* onto a single generic plate (an impressive *lanx*, and no mere *patella*) and to call that plate "satire."[2] Once crammed with the full enormity of what

---

[1] Having mentioned Ennius here, I must abruptly leave him behind, unstudied. The remains of his 4 books of satires are so slight that very little of real use can be adduced from them.

[2] These works are thus "satire" because "on the plate," and not "on the plate" because "satire."

we automatically "count" as satire because that is what Lucilius, Horace, Persius, and Juvenal told us they were writing, the plate spills over, defying our efforts to neatly categorize and contain the works we have heaped it with.

But the problem "What is satire?" has embarrassed not only professional scholars since antiquity. It was there to be wrestled with, and staged as a problem of writing, by the ancient satirists themselves. They take on that problem well before the grammarians step in with their commentary solutions, and they treat it in great detail, performing their attention to it for as long as satire is written in Rome. We can no longer determine what Lucilius' audiences may have expected from his poems by finding Ennius' title, "satires," atop his page. But we can be quite sure that Lucilius did not give them what they expected. The shift from Lucilius to Horace is, by all accounts, and especially by Horace's own, equally abrupt and disorienting, to be repeated again in the transition from Horace to Persius, and, wildest of them all, the last, from Persius to Juvenal. But the fact that each of these satirists seems free to turn his work in whatever bold new direction he likes should not lead us to assume that the genre's demands are slight (mere "friendly suggestions"), or that the stakes of their making these changes are either inconsequential, or precisely the same for each new satirist down the road. Far from it. By Horace's day, the stakes of changing satire are much larger than they ever could have been for Lucilius. For it was taken as gospel by many in Horace's audience that satire had reached its *telos* already a century before, with Lucilius, in his massive thirty books of *Saturae*. Horace's problem, as he puts it in his *Sermones* (not even calling them "satires"), is not that his audiences have no clear sense of what to expect from him. It is that they expect him to write satire just the way Lucilius, *their* Lucilius, had written it; or, better in Horace's particular case, not at all. For them, Lucilius is an unassailable classic, not to be tampered with.

Horace pokes fun at these "Lucilius fans" in his poems, putting on them the onus of his elaborately drawn out paranoia at undertaking to improve upon *their* icon. But the pressure they apply, I hope to show, is more than a clever fiction that plays within a few chiding poems where the satirist's "Lucilius problem" is taken up as an explicit theme (1.4, 1.10, and 2.1). Its influence broods over the entire work, heard in the curiously soft voice that issues from the *Sermones*' every page. For this is a voice that does not simply raise the problem of Lucilius from time to time. It is a voice that is itself an elaborately performed side-effect of that problem, and thus always expressive of it.

But Horace's critics, we shall see, are extremely persistent. They are not done away with easily, or at all, by Horace's two books of *Sermones*. Being brushed aside was not the point of their being there to begin with. Rather, they remain a nagging source of pressure, and a way of seeing the satirists' respective efforts at "satire," throughout the history of the genre. Each satirist after Horace recasts his Lucilius problem as theirs, too, to solve, because each steps into a generic arena where he is once again challenged to speak like Lucilius. But none does. Instead, every writer of satire after Lucilius fights a losing battle against him, and by trying to fight it, they perform the activity of their losing it. Without question, Lucilius remains this genre's inventor and most celebrated practitioner in antiquity. Not Horace. Not Juvenal. And certainly not Persius. Studying Roman satire is thus comparable to being left the full epic output of Ovid, Statius, and Lucan, with only the merest scraps of Virgil to help us reckon with what their works mean. But Virgil, we know, is not just "back there" for these poets, and incidentally "referred to" by them from time to time. He is an ever-present pressure put on them, and always at the heart of "how" they mean. So, too Lucilius, in the sphere of satire.

It is my intention with this book to draw the study of Roman satire out from the shadowy margins of Roman literary history, where it is usually put, by locating its most salient possibilities and effects at the center of every Roman reader's cultural and political self-understanding. To do this I set out to describe the genre's numerous shifts in focus and tone over several centuries (from Lucilius in the second century BCE to Juvenal in the second century CE) not as mere "generic adjustments" that reflect the personal preferences of its authors, but as separate chapters in a special, generically encoded story of Rome's lost, and much lionized, Republican identity, an identity that was heavily influenced, and emblematized, by Lucilius. Satire's story can and should be told this way because expectations of aggressive and uncompromised speech are not just built into the genre as its defining, "Lucilian," hallmark, they are a key defining feature of the elite, male self. I begin from a very basic, if not self-evident, premise that *libertas* ("free speech") in Rome is equivalent to, and only ever as good as, one's *libertas* ("freedom"). It cannot be otherwise: freedom "speaks" itself into the Roman ear. It exists in performance, and only there. As a result, satire's programmatic shifts, from "open," to "understated," to "cryptic," and so on, can never be purely "literary" and "apolitical" in focus and/or tone. In the pages that follow, I read these shifts as the genre's unique way of staging and agonizing over a crisis in Roman identity. The "genre question" is a question of the Roman self.

In the vagabond movement from Lucilius, to Horace, to Persius, to Juvenal, we are made to feel, and see deliberately performed before us, the ever-tightening turn of Rome's totalitarian pipe-wrench. In the pages that follow, I argue that "what happens to satire" is not just the story of these several authors' individual generic choices in response to one another, it is the tale of an inherited, "free-speaking," old-Republican enterprise that gets remade radically over time precisely because these authors feel and respond to the increasing pressures of totalitarian oversight. Inherited expectations, as a result, become vehicles for exploring the much bigger issue of "what has happened to us Romans, to our language, and to our once uncompromised freedom now that Lucilius, and all that he stood for, is long dead." This is to give an old "vertical" question, that of the satirists' individual critical responses to one another, a "horizontal" turn, by showing how these responses are both conditioned by, and expressive of, specific pressures felt in the separate political and social worlds that they inhabit. Existing general studies of Roman verse satire tend to do little in this regard, so that is where I hope to have something new to say. For it is all too easy to show how each author accesses and remakes his predecessor's (-s') efforts in generic, programmatic terms – for example, by way of bringing in Callimachus in Horace's case, or Stoicism in Persius', and so on – and to leave it at that. It is much harder to relate these changes to the specific social and political conditions in which the individual authors found themselves working.

The basic outline of the book is conventional, with chapter 1 on Horace, glancing back frequently towards Lucilius and, on rare occasions, towards Ennius. Chapter 2 treats Persius, and chapter 3 Juvenal. I tie these three chapters together "vertically" by looking not only at the standard canon of program poems, where satire's changing ways are explicitly discussed, but at the several poems, or parts of poems, both large and small, where these changes can be tracked from one satirist to the next by means of specific, comparison-inviting imitations. Sometimes these imitations can be traced to something as small as a single metaphor, such as the "talking phallus" of Horace, *S.* 1.2.69–71, or the "dew-dripping eye" of Horace, *Ars* 429–30. That eye becomes something quite shocking in Persius, by way of Lucilius' teary member. Then it becomes something altogether different again in Juvenal, with each subsequent stage of the metaphor's metamorphosis signaling something important about the way that each satirist operates, emblematizing his new purposes and modes of expression. At other times the satirists' imitations are more extensive, as in Horace's lengthy shortening of Lucilius' third book in *S.* 1.5. Among these larger imitations, perhaps the most programmatically telling, because it seems to have been the most widely used, is that of the so-called "consultation dialogue." Horace, *S.* 2.1, we shall see, looks back to Lucilius book 26 (which Horace knew as Lucilius book 1); Persius 1 looks back to both Horace, *S.* 2.1 and Lucilius book 26, and Juvenal 1 looks back to all three. Each author uses the theme of his legal trepidations to both dwell on, and perform, his remaking of his predecessor(s), and to chart out new directions for his own satiric enterprise. Similar lines of influence can be drawn from Horace *S.* 1.1 to Persius 2, and from there to Juvenal's tenth satire, "the vanity of human wishes."

Close analysis of these poems, then, will form the book's elongated spine, to the bare bones of which I hope to add some living flesh by "horizontally" embedding these works within the specific, highly charged social and political contexts that not only shed needed light on where satire's "generic adjustments" come from, but significantly color what they (can) mean. This will involve, if not a comprehensive study of the complete works of Roman verse satire, at least a free-roaming sampling of the poems that I feel best expose the hidden pressures behind each poet's "choosing" to speak the way he speaks. My method for exposing these hidden pressures is to read the poems closely, paying strict attention not only to the social-historical issues that they explicitly raise, but to the implicit political motivations, often quite topical and author-specific, that steer them to express themselves, within a given rhetoric, in certain politically telling ways. The poems of Roman satire, scholars have long recognized, stem from a context where literature is always more than "just literature," because of the roles that poets played in fashioning themselves, and their friends, by means of the poems they wrote. The problems I focus on will thus range from issues of big politics, such as Horace's refusing(?) to write Augustus' big poem, to seemingly small issues of style and self-expression, such as Persius' disdain for phrases that glide with the "liquid" sounds of the letters *l*, *m*, *n*, and *r*. Such aesthetic preferences, we shall see, are never "just personal" in what they express. At times, they are the poet's best means of becoming aggressively political.

These are the kinds of problems that I study in the pages that follow. I propose to treat these problems as meaning-filled entanglements rather than obstructions to meaning. The basic idea for reading this way is Wolfgang Iser's, though the practice of it in this book has much more to do with critical habits observed in John Henderson (especially in his work on Persius) than with reader-response theory *per se*. Along with Iser, I regard the sheer persistence of what he names "the classical norm of interpretation," i.e. demands for balance, closure, unity, and so on, over so many centuries of western criticism (from Aristotle to New Criticism, and beyond) as evidence for certain strong tendencies in the way that readers, of whatever (western) stripe, read, and for the demands that we, with them, habitually put to the poems of Roman satire, and for what we expect them to do for us. Thus, instead of insisting that traditional commentaries are wrong to obsess over the things that they tend to obsess over in their search for clear and stable meanings, I treat these obsessions as evidence for the way(s) that certain works of Roman satire tend to operate upon readers who have set themselves the task of rendering them stable, singularly meaningful, and trouble-free, i.e. acceptable *as expressions of* "the classical aesthetic." That desire to authorize them in that way has something to do not only with our being stubborn and stuck in a long, Aristotelian rut. It has to do with our being stubbornly human (not just stubbornly "western"), and thus afraid of the chaotic and the unknown. We are, at some level, hardwired to make those misguided demands.[3]

---

[3] Iser (1978) 15: "If one recognizes the fact that harmonization is an attempt to grapple with the unknown, then one can more easily understand why classical aesthetics have continued to exercise such influence on the interpretation of art."

I begin my analysis of Roman satire's meaning-filled problems with the first three poems of Horace's first book, his so-called "diatribe satires." These poems, I will argue, fail to live up to their billing as either "diatribe" or "satire" because they are too deeply embedded in, and expressive of, a parasite's-eye-view that does not fit the traditional demands of either genre. The Epicurean philosopher projected from the pages of these poems is glib, addled, and amateurish, not much of a philosopher at all. But neither is he much of a satirist.

And yet, in poems 4 and 5, this speaker stakes a powerful claim to his writing in the tradition of Lucilius. *S.* 1.4 justifies his "refining" Lucilius along Callimachean lines, and *S.* 1.5 lets us hear what his refined product sounds like. In treating these poems I will argue against the great bulk of satire scholarship that makes Horace the clear and easy winner of his battle against Lucilius. Instead I attempt to demonstrate just how impossible it is for Horace to win this battle easily, or at all, especially by making the case he makes. Losing to Lucilius, I believe, not defeating him, is the more telling point. For many in Horace's audience, his toning down of their icon would automatically be heard as a comical, freakish failure to "rank" with Lucilius in the genre he set up to speak quite differently. That, I suggest is exactly what Horace gives them: a comical, freakish performance, played in the role they had written for him. In undertaking to write satire, Horace enters a sphere of expectations where a dispossessed freedman's son and low man at Maecenas' table (constraints put on him by his critics, and by society itself) simply does not belong. Given who he (lets us believe he) is, this satirist is doomed to fail before he starts.

Seeing him struggle there, in satire's arena, unable to hoist Lucilius' long-rusted sword, is the hilarious performance to which we are treated in Horace's two books of *Sermones*. But laughing at him, we shall see, exacts a high price. For although this ambling, apolitical "friend" of the great Maecenas cannot bring himself to speak openly the way Lucilius did, he can still bury a good amount of critical aggression under the surface of his poems. And he does that without stinting. Early in the book, at *S.* 1.1.68–70, he cautions us against laughing too quickly at a miser whose constant grasping at gain likens him to Tantalus tormented in the underworld: "Why are you laughing? Change the name and the story is about you!" The poet catches us here, by deftly interposing a mirror between ourselves and the fool on the page. This is a programmatic warning. "Be careful!" he hints. These poems are loaded with traps.

Proceeding through the remainder of book 1, I test the surface of several poems to see where their traps might hide. What happens, for example, when we laugh too quickly at the shadow character of *S.* 1.9, an interloper, like the witch-hags, Canidia and Sagana in 1.8, fecklessly shooed away by one of Maecenas' scarecrows, Horace. This man wants from Horace only what we want from him, but have never managed to find in his poems. He wants to get close to Maecenas, past the gates of his white-clad mansion, so that he can see what really happens there. He wants to belong. Or perhaps he wants to dig up dead men's bones in his garden, and to stir up their power to torment and curse. Either way, this poet will not take him inside, just as he refuses to take us anywhere close to Maecenas in the poems that precede, especially in *S.* 1.5 where our desire to get close and to know more is a game played on us from beginning to end. Laughing at the fool of *S.* 1.9, we see, exacts a toll, taking us into the dark of the shadows *we* cast.

If we did not happen to find ourselves in the shadow of *S.* 1.9, we have to wonder about our being abruptly hauled off to (lit. crit.) court in the opening lines of the next poem, the book's last, where we are finally bullied into casting a vote in favor of Horace's remaking of Lucilius. There is no finesse in the pleader's final words, only brute force to expose something nasty about us before hustling us abruptly away. In the opening poem of book 2 we find ourselves in Trebatius' back room, preparing for yet another trial, and another book of poems. What will the poet's strategy be this time? Here, however, the satirist lets us know from the start that the poems of this book will be very different. By taking us behind the scenes as eavesdroppers, and away from the public confrontations of book 1, Horace lets us feel the pressures that come with his undertaking to write satire in the nervous first days after Actium. That is the principal caesura that divides book 1 from book 2, a pressure strongly felt in the consultation with Trebatius. Octavian is now watching, Trebatius warns, and he has many grand, new plans for the poets whom he counts as his friends. Virgil is certainly one of them. Will Horace be one, too? If so, how will that friendship express itself *in writing*? Or will it be expressed in "song" (*bona **carmina***, 2.1.82–3), that is, not in satire at all, but in a different "well-meaning" mode (specifically "good" songs, not bad) where expressions of goodwill towards friends of high standing do not cast such a long, parasitic shadow, because they are packaged as Pindaric song rather than satire, and thus fitted to a genre where critical reticence makes sense? The book, as a whole, shows the effects of this pressure. It will find Horace letting others speak for him, even criticizing him for not speaking, as he goes on a private search for other modes of expression, looking for a home that he can finally call "his own" (and not Lucilius'). Finally, in *S.* 2.8, he simply stands up and walks away, leaving us holding the plate.

The traps that ripple across the surface of Horace's easily ambled poems are mere etchings in the pavement compared to the mammoth caverns that break apart the terrain of Persius' *Satires*. There can be no sidestepping the extraordinary difficulty of his poems, or the bitterness of the views they express. Strangely, it is congenial Horace who stands behind much of what Persius has to say. His voice, we shall see, is filtered into Persius' nearly every line, but it is no longer congenial. The memories evoked by this voice are therefore both familiar and terribly disorienting. The honey-rimmed cups and cookies of the kindly doctors, Lucretius and Horace, have given way to a stinging, acidic decoction from Cleanthes' kitchen, to be administered straight and hot, and taken right away. The questions I put to this shift, in my study of Persius' Prologue and P. 1, concern not only the unseen pressures behind this hardening of once-congenial Horace, but the further meaningful effects of Persius' incessant "Augustan" ventriloquism within the milieu of Nero's Augustan revival. What pressures do we imagine constrain this voice, breaking it into bits that sound so grating, bitter, and disillusioned?

The pressure-cooker that reduces Horace to bitter disgust in Persius' poems is Nero's sun-drenched Rome. In the pages below I argue that the heat applied to these poems is Nero himself, the Helio-Apollo of the Palatine, whose innovations in music, literature, and governance, Persius would have us believe, commenced a new Golden Age of style without substance, and a desperate Dark Age for the Roman soul. These reforms, Persius suggests, were all the rage. But they did not penetrate past skin level, down to the inner-heart where real reform happens for this poet, and where true worth can be gauged. So Persius proposes to take us there with his poems, beneath the glossy surface, to show us the ugly underside of cosmetic reforms to Nero's brash new society that is a larger expression of the emperor's egomaniacal self. To get us there, to the very beating heart of Rome, Persius admits to owing a strong debt to Horace, whose ability to take us, his "friends," inside ourselves, by turning our laughter against us as we read, Persius contrasts to the skin-deep, but painful, violence of Lucilius (P. 1.114–18). These programmatic focalizations on his predecessors tell of the specific pros and cons that Persius sees in their respective purposes and techniques. In doing satire *for himself*, Persius suggests, he will take the best of both Lucilius and Horace, by loading his poems with ever-abundant Horatian traps that inflict tremendous Lucilian pain when set off.

Persius' second hexameter poem tests our readiness for these generic adjustments by taking us out of the public streets of Rome, where satirists have always set up shop, into her smoky, shadow-strafed temples, where lovely trappings have to be checked at the door. There he proposes to show us what lies beneath the surface of Rome's best-dressed citizens. But is it realistic to think that satire can be made to take this inward, Stoic turn? Surely the only soul that Persius has any chance of getting inside is his own. Not ours. Not Nero's. Whose nasty secrets, then, do we imagine that *we* are being made privy to in these poems?

That is the diagnostic test administered by P. 4, and the final lines of P. 6. Here the invitations to taunt Nero, and to load all of Rome's problems on his shaggy back, are some of the most tempting in the book. But to accept these invitations, we shall see, is both hazardous, and painfully self-revealing. For, in the end, these poems are not about Nero. They are, first and foremost, about Persius, charting his descent into himself in order to locate, and painfully extract, the Nero within. We cannot follow him there, because only he can enter his own soul. But, if we choose to, we can mime his journey, step for step, by making the philosopher's *katabasis* into ourselves, to see what painful surgery might be required there. Deciding to blame Nero, or to detect his cancerous effects in Persius, is to fail to make that descent. It is to become the superficial reformer that you, with these poems, deride.

With Juvenal's five books of *Satires* I will become more drastic in what I choose to include, and what, regrettably, I must leave out. I shall focus my discussion primarily on Juvenal's first book, poems

1–5, with frequent glances towards book 2, his famous protreptic against marriage (poem 6), because I regard these poems as the most programmatically absurd in the corpus of Roman satire, besides being the most read in the corpus of Juvenal. The main absurdity tossed our way in these poems is the poet's decision at the end of his first poem to step back from his promise to take up Lucilius' epic sword of satire in order to take a safer course that leads outside the city walls, along the byways of Rome's most elegant graveyards. There, among the dead, he intends to inflict tremendous Lucilian "pain" on Rome's first-century emperors and their minions by ritually flogging their corpses. This, the poet decides upon further reflection, is a road more safely traveled, so he lays it out as the path he intends to take. His first two books vent a century's worth of pent-up rage. Their volume is loud, and their hyperbole incessant. It is this rage, so extreme and late in coming, that I will take as my principal focus in the pages below.

Things are different in Juvenal's third book (poems 7–9), with the opening lines of poem 7 heralding the arrival of a hopeful new age for the city's poor and scrabbling poets, the very part Juvenal played for us in many of the poems that precede. Rome, he says, now has an emperor friendly to poets (presumably Hadrian) who intends to support literary pursuits that were neglected for many years preceding his accession. Matching satirist to emperor in this book, just as he did in book 1, the speaker tones down his damning of the unpunished dead of the Julio-Claudian and Flavian eras. Less obsessed with the first-century past, he sheathes his avenging, Trajanic sword, and begins to sport the telltale stubble of a philosopher's budding beard. In books 4 and 5 (poems 10–16), as Franco Bellandi has shown, the poet's transformation is even more pronounced, and the beard in full bloom.[4] The poor man's rage at his lot in life, once a standard source of humor in books 1 and 2, especially in poem 3, gives way in these last books to a Democritean smile, and to protestations of his now enjoying a "happy poverty" that his earlier works never dared even to imagine.

With the poet's new demeanor in poem 10 come new ways of seeing the satiric habits of books 1 and 2. Perhaps the boldest

---

[4] Bellandi (1980) 66: "Con la satira 10, in effetti, ci troviamo di fronte, sin dai primi versi, a un Giovenale radicalmente diverso da quello dell'*indignatio*."

of these new perspectives is taken in the tale of Sejanus' untimely demise, the first illustration of the poem's central theme. Sejanus, according to the story of lines 58–94, was a man who achieved his every "vain wish" for political power under Tiberius. But he ended his life in pain and disgrace because of what he wished for, and got. After he was murdered, Juvenal says, his bronze statues were brought down by ropes, then smashed to bits and melted into fry-pans, pitchers, and pisspots. His corpse was then dragged around on a hook to be gawked at and vehemently scorned by the crowds who had gathered to vent their anger. At lines 67 and following, in a move typical of Juvenal's first books, all eyes turn from the spectacle of Sejanus' corpse to the spectators themselves. One man boasts to another that he hated Sejanus all along. No doubt about it. When his friend hints that many more are likely to die in the aftermath of Sejanus' fall, the boaster comes up with a quick and easy method for coming clean after the fact (85–8):

> "curramus praecipites et,
> dum iacet in ripa, calcemus Caesaris hostem.
> sed uideant serui, ne quis neget et pauidum in ius
> ceruice obstricta dominum trahat."

"Come, let's hurry down to the river. And while his body is lying on the bank, let's kick 'the enemy of Caesar'. But let's make sure that our servants watch, so that none says we didn't do it, and then drags his terror-struck master off to court with a noose around his neck."

The fool in this story is no longer the fallen monster, Sejanus, but the man who abuses his corpse. His kicking Sejanus' body is an elaborate, politically convenient act he puts on not because he really hates Sejanus, but because he really needs to be seen hating him. The illustration is hazardous for Juvenal, for it invites us to take a very different perspective on his earlier practice of ritually beating the dead. He himself has made many a satiric pisspot out of the faces of Rome's first-century villains. How, then, can he escape from the moral of the story he tells?

This, we shall see, is not just a nagging doubt thrown our way near the end of Juvenal's career, in one of his more philosophically colored, but still hyperbolically loud and self-defeating, last poems. It is the central conundrum of his first two books, put to us from the start of his first poem as a way of drawing us into, and forcing us to deal with, a problem of much larger cultural significance; namely, the race to re-invent oneself after Domitian's fall. To show this, I shall take a fairly lengthy detour away from Juvenal's first two books *per se* into the eulogistic, epistolary, and historical works of his contemporaries, Tacitus and Pliny. There I will trace the outlines of a much larger revenge-taking industry that is the unseen background of Juvenal's strangely retroactive show. This detour will show that the most prominent writers of Juvenal's age were all absorbed into the same overriding obsession with the city's recent, traumatic past. None seems to have written anything while actually living in the past they write of. But when given the chance to write, none has much, if anything, to say about the present in which they live. The problem of their "finally" saying what they always wanted to, but never did, is especially acute, and the rhetoric extra thick, for those who seem to have thrived under the biggest "monster" of them all, Domitian. The reason for this, I contend, is that their many written reconstructions of the Julio-Claudian and Flavian emperors are perhaps less about the "monsters" they construct than they are about the writers themselves. To steal a phrase from Pliny, their monster tales are a means of "making *oneself* known" (**se** *proferendi*).

In the opening lines of his first book, I maintain, Juvenal plugs himself into one of the central literary and cultural enterprises of his day. He repeats its well-worn mantra of "finally" being allowed to speak his mind after so many decades spent seething in silence. That is, he lets us know "who he is" by fashioning himself, now, as someone he never was, an outspoken antagonist of Rome's bad emperors. Here and throughout his first two books, Juvenal vents the rage he ostensibly has built up against them, and he lets us see how good it feels for him finally to pay them back for making such a cruel mess of his life in Rome. Gauged by the enormity of the rage he lets out, the abuse he suffered must have been enormous.

But the question I put to his particular style of performance concerns its viability as an uncomplicated gesture of "indignation" when set beside the more understated and generically fitting self-professions of his contemporaries, Tacitus and Pliny. For, in Juvenal's case, not only do satire's standard rules for addressing the present in a timely fashion destabilize his stated program. The sheer volume of his voice, and the wild fictionalizing of the scenes he paints, themselves suggest that Juvenal's particular style of revenge is perhaps not to be taken as the genuine article. At best, his show of revenge rides the edge of respectability, loud-mouthing what others had done with finesse. Not only is the entire revenge-taking industry cheapened and parodically taken down by this, but our own smugness and/or gullibility in crediting any and all such expressions of "righteous" moral outrage are exposed to view. The questions put to us by Juvenal's overdoing what others had done well are many, and self-revealing. For example, they make us consider what our enjoying of Juvenal's show, and letting it count as "satire," might say about us. Where is *our* point of maximum disgust (at ourselves) "finally" reached?

CHAPTER I

Horace

THE DIATRIBE SATIRES (*SERMONES* 1.1–1.3): "YOU'RE NO LUCILIUS"

The opening scene of Horace's first satire (*Sermones* 1.1) hustles us to the front row of a street-preacher's harangue. The man who rails at us there (a genius? a fool?) has us labeled as miserable, unbalanced, driven by desires for wealth and prestige that are utterly out of sync with nature's own sense of "limit" (*finis*), "due measure" (*modus*), and "just enough" (*satis*). From the very start, and without warning, he has decided that *we* are part of the problem, that *our* greed, discontent, lust, and so on, are grist for his satiric mill. Along the way we, his fidgety accused, must face up to that central, narratological task of determining who "we" imagine ourselves to be in relation to the man who speaks from the page, and just how much we want to credit his sometimes strained and addled reasoning against us. When he says *de te | fabula narratur* ("*you* are the fool in the story," *S.* 1.1.69–70) do we run for cover by reminding ourselves that the speaker is a zealot and a know-it-all, or, even easier, that he has someone else in mind? Maybe he means his addressee, Maecenas, or the fictive audience inside the poem. Or how about the poem's first-century-BCE "intended" readers? Could he possibly really mean me?

The barrage continues into the second poem, where the penetrating philosopher / snake-oil salesman (take your pick) turns his eye towards matters of the male libido. Some men, he complains, chase after high-class matrons, turned on by the threat of being caught *in flagrante*. Others bankrupt themselves on prostitutes, preferring the thrill of a potential social disgrace. The basic moral issue, and the speaker's point of attack, remain precisely those of the preceding poem: fools willfully stray towards extremes because

15

they fail to content themselves with nature's basic, middling "enough." But what precisely is nature's basic "enough" when it comes to matters of male desire (is that really what's wanted, just "enough")? What is the "horny mean" between matrons and slaves that every idiot's penis, if it could talk (lines 69–71), would tell him to be happy with? Simply split the difference, the poet says. Halfway between paramours too difficult and too easy, between dazzling white and filth, free and slave, one finds an obvious compromise: freedwomen. What is so hard about that? One (glib) theory fits all. Such is this poet's comfortable, mock-Epicurean compromise. Unlike the Stoics, whom he abuses repeatedly in this book's initial poems, hard-nosed critics who would insist on ridding oneself of the desires that are the root cause of folly, this poet argues for having your desire, and enjoying it, too. Everything in moderation, especially moral philosophy regulating sex. Aristotle rolls over in his grave. Epicurus winces. We, quite possibly, laugh.

The third poem, the last of the book's inaugural triptych of "diatribe satires," so-called because of their strong resemblance to rambling sermons in the Cynic tradition (especially those of Bion), treats the delicate matter of criticizing faults spied in the company of friends, an issue with obvious programmatic relevance to the poet's own finger-pointing project.[1] The general message issuing from the poem is again one of balance and moderation, with the poet urging that, since all are born with faults, and since ridding oneself completely of these faults is out of the question (whatever Stoic zealots may urge to the contrary), one should be sparing in one's criticism of friends, always intending well, even finding certain defects attractive, like a well-placed mole on a girlfriend's cheek. Once again, Epicurean tenets are glibly tossed about. At times they are grossly mishandled, most famously in the mock-Lucretian "archaeology of justice" of lines 99–112, where the emergence of human language and laws is linked directly to early cave-dwellers' clubbing one another over acorns, caves, and – to make the point with a cave-man's finesse – "cunt" (*cunnus taeterrima*

---

[1] Brown (1993) 89: "The first three satires of the book form a related group, and have more in common with, and owe more to the influence of, the Greek diatribe or philosophical street-sermon than any others." For specific connections with Greek diatribe, see Freudenburg (1993) 8–21.

belli | causa, 107–8). While the basic idea has good precedent in
Lucretius, the packaging and delivery of the idea does not.[2]
Clearly, very little of what this man says can be taken at face-
value. One has to wait nearly one hundred and fifty years (until
Juvenal's sixth satire) for a scene of acorn-belching romance that
is anything like so deranged and comical.

But just as this speaker's routine threatens to go on too long and
to become just a bit too obvious, the bumbling Lucretius disappears, and his accusations towards us, his buttonholed audience,
come to an abrupt halt with the opening lines of *S.* 1.4. Here, perhaps to simulate an Old Comic *parabasis,* the clown drops his mask
(or does he? see below) and gives way to that saner, steadier voice
of a poet in his literary-critical, and now decidedly "programmatic" mode (*S.* 1.4.1–7):

> Eupolis atque Cratinus Aristophanesque poetae
> atque alii quorum comoedia prisca uirorum est,
> si quis erat dignus describi, quod malus ac fur,
> quod moechus foret aut sicarius aut alioqui
> famosus, multa cum libertate notabant.
> hinc omnis pendet Lucilius, hosce secutus
> mutatis tantum pedibus numerisque.

The poets Eupolis, Cratinus, and Aristophanes, and all the other "real
men" of Old Comedy, if anyone deserved lampooning, either because he
was wicked, and a thief, or because he was an adulterer, or murderer, or
notorious in some other way, they would brand him with abundant freedom of speech. Lucilius depends on them totally. These are the ones he
follows, changing only their meters and rhythms.

The speaker's handling of Greek and Latin literary history in
these lines is every bit as shaky as his grasp of Epicurean moral
philosophy in the poems that precede. The picture he paints of
Greek Old Comic poets branding criminals with the Roman censor's *nota* is anachronistic and far-fetched, to say the least, exaggerating the poets' public moral function to the exclusion of all
of Old Comedy's many further purposes, practices, and effects.[3]

---

[2] Martindale (1993) 9: "Horace's 'unromantic' attitude to women is often described as typi-
cally Roman, and compared to Lucretius'. The comparison is unconvincing. Lucretius'
suspicion of sexuality is fuelled by a fierce philosophic commitment; by contrast when in
Sermones 1.3.107–8 Horace writes *nam fuit ante Helenam cunnus taeterrima belli | causa* ... the
voice seems rather that of Shakespeare's Thersites. *Cunnus* functions as a metonymy for
woman, who is thereby reduced to this single orifice."

[3] For *notare* referring to the censor's *nota*, see Lejay (1966) 76.

How often, an uncooperative reader might ask, does Aristophanes name and/or disgrace murderers in his extant plays? How many adulteries does he expose on stage? When, if ever! And what of Aristophanes' abundant jibes against non-criminals, and nobodies, philosophers, government officials, bumpkins, cabbage-sellers, and so on? How are these to be construed as corrective and "censorial" in function, and clearly in the public interest?

The lines are fraught with misinformation that caricatures not only the poets of Greek Old Comedy, but Lucilius as well. For Lucilius' dependence on these poets is hardly what it is made to seem here, so utterly direct and all-encompassing that Lucilius has "merely" to adjust their rhythms and meter. At best, the statement contains a grain of truth. At worst, it represents an absurd attempt to re-invent the writers of Greek Old Comedy as agents of public moral oversight, clear and simple, and thus to commandeer them for a very late (and lost, and highly contentious) Roman cause. Such notions, whether taken as "history" or "theory," are expressive of a strained ideology of the purposes and meanings of critical jests in the comic tradition. As if to rescue the writers named for some (pipe-dreaming Stoic's?) ideal state, Greek funsters are "theorized into" dreaded Catos by these lines, and Lucilius becomes an Old Comic watchdog of public morals, a quasi-Greek. Very little of this stands up to serious scrutiny. Alien, extreme voices, I suspect, have been filtered into these lines, and play inside them. Other, hard-line views (those of certain *fautores Lucili*? see below) are being sampled and sent up.

But given that gross exaggerations stand out in the opening lines of each of the three poems that precede, as if to characterize this poet's only way of commencing (*qui fit ... ut* **nemo** *... contentus uiuat*, 1.1.1–3; *hoc genus* **omne**, 1.2.2; **omnibus** *hoc uitium est cantor- ibus*, 1.3.1), we should perhaps not be surprised that the literary/ programmatic disquisition undertaken in 1.4 should take us immediately into a world of overdone extremes: *hinc* **omnis** *pendet Lucilius, hosce secutus* | *mutatis* **tantum** *pedibus*, 1.4.6–7. The real jolt delivered by these lines, I suspect, derives less from their addled exaggerations about Lucilius, than from their daring to mention him at all. For here, quite unexpectedly, we are first given to believe that Horace actually *has* a Lucilius problem that he needs to set straight. On the heels of the diatribe satires, we may reasonably wonder how Lucilius comes into this picture at all. On what basis does the poet assume that his ironical "diatribes" will have made us think of Lucilius as his one clear rival? Why not Lucretius or, more obviously, Bion? Is that really what Horace thought he was writing, "satire" after the manner of Lucilius?

If so, how were we to know? Nowhere in the book's first three poems is Lucilius mentioned by name or his poetry explicitly called to mind – that happens first here, in 1.4, and then more prominently in the poem that follows (see below).[4] His memory, if evoked in the book's first poems, is activated by clues that are relatively general and understated, such as the steady presence (in hexameters) of a strong first-person voice, fond of vulgar expressions, and ready to criticize moral faults and, at times, to name names. While it is true that Lucilius, too, played the railing philosopher and literary critic in a number of poems, his performances in this mode were relatively few, and they worked to a remarkably different effect. They were famous not for their ironic undercurrents, but for their searing abuse of Rome's most prominent writers, political figures and men of high social standing, both living and dead. Despite his legend, Lucilius' enemies tended to be not moral derelicts and "enemies of the state" *per se*, but enemies of his friends, especially those known to be hostile to his closest and most powerful friend, P. Cornelius Scipio Aemilianus. Thus the voice he projects is not that of a barefoot preacher, but of a well-connected Roman aristocrat, powerful, unrestrained, and deeply invested in the party politics of the late second century BCE (as critical observer and commentator).

Such was the legend of Lucilius, well known to Horace, and hotly traded in his day as a kind of political/moral capital to be cornered and spent as one's own.[5] Traces of that legend can be heard to emanate from the opening lines of *S.* 1.4, where notions

---

[4] The talking penis of *S.* 1.2. 69–71 reminded Horace's third- and fourth-century scholiasts of a similarly gifted member in Lucilius (see below chapter 3). Beyond this, reminiscences are few and quite general. Fiske has argued that Horace's *S.* 1.1 draws on certain commonplaces from Lucilius book 19, and that 1.2 may be an imitation of the third poem of book 29; see Fiske (1920) 219–77. His evidence is extremely thin. Recently Scholz (1986) has attempted to prove that the first four poems of Horace's first book follow a thematic sequence found in (his elaborate reconstruction of) the first four poems of Lucilius' earliest book (book 1 in early editions, later renumbered as book 26). His hypothesis has been dismantled by Christes (1989).

[5] On the Lucilian revival of the fifties BCE, see Anderson (1963) 78–9. For Lucilian *libertas* as a potent political symbol in the forties and thirties, see Freudenburg (1993) 86–102.

of high *aristo-cracy*, and deep *poli*-tical engagement, both assumed
in the "poet as censor" metaphor, are cryptographically figured
into the impressive set of names that begins the poem, the most
famous of Greek comedy's "real Romans": *Eu-polis*, *Crat-inus*
Aristo-phanesque. But given that this was the dominant, overbearing
paradigm for the interpretation of Lucilius in Horace's day, it is
hard to see how Horace would have us believe that his poems
belong to the same tradition in anything other than a tangential
way. The contrast between the two writers is sharp, and patently
obvious from his book's first half-line: *Qui fit,* **Maecenas***, ut* **nemo**
. . . ("How come, Maecenas, nobody . . ."). With the odd juxtaposition of one name so politically resonant against another so empty,
the stage is thus set for a very different kind of satiric enterprise:
Maecenas versus *Nobody*! Why not start with Maecenas versus somebody? Surely Maecenas, one of the most powerful political figures
of the thirties and twenties BCE, has bigger enemies to contend
with than the anonymous fools and type-figures (farmers, mer-
chants, soldiers, etc.) that come in for a thrashing in this poem. If
Horace is bent upon seeming at all Lucilian in his poems, why not
begin where Lucilius began his first book, by attacking not greed
and vain ambitions in general, but the greed and vain ambitions
of a man of real significance, such as Lucius Cornelius Lentulus
Lupus, a consular senator and former censor and *princeps senatus*?
He was Lupus "the Wolf," nobody's "nobody."[6]

But even when Horace ventures to criticize by name, his targets
are, without exception, unexceptionable: mere "nobodies" such as
Crispinus, Fannius, and Hermogenes Tigellius, few of whom are
known from any source outside the poems themselves.[7] That said,
it is still clear from the book's first line that persons of real social
and political significance do appear in Horace's *Sermones* from time
to time. But these always happen to be friends of the poet, or
potential friends, rather than enemies, so they are always handled
with a light touch. Thus the critical performance of these poems,
while perhaps vaguely reminiscent of Lucilius, is anything but
purely "Lucilian." It comes as no surprise, then, that some in
Horace's audience found his efforts "gutless" (*sine neruis*) by comparison (see below).

---

[6] For Lupus' role in Lucilius book 1, see chapter 3 below.
[7] The fundamental prosopographical study of names in the *Sermones* is that of Rudd (1966)
     132–59.

But the first half-line of Horace's first poem does more than mark a shift away from the critical habits of Lucilius. Inside that shift, it urges a remarkably different sense of the satiric speaker as well, and thus it leaves us to consider the poet's non-Lucilian technique as a condition of his non-Lucilian self. He is no Lucilius, clearly. But then who, precisely, is he? Recently, Ellen Oliensis has remarked on the obvious irony that inheres in naming Maecenas so prominently in the first half-line of a poem where social climbers are freely abused: the act of naming Maecenas lets us see the social climber in Horace himself.[8] For that name, standing out as it does in his book's first line, brings us immediately to the conclusion that this speaker, despite sounding so much like Bion, is not detached from the social world he criticizes, and thus unaffected by it, as any good cynic should be. His book's dedication to Maecenas, while blunt and minimal, the least elaborate dedication in all Latin literature (a single word), carries powerful implications for the speaker's self, and the way his lessons will be received: it puts him squarely inside a world of Roman social relations where promising young poets look to men of means to provide them access to books, learned audiences, and facilities, as well as abundant political and financial rewards.[9]

Scholars have often puzzled over the poet's one-word dedication to his patron as a narratological conundrum, wondering just how we are to think of Maecenas as the poem's addressee and principal audience when so much of what follows brings to mind the deictic trappings of diatribe, with its fictional hearers and interlocutors. How can the two settings work together? Are we to think that the speaker rants for Maecenas alone (hard to imagine), or perhaps among a select group of friends, with Maecenas front and center (at a formal recitation or dinner party)? Or is the performance, rather, to be imagined as a public harangue set along a busy street? If the latter, then how is Maecenas to be imagined as addressed by it, and functioning in it?

By beginning "How come, Maecenas" the speaker immediately casts himself as someone struggling to belong in Maecenas' social world, not someone anxious to escape from it. And yet he would have us believe that his is a secure and independent voice of moral criticism in the tradition of Bion. So which is he, the dependent

---

[8] Oliensis (1998a) 17–18.
[9] The fundamental study of poetry and patronage in Rome is White (1993).

lesser friend, or the cynic free agent? How can he possibly be one *along with* the other? Such is the puzzle of the poet's hard-to-place self that lurks inside the narratological puzzle of his opening poem's first line. And not just there, but throughout the diatribe satires generally. For despite our best efforts to place this speaker cleanly inside one of the several traditions to which his perfor-mances refer, he always manages to slip free of those traditions by failing to fit them in certain fundamental respects. And thus he always leaves some large remainder of himself unaccounted for.

Recently William Turpin has demonstrated that the speaker of *Sermones* 1.1–3 shows a high degree of comic patterning in the expression of his manners, social self-confidence, and moral point of view. Taken as the sum of these expressions, he argues, "the speaker of the satires is supposed to be understood both as a com-mitted Epicurean and as a contemporary version of that stock figure of Greek and Latin comedy, the parasite, or professional guest. These two characterisations might be thought quite distinct, but for those hostile to Epicureanism or willing to be amused by it there was clearly a connection, and it is central to the character that Horace has created."[10] Thus a second tradition, that of comic party-goers and lackeys, resides uncomfortably inside the first, that of the preacher of Epicurean moral values. The self projected in these poems, like their genre (see below), is best understood not from within the narrow confines of any given tradition, but as a dialogue between traditions, and an effect of their interacting.

The moralist of *Sermones* 1.1–3 mishandles the stock ethical lessons he attempts to employ, but he does so in a way that puts a specific kind of face (a *persona* "mask") to his voice. Scanning the lessons of the diatribe satires for indications of the speaker's moral character and station in life, we see that his thoughts easily stray from the point at hand towards matters of food, sex, and getting along with friends, telltale signs of the world he lives in, and what he values, and knows. The man has a keen eye for sizing up patrons. Some, he complains, spend too lavishly on the wrong sort (and he has to reach pretty low to get lower than himself, 1.2.1–4). Others spend nothing on their poor, but deserving, friends (1.2.4–11). He knows what it is like to drink too heavily at parties, and accidentally to break expensive tableware and piss on the furni-

---

[10] Turpin (1998) 127.

ture (1.3.90–1). And he has learned the hard way not to barge in on Maecenas while he is reading or resting (1.3.63–6). Sleeping with a rich man's wife he regards as dangerous, and anathema (1.2 *passim*). Grabbing chicken from the wrong side of the plate he considers a forgivable offense, especially for someone who is "starving" (*esuriens*, 1.3.93).

Clearly there is a pattern to his digressions and bunglings that is suggestive of the world he inhabits, and who he (fictionally) is. We see that pattern again, in the course of his telling us to overlook a friend's insignificant faults, where his mind strays, leeringly, towards matters of cave-sex (1.3.99–110), and to that well placed mole on a girlfriend's cheek (1.3.40). We see it in his priding himself on his x-ray vision for attractive women, able to size them up, part by part ("ass," "neck," "thigh," "leg"), like a king shopping for a horse (1.2.83–90). Further, to round off his point about not being greedy in *Sermones* 1.1, he draws us into the only world he seems to know, and to have mastered, that of a pleasant "guest" (*conuiua*) at someone else's dinner-party (1.1.117–19). Eat just "enough," he says. Don't gorge yourself, and don't overstay your welcome. Above all, know when it is time to get up and leave – and so he does, as if to prove himself worthy of being invited again. Such lessons, not because they are unknown to the diatribe tradition, but because they presume to know so much of, and draw so freely from, the world of dinner-parties, seductions, and keeping up appearances, tend to circumscribe our sense of the speaker's range of experience, and define his specific eye-view. The end effect of these lessons is less a treatise on sane living *per se* than it is a *Parasite's Guide to Getting by in Rome*, something that straddles the domains of serious philosophy and comic nonsense.

SERMONES BOOK I AND THE PROBLEM OF GENRE

According to their legends, Bion managed to speak the truth bluntly because he had no status to lose, and Lucilius because he had none to gain.[11] One man was content to remain a social outcast, so he spoke in a way that kept him begging and in bare feet. The other was a man of unassailable social influence, so he spoke in a manner that proved just how unassailable his influence was.

---

[11] For Bion's life as street-preacher and beggar, see Kindstrand (1976).

In each case, just as in the case of the parasite figure of *Sermones* 1.1–3, style and self entail one another integrally. The speaker's habits of criticism are a condition of the social position he occupies, and the societal role he has given himself, or been handed, to play. But Horace's parasite philosopher lacks the strong social definition of a Bion or Lucilius. Neither an outcast nor a man of means, he speaks as he lives, from somewhere in the middle. And that does not bode well for his having a decisive mannner of critical expression in his poems. His middling *genus* ("status") expresses itself in the generic indecision of the *Sermones* themselves.

"Who," then, exactly do these poems give us to think they are? What generic "pedigree" do they express for themselves if not that "simply" of a Bion, or a Lucilius? The first poems, we have seen, make a run at appearing regular, but then the diatribe satires abruptly give way to something quite different in 1.4, with the poet now performing in his literary-critical, "programmatic" mode. With the fifth poem we get to experience the low-life's eye-view (complete with mosquitoes and wet dream) of the big-shots' entourage to Brindisi (or wherever it was). Poem 6 pays tribute to the speaker's freed-slave father, and to Maecenas, a man who pays no attention to status whatever, provided you are a man of some status and not as lowborn as Horace's freed-slave father (*dum ingenuus*, *S.* 1.6.8). The anecdote-poems 7, 8, and 9 take us on-tour with †Brutus and †Co., into the gardens of a crack-assed Priapus, and out for an interminable stroll with a poet on-the-make (perhaps two). Poem 10 rounds off the book by having at the "Lucilius fans" (*fautores Lucili*) one last time, with the poet-critic telling us who really counts in his world of Second-Triumviral literary criticism.

It is an odd jumble of a book. A generic puzzle, if not a morass. The title that appears at the top of page 1, *Sermones* "Talks," "Discussions," does little to set up expectations and to guide readers along a specific generic path, unless perhaps it leads us to think of Plato's "Dialogues," a genre with obvious relevance to the poems of book 2 (see below), but no appreciable connection to those of book 1. Other than this one false lead, the title selects out next-to-nothing, and triggers no significant memories of other similarly named texts. As a generic marker, the title suggests specific ways of reading and making sense of the poems only in retrospect, once we have seen how conveniently it refers to just about everything that *actually happens* in books 1 and 2: "diatribe," "gossip," "dialogue," and so on. Once we are done, the term can do just about anything *we need* it to do to explain the book.

The word *Saturae* "Satires" once did the same thing for Ennius, opening a space for him to toss four-books'-worth of disconnected occasional poems in various meters – quite possibly poems he composed as separate set-pieces intended for individual consumption.[12] Their collection and publication may, in fact, have been an afterthought. His title, *Saturae*, likely informed by Hellenistic Greek titles such as Σωρός "Pile," ἄτακτα "Hodgepodge," and σύμμεικτα "Miscellanies," does not so much set off a new genre and tell us how to read as it warns readers against harboring any too rigid generic expectations.[13] The term takes a drastic turn with Lucilius, the so-called *inventor* of satire (see *S.* 1.10.48), who established the genre's characteristic form, focus, and tone in his monumental 30 books of *Saturae*.[14] Especially influential was his trenchant, and at times obscene, moral criticism, the famous *Lucilianus modus* that became the hallmark of satire and attached itself indelibly to the term from the late second century on. So strong was Lucilius' influence on the idea of "satire" that, by Horace's day, the word is less a generic marker that works (in the usual way) by triggering a full and illustrious world of remembered texts, than it is a way of saying simply "the kind of poems Lucilius wrote."[15]

That is the problem Horace faces in his first book. "Satire," as it was handed to him, came prepackaged and complete. For his first-century audience, Lucilius *was* satire, so the idea of his writing something decidedly un-Lucilian (by way of being softer, less direct, briefer, and so on) and calling it "satire" is just a little

---

[12] Gratwick (1982) 158 points out that although "Porphyrio (*ad* Hor. *Sat.* 1.10.46) states that Ennius left four books called *Saturae* ... it does not follow that the book arrangement or even the contents of the edition known to Porphyrio were due to Ennius himself. Each book, one *Satura*, contained miscellaneous poems, mainly in the iambo-trochaic metres and diction of comedy, but also some in hexameters and perhaps Sotadeans."

[13] On the origins of the term *satura*, see Knoche (1975) 7–16; and Coffey (1976) 11–18.

[14] While the grammarians consistently cite Lucilius' poems as "satires" (*satirae* or *saturae*), it is not certain that he gave them that name. Within the existing fragments he refers to them as *poemata* ("poems," fr. 1091W), *ludus ac sermones* ("games and chats," frs. 1039–40W), and *schedia* ("improvisations," fr. 1131W), never *saturae*.

[15] Gratwick (1982) 168: "It is not until Horace (*Sat.* 1.1.1) [*sic*] that we find *satura* used generically to designate a certain kind of poetry, and what Horace means is the kind of poetry that Lucilius wrote." He means, of course, *S.* 2.1.1.

perverse, if not unthinkable. That is the problem the poet-critic
wrestles with in book 1. That is the generic question he has us
consider every time he feels around, elaborately, awkwardly, for a
label to fit his collection of poems. Proceeding through the book
we see him struggle to trigger our memories of Lucilius, most obviously in poems 4 and 5, without actually naming what he writes
"satire." The art of dodging the *s*- word becomes a game in itself:
genus hoc scribendi ("this type/genre of writing," 1.4.65), *nescio quid
nugarum* ("some trifle or other," 1.9.2), *hoc* ("this here," 1.10.46), *sint
qualiacumque* ("whatever-the-hell these things are," 1.10.88), *haec ego
ludo* ("these comic productions I put on," 1.10.37), and so on. With
each vague periphrasis we sense the painstaking avoidance of
the word we are all thinking of, the one Lucilius makes us remember.[16] By not naming the poems anything in particular, the
problem of genre is allowed to dangle and disturb; it becomes
ours to solve. It is we readers, after all, who come to these poems
with preset notions of what really counts as "satire," and with
memories fixated on and energized by the monumental Lucilius.
By repeatedly dangling the generic question in front of us, Horace
reminds us of the tremendous obstacles he faces in dealing with
us, readers who are notoriously less than willing to deal with him
(he constructs us that way, at least), because he writes poems that
recall and compete with one of our all-time favourites, Lucilius.

And yet, at the same time as these repeated circumlocutions
dangle the generic question before us, they hint at ways we might
handle the question. They invite us to look beyond the obtrusive,
too-obvious model of Lucilius, and to stretch our generic imaginations into new, unexpected directions. At the very least they
remind us of Catullus' "strange/new little book" and the similar
problems he invented, and performed himself facing, in struggling
to assign a label to his mad assortment of poems: "The book is
yours, Cornelius. You're the one who used to think that my scraps
(*nugae*) amounted to something (*aliquid*) ... Take it, it's yours, a

---

[16] Van Rooy (1965) 66 is well aware of the problem: "Though Horace had published his
first book under the title *Sermones*, we may assume that everyone, both detractor and well-
wisher, referred to his poems as 'saturae' or 'satires.'" Following Knoche, he explains
(pp. 60–6) Horace's failure to deliver the expected title in book 1 as a deliberate attempt
to distance his work from the *Lucilianus modus*, with which the term *satura* was inextricably
bound.

slim something-or-other of a book, for what it's worth" (*quidquid hoc libelli, qualecumque*). With every "this here" and "whatever it is" that Horace uses to (not) describe his work, he breaks into our memories of Catullus and his revolutionary little book. He lets our Catullan preconceptions (and these will vary considerably from reader to reader) colour the way we perceive *his* work. As we shall see shortly, it is precisely through such interlocutory, genre-constituting memories, of Catullus, Lucretius, Virgil, and others, that Horace's own book makes its best claim to being, itself, revolutionary, and new.

REMEMBERED VOICES: SATIRE MADE NEW IN *SERMONES* 1.1

To make satire his own, Horace must first dispossess others of it, those who thought it theirs alone by right of inheritance from Lucilius. To do this he must first locate and do his best to dislodge a number of inveterate readerly assumptions about what satire can and cannot do. Somehow the term "satire" has to be substantially erased and reprogrammed. We see him attempt to do this, in some obvious and aggressive ways, in the so-called "program poems" of book 1 (*S.* 1.4 and 1.10). Perhaps less obvious, but equally aggressive, are the deprogramming efforts of the first poem. In *S.* 1.1, beneath the jumbled moral lessons that direct us to observe nature's mean in matters of gain, there lies a second, parallel set of lessons concerning the natural limits of satire.[17] The "moral" sum of *S.* 1.1, we have seen, is roughly this: the poem's deluded wretches are those who cannot be content with the basic "enough" (*satis*) provided by nature. Theirs is the opposite creed: *nil satis est* "nothing is enough" (line 62). They neither understand nor respect "limits" (*fines*) set by nature. Instead they choose to waste away in resentment towards others who have more. They want their stuff in great piles too, and as long as anyone else has more, they are driven to continue their pursuit of gain with unending "toil."

All of this, I maintain, applies at a second, less obvious level, to the writing of satire: the extreme Stoics targeted by the poem have no sense of "limit" when it comes to driving home their

---

[17] See Freudenburg (1993) 110–14.

moral lessons. Horace would have us believe that they stack pre-
cepts one on top of the other until they resemble a massive, messy
"pile." Making that pile they regard as deadly serious work, so the
critic never cracks a smile. In the famous question of lines 24–5 we
are given to think that Horace's rivals have serious objections
to the idea of jesting censure: "what's to say I can't laugh and tell
the truth at the same time?" (*ridentem dicere uerum | quid uetat?*). The
critics' disapproving frown, we assume, is an unalterable feature
of their pile-making work. That miserable enterprise never ends
because the preceptive heap they are so hot to have more of has
no natural "limit." Nothing is more notoriously undelimitable
than a pile. And since angst keeps them from enjoying their stash,
it just gets bigger and bigger. That, Horace suggests, is what their
version of *satura* looks like.

Seen for this, its metaphorical potential, the poem is every bit as
"programmatic" – and right where we most expect a program-
poem to be – as the literary manifestos *S.* 1.4 and 1.10. For hidden
squarely beneath each of the poem's many "piles," and behind
every image of an in*sati*ate fool, there lies the entrenched etymological notion that satire is something "heaped high" and/
or "stuffed full" (*satur*). The idea has clear connections with the
"stuffed plate" (*lanx satura*) etymology, especially given the poem's
inordinate emphasis on food and drink.[18] Horace's rivals, whether
they subscribed to the notion or not, are clearly being made to
speak for the "stuffed-/piled-high" theory here.

Yet, it seems equally likely that the image repeated in the
poem of built-up "piles" anxiously guarded touches on a connection presumed between *satura* and Greek σωρός "pile." Among

---

[18] Romans who studied Horace's *Sermones* were fond of the etymological game. Certain
commentators whose notes have come down to us as the scholia of Pseudo-Acro prefaced
their comments on individual lines of the *Sermones* with a short excursus on the naming of
the work. First, they assert, there are those who connect the term "satire" to a plate handled by a follower of Bacchus, that is, by a satyr. Thus we are invited to think of a satyr's
unrestrained, horny, drunken ways. Others, they say, connect it with a *lanx satura* "plate
stuffed full" offered to Ceres at her annual festival. That gets us thinking in terms of
variety and fullness. And they mention still others who connect satire with being drunk,
since such poems "freely (*libere* = 'thanks to *Liber*, Bacchus') rail at the disgraces and
crimes of men, just like men when they are saturated, that is, drunk (*ut saturati homines
idest ebrii*)." We think then of the freedom that comes with alcohol-induced oblivion;
the chance finally to say whatever you really feel, regardless of all personal and social
constraints.

Hellenistic works that may have informed the naming of Ennius' *Saturae*, Posidippus' grab-bag of epigrams known as "the Pile" is generally considered one of the most likely.[19] But still more relevant to the idea of "satire" as "pile" here is the connection Horace posits between his critics and the philosophy of Chrysippus, the third-century head of the Stoa and vigorous defender of the faith against the skeptical Academy. If the critics lampooned in *S.* 1.1 really are the unbending, hyper-systematic Chrysippeans that Horace makes them out to be, both here and throughout the first book, then their version of moral criticism will indeed have possessed and proudly exhibited a "pile-like" nature.[20] In plying their moral work, they will have conjured up the relentless, syllogistic chain-arguments of Chrysippus, known generally as "soritic," or "pile-fashion" arguments.

The name derives from the so-called *sorites* paradox, the unsolvable puzzle that gave its name to a whole class of chain-arguments that proceeded by adding one syllogism upon the next, pile-fashion, until a point of inevitable, logical collapse was reached.[21] The *sorites* paradox dealt specifically with the central issue addressed in *S.* 1.1, the pile's lack of natural "limits" (*fines*). The short version of the puzzle looks like this: if one grain of wheat doesn't make a pile, then how about two? Three? Four? At some point you have to give in and say "Yes, it's a pile now."[22] But then the trouble comes in saying what precisely is magical about the magic number. What is the essential, "pile-constituting," quality that it has that the previous number does not? Chrysippus found this puzzle, developed by the Skeptics in several forms, especially problematic and worthy of study. Though it was sometimes used against him, and apparently to some effect, we know that by Horace's day the *sorites* paradox was specifically associated with Chrysippus to the exclusion of nearly everyone else.[23] It had

---

[19] See Gratwick (1982) 160.

[20] For the *fautores Lucili* as neo-Chrysippeans, see Freudenburg (1993) 109–19.

[21] On the *sorites* paradox, see Brink (1982) 80–1.

[22] The more common version of the puzzle works in reverse, with seeds subtracted from an existing pile until a point is reached where it is no longer reasonable to call the seeds a pile. The scholiasts' note on P. 6.78–80 makes clear that the puzzle could proceed in either direction (*per adiectionem et detractionem*).

[23] Brink (1982) 81: "Chrysippus' name in particular was associated with this mode of arguing." See also Reid on Cic. *Acad.* 2.49.

come to represent his peculiar brand of driving syllogistic analysis. If anyone could pile on the syllogisms, apparently, it was
Chrysippus (in 705 slapdash volumes!).[24]

To make room for his work in a world stuffed with preset
notions of what satire already is and only can ever be, Horace
must first engage in some aggressive demolition work. His first
job in *S.* 1.1 is to heave aside the "pile" that stands in his way,
covering so much of the desired space of "satire." The so-called
"pile-arguments" of Chrysippus had a long and illustrious history
in the field of Stoic dialectic, the study that Chrysippus helped
shape and exhaustively systematize. The question we are asked
to consider in *S.* 1.1 is whether or not that pile-image, with all
its built-in associations of dead-serious, dry, and unrelenting analysis, is really the best and most "natural" inroad into satire. For
although the word "satire" is never used in the poem, it is clear
that its "limits," its definitional *fines*, are being probed into by the
poem's scattered images of piles, fools who cannot get enough
(*satis*), and the dinner-guest who finally gets his fill (*satur*). To reset
notions of satire, Horace drags his rivals' precious pile out of its
intended referential space, where it derives a certain lustre from
an association with the driving dialectical methods of Chrysippus,
and sets it within new, alien fields of reference where it seems
awkward and out of place.

Put simply, there are places where piles do not belong, and in
the course of the first poem, Horace shows us where these are.
Some of these spaces, he insists, jut into the generic space he is
determined to have for "satire." Most obviously, he reminds us
that piles have all sorts of negative associations in the traditional
imagery of diatribes against greed: to want things in piles is to be
a miser.[25] How, then, can his rivals rail against misers (as writers
of diatribe must) if their own methods of censure can be labeled
as miserly? Further, Horace previews his later obsession with
compositional technique (*compositio, structura*), evident especially in

---

[24] Diog. Laert. 7.180: "He [Chrysippus] had abundance of matter, but in style he was not
successful. In industry he surpassed every one, as the list of his writings shows; for there
are more than 705 of them. He increased their number by arguing repeatedly on the
same subject, setting down anything that occurred to him, making many corrections and
citing numerous authorities" (Loeb trans.).

[25] On the *fines naturae* theme in diatribes and philosophical treatises on wealth, see Lejay
(1966) 5–9. As a specifically Epicurean principle in Horace, see DeWitt (1939) 133–4.

S. 1.4 and 1.10, by having us consider the poem's various piles as quasi-compositional artifacts. The terms he uses to picture these piles (e.g. **congesta** *cibaria, acervo quem* **struit**, **immensum** *pondus*, **constructus** *acervus*, **congestis** *saccis*) are suggestive of rhetorical theories of arrangement, where the pile-metaphor is universally negative. Thus, if we imagine "satire" as a compositionally ordered space, as Horace invites us to do here, we see that the pile-image is hopelessly inept and out of place. In compositional theory it signifies always an overblown, disconnected mess.[26]

"Finishing your work" (*finire laborem*, 93) cannot happen with a pile, because it has no "fixed ends" (*certi fines*, 106) to mark where you should stop. The inordinate emphasis on this theme throughout *S.* 1.1 draws us to consider how this poem ends itself. How does it locate its own natural *fines*? Lines 117–21 make quick work of the act of concluding, and the quickness of that ending is a key feature of how it means what it means. Instead of just ending the poem, the lines deliberately *perform the discovery* of the poem's end, and thus they help us think in new ways about satire's generic shape. By the poem's end, the pile has been substantially removed, making room for something new, and of Horace's own making:

> inde fit ut raro qui se vixisse beatum
> dicat et exacto contentus tempore vita
> cedat, uti conviva satur, reperire queamus.
> iam satis est. ne me Crispini scrinia lippi
> compilasse putes, verbum non amplius addam.

And that is why it is so hard for us to find a man who'll say he has lived out his life in happiness and, content with time already spent, will step away from life, like a dinner-guest who has had his fill. Enough now. And in case you think I've been ransacking the writing-boxes of bleareyed Crispinus, I'll add not a word more.

The poet's parting words (*non amplius addam*) remind us of the fool swept away by the Aufidus because he has insisted on drinking

---

[26] Certain Stoics would have liked the mess and defended it on stylistic grounds. On compositional theory in the *Sermones*, see Freudenburg (1993) 128–84. The pile-metaphor is well represented in Quintilian under the terms *aceruus, cumulus,* and *congeries*; cf. Quint. *Inst.* 7pr. 1 *sed ut opera exstruentibus satis non est saxa atque materiam et cetera aedificanti utilia* **congerere**, *nisi disponendis eis collocandisque artificium manus adhibeatur, sic in dicendo quamlibet abundans rerum copia* **cumulum** *tantum habeat atque* **congestum**, *nisi illas eadem dispositio in ordinem digestas atque inter se commissas devinxerit.*

from a flooded river, though his thirst required "no more than an
urn" (*non amplius urna*, 54). That muddy river is the most salient
literary-critical (compositional) image of the poem.[27] So here, at
the poem's end, we are directed away from those earlier metaphors of "flooding," "stuffing," "piling," and so on, towards the
idea of satire's basic, natural "enough." With *iam satis est* "enough
now," the poet shows that he, the poet who writes the poem and
"defines" its beginning and end, has found the very thing that
the pile-obsessed fools inside the poem were so notoriously unable
to find; that basic "enough" of nature. That is the limit. That is
the "end" and "finish" that their unwieldy pile can never have.
Having found it, he performs his definitional achievement by
doing something the fools of the poem can never do: he finishes
his *labor*. One line after the "enough now" declaration, the speaker
departs, the poem is done. Like the dinner-guest, his alter-ego in
line 119, he is satisfied, and he performs his *satis*faction by getting
up and walking away. By setting *satur* ("full") and *satis* ("enough")
in such close proximity (a "clever joining," *callida iunctura*), he has
us consider yet another etymological inroad into the genre: as
nature's basic "enough," satire acquires a new, streamlined identity (*satura* from *satis*) that derives its basic relational energy and
sense from the remembered "piles" and "plates" that are its rejected, half-erased prototypes.

   The poem's final lines shake out memories gathered from all
sorts of places. Some of these memories, we have seen, are based
inside the poem itself, drawing on what we were told there about
the misers who could not get enough, and the blowhard critics
who mimic them so uncannily. Mostly, though, in reading these
lines (as with any line of Roman poetry) we are working with
memory-banks completely erased: the works of Crispinus, Fabius,
and anyone else who may have fallen through the cracks of the
poem, too subtly handled to be noticed by us now, are completely
lost to us. We have no real memories of their works, just re-
minders and cartoon-images, with assurances from the poet that
these practitioners of whatever it was they were doing (we cannot
even know that!) were completely inept. Because genres "happen"

---

[27] On the river imagery of Hor. *S.* 1.1, see Freudenburg (1993) 185–92.

precisely through the dialogic processing of these memories, our view of Horatian satire can never look terribly like Horace's view or that of any of his intended, first-century-BCE readers (views multiple and unstable in themselves).[28]

Still, there are other memories shaken out by the poem's last lines that project from texts that are known to us quite well, and these texts bring with them their own generic and ideological associations that necessarily contribute to our sense of what this new brand of Horatian satire is all about. The most famous and best explored of these allusions is to Lucretius, who used the full dinner-guest metaphor in his diatribe against the fear of death to convince us that, when life is a drag, there is nothing to fear in dying. In commenting on the last lines of *S.* 1.1, scholars routinely make only the most obvious connection between the two passages by matching Lucretius' *ut plenus ... conuiua recedis* with Horace's *cedat uti conuiua satur*.[29] Still, as the words highlighted below attest, the points of contact between the two passages are actually more extensive (Lucr. 3.938–43):

> cur non ut **plenus uitae conuiua** re**cedis**
> aequo animoque capis securam, stulte, quietem?
> sin ea quae fructus cumque es periere profusa
> uitaque in offensast, cur **amplius addere** quaeris,
> rursum quod pereat male et ingratum occidat omne,
> non potius uitae **finem facis atque laboris**?

---

[28] Conte (1994) 5: "If we instead see every text as an interlocutor of some other text, the frame becomes animated and starts to move. Every new text enters into a dialogue with other texts; it uses dialogue as a necessary form of its own construction, since it tries not only to hear other voices but somehow to respond to them in such a way as to define its own." The fundamental study of intertextual memory as a "dialogic," genre-constructing, activity is Conte's monograph *Memoria dei poeti e sistema letterario*. His ideas are usefully summarized in the introduction to his *Latin Literature, a History*. Among recent followers of Conte, I have been most influenced by Hinds (1998) and Fowler (1997). Also Kennedy (1989) 210: "genres are only intertextual frames, only ever constructed in discourse." And thus their forms are never singular, stable, and/or final, but a mere "momentary coherence" (I owe the phrase to Dan Hooley *per litteras*). Cf. Fowler (1997) 14: "We do not read a text in isolation, but within a matrix of possibilities constituted by earlier texts, which functions as *langue* to the *parole* of individual textual production: without this background, the text would be literally unreadable, as there would be no way in which it could have meaning."

[29] For example, both Lejay (1966) 28, and Kiessling–Heinze (1961) 21 treat the *conuiua satur* as a discrete "image" added from Lucr. 3.938 rather than as a figure that functions within, and brings with it, a larger moral discourse on nature's inherent limits. For a somewhat broader perspective, see Glazewski (1971).

Why not, like a dinner-guest who has taken his fill of life, just step away, you fool, and with mind at ease take hold of rest that is free from care? But if all that you once enjoyed is now drained to the dregs and lost, and life gives you pain, why do you seek to add more of what it will be painful and unwelcome to lose a second time, and to see vanish utterly away? Why not, instead, make an end of your life and of your toil?

To my knowledge, no one has picked up on the connection between *amplius addere* of line 941 and Horace's parting *amplius addam*. Yet, in making the connection we are much more inclined to pick up on the careful dovetailing of the poem's last two lines into the moral discourse that precedes, dovetailing already signalled by the various "inside" allusions mentioned above. Taking the full allusion into consideration, then, we see that what at first looks like, and gets edited as, a detached "literary" jibe closing the poem actually extends from and takes its sense from the dinner-guest metaphor that precedes it in lines 118–19.

There is a second, hidden, feature of the Lucretian passage that bears upon the way in which the conclusion of *S.* 1.1 does its definitional work: the voice that scolds the fool for refusing to "die already" in Lucretius is none other than that of the personified *Rerum Natura* "Nature of Reality," the focus and title of that mammoth work. Thus the voice that breaks into the final lines of *S.* 1.1 is not just any standard, didactic voice *from* Lucretius, it is the voice *of* his *Rerum Natura*. With it, we think not just of Lucretian diatribe generally, but of a specific, revolutionary, six-book project that goes by the name *De Rerum Natura*. Even more, those who know their Lucretius well remember not only that the dinner-guest metaphor of book 3 is assigned to his title-character, but that she casts the fool's demand for more life in terms of his failure to "finish his labor" *finem facis atque laboris*. Thus, that central problem of Horace's first poem, the quest for limits set by nature (*denique sit **finis** quaerendi, cumque habeas plus | pauperiem metuas minus, et **finire laborem** | incipias, S.* 1.1.92–4), is recalled silently one last time at the poem's end through an allusion that is itself positioned and performed as the natural "finish" of the poet's first satiric *labor*. Horace is no (Lucretian) fool.

Sermones 1.1 is thick with voices remembered from other works. The most prominent of these, the one scholars generally have been most ready to hear, is the Lucretian voice that breaks in at several points and is most prominent in the poem's last lines. Still, there are other voices blended into those lines that generally do not get noticed, either because they are softer and, as a result, slightly less obvious, or, as I prefer to think, because admitting them makes such a mess of the views we bring to these poems about what can and cannot happen in satire. By this I do not mean to suggest that scholars are in the habit of seeing allusions and then finding ways to deny them. Rather, I think that the activity of picking up on allusions and admitting their relevance always depends first on the reader's field of view. That is, it has to do with the checklist of *possibly* relevant pre-existing texts we bring to what we are reading and actively use to make sense of it. That list, that "matrix of possibilities" preapproved as relevant, sets our notions of genre and fixes our attention in certain directions.[30] Unless an allusion to something off the list is simply too powerful to be denied, it runs a decided risk of getting ignored or pushed aside as mere "background noise."

In the case of Horace's *Sermones* it is easy enough to see how Lucretius might figure as a relevant and likely source of inter-textual meaning, since he is judged to be roughly in the same field of confrontational moral-didactic. Given that conceptual overlap, references to Lucretius are noticed readily and given plenty of room to maneuver and "mean." It is much harder, on the other hand, to see how or why Virgil's songs among the goats might be relevant to the satirist's moral, confrontational aims, and so the *Eclogues* are generally left off our genre-fixing list; not actively rejected, just something we do not expect to encounter, and so we don't. Yet, as Michael Putnam has recently shown, the last lines of *S.* 1.1 are in fact stacked with allusions to Virgil, both to his *Eclogues* and (if you believe him, as I do) to his not-yet-published *Georgics*.[31] If credited as grade-A "allusions," and thereby allowed to "mean," these correspondences give a severe jolt to pre-existing notions of genre. They make us reconsider the relevance of texts that never appeared on our genre-constituting, relational-sense-making list.

That jolt, I believe, is the key point to the Virgilian allusions that cluster about the conclusion of *S.* 1.1. For it is the very business of this poem, and especially of this conclusion, to get us

---

[30] The idea of reading through a "matrix of possibilities" I owe to Fowler (1997) 14.

[31] See Putnam (1995). For a more general survey of allusions to Virgil's *Eclogues* throughout book 1, see Van Rooy (1973).

thinking in new, streamlined ways about what satire looks like. As
Putnam has pointed out, the *satur/satis* juxtaposition that concludes the poem and signals a salient moment in the poem's genre-
shifting work itself alludes to the last lines of Virgil's tenth
Eclogue, where the image of satiation/satisfaction in eating serves
already "as a metaphor for the measured composition of a
poem."[32] There the shepherd-poet takes his leave from song with
these parting words to his muses (Virg. *Ecl.* 10.70–7):

> **haec sat erit,** diuae, uestrum cecinisse poetam,
> dum sedet et gracili fiscellam texit hibisco,
> Pierides: uos haec facietis maxima Gallo,
> Gallo, cuius amor tantum mihi crescit in horas
> quantum uere nouo uiridis se subicit alnus.
> surgamus; solet esse grauis cantantibus umbra,
> iuniperi grauis umbra; nocent et frugibus umbrae.
> ite domum **saturae**, uenit Hesperus, ite **capellae**.

It will be enough, goddesses, for your poet to have sung these things
while he sits and weaves his little basket from twigs of supple hibiscus. It
is up to you, Muses of Pieria, to make Gallus prize them beyond the rest;
Gallus, for whom my love grows stronger by the hour, shooting up like
a green alder at the first of spring. Come on! Shade weighs heavy on
us singers. Heavy juniper-shade. Darkness does our grain-crops no good
either. Home with you, goats! Now that you're full, home with you! It's
getting dark.

The parallel juxtaposition of *satur/satis* at the end of *S.* 1.1 suggests
that Horace's remaking of satire takes its cue, in some fashion,
from Virgil: he resembles the shepherd-poet of Eclogue 10 in
knowing precisely when and how to set limits to his poetic work.
More importantly, it is only set against Virgil's *goat*-dappled backdrop that the *satur/satis* of *S.* 1.1 actually makes sense as something other than a stretched etymological pun or a faintly credible
paradox. Being "full" or "stuffed" and having nature's minimal
"enough," after all, are two quite different things, and it is hard to
see exactly how Horace would have us think that these contrasting
ideas become automatically complementary just by being set side-
by-side – I will return to this, in a less cooperative vein, below.

    It is through the Virgilian allusion, I think, that we get a sense
of how these notions really can work together and contribute to
a single, non-contradictory idea. At the end of Virgil's *Eclogues* it

---

[32] Putnam (1995) 315.

is precisely when the goats are "full" or nicely "stuffed" that the shepherd-poet decides he has had his "enough" of muse-driven song. And here it matters tremendously that the full ones are goats and not a dinner-guest. That image of fat goats set against a thin, just "sufficient", muse, brings a telling intertextual relevance of its own: we think of Apollo's words to the poet in the prologue to Callimachus' *Aetia*: τὸ μὲν θύος ὅττι πάχιστον | θρέψαι, τὴν Μοῦσαν δ' ὠγαθὲ λεπταλέην ("feed your victim to be as fat as possible, but your muse, my friend, keep lean," 23–4). The poet is enjoined to produce one thing "thick," and another thing "thin." Somehow, I think, the ideas are complementary in Callimachus and not strictly exclusive. Both touch on his poetic aims as a writer of something that is not just "thin," but both "thick" *and* "thin."

The more readily accessible metaphor for the idea is that of the *deductum carmen*, which makes the art of poetry analogous to spinning thread: the poet resembles a spinner in carefully twisting a thick tuft of wool into a fine, narrow thread. Modern discussions of the metaphor stress only its "thin" stylistic implications, taking it as a symbol for a concise and refined aesthetic sense (which it is) virtually to the exclusion of any other implication.[33] But I think that misses a very important point: this is a metaphor about thickness just as much as it is about thinness. Namely, it is about the thickness that goes into and *lies beneath* the thin, fine thread of Callimachean verse and gets hidden in the process of the thread's being "drawn out" (*deductum*). All the material that made the unworked tuft of wool thick and tufty in the first place is *still there* in the slender thread, and nothing is lost from it in the process of its being worked. The thread is substantial and "full," in a sense, but it has come to resemble something delicate. And that, I think, is what Apollo's double-edged advice to the poet implies in the *Aetia* prologue. It inheres in the *satur/satis* juxtaposition that closes the *Eclogues*, and nothing is lost from that "thickness underneath"

---

[33] A more promising approach recently has been taken by Deremetz (1995) 287–314. He argues that, whereas Callimachus' "fat victims" are opposed to "thin poems" as two different types of gifts acceptable to Apollo, in Virgil the activities of feeding and thread-making are both complementary and successive, since shepherds must raise fat sheep for the production of high-quality thread. The inextricable link between these two activities, Deremetz argues, therefore adheres to the metaphor of the poet's own *deductum carmen*. He writes (p. 299): "La laine épaisse des grasses brebis, repues après leur longue errance à travers les monts, pourrait donc bien symboliser la tradition poétique antérieure à travers laquelle le poète vagabonde et qu'il étire en un long fil mince."

sense of the juxtaposition in the Horatian reuse of it at the end of
S. 1.1.

Such is the thickness, the stuffing that hides beneath Horace's
thin, satiric cloth. Hidden inside the last threads of his first poem
there is a whole, fat world of other texts, glancingly remembered,
that lend their substantial meaning and weight to something that,
at first sight, looks deceptively flimsy. Thick memories here include the several "inside" references mentioned above, along with
allusions to Lucretius, and, if I am right, a two-tiered allusion to
Callimachus *via* Virgil. Who knows what other references might
have been available to a first-century-BCE audience. In the end,
there is a strange, metalinguistic significance to ending the poem
with such a flourish of impressive, intertextual thickness. It proves
the point being made about satire's being at once "full" and "just
enough." It shows us where that fullness derives: from the cluster
of intertextual memories that get gathered up *in us* as we read.

Putnam's insight that Virgil's *Eclogues* matter to the *Sermones* in
significant, programmatic ways is both scandalous and just a little
disturbing. The scandal stems from the realization that Horace
can be just as subtle and allusive in his *Sermones* as he is elsewhere.
Scholarly narratives of Horace's poetic career often stress his early,
moral earnestness and a near-monolithic fixation with Lucilius.[34]
That makes the young Horace fairly easy to manage and compre-
hend. The preferred image for the poet in his early years tends to
look like that of his father in *S.* 1.6; a straight-talker, fresh in from
the Apulian countryside. Though a bit rough around the edges, he
can be admired for his simple wisdom and his willingness to tell it
like it is. As a poet, though, he leaves a lot to be desired. He will
come of age later when, with the help of Virgil and friends, he
transforms himself into that learned, densely allusive scholar-artist
we know so well from the *Odes.*

But here in the beginning the rules are different and much simpler: he imitates Lucilius with precision in several poems. Moral

---

[34] The most extreme example is Fiske (1920). Cf. especially pp. 25–6, where he describes
Horace's aesthetic and creative development as a process in three stages: "In the first
book of the satires Horace is trying his prentice hand. Here his dependence on Lucilius is
most clearly discernible in theme, thought, tone, and at times even in language ... The
second book of the satires ... paves the way for the epistles, in which Horace moves for
the most part quite unconsciously in the field which he has won for himself, casting only
an occasional glance backward to his former master Lucilius."

philosophers such as Bion and Lucretius he uses more generally. Comedy, both Old and New, figures into the *Sermones* for themes and characters. Rarely, though, are we required to think of specific lines from named plays. Philosophical and comic texts, not the standard canon of Callimachean writers, form the generic backdrop of Horace's early work. Since it is easy to be overwhelmed, if not turned off, by the allusive denseness and subtlety of his later *Odes*, the *Sermones* have always attracted attention of a different sort from scholars drawn to poetry of a different sort. The *Sermones* have always seemed to be that one place in Horace where we could make sense of a poem without constantly looking over our shoulders to see what tiny nuances we might be missing in poetic precedents faintly remembered.[35] How refreshing that was! And it made for a nice hometown-hero start to the tale of the poet's soon-to-take-off career.

Those dense, provocative allusions at the end of *S.* 1.1 make us question that easy narrative scheme. We are right to be scandalized by them, and to think that they pose a threat to satire's attractive, straight-talking ways. That is exactly the reaction they seem to demand, both now and, even more, in their late first-century BCE setting. They make us reconsider any prepackaged notions we might have about what satire looks like and how it goes about its "straightforward, moral" work. As I have suggested, it is significant that the poem's most salient, genre-fixing moment should also be the moment of its most intense and "thick" intertextual energy. And it is important that this energy derives exclusively (as far as we can tell) from non-satiric texts. Genres "happen" through dialogue with pre-existing texts, so notions of genre, such as those remembered and challenged in *S.* 1.1, can be realigned only when new, extra-generic voices break into the mix.[36] Generic expectations, set by the reader's personally screened list of preapproved texts, are thereby given a thorough shake, and notions of genre are then necessarily reconfigured. That reconfigurative shake, I think, is precisely what happens with the infusion of bucolic images that close the first satire.

---

[35] For example, Knoche (1975) 77 summarily dismisses an early attempt by Witte to establish a link between the chariot-race scenes of Virg. *G.* 1.512–14 and Hor. *S.* 1.1.114–16. The connection rates as extremely strong and meaningful by current standards of intertextual criticism. See especially Putnam (1995) 313–14.

[36] On genre as "happening" not "thing," see especially Barchiesi (1997).

The point is suggested not only by the fact that the dense, intertextual moment that ends *S.* 1.1 is also the moment when we are
most aware that the genre is being reconfigured, but by the extra-
generic suppositions that are themselves already inside the reference to Virgil's well-fed goats, put there by Virgil himself. As
Michael Putnam has suggested, the conclusion of Virgil's tenth
Eclogue is already obsessed with the process of generic reconfigu-
ration, and this surely contributes to the genre-shifting force of
the allusion at the end of *S.* 1.1. Putnam writes (emphasis mine):
"Virgil closes his collection of pastorals with an elaborate tribute
to his slightly older poetic contemporary and friend, Gallus. This
encomium served to enshrine Gallus in the pantheon of poets by
praising his accomplishments in the writing of elegy *through a different generic medium* to which the same criteria of refinement have
now been applied. Horace in his opening satire pays a similar
tribute to his own slightly older poetic friend, *again in a different
genre* carefully signaled by the word *satur*, of which once more new
standards of polish are henceforth to be demanded."[37] That
insight, I think, gives new force to the Virgilian allusion at the end
of *S.* 1.1. Because it refers not just to Virgil, but to Virgil's redeployment of Gallus in the pioneering of his *Eclogues*, the allusion
demonstrates not only that Horace respects his older contemporary and that his *Sermones* access Virgilian standards of polish, but
that he knows the *Eclogues* for what they advertise themselves to be:
an aggressive, perhaps equally jarring act of reappropriation and
generic invention. Such invention, Horace knows, never arises *ex
nihilo*. It stems from the redeployment of off-list texts we never
thought to encounter.

By now it is clear that, despite all protestations of contain-
ing just enough and no more, Horace's *Sermones* are in fact big,
thick poems, stuffed just as full and piled just as high as the
works they try so aggressively to discredit. Those last two lines
where the poet warns us against thinking he has "ransacked" (*com-
pilasse*, from which English "compile") the works of "blear-eyed
Crispinus" (**Cris**-*pini* ... *l*-**ippi**, 120, a cryptogram for **Chrysippus**) are double-edged, since they are themselves chock-full of
material ransacked not from Crispinus necessarily (as far as we can
tell), but from Lucretius, Virgil, Callimachus, and perhaps even

---

[37] Putnam (1995) 315.

others.[38] The reuse of material marked as "theirs" implicates the poet in the ways of his misers. It proves that his opening claim "*No one* lives content with his own lot in life" (***nemo*** ... *illa contentus uiuat,* 1.1.1–3) really does apply to everyone, himself included.[39] In his own way, the poet who speaks the lines is just as greedy and envious of what others have as everyone else. It is just that his desire for what is theirs shows itself in different, less obvious ways.

He returns to that "everyone is miserable and greedy" theme at the end of *S.* 1.1 with the image of a fool who "melts" with envy when he sees that "someone else's she-goat carries a more-swollen udder" (*aliena capella gerat distentius uber,* 1.1.110). As Putnam has decisively shown, besides recalling the "full goats" of Eclogue 10, the line recalls a striking moment in Virgil's fourth Eclogue "where the poet describes the magical abundance nature manifests for the newborn child" (*E.* 4.21–2):[40]

> ipsae lacte domum referent distenta capellae
> ubera ...

and all by themselves the she-goats will return home with udders swollen
...

And so it turns out that the object of the fool's desire, that "someone else's she-goat" he is so hot to have for himself, is *Virgil's* she-goat.[41] Inside the image, we spy the poet glancing enviously in Virgil's direction, even reaching over and taking something that clearly does not belong to him: a small snatch of bucolic *ubertas*.[42]

---

[38] The cryptogram in line 120 was suggested to me by Andrea Cucchiarelli, Denis Feeney, and Peter Nani, all working separately.

[39] Cf. Oliensis (1998a) 17: "On one side, the poet ridicules the foibles of men caught up in the pursuit of wealth or status and extols a traditional ethics of contentment; on the other, the poetry publishes and promotes the poet's own progress from the obscure margins to the shining center of Roman society. The dissonance between the preaching and the practice is audible from the outset."

[40] See Putnam (1995) 310–12.

[41] On further goat-envy in Virgil (especially *cuium pecus* of *Ecl.* 3.1), cf. Henderson (1999) 169: "This particular animal fattening nicely for sacrifice, and eventually a feast in store for somebody, *belongs to Theocritus,* word for word. Does the Latin poem belong, then, to Theocritus? ... And that may put to us the question: in what sense do we think that poetry 'belongs' to someone; that literature is a dispute and criticism and arbitration; that the arts are the sort of thing that can be 'owned.'"

[42] The term *ubertas* has a long established history as a stylistic term in rhetoric and literary theory; see *OLD s.v. ubertas* 3a. Such "richness" is thus something that a satirist might well want to ransack from a higher literary genre.

Horace's own emulatory greed is showing. But then Lucretius used the phrase *uberibus distentis* of milk-laden sheep at Lucr. 1.259, so we cannot automatically let Virgil off the hook either. He has done some cattle-rustling of his own in stocking the hills of his *Eclogues,* and who knows where Lucretius might have gotten the image? Sources behind this merest of glancing memories proliferate, pile-fashion, at the poem's end, and the whole source-tracing game threatens to spin off into infinity. That is the problem that may well be the point. The pile is back!

The satirist's wagging finger turns on himself a second time with the chariot-race scene that directly precedes the severally-tiered *satur/satis* allusions at the poem's end. Putnam has pointed out that lines 114–15 –

> ut cum carceribus missos rapit ungula currus,
> instat equis auriga suos uincentibus . . .

– bear a remarkable resemblance to the concluding lines of *Georgics* book 1 (512–14):[43]

> ut cum carceribus sese effudere quadrigae,
> addunt in spatia, et frustra retinacula tendens
> fertur equis auriga neque audit currus habenas.

So again, built into a message about the foolishness of speeding your horses ahead to catch up to the fool in front of you is an instance of the poet's own horse-powered competitiveness. The image shows him in a stolen chariot, following in someone else's well-marked tracks. We see him peer ahead to Virgil (or is Virgil perhaps peering ahead towards him?) in a hotly contested compositional race. But Virgil is not leading the race, and he has eyes that are equally green. As John Henderson has recently shown, the image of the poet struggling "along with/against the precursor-rivals – as in any horse-race" has a long history in Greek and Latin literary history.[44] Already in the late fifth century BCE Choerilus of Samos complains of being left in the dust of poets who raced ahead of him, and by Juvenal's day the chariot-race had become the stock-in-trade way of imagining the poet's "drive"

---

[43] Putnam (1995) 313–14.   [44] Henderson (1995) 108.

to compete with and match his precursors' achievements.[45] Virgil knew the motif from Callimachus (as he demonstrates later in the proem to *Georgics* 3). But among Latin precursors Ennius had a version of it, perhaps Lucilius as well. Callimachus knew it from Pindar, but he may have availed himself also of intervening sources now lost to us. Again, we are spinning off into infinity.

Clearly, as with any good, diagnostic "pile," the problem that comes with an image so intertextually "deep," is knowing where precisely to mark its beginning and end. If Virgil's use of the motif matters in *S.* 1.1 (as I think it does), then why not Virgil's source in Callimachus (or did he have it from Ennius, or perhaps Lucilius)? And how about Callimachus' source in Pindar, and so on? Who counts among precursors who used the image, and who does not, and just how much does each "possible" source contribute to the image's most recent use? What is the proper "hierarchy of reference" to be observed in our reading?[46] Such is the inherently pile-like and unmanageable nature of the image, or any image of its hyper-allusive type; it can never be probed to anything like its natural, final "bottom." *Putting a stop* to what it means, then, must always be a function of, and take its cue from, the reader's own, personalised sense of what is "too much." Limiting its sense, making it "mean," making it "genre," is an aggressive act of the sense-*maker's* will, that very human will to impose order upon, and orient oneself within, a frightening, fathomless space.[47]

---

[45] *Supplementum Hellenisticum* 317: "Blessed indeed the man who was skilled in song in those days, a servant of the Muses when the meadow was still undefiled. Now when everything has been portioned out and the arts have reached their limits, we are left behind in the race, and one looks everywhere in vain for a place to drive one's newly yoked chariot." On these lines, see Hopkinson (1988) xv.

[46] On the "hierarchy of reference" problem in intertextual studies, see Fowler (1997) 16: "The inherently multiple nature of intertextual reference means that the notion of a hierarchy of reference itself becomes questionable. In terms of a common metaphor, previous texts leave "traces" in later texts, and the relationship between those traces, whether figured as additive or combative, is a central concern of any study of intertextuality: but traces left are always multiple."

[47] Cf. Steiner (1992) 7–8, writing on Shakespeare: "And where are the confines of relevance? No text earlier than or contemporaneous with Shakespeare can, *a priori*, be ruled out as having no conceivable bearing. No aspect of Elizabethan and European culture is formally irrelevant to the complete context of a Shakespearean passage. Explorations of semantic structure very soon raise the problem of infinite series." Martindale (1997) 14, commenting on Steiner, notes: "One might add that no later text can be excluded either, if one accepts the importance of reception."

Such is the bottomless depth to Horace's slender cloth. It is here, in the pile, that Horace hides some of the most un-Callimachean aspects of his famously Callimachean program. Here he is most cluttered and torrential, like Lucilius in *S.* 1.4, and like that muddy river, *his* home-town, inspirational river, in lines 58–60 of poem 1. Here, too, as I hope to show, he will bury the barbs of some very aggressive satire, that angry, politically engaged, acerbic stuff we always sensed *should* be there. There, in that un-Callimachean pile, is where his "real" satire happens for Horace, and that is precisely where it has to happen. For by Horace's day, claims to being "new" and "slimmed down" were themselves passé, and necessarily self-defeating. They had been used too often to seem anything other than "old" and "fat." This is the bind that Horace, and the Augustan poets generally, find themselves in, in setting out to write poetry that qualifies somehow as *really* "new" and "their own." That poetry, whatever its final generic look, must depart from cliché-Callimacheanism (i.e. by constructing Callimacheanism *as* cliché) in some real sense. The satirist knows this. And it is no accident that his alter-ego in the charioteer-poet who runs so far behind in the race, and strives so desperately to catch up and get noticed, can only make his way to the front of the pack by doing exactly what Callimachus insists he must never do: he must tread a path trampled flat by the chariots of so many others before him. He must eat their dust. For Horace, and for all the poets soon to emerge (in our imaginations, at least) as "Augustans," the well-worn path is the only "new" way to go.

THE SOCIAL POETICS OF HORATIAN *LIBERTAS*: SINCE WHEN IS "ENOUGH" A "FEAST"?

Horace serves subtle fare. His plate is small, and its viands neatly arranged. But their flavours – if you have a taste for his sort of satire – are delectable and complex, redolent of remote spices, and pinches of this and that. So much endless work, easily over-looked, has gone into making his dish perfect. But the question remains whether anyone will notice. And, more importantly, whether anyone *should*. For scholars commonly allow Horace to win his every point against the *fautores Lucili* without seriously con-sidering what is at stake in his critique of Lucilius beyond matters of aesthetic refinement and careful writing. But who is to say that

Horace's "enough" should automatically count as enough for anyone else, especially for those who have developed a taste for the
gigantic stuffed plates of Lucilius? Satire's plate, both as served
by Lucilius, and by definition, is huge (a *lanx* "trencher") and
"crammed full" (*satura*), spilling over its edges like a cornucopia, or
(negatively turned) like a river in flood. The *lanx satura* metaphor
is derived from an ancient feast of Ceres, a harvest celebration
of first fruits, and thus an ancient "Thanksgiving Day" of sorts.
Variety and sheer abundance matter to this feast, not because
certain of its celebrants just happen to stuff themselves on that
day, but because this is a feast, a harvest feast, no less, and not a
philosopher's lunch. The day is thus defined by its provision of
"too much," never "just enough." And stuffing oneself is simply
what one does as a matter of observing the day's conventions.

We came to satire's "feast" expecting to stuff ourselves. But
Horace sets out lean, pretty fare on a small plate, and he tells us
that this will be his way, and thus necessarily ours, too, of observing the day from now on. Haven't we a right to be offended? The
man is messing with *our* Thanksgiving Day! Who is he to tell us
that Lucilius did not know how to throw a "proper" party, and
that getting stuffed and drunk, and maybe even losing control and
pissing on the couch, is not his idea of a good time (not on *my*
couch!), and therefore should not be ours? Lucilius threw one hell
of a party. Everyone in Horace's audience knew it. Some may
have questioned whether Lucilius' poems were decent and/or
refined, but none would have thought that decency and refinement
were what his "Satires" were supposed to be about. None would
have had the temerity to serve a scaled-down side-salad, however
brilliant, and still call the dish a Lucilian "feast."

Horace calls Lucilius "muddy" (*lutulentus*) in *S.* 1.4, comparing
him to a river in flood, cluttered with debris. Scholars generally
have let Horace have his way here, emboldened by the happen-
stance of history that has delivered Horace to us as a Golden Age
Classic, and Lucilius as a smattering of scraps. As if heeding
Horace's advice, *Historia* herself stirred a "just" editorial hand to
the task of removing the great bulk of Lucilius that Horace com-
plained needed to be removed (*quod tollere uelles*, 11). Horace gets
his way.

Inside the image of "muddy Lucilius" we hear a clever allusion
to Callimachus' *Hymn to Apollo*, and that, too, is commonly credited

to Horace as evidence of his deep learning, and his adhering to higher aesthetic sensibilities.[48] But this may be to credit him too quickly, and with far too much. For also inside the image we are given not just a clever allusion to Callimachus, but a healthy dose of the same inane theoretical reckoning about "nature's limits" that we heard so often in the first three poems. The basic criticism is, by now, utterly familiar: like a river spilling over its banks, boundaries put to it by nature, Lucilius has no sense of his satires' natural "limits" (*fines*), so he rages unchecked, and he sweeps up everything that stands in his way. The theory is easily picked apart. For what is so "unnatural" about a river spilling over its banks at certain times of the year? This is more "law" than "aberrance" as far as rivers go. And, more fundamentally, who is to say that satire, or any literary genre for that matter, either can, or should, have anything demonstrably "natural" about it? Are we to assume that the urge to write satire is somehow instinctual? Are its "limits" a secret code written in the stars, or in rivers flowing smoothly in their banks?[49]

The problem with letting Horace win his every "aesthetic" point against Lucilius is that "winning" is too clearly not his point. Rather, it is losing, in a certain style, and for certain effects. That is, Horace "plays" his debate with the *fautores Lucili* for numerous comic effects that dare us to take either side seriously enough to declare one ("our" side) a clear "winner," and the other a "loser," or the battle even worth fighting. At *S.* 1.4.86–90 Horace hints that this battle is hardly the grand, theoretical enterprise that it is commonly made out to be. To his critics' charge that he loves causing pain (*laedere gaudes*) he responds:

> saepe tribus lectis uideas cenare quaternos
> e quibus unus amet quauis aspergere cunctos
> praeter eum qui praebet aquam; post hunc quoque potus,
> condita cum uerax aperit praecordia Liber.
> hic tibi comis et urbanus liberque uidetur.

---

[48] Notoriously complacent in this regard is Freudenburg (1993) 158.

[49] The idea that satirists write from "instinct" is humorously sent up in the mock archaeology of justice of 1.3.99–112 (heard especially in the correspondence of line 106 *ne quis fur esset, neu latro, neu quis adulter* to the same criminal figures as objects of humorous abuse at the beginning of the next poem), and again, more obviously, at 2.1.24–60 (with lines 41–2 again featuring the dreaded *latrones*). In the end, such "natural" theories of genre sound much more Stoic than Epicurean, so these passages may perhaps be taken as further instances of "theoretical ventriloquism," i.e. Horace sampling alien theoretical views (perhaps even those of his own sect) and sending them up.

Often you can see them at dinner parties sitting four-to-a-couch. One of them loves casting aspersions on everyone there for any reason at all; on everyone, that is, except for the host. But once the man is good and drunk, he splatters him too, after Liber, who's always blurting out the truth, opens up the hidden recesses of his heart. That's your version of someone who is elegant, cultured, and free!

This is what the ancient grammarians' "*satura* = inebriated release" theory looks like when repackaged as a taunt.[50] We are given to assume that Horace's critics made use of the etymology in defining their (and Lucilius') work as a brand of honest, unrestricted censure targeted squarely against "the disgraces and crimes of men." Horace's less direct brand of criticism they have discredited as so much underhanded backbiting. The charge is deflected here and sent speeding back against the *fautores Lucili* in the image of an abuser too drunk to notice whom he is abusing and why.

But more important than the (quite conventional) theory that hides inside the image of drunkards squabbling at dinner, is the power that that image possesses to define a particular range of experience for the speaker who uses it, and thus to establish a highly distinct and, by now, familiar point of view. For by means of that image we are once again drawn into the narrow world of a seasoned dinner-guest, whose experience of parties and keeping up appearances is so vast and all-consuming that it makes itself felt in everything he says and does. His rules of good satire he understands as a code of decent behavior to be observed at parties, not by the host (why not take that perspective?), but by guests of low standing. His is a "parasite's theory of satire." And thus, what we often think of as a deeply learned critical debate between Horace and his detractors, with Horace always managing to land strongly on the winning side, is here cast as a squabble between lackeys at a rich man's dinner-party. The Epicurean parasite of poems 1–3 has been taking notes. And he does not like what he sees. His rivals across the table prefer getting boisterous and drunk, thinking themselves more honest and more fun. He himself prefers to enjoy the evening, and thus his satire, at a slower pace, drinking in moderation, and keeping everyone happy and on good terms.

Horace scoffs at the idea that the satirist's voice is necessarily

---

[50] For the theory, see above n. 18.

unrestrained and out of control (this amounts to yet another "lack of *fines*" complaint), like that of a party-goer in his cups, reeling under Liber's influence (Liber = Bacchus, god of wine, the tongue's *liber*ator). He claims to have a much better sense of what being "free" (*liber*) entails, and how that freedom expresses itself in satire's polite company. And yet, nothing that this man says, or stands for, in these poems suggests that he has the slightest idea of what it means to be truly "free" in the way that Lucilius was free. That is the most ludicrous part of his debate with the men whom he casts here as lackeys stacked four to a couch. Even as we see them crowded together in worn togas, and squabbling hungrily over the last bit of cheesecake, we hear both sides making bold claims to knowing precisely what true "freedom" entails.

But Lucilius' case was clearly different. If he spoke, as his legend asserts, "with much freedom / freedom of speech" (*multa cum libertate*) he did so not because he was temporarily out of his head, drunk on someone else's wine, but because he had that much freedom to draw on *in himself*, whenever he liked. He spoke who he was, in other words. And he was no lackey. Nor was he a mule-driver, as Horace pretends to be near the end of his sixth satire (1.6.104–6). And his ears never drooped, as they tend to for poor Flaccus ("Droopy") in more than one of his poems, likening him to an overburdened ass (see below). Instead, the equestrian image we most associate with Lucilius is that of Juvenal 1, where the poet remembers him as an epic hero, driving his horses at full speed over the plains of his native Aurunca, in hot pursuit of his next kill. That image, and the aggressive satiric "horsemanship" it represents, is not just a metaphor in Lucilius' case, but it refers to his actually having been a horseman in real life, an *eques*, with the requisite fortune to purchase his rank, and the requisite freedom to say whatever he wanted.[51] His *genus*, the standard Latin word for "genre," is a condition of his *genus*, the word for "stock" and "social class." The words are the same in Latin not as a matter of chance, but because the concepts entail one another so inextrica-

---

[51] Lucilius was, by all accounts, extremely well-connected, and he was exceedingly wealthy. His rambling third satire tells of his touring vast estates that he himself owned in southern Italy and Sicily. Through his sister he would eventually, posthumously, become the Great Uncle of none other than Pompey the Great. Gruen (1992) 278–9 concludes: "The poet belonged to a family that had acquired senatorial rank, secured links with major political figures, and possessed the means to play a role on the public scene ... the satirist plainly had a place in Rome's upper echelons." For Lucilius' illustrious family background, see Krenkel (1970) 18–19.

bly that to say one is also to say, and mean, the other. Thus, for many Romans in Horace's audience who knew Lucilius' *Saturae* as poetry of a certain "genre/class," Horace's ambition to "rank" as a satirist in his *Sermones* would have seemed far-fetched and foolhardy, with his failure a foregone, laughable conclusion.

But that is the way it always was in Rome, and the way it would always be: *libertas* "free speech" is equivalent to and only ever as good as one's *libertas* "freedom." Here again, the same word covers for the Romans what are for us two distinct (though intersecting) semantic territories, and there is no *Oxford Latin Dictionary* at hand to tell them to keep "freedom" in column 1 at a clear distance from "free speech" in column 7. They knew no such handy hierarchy. Put differently, "freedom" for the elite Roman male (the only ones who ever really had it in full) is not something he merely "possesses," it is something he "does." It exists in performance, that is, in the day-to-day events, situations, and rituals that generally were thought to mark a man as "free." Public invective, as an exercise in "freedom"/"free speech," ranks among the most important of these status-generating/status-demonstrating rituals. Not only does it define its target as a deviant, but, more importantly, it identifies the speaker as someone with the requisite *auctoritas* to criticize and degrade another free, noble citizen. He is himself a free, self-standing subject, with full access to the ritual that defines him as such, and full freedom to use the aggressive voice that it gives him against one of his peers.

Lucilius possessed an impressive, grade-A "freedom" in abundance (**multa** *cum libertate notabant*), so he speaks *in abundance*, freely, whatever he wants, against whomever he chooses to name a sluggard or a scoundrel, worthy of being lashed with his quasi-censorial whip. According to the strange tale of *S.* 1.4, he is as an attractive, pure-bred peach "hanging" from a noble tree (*hinc omnis* **pendet** *Lucilius*, 6), a man of deep, *old* comic pedigree and punch. As I have already remarked, this is not just a story of the famous, unrestrained *libertas* "free speech" that Lucilius is known to have employed in his *Satires* (though that is precisely the way the opening lines of *S.* 1.4 are always taken), this is also the story of the "freedom" that he possessed *in order to* speak freely. That is, Horace is telling us in these lines where Lucilius' free speech came from, and what it took for him to have it, and to use it. This also, by extension, is the story of why he himself never will.

Thus, Lucilius' project, as Horace constructs it in *S.* 1.4, is an exact mirror image of the poet's swaggering, late-republican, elite-male self: politically engaged, hyper-confident, unchecked, not niggling over details, prolific. That is Lucilius' problem, this poem says. He never had to erase anything on his page. As in life, so in his writings, Lucilius never had to take back anything he said or did. He did not own an eraser, and he was *proud* of it! And he performs that freedom to live and speak as he pleases, without apologies, by writing the way he writes – taking nothing back. What an impressive freedom that was!

That is what makes Horace's claims to have learned his habits of free speech from his father in *S.* 1.4 and 1.6 so odd and, at the same time, so programmatically telling. He claims at *S.* 1.4.103–5:

> liberius si
> dixero quid, si forte iocosius, hoc mihi iuris
> cum uenia dabis. insueuit pater optimus hoc me ...

If I have spoken too freely, or maybe jested too much, you will forgive me. My noblest father trained me in the habit.[52]

That father may have been "noblest" in terms of his virtue and good sense (*OLD* columns 1–2), but he was anything but noblest in terms of status (*OLD* columns 5–6). Horatian *libertas*, the brand of "free speech" he shows us in satire, he claims to have learned from a *libertus*, a man of severely compromised freedom. And that restricted version of free speech must necessarily *sound* very different from the Grade-A, uncompromised version of it Lucilius had access to and seems to have used in his *Satires*.

The issue of status, huge in *S.* 1.4 and 1.6, is picked up again and relentlessly driven home in the first poem of book 2. There the poet repeatedly claims to follow Lucilius in his chosen generic path only to show us just how impossible it is for him to follow that path through to its free-speaking, Lucilian end. In lines 28–9 he says to Trebatius: *me pedibus delectat claudere uerba | Lucili ritu, nostrum melioris utroque* ("I like to close off words in feet, just as Lucilius did. He was a man better/nobler than the both of us"). Scholars have scratched their heads over these lines, wondering how Horace has managed this change of heart, now thinking of

---

[52] These lines appear to be a deliberate remake of Cicero's defense of *his* use of Lucilian *libertas* at *Ad fam.* 12.16.3: *in quibus uersiculis si tibi quibusdam uerbis* εὐθυρρημονέστερος *uidebor, turpitudo personae eius, in quam liberius inuehimur, nos uindicabit ... deinde, qui magis hoc Lucilio licuerit assumere libertatis quam nobis?*

Lucilius as his poetic "better." Usually this is explained in terms of the poet's deferring to Lucilius as an older authority figure, and the acknowledged *inuentor* of the genre.[53] But then why should he include Trebatius in his assessment? He was not in the habit of "closing off words in feet." Porphyrion, in the early third century CE, sees it differently: "clearly (he means) better in status and natural talent." I think that is right. The issue is, at least partially, if not primarily, one of status, and what one is born with. It concerns the great gulf that separates Horace from Lucilius not just in terms of connections, money, and power, but especially in terms of his being able to say what he wants to say.[54] By 30 BCE both Trebatius and Horace met the minimum qualifications of a Roman *eques*, and so, technically, they could claim to measure up to Lucilius as equals.[55] In real terms, however, as these lines point out, they were nowhere close. They measured up to Lucilius as little better than municipal hicks.[56] Horace's "freedom," and thus his "freedom to speak," would always look terribly pale in comparison to that of Lucilius.

HITTING SATIRE'S *FINIS*: ALONG FOR THE RIDE IN *SERMONES* 1.5

Try as they might, Horace's *Sermones* are chronically incapable of doing what Lucilius' *Satires* did. They cannot even begin to approach his pitch of unencumbered belligerence and venom. Nor can they "bite into" (as Persius has it) the power-players and the big political issues that Lucilius so notoriously lashed at

---

[53] E.g. Kiessling–Heinze (1961) 183 annotates *claudere uerba* with: "also ohne den Anspruch, wirkliche 'Poesie' zu geben. Damit repliziert H. auf den Vorwurf *similis mille die uersus deduci posse*: ihn selbst freut es, und er tut es *Lucili ritu*, in der Weise des grossen klassischen Schriftstellers, einer Autorität, der auch Trebatius sich unterordnen muss, daher *nostrum melioris utroque*."

[54] Commentators generally dissuade their readers from thinking too crassly of money and status here, e.g. Lejay (1966) 300: "Ici il n'y a pas lieu de faire allusion à la fortune ou à la noblesse de Lucilius. *Melioris* indique une supériorité générale, surtout d'ordre intellectuel." Cf. Muecke (1993) 106: "a catchphrase, in which the meaning of 'better' need not be pressed."

[55] On Trebatius' equestrian status, see Sonnet in *RE* vi A 2253–4; for that of Horace in the period of the *Sermones*, see Armstrong (1986).

[56] There was a vast "continuum of domination" within the categories "free" and "slave" in ancient Rome, as well as within each smaller category (such as *eques* "horseman") inside these basic poles. On the "continuum" of Roman social relations, see Fitzgerald (2000) 69–86.

with hungry teeth. As I have argued, this is not just a matter of
Callimachean sensibilities keeping the poet from saying what his
Lucilian, south Italian instincts urge him to say (though it is that
too). It is also, and perhaps especially, a matter of his being a
freed slave's son, and of his never having had the remotest chance
of doing what Lucilius did. This linking of "genre" to "status" and
"style" to "self" is a central theme of the programmatic "freedom"
disquisitions of *S.* 1.4 and 1.6, where the poet's father figures so
prominently.

But I think the issue is there too, in significant but subtle ways,
in the poem that intervenes, the famous, comparison-inviting narrative of the poet's trip to Brindisi in the entourage of Maecenas.
That poem is the most obvious of extended imitations of Lucilius
in the Horatian corpus, and it is significantly placed right after the
Lucilian criticisms of *S.* 1.4.[57] Elsewhere I have argued that in
the comparison-inviting travel narrative of *S.* 1.5 Horace shows us
some of the things he can do in satire that Lucilius never could;
namely, write clean, slimmed-down verse.[58] The trip that Lucilius
required an entire book to describe, Horace gets us through in
a mere 104 lines. I stand by that assessment, but I think that the
opposite point can and should be made as well. It is, I think (and
must now admit) the more important point. For in this poem,
Horace invites comparison with Lucilius not only to show that he
can do things that Lucilius could not. He does it to show that
he cannot do some of the things that Lucilius so famously did.

A case in point concerns the strange, un-Lucilian muzzling of
the poet's political voice throughout the poem. In *S.* 1.5 the poet
makes a habit of teasing us with suggestions of having something
politically relevant and important to say, and then not saying it.
Repeatedly he balks at saying anything that really matters, preferring instead to talk about cheating tavern-keepers, croaking frogs,
whatever. That is, anything but anything that matters. And what
makes this so especially frustrating in the poem is that the journey
it describes was actually a crucial event in the political history of
the Second Triumvirate. Though you would never know it from
the narrative of this poem, Rome hovered on the brink of civil

---

[57] In a forthcoming work, Andrea Cucchiarelli describes the connection of 1.4 to 1.5 as
that of a "manifesto teorico" giving way to a "manifesto pratico." I owe much to
Cucchiarelli's fine study of *S.* 1.5 in the pages that follow.

[58] See Freudenburg (1993) 201–5.

war in 37 BCE. The delegation Horace tells of travelling with was sent from Rome to Brindisi to negotiate a peace between Antony and Octavian.[59] If that delegation should fail, Rome would tumble headlong into civil war. That is the larger political context of *S.* 1.5. But this is how Horace chooses to remember meeting up with two of the most important members of the delegation at the town of Anxur (*S.* 1.5.27–31):

> **huc** uenturus erat **Maecenas** optimus atque
> Cocceius, missi magnis de rebus uterque
> legati, auersos soliti componere amicos.
> **hic** oculis **ego** nigra meis collyria lippus
> illinere.

Noblest **Maecenas** was on his way **here**, and Cocceius, too, both sent as legates on some big business because they were good at patching together broken friendships. **I** smear dark salve on my eyes **here**. They were acting up.

The contrast of big politics with petty nonsense is set off by the antithesis of *huc ... Maecenas* to *hic ... ego*. As W. Ehlers writes, "There exists a striking contrast between the importance of the two delegations, on the one hand, and the triviality of Horace's discomforts on the other. Still, Horace's conjunctivitis is thoroughly framed by the three verses devoted to the delegations."[60]

Readers come to this poem always wanting more, but the speaker gives them *his* minimal "enough," and no more. Instead of delivering on desires, Horace simply toys with them in *S.* 1.5 by exaggerating his Epicureanism (and thus his detachment from politics) as nowhere else in the first book. In places he sounds awfully like Lucretius himself, especially when he describes the coming of night in lines 9–10 ("now night was preparing to draw shadows across the lands, and to sprinkle signs in the heavens"), and when he scoffs at the people of Gnatia for thinking that the

---

[59] Most recently, Fedeli (1994) 410–13 has made a strong case for the delegation of 37 BCE, the *pax Tarentina.*

[60] Ehlers (1985) 71 (my translation). Scholars have long regretted this failure by the poet to address the larger political significance of the journey he under-describes. Lamenting this as an opportunity lost, Gibbon quipped in his 1796 treatise *A Minute Examination of Horace's Journey to Brundisium, and of Cicero's Journey into Cilicia* (p. 16): "The maxim that everything in great men is interesting applies only to their minds and ought not to be extended to their bodies". Cf. Fedeli (1994) 412: "D'altra parte, nonostante la gravità del momento, i motivi politici per cui Orazio e i compagni di viaggio furono costretti a percorrere la lunga strada verso Brindisi restano completamente sullo sfondo."

gods involve themselves in human affairs (97–103).[61] He waves a bright Epicurean banner by obsessing over the value of friendship and keeping good company, rejoicing when good friends arrive, and weeping when they depart. His swearing to value nothing more than a pleasant friend (44) recalls a famous maxim of Epicurus himself.[62]

As we have already seen, the speaker's eyes flare up at the sight of big political issues.[63] He steers clear of them again at lines 77–81, when he catches sight of those mountains he knows so well from his childhood (*montis Apulia notos*, 77). As he approaches his home-region of Apulia we might expect him to dwell on his homecoming a bit. But unlike Lucilius, he has no country estate to visit, and no home to go back to. His father's estate was taken from him and handed over to Octavian's veterans after Philippi. For Horace, there is no going back, and there is nothing left in Apulia to dwell on. Closing in on his home-town of Venusia ("Venus-town"), though on a road that cannot take him there, he has those blinding tears in his eyes again, and he uses the same *hic ego* dodge of line 30 to check himself into a flea-bag *uilla publica* where his Venus never shows.[64] She is only a spectre haunting his dreams (*S.* 1.5.82–5):

> hic ego mendacem stultissimus usque puellam
> ad mediam noctem exspecto; somnus tamen aufert
> intentum **Veneri**. tum immundo somnia **uisu**
> nocturnam **ue**stem maculant **uen**tremque supinum.

Here, like an idiot, I stayed up till midnight waiting for a little hooker to show up. I fell asleep, still hard up for Venus. Then, lying on my back, a dirty dream came and made a mess of my pajamas and my front side.

Is it Venus, or Venusia that haunts his (Lucretian) dreams?[65]

---

[61] Clear parallels to lines 9–10 are Lucr. 5.777 *tenebris obducere terras*, and 6.864 *hoc ubi roriferis terram nox obruit umbris*. For *S.* 1.5.97–103 parallels in Lucretius are many; cf. especially Lucr. 2.646–51, 5.82, and 6.58.

[62] See DeWitt (1939) 134.

[63] Cucchiarelli (forthcoming) shows that Horace's "conjunctivitis" (*lippitudo*) has a history in Greek Old Comedy as a symbol of political incapacity, e.g. in the "blear-eyed" (ὁ γλάμων) Neoclides of Ar. *Eccl.* 395–407.

[64] There is much dispute over the exact route taken by the delegation on their southeastward trek through the mountains. See Mazzarino (1968), Desy (1988), and Radke (1989).

[65] The scene recalls the adolescent wet dream of Lucr. 4.1030–6; cf. Gowers (1993b) 59–60: "As sleep carries him away (*somnus tamen aufert* 83), we learn that we too have been diverted from Venus: her town, Venusia, lies far away on the Via Appia." Venusia is actually quite close (as the crow flies) at this point, perhaps as near as 25 kilometers. Getting there, however, as Gowers points out, would require significant backtracking: first to Beneventum, then southeast along the *Via Appia*, a two-days' journey.

Thwarting expectations is a game played *on us* throughout this poem. Recently Emily Gowers has argued that the first red herring *S.* 1.5 tosses our way is the mention of Heliodorus in line 2.[66] Scholars have generally agreed that this must be an alias for Apollodorus, a name that cannot scan in hexameters. The question, then, is which Apollodorus? Most scholars have assumed it must be the famous one, the Greek rhetor who was once Octavian's teacher. But Gowers has made an excellent case for a travel-writer less well known to us, a certain Heliodorus who wrote a poem, now completely lost, known as the "Sights" (*Theamata*) or the "Marvels" (*Thaumata*) of Italy. Horace's companion, she suggests, is not a person, but an ancient travel-guide he packs along to tell him the best features of each place he happens upon along the way. In other words, if we thought he meant Apollodorus the rhetor, we were duped. Gowers writes: "He wants to make his readers expect castles in the air, but lets them down with a bump."[67] Broken expectations are the stuff of this poem. In its own way, that wet dream of lines 82–5 is, perversely, programmatic: like that poet splayed out on his hotel bed, readers of the poem are repeatedly duped and undone by their own expectations. We keep waiting for the hooker to show, but she never does.[68]

S. 1.5 reads like a travel-guide in many ways. Among other helpful details, it tells us where the roads are especially bad, the food good, and the mosquitoes nearly unbearable. But that is where this poor-man's travel-guide always stays: in the petty details. The perspective it offers is that of a complaining Epicurean tag-along, obsessed with his own comfort, with eyes chronically flaring up at the sight of anything that matters. I think the most stunning example of the poem's penchant for teasing readers with false suggestions of grandeur comes as the entourage reaches the villa of Cocceius at Caudium. Now, as far as most Romans were concerned, Caudium was just some backwater place you hurried through on your way to somewhere else, somewhere that mattered. Still, it was a backwater that every Roman had heard of and knew

---

[66] Gowers (1993b) 54.

[67] Gowers (1993b) 54.

[68] It is generally acknowledged that Horace's nocturnal misadventures may have had some remembered parallel in Lucilius, now lost. More likely than a wet dream, in Lucilius' case, would have been a scene where the girl actually shows. Lucilius' full-scale pornographic romp would have left little to the imagination.

one very important thing about. In opening their travel-guides
to "Caudium" every Roman would expect to find some reference
to the Battle of the Caudine Forks, the most famous battle of the
Second Samnite War. Somewhere in a narrow defile near that
town in 321 BCE, a surprise battle was engaged and the Romans
were thoroughly thrashed. Defeated Roman soldiers were forced
to pass under a yoke of Samnite spears wearing only their tunics.
In other words, there is a great story to be told upon arriving at
this spot, but Horace does not tell it. Instead, he tells us about a
different battle, the one he witnessed in a local tavern, between
Maecenas' tag-along *scurra*, Sarmentus, and a scar-faced local
named Messius the Cock. A cock-fight, in other words, but all
done up in the grand epic tones we might expect the poet to use
in telling the story of the real battle of Caudium. He even calls
on the epic muses to help him "catalogue" the combatants. A
mammoth battle, all right, and right where we expected to find it.
Just not the battle we expected to find.

This poem, and this poet, are good for a laugh, but incapable of
saying anything that really matters. In *S.* 1.5 big epic themes, such
as political summits, wars, land-confiscations, and so on, are all
sights hinted at but never visited. This satire, Horace's brand of
satire, cannot go there. The last line of the poem, and the sum
of the story, is simply this: *Brundisium longae finis chartaeque uiaeque est*
("Brindisi is the end of this long journey and page," 104). This is
the most notorious letdown of the poem. Scholars have always
been puzzled by it, wondering how Horace can possibly have
meant to end it there, right where things are finally getting interesting.[69] For if the delegation described in the poem really is that
of 37 BCE, the one sent to help negotiate the Peace of Tarentum,
Brindisi is not the poem's natural "end" (*finis*). Tarentum is. So
how can he leave us hanging here in the wrong place? Since he
does leave off in Brindisi, some scholars have taken this to mean
that he cannot possibly have in mind the Peace of Tarentum.
Some have suggested the Pact of Brundisium of 40 BCE, or
Maecenas' mission to Athens in 38. But, all in all, those missions

---

[69] Gowers (1993b) 60 comments on the sudden shock of ending this way: "But Brundisium,
not Tarentum, is the end of the road. There is no doubt about that. Horace names it
as his terminus in what is perhaps the most emphatic ending in Latin literature ...
Paradoxically it is also one of the most open-ended and unsatisfying endings possible."

are even harder to make fit the details of the poem than the Peace of Tarentum.[70] That delegation is still the best option. Plutarch tells us that, on his way to negotiate that peace, Antony went first to Brindisi, so the original plan may actually have been to meet there.[71] But the citizens of that town refused to let him ashore because they were afraid to let on that they might have pro-Antonian leanings. Because of the blockade, Antony was forced to move on to Tarentum, and that is where the treaty was eventually arranged and given its name.

Of the few historical details that Horace actually lets out in *S.* 1.5, the only one that does not fit the Peace of Tarentum is the suggestion that the delegation concluded its business at Brindisi rather than at Tarentum. But that is not the necessary upshot of the poem's last lines. They may not have to tell us that at all. For perhaps the more salient point they make has to do not with where the delegation stops, but where Horace does, where he bumps into his satire's *finis* ("limit"). That is where *he* has to stop, though he clearly has much farther to go. He, that narrator of nothing that matters, in ending the poem where he does, leaves us short, at *his finis*, just as he has done so often in this poem, and in the book as a whole.

From a sympathetic perspective, we can choose to see the poet who stops too soon and says too little in a positive light, as a man who knows his limits. That is, he is a good Epicurean, comfortably at home *intra fines naturae*, as good Epicureans *should* be, and thus not much concerned that his limits do not extend out nearly as far as our own. Good for him. But from another perspective, that of one less ready to let Horace win his every point (or, to put it differently, one less convinced that his winning *is* the point), this man rates not as someone who knows his limits, but merely as a man of severe limitations, someone not up to delivering the promised Lucilian goods. For in this, his inconsequential, blatantly non-Lucilian, version of satire, there are places we simply cannot go. Places he cannot take us.

That, I believe, is the point of ending the trip so suddenly, with a flippant joke about hitting the bottom of the page, as if that

[70] The separate arguments for each treaty are examined by Musurillo (1954–5) 159–62, and Fedeli (1994) 411–12.
[71] Plut. *Ant.* 35.

matters, and thus leaving us, always, so disillusioned, and wanting more. For the shock of hitting that one-page limit, a limit never regarded as meaningful by Lucilius, has a probing, diagnostic quality to it. That is, it has a way of testing limits of a different kind, limits drawn *in us* to mark off the generic confines of "satire," and thus to separate what counts as "the real thing," from what does not. Which is it in Horace's case? How do the defining limits of his *Sermones* match up with the boundary-lines drawn in us by cherished memories of Lucilius, the genre's inventor? Do we regard Horace's newly drawn *fines*, his limits, as highly personalized re*fine*ments of the genre? Or are they con*fines*, barricades thrown up to keep this poet (and thus his audience) from going where we know that he, as a satirist, should?

In this, his low-life, non-Lucilian, version of satire, there are places we simply cannot go. Places he cannot take us. Tarentum, where Lucilius once went to visit his estates, and where the "big business" of this delegation still awaits, lies beyond the limits of Horatian *sermo*. Horace can hint at big themes in these "conversations," as he so often does, but he can never manage to deliver them. We thought he might actually land us in Tarentum, and so the joke, one last time, is on us. As the poem cuts away, leaving so much more to be said, we see the sun streaming through the slats. We, the deluded readers, are still waiting for the hooker to show.

DOGGED BY AMBITION: *SERMONES* 1.6–10

Horace never rushes to his destination in book 1. With nothing particularly urgent to do, and no appointments to keep, he maintains a steady pace in his travels, low to the ground, and painfully close to shore.[72] He ambles about the city on foot at the end of 1.6. Then again in 1.9, meandering rather than walking with purpose. Outside the city he travels by mule. The closest he ever comes to braving windswept seas is when he stalls for the night on the Pomptine marshes south of Rome (*S.* 1.5.9b–23), on a passenger barge fitted to a mule. So much for high adventure in the *Sermones*:

---

[72] On the plodding pace of Horace's trip to Brindisi, extending a five-day journey to fifteen, see Ehlers (1985) 70.

the hero's "Syrtes" is a swamp, his *Argo* a barge drawn by a mule, driven aground by a drunken sailor and a raucous fellow traveller, the deadly "sirens" of the swamp.[73]

The horses and ships not taken in book 1 are well-worn symbols of grand poetic enterprises, such as epic, and its swashbuckling counterpart in Lucilian satire, projects pushed along by mighty gusts of inspiration, like a racing chariot, or a rushing river. It makes sense, then, that they should both figure prominently in Lucilius' account of his trip to Sicily in book 3 of his *Satires*, and be taken subsequently (most famously by Juvenal) as symbols of his work.[74] The horseman speaks what the horseman knows: horses, and windswept adventures at sea. But nowhere in book 1 does Horace mount a horse or board a sea-going ship.[75] His mighty steed is always a mule, a symbol more apt for his particular brand of satire because it takes us down several notches on the "generic" scale of the Roman self, to the parodic, asinine level of who Horace is, a horseman at the bottom of his class, poorly bred, and hopelessly out of place in the world that Lucilius knew and expressed as his "satire".

That sense of the poet's displacement within his own genre/rank is figured into the image of Horace riding a gelded mule at *S.* 1.6.104–6, taking it, whenever he likes, "all the way to Tarentum" – exactly where he could not take us in the poem that precedes. The last line of this picture, the punchline, "the saddlebag chafes (the mule's) hind-quarters, **the horseman** his shoulders" (*mantica cui lumbos onere ulceret atque **eques** armos*) imitates Lucilius fr. 101W "the saddlebag pressed the nag's ribs with its weight" (*mantica cantheri costas grauitate premebat*). The pack animal in Lucilius' third satire

---

[73] For specific, mock epic features of this episode, see Sallmann (1974) 188–9; cf. Bramble (1974) 166–7: "the [ship of poetry] metaphor came to symbolise the magnitude of an author's undertaking: open sea and full sail mirror the efforts of the higher genres, while a calm expanse of coastal water, sailed by a small boat, images less energetic ventures."

[74] Horses and ships figure in Lucilius' account of his journey to south Italy and Sicily at frr. 99–100W, 101W, 119W, and 122W. For the "ship of poetry" metaphor generally, see Bramble (1974) 166–8. For Juvenal as specifically "Lucilian" satirist, driving his long-neglected chariot (Juv. 1.19–21), and taking his ship out to sea (Juv. 1.149–54), see below chapter 3.

[75] A much more detailed and far-reaching study of the symbolic value of Horace's various means of travel in book 1 has been undertaken by Cucchiarelli. My observations here owe much to his forthcoming work.

(his trip to south Italy and Sicily) is not a mule, but a gelded horse, and its load is a saddlebag, centered over its ribs, and not the horseman himself.

Horace paints the picture of his being half his mule's load to stress not only his dubious, even laughable, qualifications as a "horseman" of Lucilian rank (his being always half the joke), but his contentment with who he is, and his determination to keep a low profile in the rank he holds, and the genre he writes. Horses are for "kings" and/or "patrons" according to the barefoot philosopher of *S.* 1.2.86 (**regibus** *hic mos est*). And those who race them at the end of 1.1 are greedy fools, every bit as deluded as the merchant tossed about at sea at the beginning of the poem. But Maecenas, it seems, wants Horace to get off his mule and become something more, perhaps a senator, or perhaps a writer of a nobler genre/rank. But Horace insists in the *recusatio* of *S.* 1.6 that he cannot change who he is, and he reminds Maecenas that his having no horse is precisely what enticed Maecenas to befriend him several years before.[76] For in selecting new friends, he says in lines 50–2, Maecenas weeds out the greedy and unworthy, selecting only those who are demonstrably above personal and political self-seeking (*ambitione procul,* 52). His initial interview with his future patron he recalls as follows (*S.* 1.6.56–60):

> ut ueni coram, singultim pauca locutus,
> infans namque pudor prohibebat plura profari,
> non ego me claro natum patre, non ego circum
> me Satureiano uectari rura caballo,
> sed quod eram narro.

When I came before you I said a few halting words (for my being a shy babe kept me from speaking out more openly). I never said that I was the son of a noble father. I never said that I rode about estates on a Satureian steed. But I told you what I was.

Horace owns no "Satureian" steed. The exotic adjective *Satureiano* refers to Apulia, Horace's home region near Tarentum (= Greek *Satyrium*), where Lucilius is thought to have owned one

---

[76] Armstrong (1986) 267–77 makes an excellent case for Horace's refusal of senatorial rank in *S.* 1.6. He also makes clear that Horace was no struggling mule-driver by the mid-thirties BCE.

of his many estates, and where Horace is known to have lost his.[77] And, not by chance, the adjective utters the unmentionable *s*-word that the poet cannot bring himself to call his own because it, too, belongs to satire's real horseman. His lack of a noble horse, he tells Maecenas, is at the heart of "who he is" (*quod eram*), telling of the private, estate-less, and ambitionless world he inhabits, as well as the way he writes. He cannot claim to rank with Lucilius, or to ride the steed of his "satire". That is what Horace tells Maecenas the first time they meet, "saying a few words" (*pauca locutus*) because his few words say so much. He insists that his life as he lives it, and thus his "satire" as he rides/writes it, is low to the ground, private and, above all, "free from the miseries and grind of political ambition" (129). Later he complains that the higher poetic/political place that Maecenas would have him seek brings with it a host of new duties and displeasures for a mule-riding freedman's son. Among the first of these would be the demand that he buy up "stable-hands and steeds" (*calones atque caballi*, 103). The mule would have to go.

So Horace stays on his mule in the remainder of book 1, keeping to "who he is," and writing as if determined not to make a fool of himself by performing above his rank. We see the horseman seated squarely on his mule again at the end of *S.* 1.6, as we watch the poet take a leisurely, lonely stroll through the streets of downtown Rome, locating himself where senators haggle and real horsemen conduct their financial affairs. Horace is where he belongs here, in satire's downtown, having finally made his way into the crowded "stuffed" scene where satire happens, but his timing is completely off, and the scene he paints is anything but "stuffed" and Lucilian. He makes the point at lines 111–12 with the phrase *quacumque libido est|incedo solus* ("by whatever way I please, I make my entrance all alone"). The coupling of *incedo* with *solus* has an oxymoronic effect, for the verb *incedo* here has less to do with simply "entering" than it does with "making an entrance." It is a parade word, parodically recalling the noble statesman's daily

---

[77] For Lucilius' massive holdings in Apulia and elsewhere, see Krenkel (1970) 20–1. For the adjective "Satureian" (perhaps quoting Lucilius) referring both to the larger region of Apulia and to the city of Tarentum, see Krenkel (1970) 732. He surmises (733) that Lucilius' holdings in the region are the hidden point of the reference: "Ist die Zuweisung korrekt, wird damit der Besitz des Lucilius in Apulien bewiesen."

incessus, his showy entrance into the forum, attended by a full array of slaves, clients and friends, all decked out in the finery that best suits their rank.[78] One does not "make an entrance" all by oneself in Rome, nor does one enter "by any old way," but by the most conspicuous and spectacular avenue available. The noble-man's formal *incessus* requires a crowd of watchers, supporters, and friends, and it happens at an early morning hour when the rest of Rome's statesmen and businessmen crowded their way into the forum to debate policy and conduct the day's first business.

Horace "makes his entrance" after dusk, the first hour of *his* working day (and no one else's), after satire's crowds have left, and the circus and forum have been given over to a smattering of hucksters, peddlers, and a single, misplaced satirist. Upon arriving there he adopts a businessman's demeanor by launching a for-mal "investigation" (*OLD percontor* 1) into the price of cabbage and spelt, and "taking a stand in support of" (*OLD assisto* 3c) the "seers" (or are they *diuina* "statues"?) who have filtered into the forum after the city's real lawyers have left for the day. This is Horace's way of attending to "business" downtown, and of travel-ling the streets of Lucilian satire. With these poems he takes us into places where we know the crowds are routinely thick, and the personalities huge, and politics hotly debated. The circus and forum are satire's best place, where greed, ambition, and vanity parade about in a glorious, gaudy, daily show. But Horace takes us there after the crowds have left for the day, and he focuses our eyes on persons of no consequence, and he attends to business that does not matter. His eye-view, and thus the perspective he treats us to, is that of someone arriving on "satire's scene" too late, more at home with the low-bred, evening "crowd" (so called) who have filtered in well after Lucilius and his "kind" have left for the day. There, in Lucilius' space, he haggles for cabbage and spelt be-cause that is what he is best suited to haggle over, and because cabbage and spelt are what he intends to serve *us* for our evening "feast," setting out just two cups (117), one for him, the other for us (some feast!). And for the philosopher's lunch, just enough to ward

---

[78] For *incedo* as a parade word, see especially Serv. *A.* 1.46 (*quae diuum incedo regina*): *incedere proprie est nobilium personarum, hoc est cum aliqua dignitate ambulare*; cf. Lucr. 3.76 *claro qui incedit honore*; Catul. 42.7–8 *illa, quam uidetis | turpe incedere* (referring to a prostitute para-ding her wares); Hor. *Epod.* 15.18 *superbus incedis*; and Tac. *Ann.* 3.9 *magno clientium agmine ipse, feminarum comitatu Plancina et uultu alacres incessere*.

off hunger, and not a snitch more (127–8). Clearly the feast of Lucilius was differently apportioned and arranged, "stuffed" with the forum at midday, and with political scandals, and noblemen's names, and their outlandish feasts. But, for Horace, such spectacular ingredients are the greasy, bowel-clogging stuff of miserable ambition. The most outlandish ambition of all would be his own attempt to rank with Lucilius, and to ride *his* satire's steed.

The poet's low social standing in Rome, his fecklessness as a satirist of Lucilian pyrotechnical punch and inspiration, and his outspoken lack of political wherewithal and drive, are all metaphors for one another in the generic *self*-expression of *Sermones* book 1. Their complementary interaction is clear throughout, but perhaps most evident in *S.* 1.9, where an anonymous neoteric poet makes a full-scale assault on his counterpart in satire's neoterical nobody, Horace, as his one best way of working into Maecenas' circle of friends. Horace himself seems to have made a similar, successful advance from outside to inside several years before, helped along by his poet friends, Varius and Virgil, so the man quite naturally regards him as his ideal model of effective self-seeking, and a target worth pursuing. For his pursuer, Horace has the look of someone facing impossible odds (a dispossessed freedman's son, aiming to rank with Maecenas and Co.!), but incredibly lucky in his efforts, shamelessly driven to promote himself, and well ahead of him in the race to get ahead. He is the poster-boy of this man's own shameless ambition.

But Horace hardly looks the part at the beginning of 1.9, for here again, as at the end of 1.6, we find him wandering the streets of downtown Rome, perfectly "placed" to promote himself as a satirist of Lucilian worth, but with no particular destination in mind, and no sure sense of why he is there. As in the two "anecdote poems" that precede, one set in the gardens of Maecenas (1.8), the other on campaign with Brutus in Asia Minor (1.7), Horace locates his speaker in a place that might otherwise be thought to matter, where political agendas are sure to have been fashioned and fought over, and social maneuverings and vanities of all kinds to have been waved about for all to see. But the poet's eye-view fixes elsewhere, on the margins of events that matter (1.7), and on things spied at the dead of night (1.8), well after Maecenas' friends have made their way home for the evening, leaving his Esquiline gardens to interlopers, statues, and wolves.

He relates what he sees in these places as so much barbershop gossip (1.7.3), and an ass-splitting tale of two witches tall enough to rate with the goblin stories of Trimalchio's freedmen ("And if I'm lying, may crows shit all over my [one presumes "already shit-splattered"] head!" 1.8.37–8).

And so it is no wonder that this retailer of bad puns and witches' brew should amble into the heart of Rome in the last of his book's three anecdotes (1.9) with his head in the clouds, "rehearsing some trifle or other" (*nescio quid meditans nugarum*), like a perfectly irrelevant Epicurean poet who has absent-mindedly strayed into a space where he is utterly out of his element – a mule-driver on a horse (or is he a horseman on a mule?). Once again, Horace has made his way into satire's place, and the man who blind-sides him here deserves a good lambasting. But the speaker cannot find it in himself to go on the attack, even against a man of so little account. Inside he rages with a Lucilian rage, while outside he puts up a piddling fight in a series of nudges, nods, and hints not taken. As the sweat of this "battle" reaches his ankles, he turns to Bolanus (his slave?) with "god, Bolanus, how lucky you are to have a temper that lashes out!" (11–12).

Circumstances require that the poet step out of character here, in order to rid himself of the alter-ego who shadows him.[79] But by now he has written himself into a corner, and become too well known as the character he has played since the opening lines of *S.* 1.1. Here in *S.* 1.9 he is forced to pay the price for being "who he is" in this book, playing that fiction as the fact of his daily routine in Rome.[80] For it is precisely his much vaunted Epicureanness, his proud lack of political ambition and purpose, that is his repeated undoing in his encounter with his pesky attacker. What he needs is a bit of Lucilian fire to shake him off, and he needs to

---

[79] For the close resemblance of Horace to his shadow in this poem, and the many *self-defeating* ironies that taunt our every attempt to polarize the two and/or to laugh at them, see Henderson (1999) 202–27.

[80] We cannot know to what extent one performance, that of the poet's self in the poem, resembles his self-performance outside the poem. But the fact that all selves issue from performance (i.e. they are constituted from an elaborate, highly encoded set of performances) should make us rethink the now standard claim that *S.* 1.9 is "merely fictional." What can that mean? Part of the problem, and the uneasy fun, of the poem comes in not knowing where to draw any clear and hard line between fiction and fact. For the necessary interplay between performance and self in Rome, see Oliensis (1998a) 1–4.

have some real business to get on to downtown, and someplace to claim that he urgently needs to go. But his unwanted travel companion knows him too well for that. And so do we.

Thus the poet is forced to try to shake him/us off with an excuse that nicely suits the self he has expressed, by claiming to be urgently on his way to visit a friend sick in bed, way off across the Tiber. It is a good Epicurean excuse (cf. the "friendship" theme so prominent in *S.* 1.5, above), the best he can muster, stressing his devotion to an ailing friend. But it does not work. The pest decides to tag along. Horace hints that the man might want to reconsider because he, too, might catch whatever ails his sick friend and die an untimely death (26–7). But the brush-off is too weak, and it works to a remarkably different effect. For it only goes to prove to the man who stalks him what a deeply devoted friend Horace is to those whom he chooses to get close to. Thus, because of the excuse, he is doubly committed to shadowing him and winning his case. "If you are *my* friend" (sc. "as much as you are the friend of that man across the Tiber") he says in line 38, "you will stay with me *here* for just a while." Apparently the man has some legal troubles to attend to downtown, so he needs Horace's help. But Horace insists that he is completely ignorant of standing before juries and handling details of Roman civil law. The man hesitates for a moment – for once, Horace's Epicurean-ness seems to work to his advantage. But, in an instant, the man decides that he has more to gain by sticking with Horace than he has to lose by forfeiting his case.

The burden of being "who he is" dogs the poet at every turn in 1.9, and it undoes him in his efforts to disentangle himself from his (own) shadow. His Epicurean-ness backfires yet again when his "friend," Fuscus Aristius, arrives on the scene in line 60, only to take his hints and nudges too well. For, seeing that Horace is in trouble, Aristius decides to have a little fun with him by leaving him to hang by his own Epicurean noose. He insists that he must rush home in order to observe the Sabbath, and that leaves Horace to respond in the only way he can, exactly as Aristius, and the pest, and we ourselves, knew he would: "I have no truck with religious mumbo-jumbo" (*nulla mihi ... religio est*, 70–1). Because Aristius knows Horace right down to his shadow (*illum | qui pulchre nosset*, 61–2), he is able to make his own quick escape. Playing off

the knowledge that Horace can have no urgent business to rush off
to downtown, and no "members only" superstitions to observe
elsewhere, Aristius quickly does what Horace cannot: he disen-
tangles himself from the man who attempts to shadow him. Once
again, Horace is forced to pay the price for writing himself into a
role that predicts his every move.

The poem's last lines, just as the first, put us in the capricious,
bottom-feeding world of a Roman mime play.[81] Out of the blue,
the shadow's legal adversary arrives on the scene to haul him
off to court. Immediately the curtain rises, and the play is over.
One possible, hidden irony of this last-minute "mime" rescue, as
Tadeusz Mazurek has recently shown, is that by allowing the
man's adversary to touch his ear, Horace commits himself to
appearing against him in court. In other words, in order to disen-
tangle himself from the man who intends to follow him "way
off across the Tiber," the very man whom he refuses to help by
claiming to have no business in a Roman court of law, Horace
first must shadow the man straight back into court and stand up
against him there as a witness for the prosecution.[82] Everything he
sought to avoid by running away from this man he runs straight
into by "escaping" him.[83]

The poet's reluctant return to court is left to the imagination at
the end of 1.9, signalled by the touch of Flaccus' too compliant
ear. But we see the poet make another sudden return to court in
the lines that follow directly in the book, at the top of the next
page. Here, in the legal *praescriptio* that introduces *S.* 1.10 (perhaps
spurious, but designed to counterbalance the *subscriptio* at the
poem's end), Horace announces that he fully intends to pursue his

---

[81] The clamoring, last-minute escape was the stock-in-trade of mime plays; see Mazurek
(1997) 12–13. The first words of line 2 *nescio quid meditans nugarum* appear to quote a mime
of Laberius (Bonaria fr. 132, *nescio quid nugarum*). The word *nugae* has a clear Catullan
resonance (though he uses it only once). Newman (1990) 30–6 demonstrates that the term
is directly relevant to the mime stage. He cites the earliest usage of the term (p. 30) on a
tomb of a mime-actor who died in the late third century BCE (*CIL* 1.2.1861) where *nugae*
refers to the "fast-talking nonsense" of the mime play's hucksters and slaves.

[82] Mazurek (1997) 1: "the satirist does not truly escape from the Pest. On the contrary, after
agreeing to witness the seizure, the satirist would immediately accompany the two
litigants to court ... Apollo has not saved the satirist in the manner generally assumed by
Horatian scholarship; rather, he has entangled him in a tumultuous lawsuit."

[83] At the very least, that touch of Horace's ear commits him to playing some small, technical role in the plaintiff's case – if only to vouch for his having used proper force in
hauling his delinquent defendant off to court.

indictment against the poet who has dogged his every move since the beginning of *S.* 1.1 (*S.* 1.10.1–3A):[84]

> Lucili, quam sis mendosus, teste Catone,
> defensore tuo, peruincam, qui male factos
> emendare parat uersus.

Lucilius, with your defender, Cato, as my witness, I will prove how full of fault you are. He aims to clear your crooked verses of their faults.

Perhaps he thought he could wander into Lucilius' territory without having to be detained downtown. But he made trouble for himself in *S.* 1.4 by lodging an elaborate complaint that he must now return to court to draw out and defend. He has defamed his noble precursor, Lucilius, so he must now "prove beyond a shadow of doubt" (*peruincam*) the case he undertook when he called him a sloppy composer. And he must deal with the trouble he stirred when he failed to speak in the deferential tones expected of a freedman's son.

Taking Valerius Cato, Lucilius' most recent editor and ardent, neoteric "defender," as his chief "witness," Horace goes on the attack in the second act of his *in Lucilium*: "Yes, I *did* say that Lucilius' verses run on sloppy feet!' (*S.* 1.10.1–2); "I *did* say that the man is chock-full of mud!" (50). And so on throughout. The defense of his former indictment is elaborate and detailed. But the decisive, case-ending move comes in lines 81–8, where Horace offers the names of certain noble bystanders who "applaud" him from the crowd (*nam satis est equitem mihi plaudere*, 76). "These are my friends," he says, "those who happen to be here with me today, and like what I have to say." Enter Maecenas, Varius, Virgil, Octavius, Pollio, Messalla, and so on. "And I have plenty of other supporters of this caliber besides these," he warns. "So just you go ahead and tell *them* they are wrong!" After that there is nothing left to say: "Now off with you, boy, and be quick about appending these charges to my indictment" (92).[85] The case is closed.

---

[84] Brink (1963) 167, n. 1 expresses the standard view that these lines are "spurious but contemporary." Whoever wrote them was keenly aware of the legal overtones issuing from the poem to which they are attached as a quasi-*praescriptio* that defines the scope of the suit, and names the parties involved; cf. *OLD praescriptio* 2a–b.

[85] Commentators generally overlook the strong legal coloring of the book's last words, *subscribe libello*. Besides a Catullan "little book," a *libellus* was also a formal, legal complaint; see *OLD libellus* 3c–d. For *subscribere* in the sense "to specify details of a crime," see *OLD subscribo* 4 and *OLD subscriptio* 4.

Horace warned his detractors at the end of 1.4 that he intended
to bring a "great band" of poets to his aid if they should persist in
opposing him: "And, just like the Jews, we will *force* you to join our
crowd" (*ac ueluti te | Iudaei* **cogemus** *in hanc concedere turbam*, 1.4.142–
3). Here, at the end of the book, he delivers on that threat by
parading before us an impressive set of poet-friends, whom only
the most politically oblivious and/or suicidal of adversaries would
dare to oppose. As commentators on these lines are wont to point
out, his cast of supporters happen to be some of the most powerful
political figures of late triumviral Rome, so he leaves his oppo-
nents stunned, and with nothing more to say. Who would have
thought that he, the dispossessed mule-driver, could hail such an
impressive list of friends into his defense? This final brandishing of
the poet's elite connections, so unlike anything that precedes in
the book, is not a matter of his putting a few finishing touches on
his case. It is about his *winning* it, Roman style, in one bold stroke,
by flexing the impressive muscle that his multiple friendships
provide.

The poet who speaks these lines has little of the soft-spoken
Epicurean about him. His dramatic *praeteritio* (*amicos | prudens prae-
tereo*, 87–8) is the final, decisive say of someone politically astute,
and well attuned to the ways of winning in Rome's courts. No
wonder the shadow refused to be put off. Horace has ended his
case against Lucilius, the case that is the book itself, in a single,
deft stroke. The surprise ending recalls the "mime rescue" of the
previous poem not only in formal ways, but in the way it deftly
muscles aside a problem that has shadowed the poet for some
time. But this time it is we, the poet's devoted audience, who must
feel ourselves strong-armed by the poet's courtroom thugs, and
quickly hastened away. In the end, *we* prove to be his most persistent pest, because we are still here, dogging him, and because
ultimately it is our desire to be seen with the crowd he names,
his crowd, that allows him to win his case. For, to concede to his
strong-arming is first to acknowledge that this is the crowd we
want to belong to. It is to have that much of the self-seeking
"pest" in ourselves.

Certainly anyone who harbored hopes of getting inside the
circle(s) of Maecenas, Pollio, Messalla, and Virgil, and of belonging
to their literary set, would have felt enormous pressure to concede
to Horace's final non-argument – just as we still do, so impressed

by the poet's naming *Virgil* in his list! For, to do otherwise would have been politically imprudent, putting one in league with the irrelevant "Bug," Pantilius, and the droning school-teachers, Demetrius and Tigellius, persons, he tells us, of no account, and with no decent advantages to offer the recitation set's most promising young stars (like ourselves). That is the downside of not letting Horace win his case against Lucilius. But to concede to his bullying out of hand is equally hazardous. For, with that concession we admit that we, too, like the shadow of 1.9, are driven to belong to Horace's "right" crowd, and to make our way into Maecenas' good graces by striking up a friendship with one of his favored young poets. "If dearest Virgil, or Maecenas, takes Horace's side, then clearly there can be no question of how I will vote – but, of course, my decision to rate these *Sermones* as good, noble poetry, and a clear improvement on Lucilius, has *nothing* to do with the company Horace keeps (Is Maecenas watching? Do you think he saw me?)".

The key to Horace's own success with Maecenas, he tells us in *S.* 1.6, was his contentment with "who he is," and his having no shameless ambitions to show for himself. He never pushed to get ahead, he says, and that caught Maecenas' eye, because Maecenas would have nothing to do with eager self-seekers, and he was a master at weeding them out. But, by now it is clear that a single grasping interloper may have made his way into Maecenas' snow-white mansion (*domus hac nec purior ulla est,* 1.9.49). And that, right under the master's discerning nose, in the person of Horace himself, the man who makes such a *show* of his having no drive to get ahead. For the clear irony of his magnificent success with Maecenas is that it is specifically his demonstrated lack of ambition that he cites as the key to his getting ahead. Because he showed himself insouciant about success, he succeeded, marvelously, to the point that he is now the target of other men's shameless ambition, and their model for what it takes to get ahead with Maecenas. Thus, there is a hidden pandering to be spied in the poet's every nonchalant move, in his having no business downtown, and in his giving himself nowhere in particular to go. His every claim to being happy with "who he is" and ambition-free totters under the weight of its own irony.

To sense this irony, one need only consider the experience of a hostile audience reading through the book's final lines. Half-way through his list of jaw-dropping names, the poet claims to be above reproach (*ambitione relegata* "with all self-seeking banished," as if relegated to a distant island, 1.10.84) in naming the likes of Pollio, Messalla, and so many others, so prominently at the end of his book. But by this point in the poem we, his skeptical readers, have scrolled to the book's last page, so we know the end is very near. Down below, peripherally seen, a few more lines, then a blank space, perhaps even a short sign-off in colored letters. As we read these lines, then, we are keenly aware that these are the book's last, emphatic words. And what do they emphasize? Name after name of Rome's political and literary elite, friends of the poet, most of whom are unmentioned earlier in the book. Just how "ambition-free" is this friendly display? Clearly, what some may have insisted is a "pure" gesture of deference (largely because Horace says it is "pure"), others will have regarded as a last-minute, name-dropping frenzy, a way of stuffing in all the most relevant names before hitting the big, white blank at the page's end.[86] Even the most compliant of readers, though they would never themselves read that way, will have sensed that others both could and did.

Such is the problem Horace faces in attempting to free himself from his shadow, the shadow of his own shameless ambition, in *S.* 1.9. His every claim to being ambition-free has in it the potential to say the opposite to his pursuer, a man so like his readers, and so like himself. The man attempts to bribe Horace in lines 45–8 by telling him "You'd have a great helper to play the role of your assistant if you were to, say, 'introduce' the man. Hell, you'd clear everyone else out of your way!" With these words, the man has labeled Horace as a charlatan out for a big payday, for he compares him to the lead actor in a mime play, to whose lead he himself is willing to play "the second part" (*secundas*, sc. *partes*, 46) in what he clearly regards as an elaborate scheme to bilk rich Maecenas of his excess cash (cf. Encolpius and Eumolpus in Croton).[87] When Horace says that Maecenas allows no jockeying for power in his household, and that each of his friends enjoys his own, secure place there (*est locus uni | cuique suus*, 51–2) so that none of them are tempted to put on airs and advance themselves ahead

---

[86] Oliensis (1998a) 61–2 takes precisely this view of the book's close; cf. Rudd (1986) 139.
[87] For the stage metaphor of these lines, see Brown (1993) 180.

of the rest, the man takes this as a clever hint, a nudge that requires no wink. For he is quite sure that things do not work that way in Rome, and he regards the story of Maecenas' egalitarian garden as a beautiful, tall tale, *uix credibile* ("scarcely believable," 52). He persists in thinking that, under these words, Horace is really telling him to get busy, to wear his ambitions on his sleeve, and to use whatever means he can find ("start by bribing his slaves!") to make his move on Maecenas.

By now we know that this is not a simple problem of the fool's being a fool, or of his being unable to take a hint. It is a matter of his construing Horace's every word *as* a hint, and of his having no way to tell (and why should he?) when Horace might *really* happen to mean what he says. This is the bind that ensnares the poet in his struggle to free himself from his shadow. He has fallen into a trap of his own making, and his every effort to free himself only pulls the knots tighter, because that is the way he has set the trap to work. So it is no wonder that both shadow and poet should be dragged off to court in one and the same motion after the poem has ended. That is the way it has to be. The two men are so hopelessly entangled that where one goes, so must the other. And not just here, but in the book as a whole. For, as we have seen, the problem of the poet's own self-seeking commences with the book's first words, "How come, Maecenas," and it shadows his every nonchalant move, going with him wherever he goes, right down to the name-dropping frenzy that *makes* the book end.[88]

BOOK 2 AND THE TOTALITARIAN SQUEEZE:
NEW RULES FOR A NEW AGE

The opening lines of book 2 give the paranoiac's view of his recent critical reception:

---

[88] One of the most ironically self-incriminating moments within these bookends comes in the mime play of *S.* 1.9, when the shadow matches his movements to those of the poet who dodges him by promising to "clear the path" for Horace if he should give him the entrance he desires. As Brown (1993) 180 points out, *summouere* is the technical term "for clearing a path, as lictors would for a consul, implying that the other members of the circle are seen as an obstruction." The shadow, in other words, mimes the movements of Horace himself, by promising to do for Horace what Horace himself does for Maecenas right under *our* noses. In the apotropaic fiction of this poem, he attempts to clear Maecenas' path of an unworthy, self-seeking flatterer by pushing him out of his path, and keeping him well outside his garden walls.

Sunt quibus in satura uidear nimis acer et ultra
legem tendere opus; sine neruis altera, quidquid
composui, pars esse putat similisque meorum
mille die uersus deduci posse.

There is a whole class of people who think I'm too harsh in satire, and
that I am stretching the genre past its legal limit. There is another faction that thinks whatever I have composed is gutless, and that verses just
like mine can be spun off a thousand per day.

Horace's first book, with all of its pile-hiding, slimmed-down
pretensions, has bored some of its readers and offended certain
others. Some think it too thick, others too thin. That split reception comes as no surprise, since it was forecast clearly and often in
the first book. And because the opening lines of book 2 pick up
on a familiar theme, they lure us into thinking that the second
project will be about the same business as the first. For that initial
moment, we find ourselves in a familiar landscape, surrounded by
the well-worn theoretical debates of book 1, and so we settle in for
a second round of more-of-the-same. But then we hit these words
at the end of line 4: "Trebatius, give me your expert advice. What
am I to do?" Four lines into what seemed to be a too-familiar
poem, we are jolted out of our old readerly habits. We realize that
everything we have read to this point, however familiar it may
have seemed at first, has to be gone over again and imagined in a
different way: the speaker, it turns out, was not talking to us at all,
but to someone else inside the poem. Someone we did not even
know was there.

   We failed to imagine that he could be there because he never
was in book 1. There the basic narratological setup was different:
the direction was always from the speaker on the page directly
to us, the audience outside the poem. But here the direction is
between characters inside the poem, and we, the newly excluded,
do not figure in the narrator's imagination in any explicit way.
Suddenly we find ourselves in a narratological no-man's land,
eavesdropping, and not quite sure whether we should even be
hearing what we are hearing. That opening, by so deftly drawing
us into our old readerly ways, then shaking us out of them, alerts
us to the very different narratological and programmatic makeup
of the second book. It tells us that, despite initial appearances,
what we have here is no mere rehash of something already done.
It is a separate, contrasting project that actually dwells on and

makes the most of its not being quite the same as book 1. Its most salient defining feature, in fact, the key to its relational identity, is that contrast with the first book.

So often book 2 is treated as something of a generic letdown: the bumpkin cousin of book 1, too indecisive (by comparison), giving too little of the poet's personal biography (by comparison), and much too overrun by extremist talk and weird obsessions with food (much less of that in book 1).[89] In other words, this is satire that flirts with its old ways but never manages to deliver them, and by not delivering them it performs its own failure. That performance, I maintain, is the point. It has an unsettling, diagnostic effect on its audience: it makes us wonder what has happened to the old ways of book 1, and to that more direct, public "prosecutorial" satirist who seemed so sure of himself there. Why do the old rules no longer apply?

These are the hard, necessary questions that arise from our memories of the first book. Such questions, I maintain, are not problems that inhibit our understanding of the book – obstacles to be removed to get at what it "means" – they are the point; they are *the way* it means. Their necessary, chafing work, we have seen, begins with that abrupt narratological shift that leaves us in no-man's land in the first lines of *S.* 2.1. As I hope now to show, the problems of difference and inadequacy are cracked open as the central programmatic issues of the book in the opening dialogue between the poet and his not quite "with it" legal consultant, Trebatius.

In book 1, the poet took his problems directly to us, and we, his public, were always his first option for hearing his jests and sorting through his complaints against his rivals. There, in that very different world, moral and aesthetic issues were ventilated in the streets, negotiated directly between speaker and audience. In book 2, however, with the introduction of Trebatius, we are forced to consider them as matters best settled in private, between a writer and his trusty lawyer, both of them cloistered off in the recesses of the legal expert's house (the setting we should assume in *S.* 2.1). In other words, we are made to consider the many legal and political

---

[89] Fraenkel (1957) 145 takes the dimmest view of the book: "Being Horace, he checked himself, and when he realized that the natural stream of his *sermones* had ceased to flow, he abandoned the writing of such poems."

dimensions of the moral and aesthetic issues of book 1 that, in that book, we were left completely free to ignore. It is not that these further implications were not already there in that book – they are never not there in Rome. It is that, within that very different setting we were never made to consider their relevance. In striking contrast, then, from the start of this new project, stylistic and generic choices are constructed as politically-loaded acts, with potentially big, legal consequences. Somewhere in the process of moving from book 1 to book 2, the tables have been turned, and we are not quite sure why. If you have a literary problem now, what you need is not an erratic public, ready to hear and react, but a lawyer. Someone who can save your neck!

It is a funny proposition, to be sure, and scholars have rightly cautioned against taking the scenario at its face value.[90] Still, to insist that the scenario has nothing "real" or "serious" about it may be to miss a very important point. For perhaps not quite knowing how to take it is the sharp side to the joke, and the way it performs its diagnostic work. Perhaps the audience of 30 BCE, a terribly shaken and nervous age, did not know precisely how to gauge its seriousness either. Some may have asked themselves, "Should I be laughing at this, or wincing?" "Does he really need a lawyer, or is he just pretending? Surely it's a joke. Isn't it?" One can imagine the readers of that rattled age doing their best to sweat out a smile. The scenario rides that fine edge separating fiction from what can be imagined as one's lived (or soon-to-be lived) experience.

Trebatius' first advice to the poet is clearly his simplest and best option: "Keep quiet," he says in line 5.[91] That is to say, only shut down that offending satiric machine of yours and you might just save your neck. And not merely that: it is clearly implied that he is to give up writing altogether. That is just how tightly strung the (pretend?) literary world of this poem is imagined to be. So by line 5 we eavesdroppers are wondering just how and why things got to be as bad as they are made to seem. What is behind the literary

<hr>

[90] Much quoted is Rudd (1966) 128, concluding his passage-by-passage study of the poem: "So ends the most brilliant piece of shadow-boxing in Roman literature."

[91] Leeman (1982) argues that due attention is paid to the rhetorical *status* of Horace's case throughout the poem, ranging from the surest and best line of argument in lines 5–6, the *status coniecturalis*, to the weakest defense in the poem's last lines, the *status conuiuialis*.

shakedown, and the widespread torquing of nerves, even if they are only pretend?

The answer comes in the second of Trebatius' "safety first" legal options. To the satirist's objection that the recommended shutdown would ruin his sleep, Trebatius counters with option B (10–12):

> aut, si tantus amor scribendi te rapit, aude
> Caesaris inuicti res dicere, multa laborum
> praemia laturus.

Or, if you are so driven to write, "dare" to relate the military achievements of invincible Caesar.[92] Then you're sure to carry off abundant prizes for your labors.

This is the "real world" of Roman politics injected in a big, precipitous plunge. Without actually saying so, Trebatius reminds us that Actium has happened just months ago, and he alerts us to the "unhealthy" potentials of writing in such an uncertain, rattled age. The post-Actian squeeze is on, and the old safety rules no longer apply. If we take Trebatius' hint, Octavian still has a lot of "settling" to do, so goose-stepping in his victory parade is likely to be the best and safest way to go. The big, panegyric epic, he says, will mark the vulnerable, unclaimed poet as clearly on his side, the only side that counts any more. Such a project, he suggests, may even bring with it a handsome share of the "booty."

Trebatius' advice to the poet is apparently modeled on the bottom-line urgings of an unknown interlocutor to a poet (perhaps to Lucilius) in book 26 of Lucilius' *Satires* (originally published as book 1). There, in the first book of his first published work, the Trebatian alter-ego urges his poet to cash in on his poetic skills by writing panegyric epics that glorify the military achievements of two of Rome's most successful generals (Lucilius frr. 713–14W):

> hunc laborem sumas laudem qui tibi ac fructum ferat . . .
> . . . percrepa pugnam Popili, facta Corneli cane.

---

[92] Mention of the poet's "daring" to write Caesar's praise is highly ironic. Kiessling–Heinze (1961) 180 annotates *aude* in line 10 with "denn das Epos ist für die Auffassung der Zeit der Gipfel aller Poesie, und die Taten Cäsars . . . sind der denkbar erhabenste Stoff." On the other hand, it is clear that the poet's "daring" in this case has to do with his desire to find a safe mode of writing. Thus, the most daring and reckless of epic enterprises is also the most compliant and free of risk.

take up this task in order to win praise and profit for yourself ... bluster on about Popillius' battle, and sing the achievements of Cornelius [Scipio Aemilianus].

The consultant may have preceded his advice by urging the poet to steer clear of satire, just as Trebatius advises in the remake of *S.* 2.1. We cannot be sure. But a second fragment from the same book is likely to represent the first part of the poet's refusal (Lucilius fr. 691W):

> ego si, qui sum et quo folliculo nunc sum
> indutus, non queo ...

If I for my part, given the puny little husk I am now clothed in, am unable ...

By retrojecting Horace back onto Lucilius (always a dangerous business), we can see how the fragments quoted above just *might have* gone together.[93] Even if we leave them apart, it is still clear (and commonly acknowledged) that the Horatian consultation dialogue of *S.* 2.1 follows a model in Lucilius book 26 in several significant details.[94] Most prominent of these, as we see in frr. 713–14W, is the gruff, bottom-line coloring of the consultant's advice. In the Lucilian model, that advice is crass and opportunistic, and I think the same can be said of the Horatian version as well. Seeing Trebatius' advice as a call to virtue, flattering to Octavian, or merely innocuous, takes some effort, but it can be done. Still, we can never really know just how much that advice might have rung true, rankled, or offended in its original setting. Could it have elicited a wholehearted laugh without the merest twinge of angst? How easy would it have been to brush it aside as merely so much "outrageous fiction"?

Again, not quite knowing how to place it as "real," "potentially real," or "just pretend" may be the point, and a necessary function of the poem's diagnostic work. In the fiction of the poem, a fiction(?) that bleeds into the readers' day-to-day world, the pressure is on to tell the story of Octavian's recent military success. And not just any version of it, but the big, glorious version that renders him "invincible," a mere stone's-throw from heaven. Trebatius' advice, crass or not, makes us ask, is that pressure real, or just a

---

[93] I follow Kiessling–Heinze (1961) 180 in assuming a connection between the passages.
[94] See especially Fiske (1920) 369–78.

twisted thought in the poet's head? And where is the pressure coming from? Do we assume that Octavian is actively requesting panegyric poems like the one Trebatius has in mind? Is he perhaps looking to drum up some side-entertainments for his triumphal return home? Or does the pressure come from some other source, such as the general crush of poets racing to "cash in" on Octavian's success by coming out decisively on his side? Such questions, I maintain, are not obstacles to the poem's meaning (problems to be removed), they *are* what it means, and *the way* it means.

Trebatius' advice to the satirist that he "do one up" for Octavian has in it a number of subtle intertextual cues that generally do not get noticed and/or make their way into scholarly discussion of the poem, either because they are just too subtle to be noticed, or, more likely, because they are not part of that matrix of possibilities generally preapproved as "relevant" to the reading of Horace's *Sermones*. Most notably, the advice recalls at least two passages from the initial pages of Virgil's third book of *Georgics*, a work technically not yet published, and therefore locked out of most readers' fields of view. Yet, I think those intertextual cues really do inhere in these lines, and that they deserve to be fleshed out, because doing so levers us into seeing the epic project proposed by Trebatius in some very different terms. His advice (10–12) –

> aut, si **tantus amor** scribendi te **rapit**, **aude**
> Caesaris in**uict**i res dicere, multa laborum
> praemia laturus.

Or, if you are so driven to write, "dare" to relate the military achievements of invincible Caesar. Then you're sure to carry off abundant prizes for your labors.

– employs the same nexus of passion, daring, and being "swept off" to victory as Virgil uses to describe the founding chariot-race at the Panathenaic games (*G.* 3.112–14):

> ... **tantus amor** laudum, tantae est **uictoria** curae.
> primus Erichthonius currus et quattuor **ausus**
> iungere equos **rapidusque** rotis insistere **uictor.**

... so great is the desire for praise, so great is the concern for victory. It was Erichthonius who first dared to join four horses to a car and to fly to victory standing above speeding wheels.

Thus, behind Trebatius' advice to the satirist is the image of
Erichthonius, the inventor of chariot-racing and a founding
champion.[95] Again, as in *S.* 1.1, we are invited to consider the
poetic enterprise as a kind of athletic competition: the poet is a
competitor in a chariot-race, speeding his horses ahead to "carry
off" the prize. But the idealizing that comes with that remembered
image of Erichthonius is undercut severely in the Horatian remake by the suggestion of the poet's cowardly "daring" and his
utter venality. His is a race for cash.

The epinician underpinnings of Trebatius' advice are suggested
a second time by the corresponding proximity of "prizes" to "telling Caesar's tale" at *G.* 3.46–50.[96] Horace's **Caesaris** *inuicti res*
dicere, *multa laborum* | ***praemia** laturus* matches Virgil's

> mox tamen ardentis accingar **dicere** pugnas
> **Caesaris** et nomen fama tot ferre per annos,
> Tithoni prima quot abest ab origine Caesar.
> seu quis Olympiacae miratus **praemia** palmae
> pascit equos, seu quis fortis ad aratra iuuencos ...

But soon I will put on my arms to tell of Caesar's fierce battles. With
that glorious telling, I will carry his name through as many years as
Caesar is himself distant from the birth of Tithonus. Whether someone
raises horses, intent on the prize of Olympia's palm, or another raises
bullocks, hardening them for the plow ...

Virgil leads up to this famous promise by setting his forthcoming
project against a list of those "already done to death" epics he is
determined not to repeat. This is his version of the "steering clear
of the well-worn path" motif, that rejection of triteness that is
itself the tritest of rejections. As John Henderson has recently
shown, Virgil does not simply "cue us" with learned allusions in
the proem of *Georgics* 3, he uses these allusions to show "*how poetry
proceeds through processing poetry*. Not the incorporation of his 'what,'
but the 'how' of poetic massaging."[97]

In other words, Virgil has seen what Horace was getting at in
the horse-race scene at the end of *S.* 1.1. In his competing version
of the scene in *G.* 3, we again see the odd coupling of the poet's
determination to steer clear of the well-worn path with the meta-

---

[95] On these lines, see Thomas (1988) 60.
[96] Though sometimes cited as a general "cf." in the commentaries, the passage has never
been taken as a specific and meaningful allusion.
[97] Henderson (1995) 107.

phor of his poetic chariot-race, the contest that puts him on-track with so many others: *temptanda uia est, qua me quoque possim | tollere humo uictorque uirum uolitare per ora* ("I must attempt that path whereby I, too, might ascend above the ground and fly before men's faces as champion," 8–9). Again in lines 17–22, as R. Thomas points out, "The imagery combines elements of epinician and triumph, as V. imagines the games he will set up to celebrate the foundation of his temple – games which will supplant those at Olympia and Nemea."[98] In these lines, and throughout the proem generally, the poet figures as both military champion and athletic victor. Not in the present, but in the future, i.e. not in the *Georgics*, but in the *Aeneid*.[99] For now, he insists, the big epic project is far off, and he knows that his *Georgics* have a long way to go. He snaps out of his futuristic fancy, back to hard drudgery of the farm, that "soil" he is so determined to "rise above" (*tollere humo*), with the lines quoted above. To get back on-task, he reminds himself, and us, that some farmers raise horses destined for Olympic glory, "the prize of the Olympic palm," while others raise mere cattle for pulling the plow. For now, it seems, cattle are a more pressing concern. His Olympic horses are still being fed.

Callimachus begins the second half of his four-book *Aetia* with the story of Hercules' founding of the Nemean games, a foundation-myth "slendered down" by being set within the hero's visits to his poor, mouse-infested host, Molorchus, at Cleonae.[100] Virgil begins the second half of his four-book *Georgics* by remembering and "leaving behind" both Callimachus' "groves of Molorchus" and Pindar's charter-games of Olympian 1 (*Alpheum linquens lucosque Molorchi*, 19). Instead, he imagines the founding of his own, new games on the shores of his native Mincius, and he forecasts a grand, epinician labor that he will champion when his horses (no mere goats this time, nor plow-cattle) are well-fed and ready. Horace, then, in beginning the second half of his two-book *Sermones*, recalls those same charter-races with the thinnest of thickly resonant allusions (to Virgil, to Callimachus, to Pindar,

[98] Thomas (1988) 42.
[99] Cf. Gale (1994) 103: "Virgil's *recusatio* (to use the term loosely) in the proem to *Georgics* 3 contrasts the projected military epic represented by the marble temple with the *Dryadum siluas saltusque ... intactos* of the *Georgics*. The opening lines ... suggest that the poet regards his present work as belonging to a more humble genre than either mythological (3–8) or historical/encomiastic (10–39) epic."
[100] On the *Aetia* prologue processed inside the proem of *Georgics* 3, see Henderson (1995) 107.

endlessly, one through the other) at *S.* 2.1.10–12. And just as in the first poem of book 1, the poet again paints for us the image of a literary race that he refuses to join.

Yet that refusal itself shows him in a competitive mode, peering ahead (or right alongside) to his nearest, most admired competitor, Virgil. Just as that first poem of book 1 took so much of its relational sense from the goat-powered *Eclogues*, book 2 opens by locating itself against the now more relevant *Georgics*. That glance towards the *Georgics*, fleeting as it is, will have a powerful influence on the history of later Latin satire. For in the early second century CE, Juvenal will fashion his own, challenging version of the "already done to death" theme of *Georgics* 3.[101] A curious choice for a writer of satire. The story of that remake is usually put in terms of Juvenal's processing of Virgil's (already processed) remake, through the intermediary of Persius. That seems reasonable enough. But, the presence of the same theme, pregnant with Virgilian allusions, already in Horace *S.* 2.1 complicates the smooth linearity of that scheme. Since *S.* 2.1 is the more obvious, accepted model for Juvenal's first poem, the story of Juvenal's remake may have to be rewritten to include not just his reading of Virgil (and all stops before and in between), but his exceptionally deep reading of Virgil *through* Horace. Or is it of Horace *through* Virgil? The temporal proximity of *Georgics* book 3 to *Sermones* book 2 means we cannot really say in which direction the influence is running. I take it as running both ways.

The most obvious difference that separates Horace's treatment of the "avoiding triteness" theme in *S.* 2.1 and Virgil's treatment of it in *G.* 3 is that, in Virgil's version, the poet actually undertakes to write that big, epic project. He cannot get to it right away, but "soon," he says, he will give it his full attention. Virgil postpones, while Horace rejects. And in rejecting, he follows the standard "not just anyone can do it" *recusatio* of the later "Augustans" (himself included).[102] But his refusal, standard as it seems, hides an uncharacteristic intertextual twist. It has in it an allusion to that certain someone else *who can* write the epic: Virgil. That is his project, marked as his already from the opening lines of *Georgics* 3.

What Horace, in satire, makes look terribly crass (a race for

---

[101] Henderson (1995) 104–8.
[102] On the standard Augustan refusal, see Wimmel (1960).

cash), Virgil in his *Georgics* manages to make look grand and desirable (for those who want it that way, anyway – see below). This is not just a matter of things looking different in different genres. It is a matter of things *having to* look different in different genres. Horace here is showing us the limits of satire. It is a genre that locks him into the crass, cynical mode of Trebatius; the genre that cannot praise, or even begin to open up to the new expectations and pressures of the post-Actian age.[103] Soon enough, it seems, satire will have to go. But the *Georgics* will have to go too. That lofty proem of *Georgics* 3 makes clear that there is a grand, epinician task to be done, but the *Georgics* themselves cannot handle it. The poet does not refuse the job, the genre does. And so Virgil, too, just as Horace in *S.* 2.1, shows us the limits of his chosen genre. As he slips momentarily into the world of his projected epic, he shows us how out-of-place epinician flights of fancy are within a georgic mode. The proem to book 3 is a complex and high-flying excursus that seems to not quite belong; a slick, "look-at-me" intrusion into what has been set up, so far, as a down-home, country landscape.

Perhaps that is why we are invited to remember that proem in the opening lines of *S.* 2.1. For in both poems, the coming of a new, post-Actian age is something both performed and powerfully felt. In Virgil, just as in Horace, we are made to experience it by being abruptly shaken out of our old readerly habits. The genre as we have come to know it, in both poems, is momentarily missing, and we are put in a strange, new landscape that we do not quite understand. In the case of *Georgics* 3, for example, one might well wonder, "Wasn't this supposed to be Maecenas' party?" But here he has been made a bystander at someone else's parade. The standout image is that of Caesar ensconced in his soon-to-be built, Italian temple. That is the new focal point, the shiny temple to which the poet is determined to drive his chariot in triumph. But why go there now? Virgil knows that, in the present work, he cannot stay there long, so he forces himself to rein in his horses in lines 46–50 and get back to the serious work of the farm. Still, that detour has a lasting impact on the way we finish off our reading of the poems. Now as we read books 3 and 4, we sense that the *Georgics* are no longer enough. They may even be getting in the

---

[103] On satire as *carmen maledicum*, see below chapter 2.

way. The epinician incursion of book 3, so high-flying and out of place, lets us feel clearly that the clock is ticking. Virgil had to go there, if only for a moment, for the pressure is on to produce a new kind of poetry, something triumphal, in an over-the-top, epinician mode.[104] The more cynical of his readers will see the poet buying himself some time with the proem, producing just a little taste of the blustery, flag-waving work to come; a little something to relieve the pressure. Is that a perverse way of reading? Should we scourge ourselves soundly for thinking that perhaps Virgil has overdone it just a bit here, and for worrying that he really might write an epic that looks like that? We cannot know, and he is not telling. No matter. For now, he says, there is still a lot of plowing to be done.

PANEGYRIC BLUSTER AND ENNIUS' *SCIPIO* IN HORACE,
SERMONES 2.1

Horace is no athlete. The rigors of that big epic contest, he tells Trebatius, are simply beyond his strength: *cupidum, pater optime, uires | deficiunt* ("the desire is there, noble sir, but I haven't the strength needed to pull it off," *S.* 2.1.12–13). But then, paradoxically, he goes on to give a three-line slice of the kind of poetry he hasn't the strength to write (13–15):

> neque enim quiuis horrentia pilis
> agmina nec fracta pereuntis cuspide Gallos
> aut labentis equo describit uulnera Parthi.

For it is not just anyone-you-please that can describe troops in their ranks bristling with javelins, Gauls dying with a shattered lance, or the wounds of a Parthian as he slips from his horse.

A stunning little vignette, and quite remarkable for someone claiming to be incapable of that sort of writing. But exactly what kind of story is he refusing to write? Commentators on these lines have always been taken aback by his response, openly confused by his too-obvious failure to say what we expect him to say. The scenario we are asked to imagine is this: here we have Horace, sometime in 30 BCE, asked to tell the story of Caesar's recent military exploits, the wars that have rendered him "invincible." In refus-

---

[104] Thomas (1988) 36–7: "The proem is if anything an 'anti-*recusatio*', capturing, as no other passage of V. does, the moment at which the inevitability of the *Aeneid* must have come to him."

ing, he takes four lines to recapitulate and run us through the most notable of those achievements. Just the highlights. So what does he choose to remember? The grand, illustrious wars Octavian fought against the Parthians and Gauls. At this point, most readers respond with "Did I just miss something? I don't quite remember those wars. When did they even happen?"

The more obvious question they ask, the one that really chafes, is "Where is Actium?"[105] That is the scandal of the vignette: not what it says, but what it so obviously does not say, and the strange, misty way it manages not to say it. The problem has long been recognized by commentators, and they have dealt with it in a number of creative, but, for me, mostly unsatisfactory, ways. The main options they serve up are these: first, they argue that the vignette is a case of typical rhetorical flourish (which it obviously is), and that, because of this, we should *not be surprised* by its lack of specific detail.[106] Others have insisted that the mention of Gauls and Parthians recalls two of the less well-known campaigns fought by Octavian; or, if not these, then perhaps wars he was determined to undertake after his triumphal return home. That may be right too. But again, the explanation comes with assurances that the vignette is only superficially surprising, and that any shock we might initially experience can be easily defused. A third tack has been to argue that Horace's three-line vignette really *is* about Actium, just not in any obvious way. Some have pointed out that the description complies with the rhetoric of the new regime, where the stress is always on the foreignness of Caesar's enemies at Actium.[107] Again, the explanation may be right, but does it really satisfy? Does it put our "Why not Actium?" questions securely to one side and allow us to advance worry-free in our reading?

The common motif playing inside these various reasonable explanations is that the problem admits of a quick and obvious "solution" (but we are not quite sure which one), so we do better to downplay and quickly get past our worries than to allow them

[105] Muecke (1993) 103: "Why Gauls and Parthians? Why not Actium?"
[106] E.g. Lejay (1966) 298: "Parthes et Gaulois sont évidemment des types, mais des types choisis d'après les préoccupations du public romain au temps de cette satire." Cf. Fedeli (1994) 536: "La caratterizzazione della poesia epica nei vv. 13–15 è realizzata, oltre che con la presentazione dei tradizionali nemici, con la presenza dei suoi ingredienti obbligatori."
[107] For the proponents of various "historical" solutions to the problem of lines 13–15, see Muecke (1993) 103–4.

any lasting semantic effect. Horace's failure to mention Actium, they tell us, "makes sense," so we have no good reason to feel scandalized by being tossed a version of Octavian's story that looks just like so many other similar stories of the Roman epic tradition, with valiant Romans slaughtering the barbarian hordes on the fringes of the Roman *imperium*. That story, in fact, as Horace tells it here, is pushed so far from Rome that one would be hard-pressed to invent wars with Romans actually fighting in them that could be any farther off than these and still have a chance of seeming "real." The Gauls were at one far end of the Roman frontier, the Parthians at another.

But maybe that is the point. Maybe the description challenges our compliance by pushing us just a bit too far off the map, making it just a little too hard for us to comply and brush aside those nagging doubts that tell us we are being hurried along by the description, if not actually duped and ripped off. If readers of the passage really do ask the "Why not Actium?" question, as commentators generally admit they must, then why not, instead of insisting that the question can be gotten around easily by looking at the passage just so – squinting, with head cocked hard to the (compliant) right – why not examine the question for what it does? That is, the way it makes us experience and wrestle against an awkward moment in our reading. The absence from this description of Rome's recent *civil* wars, the reality that features Romans killing Romans not terribly far from home, really is a problem, one that does not admit of a deft, brush-aside "solution." Let's admit that. It may just be the point, and the way the poem figures to get under our skin.

What we are given to consider in these lines, instead of the awful reality of civil war, is a far-off tale that hovers somewhere in the never-land of Actium's glossy retelling, or of those "projected foreign wars" done up in typical rhetorical flourish. The commentaries are good at pointing this out. The question they do not allow is: are we supposed to be satisfied with it? Or is feeling ripped off an option we can actually allow ourselves to explore? In hearing Octavian's story told the way Horace tells it (if it is the story of Actium – and even if it is not, it *should* be), we feel powerfully that limits are being set up around an angst-ridden space, barriers to keep us from seeing what we know is inside. How do we respond to being patronized, and being told we must not go there? Do we heed the commentators' urgings to "move along" and not be terribly troubled by it ("Pay no attention to that man behind the curtain!")? Do we allow ourselves to take the Horatian vignette as the tale of Actium, the real thing, just done up more distantly so that no one takes offense? Or do we see it, perhaps, in more sinister colors; as the tale of how that tale, the bloody-awful, real one, now *has to be* told? The one and only way, adhering strictly and compliantly to the rhetoric of the new regime. Do we sense here any hint of goose-stepping, or of the unbearable new pressure to march in step? We know that, in the magnificent triple triumph of the following year, great pains were taken to avoid any suggestions of civil war.[108] The message was broadcast clearly over three days: "This was a *foreign* campaign, fought valiantly against the Illyrians (celebrations day one), the client kings of Asia Minor and the Near East (day two), and the Egyptians (day three)." Mark Antony and his Romans were never there. Their disappearance an unresolved, unrelated mystery.[109]

The range of readers' reactions to the vignette of lines 13–15, if not endless, is quite extensive. Still, it is hard to imagine them not reacting to it, or giving the lines a mere yawn, or a compliant smile. Virgil's matching version of Octavian's soon to be told tale in the proem to *Georgics* 3 resembles this one both in its grand heroic tones and, more importantly, in its being set securely in far-off places (*G.* 3.26–31):

> in foribus pugnam ex auro solidoque elephanto
> **Gangaridum** faciam uictorisque arma Quirini,
> atque hic undantem bello magnumque fluentem
> **Nilum** ac nauali surgentis aere columnas.
> addam urbes **Asiae** domitas pulsumque **Niphaten**
> fidentemque fuga **Parthum** uersisque sagittis.

On the doors [of my temple] I will fashion, out of gold and solid ivory, the battle against the Ganges' tribes, and the arms of their conqueror, Quirinus. And on this side will be the Nile, huge and flowing with war, and columns will rise up with the bronze (prows) of ships. I will include, too, the captured cities of Asia, Niphates driven off, and the Parthian who trusts in flight, shooting his arrows behind him.

---

[108] See especially Gurval (1995) 25–36.

[109] Dio 51.19.5 indicates that Romans who witnessed the Triple Triumph were fully aware of the war's being refashioned by it; cf. Tac. *Hist.* 4.4 on the scandal of triumphal honors being awarded after the civil wars of 69 CE: "with many fine words, Mucianus was granted triumphal honors for a war waged against fellow-Romans, though his campaign against the Sarmatians was made the excuse."

Again the story comes in a glossy, idealized package. But its potential to rankle, I suspect (and I am fully prepared to be wrong about this), is less than that of Horace's version. Virgil fills in the map of the world just enough so that we can at least imagine he really does mean the war against Antony. His mention of the Nile, at least, lets us think of Cleopatra and, by extension, of her presence at Actium. As I suggested above, I think it is the perceived intrusiveness of this glossy material more than its being too oppressively glossy (it is just a little oppressively glossy) that gets us feeling the pressures of the post-Actian age and asking some rather hard questions about how Virgil figures in it.

Slightly later, in the first poem of *Elegies* book 2, Propertius will address the issue of telling Caesar's tale with a version of the "done to death" motif that cues us to his reading of Horace and Virgil. Despite those cues (and precisely *because of* them), his version of the project looks terribly different (Prop. 2.1.17–19, 25–8):

> quod mihi si tantum, Maecenas, fata dedissent,
>   ut possem heroas ducere in arma manus,
> non ego Titanas canerem, non Ossan Olympo
> . . . .
> bellaque **res**que tui memorarem **Caesaris**, et tu
>   Caesare sub magno cura secunda fores.
> nam quotiens Mutinam aut **ciuilia busta** Philippos
>   aut canerem Siculae classica bella . . .

But, Maecenas, if only fate had granted me the strength to lead heroic troops in arms, I would not, for my part, sing of the Titans, nor of Ossa stacked on top of Olympus ... I would remember the wars and achievements of your man, Caesar, and, in his massive Caesarship, you would become my second care. For as often as I sang of Mutina, or of the citizens' corpses at Philippi, or of the sea-battles of Sicily ...

Propertius goes on to mention battles in Etruria, Egypt, and Actium itself. No more Parthians and heroic gloss. This is a story about Philippi, the town of Mutina right down the road, and those many fields of Roman corpses. It is less a refusal than a threat, with the poet claiming that he can tell the story, but *this* is what it will look like. "Do you still want me to tell it, Maecenas? Or is it maybe not what you had in mind?"

Horace responds to Trebatius' advice that he tell Octavian's story with a sample of the kind of poetry he claims to be incapable of writing. The refusal shows him momentarily entering into, what I take as, the "expected," "compliant" mode, with a lot of vague, epic-talk – precisely the kind of talk he would *have to* employ in taking on the project. But there is more to these lines than suggestions of epic gloss, and they do more than just sound like what grand-style epic sounds like. For as I hope now to show, they recall a passage of Ennius that had been famously criticized by Lucilius, and thus, in one motion, they allude to both of Horace's principal forerunners in the genre of satire. But this critically resonant allusion does not simply introduce Ennius and/or Lucilius as generic models. It raises one of the principal themes of the poem and, in a sense, of the entire book: the poet's anxiety over his relationship to powerful friends. The allusion points to two quite different forms that such friendships could take, in the models of Ennius' friendship with the Elder Africanus, and Lucilius' friendship with the Younger. And it once again points to the powerful distorting effects that such friendships can and commonly did have on a poet's voice. All of this becomes terribly relevant in the course of the poem as Horace turns to examine his own relationship to Octavian, and the pressures that that wildly uneven relationship would soon exert on his poetic voice, especially his satiric voice. It is with the help of Ennius and Lucilius, both under the surface of this vignette, that he probes into the question of *his* place in the power-configurations of post-Actian Rome.

In her commentary on *S.* 2.1, Frances Muecke asserts that the phrase "columns bristling with javelins" in lines 13–14 is "reminiscent of archaic epic."[110] She quotes two instances of the same metaphor in Ennius, and one in the epic-loving Livy to prove the point. That is where the matter is left, and that is pretty much all that any of the major commentaries (and I think that hers is now the best on book 2) have to say. Still, I think more can and should be said. For if you actually go to the fragments of Ennius you find that he has the "bristling" metaphor of soldiers in arms at least four times, maybe five (depending on how you read fr. 309Sk.).[111] That is quite a lot, given the little we have left of Ennius, and it makes me think that Ennius was abnormally fond of the metaphor.

---

[110] Muecke (1993) 103.
[111] Definite uses of the metaphor are found at *Annales* frr. 249, 267, and 384Sk., and *Scipio, Remains of Old Latin* fr. 6.

In contrast, Virgil, who has left us more than ten times the number of epic hexameters, has the metaphor only once, at *Aeneid* 11.601–2: *tum late ferreus hastis | horret ager* ("then the field, iron far and wide, bristles with spears"). The metaphor, common in Ennius, is unique in Virgil, and so it is not surprising that his ancient commentators felt compelled to comment on it. For example, Servius (*ad loc.*) glosses Virgil's *hastis horret ager* ("the field bristling with spears") with the following:

> terribilis est: est autem uersus Ennianus, uituperatus a Lucilio dicente per inrisionem, debuisse eum dicere "horret et alget."

It inspires terror. It is, moreover, a verse from Ennius that was lampooned by Lucilius, who remarked derisively that he (Ennius) *should* have written *horret et alget* ("it bristles and it freezes").

In other words, when Servius sees this metaphor, the *only* time he sees it in the *Aeneid*, he thinks immediately not of "archaic epic" generally, but of Ennius in particular. And he remembers that Lucilius, at one point in his *Satires* (usually this is put in book 10, but I suspect it may belong to book 26) aggressively mocked Ennius for using that same metaphor in one of his works.[112] We shall see which work that is in just a moment. That information, by itself, is enough to suggest a change in the way we read Horace's "vaguely epic" *horrentia pilis* "bristling with javelins" in line 13 of *S.* 2.1.

But there is more. Servius goes on to provide further information that makes such a change even more pressing. He writes: *unde Horatius de Lucilio "non ridet uersus Enni grauitate minores?"* ("on the basis of that, Horace says of Lucilius 'Does he not laugh at the verses of Ennius that fall short of their weighty theme?'"). The circle is now complete: from Ennius, to Lucilius, to Horace. Servius claims that that specific critique of Ennius stands behind the

---

[112] Neither Marx (1904) nor Krenkel (1970) assign the fragment to a specific book. Fiske (1913) has argued that book 26 of Lucilius contained a literary polemic against certain grand-style writers of his day, such as Pacuvius, whether along with, or in the form of, an eisagogic treatise on style (likely parodic) later imitated by Horace in his *Ars Poetica*, then by Persius in his first satire. But the scholiasts of Persius' first satire also relate that it was upon reading Lucilius' tenth book disparaging "poets and orators of recent date" that Persius set himself to writing satire. Thus, it is difficult to say in which of these two books, if either, the disparagement of Ennius' "bristling" metaphor was found. For crucial metrical considerations, see below.

apology of *S.* 1.10.54 (which he quotes). In other words, Ennius' description of a field "bristling with javelins," something like the one we see in *Aeneid* book 11, is the very thing that set Lucilius off against him in one of his *Satires*, and it is precisely *that* critique that Horace recalls when he describes Lucilius' censure of Ennius in *S.* 1.10. That was the previous satire, the last poem of book 1. And so it is unlikely that an imaginative reader of Horace, someone aware of the whole story behind that earlier interchange, could be kept from recalling it here, in the first poem of book 2. The metaphor, we have seen, sets off distinctly Ennian bells, even when it appears in Virgil. And not just that, it recalls Ennius (according to Lucilius) at his very worst – the line that Lucilius found so egregiously bad and rendered even worse by tacking on the deflating *et alget* ("and it freezes").

What makes that two-word tag so funny is not immediately obvious, but here again the ancient commentators on Virgil prove invaluable in helping flesh out the details of that famous interchange. The commentator this time is Servius' contemporary, Macrobius, who glosses the "bristling field" metaphor of *Aeneid* book 11 (the same one we saw above) with the following: *mire se habet. sed et Ennius* ("it is strange. But Ennius has it too").[113] Again, to meet the metaphor is to think automatically of Ennius, so Macrobius proceeds to give a short sampling of the metaphor's use in Ennius, concluding his list with the following example: *in* "*Scipione*": *sparsis hastis longis campus splendet et horret* ("in his *Scipio* (Ennius writes): the plain glimmers and bristles with long scattered pikes"). This is the line, I am convinced, that Lucilius made fun of in his twenty-sixth (or tenth) book.

Others before me have made the connection, so I am not being terribly adventurous in suggesting it.[114] The evidence for it is strong. First of all, among the various Ennian passages sampled by Macrobius, it is the only version of the metaphor that contains the form *horret*, and we know that Lucilius poked fun at Ennius by saying he should have said *horret et alget*. The other versions all have different forms of the word that do not match up. Secondly, if you ever needed to find a Latin epic hexameter that would set a lampoon-writer racing to find his pen, this is it; that is, if it really

---

[113] Macr. 6.4.6.   [114] E.g. Marx (1904), vol. 2, 376.

is a hexameter.[115] At least one scholar has suggested it may not be,
even though, as we have it, it scans as one (a bad one) and cannot
quite be made to scan as anything else. The two other most reliable quotations from the *Scipio* are in septenarii, and this line
nearly scans as a septenarius.

But let us just suppose for a moment that it really is a hexameter. Most scholars think it is. From a later, Virgilian standpoint,
Latin hexameters do not get much worse than this one. First you
have that grinding rhythm that comes from clustering together too
many words of the same size and metrical shape. The repetition
brings with it the agreement of ictus and accent across the whole
line – something Virgil avoided utterly. Exaggerating a bit, the
rhythm is: *spársis hástis lóngis cámpus spléndet et hórret.* The line is
virtually caesura-less (the weak one in the fifth foot does nothing
to break up the monotony).[116] There is a lot to make fun of here,
in other words, even if this is not a hexameter. But the thing that
Lucilius chose to parody seems not to have been the rhythm, but
the homoioteleuta, that is, the way so many successive words end
with precisely the same sound. This gets taken to a ridiculous
extreme with the addition of Lucilius' *et alget*, a phrase that em-
phasizes the line's grand-style "frigidity" both in its meaning ("it
freezes") and by its droning sound (the repeated *et . . . -et*). With
that tacked on the line reads "horribly" *spars**is** hast**is** long**is** campus
splend**et** **et** horr**et** **et** alget.*

For Lucilius, this was Ennius at his worst, and from a later,
Virgilian perspective, we can see why he thought that. Still, there
is one other detail in Macrobius' note that I regard as far more
important and revealing than the line itself or the evidence it pro-

---

[115] As it stands, the passage is either an exceptionally bad, but actual, hexameter line, or an
iambic cluster that resembles, but fails to scan as, a septenarius. For difficult metrical
considerations, see Courtney (1993) 26–9. If the line is a hexameter, it probably belonged to book 10; and if a septenarius, to book 26. It is also possible that Lucilius
changed the line from a near-hexametric septenarius into a true, but bathetic, hexameter, or vice versa, from a near-septenarian hexameter into a quasi-septenarius. The remaining fragments of Ennius' *Scipio* are in septenarii. Courtney concludes (p. 26): "this
may be presumed to have been the metre of the poem."

[116] Courtney (1993) 28–9 takes the absence of a caesura in the second, third, or fourth foot
as evidence that the line cannot be a hexameter. But arguments based on precedents of
acceptable style may not work here since Lucilius seems to have quoted the line specifically because he found it (or rendered it) awkward and unacceptable.

vides about Ennius' sometimes questionable verse-technique. It is the passing remark that the line comes from Ennius' *Scipio*, not the *Annales*. The *Scipio*, it seems, was either a panegyric epic or, like the *Ambracia* later, a *praetexta* that celebrated the heroic deeds of a contemporary warrior and politician. Both the Elder Scipio and Fulvius Nobilior, heroes respectively of the *Scipio* and the *Ambracia*, though men of much higher social standing than the poet, were counted as his personal friends. In traveling with them on their military campaigns and writing works celebrating their exploits, Ennius (as far as we can tell) introduced the model of Hellenistic court-panegyric into Rome, and we know that this innovation was vigorously protested by the Elder Cato already in Ennius' own day.[117] Such protests, however, were to no avail. Roman panegyric epic was there to stay, and Ennius was permanently inscribed as its founder.[118]

What potential effects, then, does this complicated history of a metaphor have on our reading of Horace's epic vignette in *S.* 2.1? Perhaps most obviously, it shows that the vignette is not what it has commonly been assumed to be: it contains more than vague epic talk, and it does more with that talk than just reproduce its distant, celebratory sounds. For when Horace is urged by Trebatius to compose a panegyric epic for Octavian, he does more in refusing than just call to mind the tedium of such an enterprise, or the overdone character of panegyric generally. Rather, he cues us with a memory from one of the most important poems in the history of Latin panegyric.[119] And it is not just any random scene he alludes to, but a scene with a well-known critical history; Ennian bluster at its very worst. By bringing in that "bristling with spears" metaphor famously lampooned by Lucilius, Horace shows that his refusal to write panegyric epic is not just a matter of flagging strength, the standard Callimachean dodge. He gives an actual, remembered sample of just how thankless and unforgiving such enterprises could be. He introduces the model of Ennius, a man of exceptional talent, who went down the panegyric road

---

[117] See Skutsch (1985) 1–2.
[118] For a survey of panegyric epic in Rome, see White (1993) 78–82.
[119] The *Scipio* is often assumed to have been a non-dramatic *laus* with poems in several meters. See Gratwick (1982) 157. It may in fact have been a *praetexta*. Again, metrical difficulties in the remaining fragments make the problem irresolvable.

in his dealings with men of exceptional power – the very thing
Horace is being asked to do in the fiction(?) of *S.* 2.1: to become
Ennius to an even bigger Scipio, Octavian. With that vignette, he
shows us how Ennius dealt with *his* Scipio at an early stage in his
career, and he reminds us of the strange, unfortunate effects that
that relationship had on his poetic voice. From a later standpoint
(at least as far as Lucilius was concerned) Ennius' sometimes-too-
precious efforts at glorifying his patron were credited to him not as
groundbreaking and ennobling, but as laughable, and a permanent blot on his otherwise stellar record.

Similar critical demons, I suspect, hover about the images of
"invincible Caesar" in line 11, and that wounded Parthian slipping
from his horse in line 15. Leaving the details to the notes, I contend that these images, like that of the "bristling fields" set between them, cue us to some famously overdone moments in the
history of Latin panegyric epic.[120] Thus the entire interchange of
lines 11–15 is littered with other poets' critical trash and memories
of their descent into infamous bluster. Panegyric epic, then, is a
potentially disastrous enterprise. Not something to be refused simply because it is too difficult and/or artificial, as the lines superficially assert. It is to be refused also because the comfort it buys is
purchased at a very steep, unrefundable price.

---

[120] Other possible "taunting" redeployments hidden in *S.* 2.1 include *inuicti* ("unconquered/
invincible") in line 11. This epithet of gods (Jupiter, *C.* 3.27.73), epic heroes (Achilles,
Epod. 13.12), and champion athletes (the pancratist Glycon, *Ep.* 1.1.30 *inuicti membra
Glyconis* = *AP* 7.692 Γλύκων ... αἵ τ' ἀνίκατοι χέρες), had been infamously attached to
the name of Scipio Africanus by Ennius, who appears to have made wide use of the
noun–epithet phrase *Scipio inuictus* in his hexameter poems, especially in his panegyric
Scipio; see Bettini (1979) 19–20. Because *Scipio* cannot scan in hexameters without under-
going the harsh elision of its final long *-o* into a short vowel beginning the next word,
Ennius resorted to a prosodic hiatus that, though it displayed an awareness of Greek
precedents, sounded terribly uncouth to most Roman ears: Cicero makes a special case of
Ennius' *frequent* use of this awkward noun–epithet phrase at *Orator* 152–3 *at Ennius* **saepe**
[sc. *hiabat*] *"Scipio inuicte"* ... *hoc idem nostri saepius non tulissent, quod Graeci laudare etiam solent*.
This famously awkward precedent in using "invincible" (slightly overblown in itself) as
Scipio's epic epithet surely stands behind Trebatius' advice here: the recommendation
thus conceals a warning against the panegyric writer's easy descent into infamous bluster.
   Yet another taunting redeployment lurks in *labentis ... Parthi* in line 15. The phrase
recalls a passage from book 1 of Furius Bibaculus' *Annales Belli Gallici*, a neo-Ennian
"Annals" devoted to Julius Caesar's Gallic campaigns = fr. 8 Courtney: *ille graui subito
deuictus uolnere habenas | misit equi lapsusque in humum defluxit*. For the lines' imitation of
Ennius, see Courtney (1993) 195–6. Elsewhere in Horace verses of Furius are scathingly
abused; cf. esp. *S.* 1.10.36 and 2.5.41. Does the allusion here hail that famously abused
epic as the bellwether of a thriving, neo-Ennian epic industry?

COMING TO TERMS WITH SCIPIO: THE NEW LOOK OF
POST-ACTIAN SATIRE

But there are other options at hand for poets feeling the squeeze
from powerful friends. Trebatius points out that Lucilius was
especially "wise" in his dealings with the Younger Africanus. For
instead of lathering him with praise, as Ennius did for the Elder
Scipio (and Bibaculus did later for Julius Caesar), Lucilius admitted into his *Satires* glossed-down scenes from his day-to-day life
with Scipio, depicting him there as a "fair" and "brave" friend
(*S.* 2.1.16–17):

> attamen et iustum poteras et scribere fortem
> Scipiadam ut sapiens Lucilius.

But you could have described him as fair and brave, as wise Lucilius did
for Scipio.

The third-century scholiast, Porphyrion, detects a contrast here
between Ennius and Lucilius. He comments at lines 16–17:
"Ennius wrote about wars, while Lucilius told stories from that
man's [Scipio's] private life." From what has been said above
about Ennius' hidden role in the lines directly preceding, we can
see why he might have thought to bring Ennius into the picture
here.

And so the question moves from the poetry of Ennius and the
"wise" Lucilius to that of Horace himself: how will he come to
terms with *his* Scipio? Can his satire handle partisan stroking even
of a softer, less assuming type? Lucilius worked it into his *Satires*,
so there is no dodging the issue by claiming that the genre is not
set up for it. Lucilius *is* the genre! Backed into a corner, Horace
counters with this excuse (*S.* 2.1.17–20):

> haud mihi deero,
> cum res ipsa feret. nisi dextro tempore Flacci
> uerba per attentam non ibunt Caesaris aurem,
> cui male si palpere, recalcitret undique tutus.

I won't let myself down when circumstances suggest. But unless the time
is propitious, Flop-ear's words won't pass through Caesar's ear when it is
pricked-up and attentive. Unless you pet him just right, he will kick back
till he is safe on all sides.

The lines have an unusual and disorienting intertextual charge, for the opening boast, "I won't let myself down," quotes none other than the money-grubbing shadow of *S.* 1.9.[121] At a point midway through that tedious contest between the meandering poet and the man who just won't take the hint and go away, the shadow uses precisely the same boast to counter the poet's suggestion that he give up on his quest of Maecenas (*S.* 1.9.56–8):

> haud mihi deero:
> muneribus seruos corrumpam; non, hodie si
> exclusus fuero, desistam; tempora quaeram.

I won't let myself down: I'll bribe his servants with gifts. If I'm locked out today, I won't give up. I'll watch for times.

Like his obnoxious alter-ego in *S.* 1.9, the poet of *S.* 2.1 is determined to succeed in his conquest of Octavian. He, too, is looking for just the "right time" (*dextro tempore*) to make his move. The parallels are close, yet commentators have routinely found ways to keep them from meaning too much. Their preferred solution has been to write the problem aside with "cf. *S.* 1.9.56," but Muecke has recently given that game away by putting an exclamation point behind her cf. ("cf. *Sat.* 1.9.56!").[122] With it, she lets on that there is a price to pay for making that connection; that the cross-reference has tremendous power to offend. A more telling punctuation might be "cf. *S.* 1.9.56–8?!" for that gets at the way the "allusion" (if that is what it really is – and it really (potentially) is) challenges readers to make something of the obvious situational and verbal parallels connecting Horace's words to those of the shadow. It pushes us to consider first whether we want it to be an allusion (and therefore meaningful), or just an accidental and mostly meaningless "cf." (interesting background noise). A decision has to be made; a decision that probes into the politics and personal preferences of individual readers. Because the parallels do not seem to fit, their potential to offend gets us thinking twice about whether we want to credit them as an allusion, and so the commentator's task of determining how to rate them, in the end, is every reader's task. They constitute an awkwardness to be felt

---

[121] In line 18 *cum res ipsa feret* might also be taken as "when my resources allow it." Cf. Oliensis (1998a) 43: "the surface message of this opening exchange is that Horace's chosen branch of poetry has brought and continues to bring no advantages."

[122] Muecke (1993) 104.

and wrestled against, an awkwardness that is the way the "allusion(?!)" means.

But how can that possibly be the right image to bring in here? If we grant that these parallels amount to something, we have to ask ourselves just how much of that earlier, seedy image of the poet's shadow, so funny there in *S.* 1.9, we will allow ourselves to see here in 2.1. Just how much of his grating, pandering voice will we allow ourselves to hear inside the poet's promise soon to take up Octavian's cause? As with any allusion, but especially with this one, the problem comes in stopping it from meaning too much. Where does the bore end and Horace begin? And how do we know when we have the proportions of "bore" to "Horace" just right? The allusion has an obvious diagnostic force in that it makes *us* responsible for finding these limits, and for determining just how much bore we can stand to see in the character of *our* Horace. But why have us consider him that way at all? What can be the point of casting him, potentially (depending on what we let happen), and just for a moment, in such an ugly and damaging light? Perhaps the point of the allusion is to make us adopt an alien, unsettling perspective on someone we thought we knew quite well: this is what Horace looks like, what he *has to* look like, in the the eyes of an envious outsider. That look is the price he pays for his success with the new regime, and for even considering a post-Actian reprise of Lucilius' brand of "stroking" praise.

But why should he *have to* look that way? Lucilius managed to paint his connection with Scipio as a close, egalitarian friendship without any hint of sycophancy. That is the story as we know it, at least, and it is a most unusual story for a poet of the second century BCE. But perhaps here, for once, hidden in that unsettling, built-in image of the pest, we have another take on that famously balanced friendship between equals and soul-mates, the stronger of whom just happened to be the most powerful political figure of his day. But if not that, then maybe this whiff of stench from *S.* 1.9 simply shows us what Horace is doomed to look like and sound like if he ever actually takes on the cause of "petting" Caesar with his poems as he (playfully? ironically?) promises to do here. With it, he reminds us that he is no Lucilius, and that his son-of-a-freed-slave, post-Actian version of satire can never look terribly much like its free-speaking, late Republican counterpart in Lucilius.

"When the time is propitious." That is when Horace will try
his hand at poetry of a more partisan, "petting" sort. This is not a
refusal, but a postponement, and so it reminds us again of the
proem to *Georgics* 3, where Virgil promises to take on an epinician
task that, he says, he cannot get to right away. In doing that,
Virgil makes a point about generic incompatibility: the plowing
genre is unsuited to the high-flying, horse-powered task. A similar
point, I think, is being made here in *S.* 2.1. Not that satire is no
place for partisan stroking; Lucilius showed it could be. It is that
Horace is no Lucilius, and that the differences separating them in
time, social standing, and so on, have a direct and powerful impact on what his version of satire must look like. If Lucilius could
flatter *his* Scipio in satire, it is because times were different then.
Actium was far off, and Lucilius was no son of a freed slave.[123]
Status, we have seen, matters terribly to the writing of satire in
Rome. It always did and it always would.[124] Having reckoned with
it as a huge issue in book 1 of the *Sermones*, we sense it here again,
bigger than ever, at the beginning of book 2, within the "fiction"
of the poet's paranoid helplessness and handwringing.[125] In the
lines quoted above, Horace underscores the point of his second-
rate status in the lowly image of his long, floppy ears. The contrasting image is that of Caesar's pricked-up and extra-sensitive
ears. With it, Caesar is imagined as a high-strung horse, ready to
kick out at anyone who pets him badly. But Horace, with those
long, drooping ears, resembles an ass, a low-breed animal, and
notoriously flop-eared. The image is helped along by a previous
pun on the poet's cognomen, *Flaccus* "droop-eared," at *S.* 1.9.20–1.
There, when the pest insists on following along wherever Horace
is headed, the poet likens himself to an ass whose ears sag when he
is set with a burden that exceeds his strength: *demitto auriculas, ut*

---

[123] Gruen (1992) 278–9 "The poet belonged to a family that had acquired senatorial rank,
secured links with major political figures, and possessed the means to play a role on the
public scene ... the satirist plainly had a place in Rome's upper echelons." For Lucilius'
illustrious family background, see Krenkel (1970) 18–19.

[124] For the status of poets in second- and first-century Rome, see Badian (1972), Gold (1987)
39–67, and White (1993).

[125] The threat of legal proceedings that is the premise of Horace's consultation with
Trebatius in *Sermones* 2.1 is itself an indication of the poet's inferior social status in comparison with Lucilius. Crook (1967) 253–5 indicates that Lucilius would have been
immune from such prosecution.

iniquae mentis asellus | cum grauius dorso subiit onus ("my ears start to droop, like those of a little ass, upset when too heavy a load is set on his back"). Drooping ears here, as elsewhere in Latin literature, are a symbol of flagging strength.[126] In *S.* 2.1 the source of drooping ears, that too-heavy load, is Caesar, and the crushing weight of his post-Actian self. Praising him, Horace suggests, is a burden too heavy for *his* satire's *asellus*.

But I suspect there is another side to this dodge than the issues of status and of the careful "timing" of one's praise to the well-bred Octavian. For the phrase *nisi dextro tempore* "unless the time is propitious" translates exactly the sense of Greek καιρός "the right/propitious moment." And when connected to the theme of the poet's praise, the word carries some very specific resonances. Most notably, it recalls Pindar, who deployed καιρός as a poetic principle central to his epinician program. For him the term signifies that ideal "balance" to be achieved in singing praise that is neither tepid nor bombastic.[127] So buried here, in a message about the right "timing" of praise to Octavian, there may be a further note about the ideal "tempering" of that praise, the καιρός that Pindar strove so hard to achieve. And there may also be something here about the rhythmic "pace" appropriate to those projected poems of praise. We know that Horace can and did use *tempus* of metrical "time," as he does at *S.* 1.4.58 *tempora certa modosque* ("fixed times and measures"). He seems actually to pun on that sense of the word at *S.* 1.9.56–60 by putting the pest-poet's boast *tempora quaeram* ("I will seek out times") smack in the middle of the five most monotonous hexameters he ever

---

[126] For drooping ears as a symbol of flagging strength, cf. Virg. *G.* 3.500 *demissae aures* (of a sick horse), and Statius, *Theb.* 11.745 *demissas aures* (a lion weakened by age). For the ass as notoriously flop-eared, see Apul. *Met.* 9.15 *(asinus) auribus grandissimis praeditus*.

[127] The phrase *nisi dextro tempore* touches on not only (1) the proper "timing" of praise to Augustus, but (2) the ideal "tempering" of that praise, and possibly (3) the rhythmic "pace" appropriate to it. Roman writers often spoke of new works as potential disruptions into their patrons' busy lives. Those seeking the ear of Octavian/Augustus found the "right moment" particularly elusive; see esp. Vitr. 1 pref. 1 *metuens ne non apto tempore interpellans*, and *Ep.* 2.1.3–4 *in publica commoda peccem | si longo sermone morer tua tempora, Caesar*. For καιρός "tempering" in Pindar, see Willcock (1995) 17, and Burton (1962) 46–8. For *tempus* as metrical "time," cf. *S.* 1.4.58 *tempora certa modosque*, OLD *tempus* 13, and LSJ χρόνος IV.2. In this punning sense, the deferral to another "time" alludes to the poet's metrically diverse efforts in his forthcoming *Odes*. On Aristotelian *decorum* as a poetic principle in the *Odes*, see Lowrie (1997) 80–1.

wrote.[128] The fact that lines 57–9 (quoted above) all have a molossus after a strong caesura in the third foot suggests that the pest is trapped in a decidedly neoteric, temporal rut.[129] At any rate, if we allow for any of this punning, metrical sense of the word at *S.* 2.1.18, "when the time is propitious" can be taken to signal a non-hexametric enterprise. Namely, it refers to the metrically diverse, Pindarically "tempered" efforts forthcoming in the *Odes.* That, in other words, is when the "time" will be right. That is where the poet will finally shed his satiric skin and come to terms with his Scipio, Octavian, by taking on that bigger, public voice that the pressures of the post-Actian age now demand. Just as Virgil defers to a big, forthcoming work at *Georgics* 3, Horace looks ahead to his. The clock is ticking, and the *Sermones*, it now seems, are no longer enough.

But just how easy will that projected shift be? What will the new generic self look like, and what will its/his making imply? These are some of the central, genre-shaping questions of book 2, a book obsessed with the issues of coping and self-fashioning in the uncertain days just before Actium and immediately after. In it, we are invited to eavesdrop into the lives of this society's various "losers," to watch them struggle to patch together new lives for themselves, and to become new selves, in a world where options for selfhood are now severely limited, and where the old definitions no longer apply. Damasippus, the Stoic pedant of 2.3, lost a fabulous sum, but he found consolation in philosophy, having no idea how obnoxious he would come to sound. Catius, his Epicurean counterpart in 2.4, is determined to place himself among Rome's gourmet elite, and to get invited to all their most elegant dinners by being the city's premier arbiter of good taste. But heading up the list of once-ruined is Ofellus in 2.2, a vividly remembered friend who lost his land in Octavian's confiscations after Philippi.[130] Amazingly, he does not care. He lives out his life

---

[128] On the exceptional metrical monotony of these lines, see Nilsson (1952) 178, n. 2.

[129] On this particular feature of the neoteric hexameter, see Wilkinson (1963) 127–30. The habit of shaping lines this way stems not from any preference for the molossus after a third strong caesura *per se*, but from the strong neoteric liking for the agreement of ictus and accent in the fourth foot of hexametric lines. A molossus (whether an individual word or so-called "metrical word") after a strong caesura in the third foot necessitates that agreement.

[130] For the book's chief philosophizers as searchers and/or victims, see Oliensis (1998b).

just as happily as ever, and he makes no effort to win back his old land or self. As far as he is concerned, he never lost them. His is a stunning first image of contentment in a sea of competitive pandering and regret.

But what of Horace? Which of these lost souls does he resemble? Perhaps most unnerving is the way that each, in his own way, echoes voices remembered from book 1: the poet railed at us there, several times, and in the high tones of a Damasippan diatribe, though never quite so relentlessly. And he attempted to impress us there, too, with his fine neoteric learning and recherché recipes for satire. Are these featured speakers of book 2, then, extreme versions of the poet's own self, cartoon images drawn from the way envy reads and unfairly pegs? Perhaps here we have a select sampling of the ways he came to sound after readers filtered out what they chose to hear: a voice, at once ideal, pedantic, parasitic. Take your pick. In S. 2.5 and 2.6 we are reminded that the "loser's" problem of getting back into the game, or of choosing not to, is primarily, and centrally, Horace's problem. Though the poet himself is apparently not "in" the mythic consultation of 2.5 in the way that he is in all the book's other poems, the dialogue's uncanny relevance to what precedes and follows invites us to see him there, taking it all in, under the guise of the bewildered Odysseus. Like Ofellus and Odysseus before him, this poet has lost an estate while away at war. He, too, must struggle to cope, and to make his way home in hostile seas. In the very next poem he, the poet, arrives. We see him happily at home in a Sabine retreat, the very thing he prayed for, and so we are given to think that his search is finally over. But Teiresias' cynical advice carries over, staining that pretty, votive picture, so we are left to wonder "at what cost this success?" Did he, our hero, sell out and pander his way to the top, just as Teiresias said he should? And what role might his poetry have played in that pandering? In 2.7 we see him scrambling to put himself together for a night on the town, giddy that he should be thought to rank as Maecenas' best available afterthought. "Who is the real slave here?" Davus asks. In 2.8 we get a mock-epic battle, a battle for revenge inside a dining hall, and with it, a glimpse of how utterly boring and demeaning those tag-along dinners could be. Not that the food was not good, and the service superb. But the vainglorious prattling of the host was just too much, for in it, I suspect, the poet-friends of Maecenas could hear something of themselves. The fall and recovery of the host, in the end, echoes their own efforts *ut arte emendaturus fortunam* "to correct fortune by means of art,"[131] and to make Maecenas take notice and marvel at their special "compositional" skills. This, then, is the larger scene of soul-searching and doubt that makes book 2 the lost, devious cousin of book 1.

BIG FRIENDS AND BRAVADO IN *SERMONES* 2.1

Horace cannot do everything Lucilius did, and he cannot go everywhere Lucilius went. When he tries, he never quite gets it right. Instead he manages to look very different, like someone trying, but clearly not up to the task of delivering, the Lucilian goods. After his long excursus on his "natural" urge to write hard-hitting satire just like Lucilius wrote (lines 34–46, see above n. 49), and after hurling a few insults against enemies of no particular significance (and *that* is their significance – see below), the poet boasts to Trebatius that he is more determined than ever to speak his mind this time, no matter if that means certain exile or death (57–60). Trebatius, worried about the safety of his client, breaks in with (*S.* 2.1.60–2):

> o puer, ut sis
> uitalis metuo et maiorum ne quis amicus
> frigore te feriat.

Oh, my son, I'm afraid you may not survive, and that someone with better connections will cause you to be frozen out.

Interesting here is the nature of the threat Trebatius perceives. He is not worried that the poet will offend someone higher up on the social scale, but a mere lesser friend of someone higher up (*maiorum quis amicus*); that is, someone with bigger connections than Horace has, who can, if insulted, use those connections against him.[132] The picture he paints, in other words, is not of a modern-day Lucilius taking on the biggest political figures of his day, but

---

[131] See especially Oliensis (1998b) 100. For Nasidienus' "compositional" cookery, see Freudenburg (1995).
[132] Muecke (1993) 110 deftly observes: "The words could also be taken more simply as 'a friend of the great', i.e. someone well-connected."

of someone whose sights are fixed on targets much lower, on the likes of Cervius, Canidia, Turius, and Scaeva, who were assaulted in the lines immediately preceding. From what we can tell, these figures do not count for much in the Roman political and social scene of the late first century.[133] But these are the targets Horace takes on, the ones he is stuck with. For all of his Lucilian bravado, these are the only ones he can manage to attack in this poem: quintessential nobodies. Their more influential, "bigger" friends are the ones who really matter.

But the idea of someone actually having bigger friends than Horace draws this response from the poet (*S.* 2.1.62–70):

> quid? cum est Lucilius ausus
> primus in hunc operis componere carmina morem
> detrahere et pellem, nitidus qua quisque per ora
> cederet, introrsum turpis, num Laelius aut qui
> duxit ab oppressa meritum Carthagine nomen
> ingenio offensi aut laeso doluere Metello
> famosisue Lupo cooperto uersibus? atqui
> primores populi arripuit populumque tributim,
> scilicet uni aequus Virtuti atque eius amicis.

What's that? When Lucilius first dared to compose songs in this generic mode and pull back the hide in which each person was parading about, gorgeous on the outside, though ugly within, Laelius was not offended by his talent, was he? Or how about that man who drew his name from the defeat of Carthage? They were not hurt when Metellus got lashed, were they, or when Lupus was swamped in shame-bringing verse? No, just the opposite. He bit into the leaders of the people and the people themselves, one tribe at a time. Obviously he was fair only to Virtue, and to Virtue's friends.

The lines set up a contrast between the kind of persons Lucilius is remembered to have lampooned, and those actually insulted by Horace in the lines directly preceding. Horace's nobodies, the mostly innocuous "Deer" (Cervius) and "Dog" (Canidia) of lines 47–8, are set against Lucilius' truly menacing "Wolf" (Lupus).[134] Lucilius took on the biggest of foes, and he had nothing to fear

---

[133] See Rudd (1966) 132–59.
[134] L. Cornelius Lentulus Lupus, a consular senator and former censor, was *princeps senatus* in 131–125 BCE. His death is the occasion for the mock *concilium deorum* in Lucilius' first book, later imitated by Seneca in his *Apocolocyntosis*, and Juvenal in his fourth satire.

from making them suffer. His friends, Laelius and Scipio, "took no offense" at his verse, but why should they? Metellus and Lupus were their bitterest enemies, quite apart from anything Lucilius ever said about them. And, conveniently, they themselves were never "bitten into" by his verse, only "stroked" by it. The last line of the passage is commonly taken as a moral defense of Lucilius' brand of hard-edged satire: for, at one level the message reads, "if Lucilius ruined the reputations of Lupus and Metellus, they must have deserved it. He was meticulous about being fair to Virtue and Virtue's friends." But, then, are we really supposed to blank out the fact that the Younger Africanus promoted his connections with Virtue so much that his name became, for his supporters, synonymous with Virtue?[135] What effect might that insight have on the way we take the message of Lucilius' scrupulous moral view, his commitment to remain "fair only to Virtue and Virtue's friends?" If we failed to equate Virtue to Scipio in that phrase, there is no getting around it in the lines that directly follow (*S.* 2.1.71–4):

> quin ubi se a uulgo et scaena in secreta remorant
> uirtus Scipiadae et mitis sapientia Laeli,
> nugari cum illo et discincti ludere, donec
> decoqueretur holus, soliti.

No (he did not offend them). Instead, whenever Scipio's Virtue and Laelius' soft Wisdom would step aside from the public stage and move off into a private setting, they would fool around with him and play games, care-free, while waiting for the cabbage to cook.

No high-powered *cena*, this. Off on their own, Messrs. Virtue and Wisdom do not bother trying to impress one another, or anyone else. Theirs is the carefree, recreative play of soul-mates and equals. Of course Lucilius has nothing to fear in offending Metellus. He is tight, just *that* tight, with the most powerful political figure in late second-century Rome. In his note on line 72, Pseudacron comments that Scipio was so "unassuming towards Lucilius and close to him (*ciuilis ... et carus Lucilio*) that Laelius

---

[135] Rudd (1989) 114: "In the 2nd cent. B.C. Scipio Aemilianus had built a temple to *Virtus* (Plut. *De fort. Rom.* 5; *Moralia*, Loeb IV); and to judge from H. *S.* 2.1.70 ... and *S.* 2.1.72 ... he was addressed in some such terms by Lucilius." The irregular patronymic *Scipiada* is Lucilius' "mock-epic" solution to the problem of naming Scipio in hexameters (see note 120 above); cf. Lucil. 424W *Scipiadae magno*, and 254–5W *Cornelius Publius noster | Scipiadas*. The form probably derives from Ennius; see Skutsch, *Studia Enniana* 150.

once happened upon him running around the dining room couches, chased by Lucilius, who was attempting to strike him with the tip of his twisted napkin."

But where does that leave Horace? Just how tight is he with the power-players of his day? Can we really think of him as anything like Octavian's most intimate friend? Do we imagine that he could have chummed around with Octavian, chasing him around the kitchen table while waiting for the cabbage to boil? It is a problem, a big problem, and Horace knows it. He follows that homely image of Lucilius' boiled cabbage with assurances that, even though he cannot match Lucilius in status and raw talent, he can at least claim to have had some powerful friends (*S.* 2.1.75–8):

> infra Lucili censum ingeniumque, tamen me
> cum magnis uixisse inuita fatebitur usque
> Inuidia et fragili quaerens illidere dentem
> offendet solido.

Now, whatever I am, even though I fall below Lucilius in status and natural talent, still Envy will have to admit, however much she may begrudge it, that I have lived with powerful men all along. So when she seeks to sink her teeth into me, she will hit on something rock-hard.

"I have big friends too," Horace says. He admits that he is no match for Lucilius in certain respects, but his friends, he says, are every bit as good, if not better than those of Lucilius. And so it seems that he, too, has nothing to fear in abusing the wicked. They cannot bite him without cracking a few teeth.

But there is an odd note struck by the phrase *cum magnis uixisse* at the beginning of line 76, and that passing *usque* tacked suggestively onto the end. For to "live with" (*cum ... uiuere*) the great is not necessarily to be on equal or intimate terms with them. The phrase has culinary shades that contrast strongly with the preceding image of soul-mates at play, waiting for the cabbage to cook. It recalls the *conuiua* ("dinner-guest"), or the *conuictor* ("companion"), whose access to the host is carefully regulated, and whose intimacy with him is determined by the seat he has been asked to take.[136] Intimacy, for him, is only as permanent as his latest

---

[136] White (1978) 80, n. 2: "*convictor* and *convictus*, although they can refer to the *actus convivendi*, tend in ordinary parlance to evoke the narrower context of the *convivium*, and to describe dinner parties and persons who happen to be present at them."

invitation. Even more, that *usque* "all along" at the end of line 76, reminds us that Horace has been a friend of the great not just lately, but for some time. But that is the problem: it tempts us to think *way* back, to the friendships he enjoyed before Philippi. Can we allow ourselves here to think of his life with Brutus, and of the way that "rock-hard," "teeth-cracking" friendship blew up in his face and lost him everything he ever had? The mention of Envy's ill-will towards his intimacy with men of power is reminiscent of *S.* 1.6.46–8, where Brutus clearly is a factor:

> quem rodunt omnes libertino patre natum,
> nunc quia sim tibi, Maecenas, **conuictor**, at olim
> quod mihi pareret legio Romana tribuno.

Everyone gnaws on me, taunting me with being the son of a freed slave. They are envious now because I am your companion, Maecenas. They were before because I was a military tribune, put in command of a Roman legion.

In moving from book 1 to book 2, Horace has graduated from Envy's "gnawing" (*rodunt*) to merit her full, teeth-cracking, Lucilian "bite" (*inlidere dentem*).[137] His earlier legionary command came from Brutus, whom he leaves tactfully unnamed.[138] Burnt once, and too confident in that earlier friendship, how safe can he really think he is this time? Just how far can he depend on these new, rock-hard friends?

Trebatius can find no obvious flaws in his client's line of defense. There are no fissures for him to "split apart."[139] Still, he is worried, and he warns the boastful young man that he should not be so cock-sure about having nothing to fear. Those friends of his, he suspects, the unnamed "big ones" of line 76, may not be big enough to get him off a charge of composing *mala carmina* "malicious/harmful songs." That was a capital offense in Rome, and a breach of Rome's oldest, most "sacred" laws, the *XII Tabulae* "Twelve Tables." Still, the threat of a capital trial does

---

[137] Kiessling–Heinze (1961) 189: "*inlidere dentem* steigert das *rodere* (1 6,46)." The *fautores Lucili* are thus imagined as injured by their own envious biting.

[138] For the poet's overt lack of tact in the next poem, where Brutus figures as a "star" character (*solem Asiae Brutum, S.* 1.7.24) by being named four times (and nowhere else in the *Sermones*), see Henderson (1994).

[139] Rudd (1966) 130: "The technical precision of *diffindere* is marred by the fact that it echoes *fragili quaerens illidere dentem* and therefore evokes a picture of the great lawyer trying to crack a nut with his teeth."

not seem to worry the poet. He responds with that famously flippant pun that closes the poem (*S.* 2.1.83–6):

> **Hor.:** esto, si quis mala; sed bona si quis
> iudice condiderit laudatus Caesare? si quis
> opprobriis dignum latrauerit integer ipse?
> **Treb.:** soluentur risu tabulae, tu missus abibis.

Hor.: And that's as it should be, if someone writes "bad" songs. But
what about someone who writes "good" songs and merits the praise of
Caesar when *he* is judge? What if he barks at someone who deserves to
be taunted, while he himself is without fault?
Treb.: The charges/tables will crumble from the laughter, and you will
be free to walk away.

Horace is dropping names again. But this time, in clear contrast to
the elaborate name-dropping that closes his case in book 1, he
needs only one name to make his legal troubles dissolve. By now,
that name far exceeds the full collective force once exerted by
his former *turba* ("crowd") of poet friends. Horace says the magic
word, "Caesar." And with it his legal worries disappear. Trebatius'
threat of *ius iudiciumque* "law and judgment" in lines 82–3 reminds
Horace that Caesar recently had been awarded the final say in all
cases of appeal.[140] He was now the ultimate *iudex* "judge" of poets,
criminals, and everyone else in Rome, so to win praise *iudice
Caesare* "with Caesar as judge" was tantamount to having your
case won. Hearing the C-word, Trebatius must finally concede
that the poet has nothing to fear. It turns out that he had a trump
card he was hiding all along, and when he plays it, he leaves the
jurisconsult with nothing more to say.

But that is one of the more disturbing facets of this cut-away
ending: the way all those well-considered worries of Trebatius
simply melt away with the mention of Caesar at the poem's end.
His worries no longer count for anything because they are based
on his intricate knowledge of a legal system that no longer works
the way it once did. By the end of this poem Trebatius looks
terribly old, much older than he really is. He is a pre-Actian holdover (*Trebatiosaurus Protoactianus*), a lumbering relic who thought he
could bring his outmoded knowledge of the way Roman law used

---

[140] On Octavian's appellate jurisdiction of 30 BCE, see Muecke (1993) 114.

to work to the analysis of this case. He goes at it in the standard jurisconsult's way, with a straightforward inquiry into the legal *status* of his client's case: the *status coniecturalis* does not fit (= his first suggestion, that the poet cease writing altogether), so he tries the *status definitionis* (= suggestion no. 2, that he write epic poetry), and the *status qualitatis* (= suggestion no. 3, that he write "stroking" satire).[141] Everything is by-the-book for Trebatius, but he does not seem to realize, until the very end, that the book no longer matters. The Roman legal scene is no longer as it was before Actium, when an appeal to one man's judgment could not override the entire system.

But things are much different now, and much more efficient, with Caesar himself determining what constitutes "bad verse" in Rome. His aesthetic sense, and his alone, has exceptional powers to shape literary thinking and practice, for his critical judgment is also a "verdict" (*iudicium*), an aesthetic choice with the power to exonerate or exile. In him the roles of literary critic and courtroom judge ultimately, scarily, coalesce. It is no wonder, then, that the last scene of the poem is that of a trial broken apart – quite "illegally," one might suppose, from an old-style, Trebatian standpoint – by laughter resounding on all sides. That laughter is so unanimous and telling that the defendant does not bother to wait for the formal conclusion of his trial. He simply walks away, and who is to stop him? Caesar has voiced his approval, so the charges simply "crumble" into the courtroom dust, shaken apart by the guffaws of so many critics picking up on Caesar's cue, wanting to be heard approving of whatever *he* approves of. "If he laughs, then so will I. Extra-loud!" Case closed.

In the final lines of this poem we watch not only the dissolution of a trial fictionally projected, but of the legal system that the trial represents; for those *tabulae* ("tables") that crumble away from the strain of so much nervously overdone laughter represent not only the specific "charges" of the case, but those ancient, most sacred laws on which the charges were based, the *XII Tabulae* ("Twelve Tables") alluded to in lines 80–3. Scholars have long wondered whether we should take the last line's "crumbling tables" in anything like this sense, for it is usually the *res* "case" that laughter

---

[141] See Leeman (1983).

has the power to "dissolve = resolve" in theoretical discussions of humor's use in the courtroom.[142] Here, though, the metaphor is altered and given an added visual impact, so that we actually see "tables crumbling." But which tables? Most scholars opt for the obscure praetor's tablets on which formal accusations and sentences were inscribed.[143] That makes *tabulae* equivalent to the charges or *res* "case," and a natural, harmless substitute. But the proximity of the *XII Tabulae* in lines 80–3 has bothered some scholars, and several have allowed for the spillover of this sense into the image of crumbling tables in the final line.[144] Most recently P. Fedeli has argued: "It seems to me inevitable that, after a citation from the laws of the Twelve Tables and various allusions to these same archaic laws, Horace here has precisely these tables in mind."[145] His is a compelling argument, and a sensible way of reading the poem's last line. But the case is overargued even leaving aside its outmoded rhetoric of reading Horace's mind. For the image of crumbling tables that closes the poem is, I think, just open-ended enough to make us hesitate between options that are equally sensible, pulling us *both* this way *and* that. In the end, the case for "tables = indictment" is just as strong as that for "tables = laws," so it is hard to see how the problem can ever be decisively dismantled and shelved. Moreover, it is hard to see the hermeneutical advantage of doing so, for to control the image so tightly may be to deprive it of its diagnostic force. In this "suspended" image we again have a case of satire's diagnosing us, probing into the way we read by making us aware of the process of our reading. That choice between valid options leaves us uncomfortably poised, wondering whether we should go this way or that, and at that moment of suspension we are most aware of our role as *sense-makers* in the reading process. Hesitating, filtering through options, and deciding are not impediments to meaning in this case; they are the built-in way this image means.

But how unsettled *should* we be by images of Caesar hovering

---

[142] E.g. Cic. *De orat.* 2.236 *odiosas que res … ioco … dissoluit*; Quint. *Inst.* 5.10.67 *cum risu quoque tota res soluitur.*

[143] Palmer (1955) 253–4, and Lejay (1966) 289–90.

[144] Mueller (1891) 155: "d.h. man wird die Gesetze (vg. Vers 82f.) unter Gelächter abthun, für nichtig erklären." Cf. Schütz (1881) on these lines.

[145] Fedeli (1994) 552 (my trans.).

over the courts and the literary world as superordinate "judge," and of law-tables crumbling from laughter? Just how offensive is this ending, really? The best answer I can find is, "It is *really* every bit as offensive as you think it is." Sharp edges can be gotten around, as in the case of those crumbling tables. They can be taken to represent the indictment and nothing more, and that is a valid way of reading. But in choosing to see the image that way other options have to be sifted through. If we felt the cross-referential tug of the Twelve Tables in the preceding lines, at what point, and on what basis, did we say, "No, that cannot be right?" Fedeli himself who argues so aggressively for the connection, backs away from its sharper edges by quoting Pasoli with approval. He glosses *tabulae* with: "The law-tables (that is, "the severity of the law-tables") will dissolve in an outburst of laughter."[146] Not the laws themselves, in other words, just some of their protruding, Draconian edges. The suspended image makes us look into and locate the limits of what we can handle.

BOOK 2 AND THE HISSINGS OF COMPLIANCE

There is plenty of laughter at the poem's end, enough to break apart the poet's imagined legal worries and the trial that threatens to take him down. But is anyone outside the fiction laughing? I see sharper edges built into the poem, especially in its conclusion, and I am rather amazed that scholars have generally heard no unsettling overtones in that final outburst of laughter. Most take the poem and this ending for what, I think, they blatantly are not: a contented, unquestioning assertion of Horace's new-found confidence in his satiric enterprise. That confidence comes with having Caesar as his friend, and it shows itself in the poet's telling us here to expect something fiery and Lucilian in the second book. With one hand on Lucilius' sword, he is now ready to attack if provoked, and he does not care if that means a backlash of rage or even a capital trial. That, in other words, is one way of reading *S.* 2.1, and I am ready to admit that a fresh burst of confidence really does seem to be there. But then the problem comes in explaining why the book fails so miserably to deliver on the promises of the opening poem. Rudd, for one, explains it as a case of

---

[146] Fedeli (1994) 552 (my trans.), quoting Pasoli (1964) 471.

Horatian discretion; his not wanting to make trouble for the new regime. He insists, "Horace does not really intend to come to blows. To use a word from an early article of Fraenkel's, it is all *Schein-polemik*. He has disposed of his problem by a joke."[147] No need to be upset by any of this. Horace was just pretending to show Lucilius' teeth. He never meant to bite anyone in the first place. Not really.

That is one way of treating the question: it was all just shadow-boxing, a trick played on us – and we were delighted to play the role of his gullible stooge. But maybe we should not be so quick to laugh the matter off and let Horace "dispose of his problem" so glibly, on us, with a joke. For if this really is a joke, it is a joke with explosive potential to unnerve and offend. We might ask ourselves if, in 30 BCE, hard on the heels of Actium, Romans really needed this kind of a laugh, the poet playing them for fools by claiming to take up the Lucilian cause and speak his mind, only to back off with, "Now watch me be a good boy and muzzle myself in deference to my powerful friends. I never really meant to revive those old-style, republican freedoms you think so highly of after all."

Rudd is right to insist that Horace has a problem. But it is a problem that does not take to being laughed off by a bad pun, leaving him free to walk away from the generic/Lucilian re-sponsibilities he sets up with such care in *S.* 2.1. As he makes clear in the poem, his is a genre that has to bite, and bite hard – hard enough to crack a few of the satirist's own teeth (as Persius later has it). Persius takes that teeth-cracking image from the middle of *S.* 2.1, where Horace claims that Lucilius "bit into" (*arripuit*, 69) the people and their leaders one tribe at a time, like an epic poet cataloguing ships.[148] But by the end of that same satire the poet counters with a contrasting image of himself that is less threat-ening by far: all "bark" (*latrauerit*, 85) with no Lucilian bite. So if we were taken in by the bravado of his promising to write searing, death-defying verse, we have to wonder "why this metaphor here?" and "where is the scandalous verse he promised?" Why does he fail to deliver? And this is a problem that cannot be flicked

---

[147] Rudd (1966) 129.
[148] Wills (1996) 39 posits a connection between the formal features of line 69 and *Il.* 2.493, "the line which introduces a more famous catalogue, Homer's catalogue of ships." It is possible, then, that Lucilius' tribe-by-tribe attack was headed by (or shaped as) a mock epic catalogue of Roman tribes and their vices.

aside with a bad pun. Bentley was so offended by the poet's lack of "bite" in line 85 that he corrected *latrauerit* to read *lacerauerit* ("lash/attack"). He writes: "I contend that this metaphor, derived from worthless dogs that apparently bark but do not bite, has no place here at all."[149] As I hope now to show, this problem of too much bark and too little bite spills over the borders of the first poem into the second, and from the second to the third, and so on, until the last, befuddling lines of *S.* 2.8, where we are abandoned mid-feast, still waiting for the satirist to show.

The first words we encounter after the break-up of *S.* 2.1 are these (*S.* 2.2.1–3):

> Quae uirtus et quanta, boni, sit uiuere paruo
> (nec meus hic sermo est, sed quae praecepit Ofellus
> rusticus, abnormi sapiens crassaque Minerua) . . .

What a virtue it is, fine sirs, and how great a virtue it is to live on little (this is not my talk, but the teachings of Ofellus, a philosopher from the countryside whose intellect was unschooled and roughly spun) . . .

The division of the theme into "what" and "how great" recalls the discussion of *eros* in Plato's *Symposium*, a topic proposed in two aspects, part philosophical inquiry, part encomium.[150] The plural vocative *boni* "fine sirs" in line 1 is reminiscent of the mildly censorious ὦ ἀγαθέ "my good man" common in the dialogues of Plato.[151] Further, the side-step signalled by *nec meus hic sermo est* "this is not my talk" is a narratological layering device well known from the dialogues of Plato, fictional "talks," like this one, remembered from the author's youth. We see it, for example, at Plato, *Symp.* 177A, where Eurymachus disclaims authority for what he is about to say with a quote from Euripides' *Melanippe*:

ἡ μέν μοι ἀρχὴ τοῦ λόγου ἐστὶ κατὰ τὴν Εὐριπίδου Μελανίππην· **οὐ γὰρ ἐμὸς ὁ μῦθος**, ἀλλὰ Φαίδρου τοῦδε ὃν μέλλω λέγειν.

The start of my speech follows Euripides' *Melanippe*: "**for the story is not mine**." But what I am about to say belongs to Phaedrus here.

---

[149] Bentley (1869) 432 (my trans.). He then adds: "you could correctly assert 'if a bad and worthless man should bark at a good man,' but hardly the reverse, 'if a good man should bark at a worthless man.'"

[150] See Plato *Symp.* 194E and 177 C–D.

[151] The plural vocative *boni* occurs only here, perhaps modeled on the Greek ὦ ἀγαθοί (rare). The singular ὦ ἀγαθέ is relatively common, especially in the dialogues of Plato. In Latin as in Greek, such an apostrophe often carries an authorial, slightly censorious tone; cf. Damasippus' *o bone* (*S.* 2.3.31), Lucr. 3.206, Pers. 3.94, and LSJ ἀγαθός 1.5.

The disclaimer leaves us several times removed from the source of the notion, with Plato, the author, saying that Apollodorus told Glaucon that Eurymachus (quoting Euripides) said that Phaedrus said a certain idea-**X**.[152] The idea is filtered through a confusing array of tellers, so the sequence of layering is easily lost track of. At any given point we are likely to forget that it is there, and so slip into hearing what Eurymachus says as just that: what *Eurymachus* says. Moreover, the existence of such thick narratological layering means we can never quite know how Plato himself relates to the ideas he has his characters consider. It is all his fiction, but filtering Plato out of that fiction is a notoriously difficult problem.

But the question "Where is Plato?" is especially irresistible in the case of Socrates, the featured character of the Early and Middle Dialogues who, because he so often gets the better of his fellow interlocutors, is commonly thought to be the one direct conduit to Plato's own mind. Since Socrates claims to know nothing himself in these dialogues, he is especially fond of quoting knowing assertions heard from others. For example, at *Symp.* 201D he begins his contribution to the evening's round-table by introducing the character of the Wise Diotima:

I shall try to go through for you the speech about Love I once heard from a woman of Mantinea, Diotima – a woman who was wise about many things besides this ... she is the one who taught me the art of love, and I shall go through her speech as best as I can.

Again we have a disclaimer, "not my speech, but hers," that leaves us several times removed from the source of the speech: Plato says that Apollodorus told Glaucon that Socrates said that Diotima said **X**. But scholars have long thought that this Diotima never really existed, so tracing "her" ideas to their source can never be as easy as peeling away the layers starting with Apollodorus. Most recently, Nehamas and Woodruff have asserted "Diotima is apparently a fictional character contrived by Socrates for this occasion."[153] And that is right. But what does it mean? The dialogue itself is Plato's contrivance, every bit of it, so isn't Diotima,

---

[152] Cf. Plut. *Mor.* 661B, also set at the symposium. In each case the speaker proposes a topic for philosophical discussion, then disclaims any personal authority for what he is about to say, pointing elsewhere to affirm its veracity. Socrates, who claimed to "know" nothing, was especially fond of such "validating" disclaimers; cf. Plato, *Symp.* 212B.

[153] Nehamas–Woodruff (1989) 45, n. 62.

in the end, *his* fictional invention rather than Socrates'? Or are we to think that Socrates really did invent her, and that Plato merely reports someone else's fiction? Or maybe she really did exist. Again, the narratological traps built into this kind of deeply layered dialogue are unavoidable and confounding. In the end, there is no automatic access to Plato through any of his characters, not even Socrates. And that is what makes Horace's reprise of Plato's "this is not my speech" so frustrating and unsettling at the start of *S.* 2.2. For directly on the heels of his promising us a feast of straight-talking abuse, the satirist goes immediately into hiding, letting someone else take all the risks. But we know he is there somewhere. We are just not sure how to filter him out of the narratological muddle. In the end, that side-step of "this is not my *sermo*" suggests that the relationship of Horace to his invented (or really remembered?) Ofellus is every bit as problematic and inscrutable as that of Socrates to the Wise Diotima, or of Plato to Socrates.

Because the opening lines of *S.* 2.2 are so obviously thick with memories of Plato, the disclaimer "this is not my talk" draws attention to itself as a metalinguistic comment on the new "someone else's" character of Horatian *sermo*. Clearly the claim is right: this is *not* his brand of dialogue; it is Plato's, and nothing at all like the risk-taking *satura* we were given to expect in the surprise opening line of *S.* 2.1. Here, in deliberate contrast to that false start, the telling generic term is back to *sermo*, something to recall not only Plato, but the softer touch of Horace's own *sermo* in book 1. Such is the ironic tension built into the claim "This is not my *sermo*." On the one hand the idea is patently false: of course it is his *sermo*! It has to be. Everything that happens in this book is Horatian *sermo* and nothing else. Since he wrote it and gave it the name, it cannot reasonably be thought to belong to anyone else. Still, in a sense, it really is someone else's, since the words on the page belong mostly to others, he claims, with the author standing aside to let them do the talking. Yet we know that their talk is always and only his talk. But knowing precisely how to figure it as his talk is a problem with no automatic solution. It is a problem that *means* to baffle, the central redefining irony of book 2: this *sermo* is, at once, both his and not his. Such a narratological tack allows for a minimum of risk (since someone else is always made to

offend or look like a genius or fool) with a maximum of detachment and open-ended irony.

The third poem again opens with someone else doing the talking. This time it is Damasippus, a pushy Stoic neophyte who
berates the satirist for his sleepy, drunken ways (*S.* 2.3.1–6):

> Sic raro scribis ut toto non quater anno
> membranam poscas, scriptorum quaeque retexens,
> iratus tibi quod uini somnique benignus
> nil dignum sermone canas. quid fiet? at ipsis
> Saturnalibus huc fugisti sobrius. ergo
> dic aliquid dignum promissis: incipe. nil est.

You write so infrequently that in a whole year you call for parchment
less than four times, unweaving all that you've written and raging at
yourself because (as you say), indulging in too much wine and sleep, you
sing nothing worth mentioning. What will come of it? Still, you have
made your escape to this spot and kept yourself sober in the middle of
the Saturnalia. So say something worthy of the promises you made. Go
on, start! Nothing.

The subjunctive *canas* ("you sing") in line 4 lets us know that
responsibility for most of these charges belongs not to Damasippus,
but to Horace himself.[154] In other words, we imagine that the poet
inside the fiction has been chiding himself for failing to produce
anything that *he* thinks is "worth mentioning" and that Damasippus
simply repeats charges he overheard and seems fully to agree
with. But the first charge against the satirist's sluggish rate of production stands outside the *quod* clause, so it does not necessarily
represent part of the satirist's self-chiding. Nor is it particularly
damning, for what Damasippus sees as a playboy's failure to buckle
down and produce vast amounts can be taken as an allusion to the
poet's Callimachean aesthetic sense; that is, his determination to
produce small amounts, finely crafted.

But what of the accusations inside the *quod* clause, charges not
so easily turned to the poet's advantage or written off as someone
else's fanatical rantings? How do they figure as programmatic
commentary on the way he now writes? Within the charges we are
presented for the first time with an image of the satirist completely

---

[154] On this use of the subjunctive in "informal indirect discourse," see Allen–Greenough
(1888, repr. 1988) 385 = §592.3.

disengaged from city life (cf. the lonesome meanderings downtown in book 1), running off to escape the rough-and-tumble of Rome at the height of the Saturnalia, a festival which for the Romans, just as much as for Bakhtin later, came to symbolise the quintessential satiric moment, the time for all good satirists to hit the streets and ply their trade.[155] In running off to the countryside and maintaining an unseasonable sobriety, Horace neglects his sworn charge as satirist to get good and drunk and rail away at the vice he spies all around. And so he sings "nothing worth mentioning," that is, "nothing worthy of *sermo*," the kind that rails and bites. According to Damasippus, his is an egregious case of dereliction of duty; he made "promises" (*promissis*, 6) that he did not keep. Setting out for his villa, he had a terribly "menacing" (*minantis*, 9) look. But all of that, Damasippus complains, has by now fizzled into nothing.

It is as if Damasippus has been there all along, reading over our shoulders as we moved from the threats of *S.* 2.1 to the ironies and narratological obfuscations of *S.* 2.2. He breaks in here, the disgruntled reader *in us*, to let us know that he is not pleased; he is an unwilling stooge, a reader who refused to let Horace dispose of his problem with a joke played at his expense. He has fixed ideas of what writing "satire" entails, and he is sure that what little Horace has managed to produce is not it. And somehow he has convinced himself that Horace's *uillula* ("sweet little villa," 10) that he now enjoys in isolation has something to do with the dulling of his satiric drives. That *uita meliore* ("more noble life," 15) he now leads, tucked away in the countryside, has made him flabby and easily distracted. It has taken him away from Rome's grimy streets where, as a satirist, he simply needs to be. Such criticism, I suspect, touches on an increase in the poet's activities outside the genre of satire as a writer of "more noble" *carmina* (a case I will argue elsewhere), but it also refers to the ever tightening squeeze put upon his satiric voice by his now famous and handsomely

---

[155] See Bernstein (1987); Freudenburg (1993) 211–35; and Gowers (1993a) 133–6, and 159–60. At the very least, Horace introduces the symbolic notion of the Roman Saturnalia as *his* satiric time by making the festival the fictional occasion of both *S.* 2.3 and 2.7. Owing to Horace's inferior social status (whether real and/or elaborately performed), the symbol fits his version of the Lucilian enterprise much better than it fits Lucilius' own. For Lucilius, as his story is told, could say whatever he wanted, *whenever* he wanted. Even so, Lucilius seems to have spoken through servile *personae* in various satires; see Freudenburg (1993) 213–15.

rewarded friendship with Maecenas. He speaks softly now, and indirectly, from the seclusion of his country villa. Damasippus chides him for it, since it is hard to see how any of it ranks as *sermo*. He gives him one last chance to deliver on his promises, but the poet has nothing to say. Damasippus, then, takes over. He gives the slack-wit playboy (and us) a clinic in how satire of the long-winded, brow-beating type *he* expected to find is to be done, i.e. *sermo* as ranting diatribe.[156] Horace is pushed aside and forced to take notes, the satirist becoming the satirized (a position he holds throughout much of the book). His silent submission to Damasippus' memorized rantings (Horace hears it from Damasippus, who heard it from Stertinius) both causes and proves the point of his dereliction of duty.

Damasippus has the poet pegged, he thinks, right down to the contents of his travel-bag. He chides him in lines 11–14:

> quorsum pertinuit stipare Platona Menandro,
> Eupolin Archilocho, comites educere tantos?
> inuidiam placare paras uirtute relicta?
> contemnere miser.

What was the point of packing Plato with Menander, Eupolis with Archilochus, and taking them along as your mighty travel-companions? Are you planning to appease Envy by leaving Virtue behind? You will be viewed with contempt, a wretch.

The "sweet little villa" that gives him his new and better life makes people jealous, Damasippus says. And that jealousy cannot be defused without some proof of his actually deserving what he got. But Damasippus sees no trace of "virtue" in Horace, no satiric vigour, so he has to assume it was "left behind" like some forgotten pair of socks that did not make it into the bag. He cannot see it because he equates it with something Horace has failed "miserably" to produce: endless reams of lectures against vice; hard-hitting Stoic diatribe. And because Horace cannot produce it, Damasippus undertakes to produce it for him, and so we have the rest of the poem, *ad nauseam*, the second longest lecture Horace (n)ever wrote.

But there is an odd note struck by the choice of "travel-companions" stuffed into Horace's bag, a split between generic

---

[156] On *sermo* as "diatribe," see Fiske (1920) 143–51, and 346.

identities that suggests that Damasippus has read too gullibly, and
that perhaps these poems really can deliver on some of their
promised Lucilian bite. Peeking into the bag Damasippus sees
Plato packed with Menander, and Eupolis with Archilochus.
Scholars have long assumed that in this list we have a direct
glimpse into the workshop of Horatian *sermo*; a tell-tale peek into
his generic toolkit. And it makes sense to think that, since we have
seen already that memories of Plato play a prominent role in
resetting our notions of genre at the start of *S.* 2.2, telling us to
whom this "someone else's" *sermo* principally relates. A look ahead
to the poems that follow suggests that Plato's role as a source of
intertextual memories only increases as the book proceeds. *S.* 2.4,
for example, is an extended parody of his *Phaedrus*, and *S.* 2.8 is a
mock *Symposium*, and these are only two of the most obvious and
extended of the book's many Platonic memories.[157]

Similarly Menander can be thought to belong in this bag
because so much of the book draws on the themes, type-characters,
and techniques of Roman popular comedy. *S.* 2.7 features the
rantings of Davus, a comic slave type with a comic slave's name,
and *S.* 2.8 is a miniature comedy (in 5 acts, according to one
scholar) told by a contemporary writer of comedies.[158] So here
again Damasippus' list of pack-along comrades makes sense. But
what about Eupolis and Archilochus, writers from the distant far
side of the Hellenistic divide? Theirs was, at least in theory, a
Golden Age of democracy and free speech, so their works are
known primarily not for ironic undertones or studies in character,
but for their direct and unrelenting abuse of personal enemies and
enemies of the state. How can they possibly be thought to belong
here, in a list that begins with models from a toned-down, tightly
regulated age, models that seem to fit book 2 so well?

The list fights with itself. The pairing of Plato with Menander
makes sense by itself. So does that of Eupolis with Archilochus.
But when all the names are tossed into the same bag the result is
an unstable mix; the pairs split off and repel one another, so it is
hard to see how they could ever be thought to belong together and
contribute towards a single generic idea. But there it is. And it is
my contention that this jumble of opposites really does make sense

---

[157] See especially Gowers (1993a) 138–40, and 161–79.
[158] On the "acts" of *S.* 2.8, see Schmidt (1937).

in Horace's case. For, as we have seen already, the calmness that rides over the surface of these poems is often delusory, and although it may give us to think that this poet really is the sedate, adaptable Epicurean he is frequently made out to be, that easy-going demeanor routinely hides a sea of Archilochean venom and regret. There clearly is some bite in these poems, as we saw in the hidden recesses of *S.* 2.1. Lucilius, the Roman Eupolis, really is there, just in ways we didn't expect. He has been stuffed into a narrow, hidden space that cracked open when the squeeze took place – into the open-end, that yawning, overdetermined gap, of subtle, bottomless allusions and Socratic irony. That is one place where he hides and where "real satire" happens in these poems, but it is not the only place. For while it is true that these poems do conform to the social and political pressures of a new, post-Actian age, and that they pull back from the Lucilian promises of *S.* 2.1, it is also true that they perform the activity of that compliance, and of their being made to fit an essentially un-satiric mold. As that squeeze takes place, we hear the sounds of resistance in the unnerving hissings and pops of a forced, unnatural fit. And that noise is itself a searing commentary, a "real satire" on the the way old freedoms get lost and power ultimately gets its way. In the end I think this poet is not so ready to adapt, and he finds all sorts of ways to let us know that.

NASIDIENUS' DINNER-PARTY: TOO MUCH OF NOT ENOUGH

A case in point, and perhaps the most natural place for me to end this study of Horatian satire, is with the last poem of book 2, the story of Nasidienus' dinner-party gone terribly wrong. The poem starts with an allusion to Plato, with lines 1–5 recalling the culinary metaphor of Plato, *Ti.* 17B.[159] What follows is a feast served up à la Plato, with the guests at Horace's feast getting increasingly into their cups, all the while trading off philosophical musings with the host. By the evening's end, the host and several of his guests have managed to look terribly stupid. In the poem's first lines we learn that the tale's teller is Fundanius, a writer of comedies whose penchant for comic fiction is evident in his description of the feast, which he casts as a miniature comedy complete with

---

[159] See Gowers (1993a) 162–3.

hard-drinking parasites, a braggart Epicurean cook, and a falling
stage-curtain. So far, then, just a few lines into the poem we have
a fairly obvious blend of Plato with Menander; a calm comedy of
manners with Eupolis and Archilochus nowhere in sight. But the
potential for scathing attack is always there inside the guests'
carefully guarded rage, and we perceive it building with the esca-
lation of the host's culinary cannonade. With every bite of this glorious food the guests edge closer to the point where they can take
no more. Finally Vibidius says to Balatro in line 34 "Unless we
drink him out of house and home, our deaths will be unavenged."
Fine epic parody.[160] And so he demands that bigger drinking cups
be passed around. Next, Fundanius gives a mock-epic take on the
host's reaction (*S.* 2.8.35–41):

> uertere pallor
> tum parochi faciem nil sic metuentis ut acris
> potores, uel quod maledicunt liberius uel
> feruida quod subtile exsurdant uina palatum.
> inuertunt Allifanis uinaria tota
> Vibidius Balatroque; secutis omnibus imi
> conuiuae lecti nihilum nocuere lagoenis.

Then the supply-officer's face turns white, he fearing nothing so much as
fierce drinkers, either because they abuse too freely, or because strong
wines deaden a discriminating palate. Vibidius and Balatro dump over
their casks entire. Everyone else follows their lead, but the guests on the
low table do no damage to their wine-flasks at all.

The invited guests – not Nasidienus and his low-table lackeys –
are now well beyond the point of having had "just enough." They
are soused to their souls, *conuiuae saturae* "dinner-guests stuffed"
with too much wine and a good deal of food, now brimming with
venom for the pounding they have suffered from their host's be-
littling blather. Here, then, the narrative reaches its saturation
point; that is, the point of its finally becoming *satura* and being no
longer capable of holding back. When the next course is brought
in, the *pièce de résistance*, we fully expect the balloon to burst, especially since the dish is served with so much vainglorious fanfare.
The host claims he can taste a difference in eel-flesh, pregnant eel

---

[160] The expression is one of grand, heroic pathos; cf. Cassandra at Aesch. *Ag.* 1279 οὐ μὴν
ἄτιμοί γ' ἐκ θεῶν τεθνήξομεν ("we shall not die without vengeance from the gods"). Also
Virg. *A.* 2.670, and 4.659.

being far superior to non-pregnant ("can't *you* tell?") and he demonstrates his genius beyond any doubt in the details of an oh-so-subtle sauce. It is all amazingly snooty, but no one says a word. The tapestry above the table falls and brings a dusty ruin to the entire dish. Nasidienus hangs his head and wails inconsolably, "as if his son had died an untimely death" (58–9).

Nomentanus, one of Nasidienus' regular guests, steps in to hearten his fallen comrade. With searing irony, Fundanius refers to him as *sapiens* "Mr. Stolid Philosopher," putting him in the unlikely role of the Stoic sage (*sapiens*), renowned for his imperturbability and indifference to disaster. The emotional outburst that follows subverts the image. Nomentanus chimes in with (*S.* 2.8.61–3):

> heu, Fortuna, quis est crudelior in nos
> te deus? ut semper gaudes illudere rebus
> humanis!

Oh, Fortune, is there a god in heaven crueler towards us than you? How you love to make a game/spectacle of human affairs!

Hearing that, Varius can barely contain himself. He stifles his laughter by burying his face in his napkin. And there it is. That is the "outburst" we have been waiting for all along. That is the sum-total of outright ridicule to which these fools will be subjected: a scoff instantly smothered.

The stage was set. The guests were *saturati* "drenched." But satire never showed. Why not? Commentators on the poem often express regret that Maecenas has no role to play here.[161] He is clearly the standout name on the guest-list, but he does not figure in the action or conversation of the feast in any noticeable way. A curious omission, and commentators are right to be bothered by it. But I think that the point of his absence is not, as some have argued, to clear him from responsibility for the evening's embarrassments; rather, it is to show just how forceful his presence really is. Maecenas does not say or do anything at this party because he *does not have to*, and yet everything that happens at this feast, except for the tapestry's dusty ruin, happens precisely because he is there,

---

[161] This is often taken as a matter of Horace's gracefully distancing Maecenas from direct involvement in the evening's manifold embarrassments; e.g. Lejay (1966) 583: "Mécène est l'objet des honneurs et des prévenances de Nasidiénus. Mais Horace se garde de le mêler trop directement aux incidents du repas."

sitting in the seat of honor, forming judgments, watching in silence. Nasidienus and friends are scrambling to please him, but to please him they are also stuck with trying to please his erratic *umbrae* "tag-alongs." But even they feel the gravitational pull of the evening's celebrity guest; they, too, are being controlled in unseen ways. Varius wants to burst out, but he cannot. Maecenas is watching. Since he is the one being wined and dined, he is the one on whom the tag-along's bad behavior will reflect.

Such is the world of book 2: a feast ripe for satire, where unchecked laughter is not an option. It has to be smothered. Or as Balatro, the sneering "Buffoon" of the middle couch, demonstrates, it can be hidden. To match the whining outburst of "Mr. Philosopher" stroke for stroke, Balatro again raises the issue of the eel's demise to the level of a grand, philosophical discourse (*S.* 2.8.65–74):

> "haec est condicio uiuendi" aiebat "eoque
> responsura tuo numquam est par fama labori.
> tene, ut ego accipiar laute, torquerier omni
> sollicitudine districtum, ne panis adustus,
> ne male conditum ius apponatur, ut omnes
> praecincti recte pueri comptique ministrent?
> adde hos praeterea casus, aulaea ruant si,
> ut modo, si patinam pede lapsus frangat agaso.
> sed conuiuatoris, uti ducis, ingenium res
> aduersae nudare solent, celare secundae."

"This is a stipulation of living," he said, "and that is why your reputation will never match up to your hard work. Imagine, you, torturing yourself, torn up with every conceivable anxiety – making sure that the bread doesn't burn, that the sauce is well seasoned when served, and that your slaves keep busy and comb their hair – and you do it all for *me*, to make sure that *I* have a good time! And consider other disasters besides: what if, as just happened, the tapestry comes crashing down, or if some oaf in charge of supplies loses his footing and breaks a plate? But, for the feast-marshal – the part you're playing now – a setback exposes talent, while success hides it."

With the emphatic *eoque* ("and for *this* reason") in line 65, Balatro counters Nomentanus' claim that fortune is a divine, calculating entity. He speaks as an Epicurean (a match for the glib philosopher dinner-guest of book 1), construing the accident as evidence for life's essential instability in a material universe where crashings and fallings (*casus ... ruant ... lapsus frangat*, 71–2) mock all pretensions to stability, neatness, and arrangement (*conditum ... prae-cincti recte ... comptique,* 69–70).[162] And all of this, the deepest truths of his chosen philosophy, he infers from the eel's untimely demise. This is all superb irony. In stark contrast to Varius, who stifles a paroxysm of laughter, Balatro conceals his ridicule beneath a web of encouragement, charming his host in the very process of mocking him: "and you did it all for *me*, so that *I* would have a good time." But we know that Balatro was not even invited, so none of it was for him! Such is his ability to ridicule in oblique ways and "suspend everything from his nose." That metaphor warns us to be especially wary of this man's speech. It refers, I think, to Greek μυκτηρισμός ("turning up the nose," "sneering"), one of ancient rhetoric's "four ironies."[163] In being marked by such skills of "suspension," Balatro resembles Socrates, the most famous ironist of all, whom Seneca describes at *Ben.* 5.6.6 as:

uir facetus et cuius per figuras sermo procederet, derisor omnium maxime potentium, maluit illi *nasute negare* quam contumaciter aut superbe.

A facetious man, and one whose talk was carried along by innuendo. He made fun of everyone, especially men of importance, but he preferred *to refute them with nose extended* rather than with aggressive, high-handed arguments.

And so if we thought Socrates was absent from this Horatian symposium, we were wrong. He is there in Balatro, the man who out-noses "Mr. Nose" (*Nas*idienus = "Snooty"), getting the best of him with an upturned "Socratic sneer" (Σωκρατικῷ μυκτῆρι). But perhaps Horace is there, too, hidden inside his remade Socrates in some ultimately unfilterable way. As Persius clearly saw, he looks terribly like that Epicurean funny man in being so closely watched by Maecenas, and forced to speak in understated but cutting

---

[162] Cf. Epicurus at D. L. 10.134 "He [the wise man] conceives of chance neither as a god, as the masses suppose (for a god does nothing marked by disorder) nor as a cause, however uncertain" (τὴν δὲ τύχην οὔτε θεόν ... οὔτε ἀβέβαιον αἰτίαν). For *ruina* as an Epicurean term see Lucr. 1.1107, 2.1145, 6.572, and Reid on Cic. *Fin.* 1.18. On the the *stabilis uita* of the Epicurean sage see Kenney on Lucr. 3.65–73.

[163] Alex. *De Figuris* 2.23.8 lists μυκτηρισμός ("turning up the nose," "sneering") as one of the four "ironies." Quint. *Inst.* 8.6.59 defines *mycterismos* as *dissimulatus quidam sed non latens derisus*; cf. *A. G.* 9.188.5 Σωκρατικῷ μυκτῆρι ("Socratic irony"), and Lucian, *Prom. Es* 1 "take care that no one detect in your praise irony and an Attic sneer" (εἰρωνείαν ... καὶ μυκτῆρα οἷον τὸν Ἀττικόν). For "weighing/balancing" symbolizing ironic expression, cf. Tac. *Ann.* 13.3 *Tiberius artem quoque callebat qua uerba expenderet, tum ualidus sensibus aut consulto ambiguus.*

ways.[164] His words, we have seen, are equally guarded and muf-
fled, and they too run the risk of being heard as so much compliant stroking: "You're a great man, Nasidienus, you *really* are."

But Nasidienus does not get it, and that is the risk one takes in
speaking this way. He hears the ludicrous "feast-marshal" analogy
not as a put-down, but as a compliment, his cue to pick himself up
from defeat and get back to the serious business of winning the
battle for Maecenas – there is thus much of "the shadow,"
and Horace himself, in him. He compliments the "kind-hearted"
Balatro for his encouragement and calls for his shoes. "Then,"
Fundanius reports, "on each couch you could have seen the whispers divided off in private hearing." The alliteration of **s** and **r**
in this line (*stridere* **secreta** *diuisos* **aure** *susurros*, 78) recasts the
sounds of a hushed murmur, while the mannered separation of
epithets and nouns (**A***B***a***b*) depicts the actual "dividing" of whispers in "private" (lit. "withdrawn," "isolated") hearing. But this is
indecipherable noise to us, exactly what we do not want to hear
at this point in the narrative. Those whispers are the good stuff,
the searing, drunken "payback" we have been waiting for since
line 34. But we do not get to hear what they say. Once again the
sounds of real satire are suppressed, and we experience only the
indistinct hissings that remind us of how much we have missed.

Despite the setback of the eel's untimely demise, Nasidienus refuses to concede defeat. He returns at the head of a sacral procession, invigorated, and ready to take back what Chance stole away.
Behind him are his slaves lugging a magnificent *mazonomus* "trencher" big enough to carry all the delicacies of lines 86–91. But
the effort is wasted. His guests put up with it for a little while,
but then, without a word, they stand up and make for the door
(*S.* 2.8.93–5):

---

[164] Pers. 1.116–18 draws upon this scene, putting Horace in the role of Balatro: "That wily
Horace touches on his friend's every fault while making him laugh, and once admitted
he plays about his conscience, an expert at suspending the public from his well-blown
nose" (*callidus excusso populum suspendere naso*). This is the only instance of the *suspendere
naso* metaphor outside of Horace (who has it twice). Thus, it is no coincidence that Persius uses the metaphor to describe Horace. With it, Persius suggests that, in his charac-
terization of Balatro, Horace may have distilled something of his own satiric persona
(or, at the very least, that he sees a connection between them). The metaphor which
Persius redeploys to connect them underscores their shared mastery of oblique, inoffen-
sive ridicule, making this an essential quality of Horatian satire.

quem nos sic fugimus ulti
ut nihil omnino gustaremus, uelut illis
Canidia afflasset peior serpentibus Afris.

We fled from the man, taking our revenge by tasting not a single one of
these delicacies, as if Canidia had breathed on them, she more foul than
African snakes.

Here, finally, is the "revenge" Vibidius hinted at in line 34, but it
is not at all in the character of a drunkard's unbalanced assault. It
is prompt, open-ended and, above all, silent. Who knows whether
Nasidienus, a man of proven gullibility, actually took the hint this
time and felt the sting of his guests' parting insult. Fundanius does
not tell us. All we know is that the food he worked so hard on preparing was left steaming on the tray. It had to be, because the idea
of eating any more of it was, by now, completely unthinkable to
his guests. Somehow this gorgeous food, meticulously prepared
and presented, had come to reek of witch's-breath, and the guests
could take no more. Their every bite had to be forced down while
biting the tongue, and taken with an unstinting splash of the
listener's own bile.

It is an ugly image to end with, witch's-breath; something to
suggest the feasters' ultimate frustration and jading. But letting go
with pent-up ridicule is not an option for these closely watched
guests, so the best they can do to relieve their bilious stomachs is
to take no more of what ails them. They walk away, unpurged.
And that is the way it is for us, the readers of book 2, as well. The
long-winded diatribes (2.3 and 2.7) and intricate lectures on the art
of fine dining (2.2, 2.4, 2.8, and much of poems 2.6 and 2.7) that
make up this book have kept us pinned to our seats, waiting for
the real satire to happen. But it never does. And this from a book
that, like its miniature in the feast of *S.* 2.8, opened on a note of
such outright ferocity: in *S.* 2.1 we were treated to a whole roasted
boar, savage country fare, set amid various acidic (*acria, S.* 2.8.7)
vegetables served not to sate, but to "pique the jaded appetite/
anger" (*lassum peruellunt stomachum, S.* 2.8.8–9). But what followed
was a feast of innuendo, secret recipes and open-ended digs, rich,
enigmatic foods that stick in the craw and clog the bowels. And so
it makes sense that, at the precise moment when Fundanius and
friends walk out on Nasidienus, we, the jaded readers of book 2,

walk out on Horace. That last *mazonomus* "trencher," a veritable *lanx satura* "plate stuffed full" with "wickedly" good delicacies, all meticulously prepared and arranged for Maecenas' enjoyment, puts us over the top as well.[165] For by now we have had too much, and we are sickened by the thought of taking any more. What we really need is a cure, something to purge the system and soothe the soul; a no-nonsense plate of cabbage, cooked in the kitchen of Lucilius.

---

[165] The *mazonomus* was an immense serving-tray, commonly used for the wholesale distribution of food and gifts at public festivals; cf. Nem. *Auc.* 17, Ath. 4 149b, 5 197f; the word occurs on numerous inventory lists from temples in the Greek East, e.g. *IG* 7.3498.50, *OGI* 214.50. Here the trencher is carried by an indefinite number of slaves and is large enough to hold all of the delicacies described in vv. 86–91.

CHAPTER 2

Persius

OF NARRATIVE AND COSMOGONY: PERSIUS AND THE INVENTION OF NERO

Neronian satire. Generally we take that to mean "Persius." But let's allow the idea to sink in beyond that. Without Persius to tell us what "Neronian satire" actually entails, the words may be felt to repel one another because, for us, with Neronian imaginations configured by the tales of the moralizing historians Tacitus, Suetonius, and Dio, it is hard to imagine Nero taking an open view towards the writing of satire in his narrowly scrutinized Rome. The ambition has the look of a scripted death-wish, especially since, we are quite sure, Nero himself would have to be any "real" satirist's chief target. The historians assure us that he was a sadistic monster, fed fat on flattery and on the sweet blood of his many enemies, erstwhile friends, rivals, and all the various nobodies who happened to get in his way on one of his many bad days. Satire under Nero? Who could have ever come up with such a warped ambition, and what would that "satire" look like?

Putting the question that way, with emphasis heavily on the absurdity of the enterprise, allows us to feel a bit more comfortable with our almost unbearable, but only non-Menippean solution: Persius. The poems of Persius, some scholars are quick to remind us, look the way they look because they were produced under Nero: six small hexameter poems and a choliambic Prologue, truncated, veiled, and safely "philosophical." This is the new look of non-suicidal satire under a tyrant, poems that turn inside, to problems of the human heart, not just because the dogmatic young man who wrote them thinks those problems matter, but especially because the larger social and political problems "out there" in Nero's Rome are now off limits, marked off as a sacred space not to be pissed in (P. 1.112–14). If this new breed of satirist addresses Rome's "one big" problem at all, as the genre makes clear he should, he must do so in veiled, understated ways, by letting our imaginations run wild; telling us, for example, that everyone in Rome has ass's ears, and leaving it to us to decide what that means.

Such is the sum of Persius as "Neronian" satirist: Nero is the "cause" to his *Satires'* unfortunate "effect."[1] The formula is neat and easy to apply, and though perhaps true in its general contours, I suspect there is good reason to be unsatisfied by it. First off, this way of reading Persius against his culture makes the most exotic and un-inevitable of all Latin poetry books seem somehow the product of a standard cultural reflex, natural and inevitable. But even more disturbing is the way the formula depends on "the fact" of Nero's actually being the glowering egomaniac of the historians, as if that Nero can be taken for granted as the driving force "out there" in Rome, making Persius write the way he writes.[2] In other words, defining Persius as "Neronian Satirist" is a bit too easy if we can claim from the start to know precisely what the "Neronian" half of the formula entails. In contrast, I maintain that Persius, much as he may have wanted to, could not rely on any handy monster-narrative of Nero in writing these poems. At best, the story of Nero as we know it from the historians was under construction in Persius' day, existing alongside a number of competing stories that were eventually selected out and tossed aside as yesterday's garish trash.[3] Perhaps most notable of these discredited narratives was the story of Nero as Rome's Apollo, bringer of enlightenment and a new Golden Age, a story that gets scoffed at now, but that had many believers in Persius' day.[4] That

---

[1] But not the standard sum. Most scholars treat Nero as a peripheral factor in Persius' case, focusing instead on Persius' philosophical aims and youthful earnestness as the main factors behind his abrupt style, and the genre's sharp, inward turn. Typical in this regard are Witke (1970) 79–113, and Knoche (1974) 127–39. In contrast, Sullivan (1985) 74–114 figures Persius' crabbed style, and much of his content, as explicitly anti-Neronian.

[2] On the manifold inadequacies of the standard myth(s) of Nero, see Elsner–Masters (1994). Still useful in this regard is Warmington (1969).

[3] Sullivan (1985) 25–6: "It is small wonder that the senatorially biased histories that have survived make Nero out to be a monster. Yet Josephus and Martial suggest that there were also histories that put Nero in a far more favorable light; indeed for many years after his death parts of the Empire awaited his miraculous return with hope and credulity ... significantly, the unknown author of the *Octavia* has to go out of his way to stress Nero's alienation from the people in 62."

[4] On Nero as bringer of a new Golden Age, see Griffin (1984) 37–66.

glossy version of the tale premiered at the boy-emperor's accession in 54, and it continued to grow in volume and sophistication over the course of his reign, energized by the boundless rhetorical imagination (and cash) of the imperial myth-making machine. Still, it was a story always under construction, and always on the verge of extinction. And so, along with a number of gorgeous buildings that had been (and were still being) built to second and solidify it, the story itself largely burns away in the fire of 64. That happens two years after Persius' death. He writes, still, against enormous tides of enthusiasm in Nero's favor, and from within the litigious muddle of every attitude in between.

And so I would like to rephrase the question of what makes this satirist and his work "Neronian" by treating "Neronian culture" not as something we can take for granted, a singular, well-defined force "out there" that exerts its pressure, predictably, on Persius' satiric enterprise and makes his poems look the way they look – proving, in turn, that Tacitus, Suetonius, and Dio were right all along. Instead, I would like to consider the possibility that Persius' *Satires* themselves play a role in making Neronian culture look the way it looks; in other words, satire as a (counter-)myth-making act, constructive of culture rather than, simply, the result of it (which it is, always, also). For if writing satire in Nero's Rome seems a weird idea, perhaps it is because these poems undertake to impress us with their utter weirdness: their stiflings, contortions, and inward turns, in other words, do not simply result from "Neronian culture" as that oppressive, vain, and threatening force "out there" we always assume it was. They construct it as such. And that is, at least in part, the point. They flash before us the sights and sounds of what can only be read as Nero's Rome. Gowers has made the point well: "Neronian literature, more than that of any other period in Rome, demands to be read in the shadow, or rather, glare, of its ruler. The sun-king always penetrates the dark studies and rural retreats that confine Neronian writing."[5]

But the sights these poems give us to see are, for the most part, terribly disorienting and hard to look at, and the sounds they give us to hear grate on the ear. The poems land us in that *aegri somnia* ("sick man's dream") of Horace, *Ars Poetica* 7, a Daliesque world of psychedelic images, disjointed, cluttered, and frequently pornographic. It is the counter-image to Horace's neatly unified

---

[5] Gowers (1994) 131.

picture-poem, with head joined neatly to neck, and neck fitted tightly to collar. Here the poems, and the world they picture, are glaringly "out of joint," a point that Persius drives home with his famous *iunctura acris* ("harsh joining") metaphor (P. 5.14) to oppose Horace's *callida iunctura* ("clever joining") analogy of *Ars* 47–8.[6] The world they construct "out there" is the ugly underside of the Golden Age, the story that Nero's glossy, smooth-jointed tale does not tell. In making that myth, Nero & Co. sought frantically for new forms of expression, bringing about an age of hectic experimentation in the spheres of literature, architecture, and the arts.[7] One key element of this experimental frenzy, but by no means the sum of it, was the revival of literary forms that had special connections with Augustus, Rome's deeply revered first emperor – and the only non-hypocrite, -psychopath, or -dimwit in the Julio-Claudian set, according to the promotional rhetoric of Agrippina and Seneca.[8] Much of Nero's early success derived from his being the direct descendant of Augustus (his great-great-grandson) and the clear "Julian" solution to Rome's mostly "Claudian" problems (Tiberius, Caligula, Claudius).[9] Hoping to contribute to this project, Calpurnius Siculus wrote pastoral poems patterned after Virgil's *Eclogues*, including a reprise of *Ecl.* 4, with shepherd-poet singing the praises of Rome's new boy-king and heralding the coming of his Golden Age.[10] Caesius Bassus, Persius' friend and posthumous editor, wrote neo-Horatian *Odes*, and Lucan, another friend, wrote a national epic that recalls Virgil in its nearly every

---

[6] On Persius' reprocessing of Horace's metaphor at P. 5.14, see Hooley (1997) 73–4. For a summary study of P.'s metaphorical imagination and technique, see La Penna (1995) 327–40.

[7] See Sullivan (1985) 19–73.

[8] Morford (1984) 8: "Culturally the new reign was to represent a renaissance of literature and the arts, fields in which Nero had a deep interest and some ability. It was to be politically and culturally a new Augustan age, and Nero, so the court-poets wrote, was a new Apollo on earth to preside over the Golden Age of Roman culture."

[9] For Nero as the champion of the *gens Iulia* over the *gens Claudia,* see Wiseman (1982) *passim,* esp. 57–8, and Eden (1984) 10. On the "Augustan constitutionalist" rhetoric of Nero's youthful accession, see Rudich (1993) 1–14; cf. Griffin (1984) 73: "Agrippina was a formidable adversary. She had political allies at all levels, acquired during Claudius' reign, and she knew how to exploit her Augustan lineage and descent from Germanicus to the full." Cf. Tac. *Ann.* 11.12 *ex memoria Germanici,* and 12.2–3, where Nero's early success is put in terms of his descending from the good branch of the Claudian house.

[10] For a summary of recent scholarship on the history and date of Calpurnius Siculus, see Fugmann (1992). Attempts to establish a third-century date for these poems are highly problematical. The most egregiously smug and over-argued of these attempts (besides being a typographical nightmare) is Horsfall (1997).

line – though with results that are remarkably non-Virgilian. And that is why I think it matters greatly that Persius should obsess so relentlessly over the Horatian character of his project, breaking into our memories of Horace in what seems to be his almost every line. Those memories suggest that he, too, has a little something to contribute to Nero's neo-Augustan project, and that his poems draw at least some of their energy and meaning from that larger mythmaking enterprise.

But his particular "contribution," in the end, can hardly be what Nero had in mind. The problem comes in its looking the way it looks, a "half-pagan's" graceless, lopsided gift, so reminiscent of, and yet so terribly unlike, its Augustan model. It is the same problem we encounter in putting Lucan against Virgil and in seeing Rome's heroic story put the way Lucan puts it. We are struck by the idea that *this* is what national epic has come to look like in Rome: godless, bloodthirsty, its "heroes" stripped of noble motives and glory. And with so much sameness hinting constantly at difference, we have to wonder what brought on this infusion of so much silver into Virgil's solid gold. Perhaps that is the jarring point to Nero's being made the poem's beginning (its muse) and its end (the imperial end-product to which the story leads). But the same disturbing uglification is evident in the *Satires* of Persius as well. These poems paint a world that has bottomed out, far worse than anything we saw in Horace, with the poet insisting from the start that his brand of didactic now has no audience and satire does no good. The whole enterprise, he tells us in poem 1, is a waste of words, secrets spoken into a hole. His world is fake, soulless, and rotten to the core, and that rottenness, he gives us to suspect, comes from the top down, devolving, in the most obvious instance, from the experimental workshop of Nero's literary coterie. That is where literary enthusiasms are generated and literary tastes filed to perfection. But what, from one angle, looks like an exciting new world of governance and good taste, with emperor and aristocrats performing "in concert" to the rhythms of Nero's pounding new beat, from another angle, Persius' angle, looks like nothing more than a cheap pornographic sideshow featuring Nero's outsized dick performing spectacular feats of multiple-penetration on Rome's eager and amazingly orgasmic aristocracy. It is a jarring spectacle, hard to look at. But we look at it, disgusted and turned on, and disgusted at *being* turned on, all the same.

That is the weird, alien take on Nero's culture that these poems seem to push for. They lure us into imagining that this is the reality "out there" against which the satirist must rail, or worse, shake his head in hopeless disgust. But, as mentioned above, I regard this take on "Neronian culture" as just that, a take, and not necessarily the indisputable reality that is the "cause" to Persius' "effect." And that is where I differ most significantly from the majority of scholars who have treated the question of Persius' many political digs. I contend that the *Satires* themselves play a crucial role in configuring our Neronian imaginations, just as they did for Persius' first-century audience(s), constructing a reality (i.e. a narrative economy of P.'s own making) in which they work and make sense, wherein a satirist is forced to talk the way Persius talks. But in saying that, I do not mean simply to reverse the poles of cause and effect, in a deft conversion from "Nero making Persius" to "Persius making Nero." It can never be that simple, especially since the forces of cause and effect seem always to run both ways when the question concerns a poet's relation to his/her culture. It is the same problem we face, say, in reading Ovid's exile poems against "the culture" in which they were produced. With *Tristia* 1.1, for example, we ask, does Augustus seem to us here, as he always does (and this is generally the story we tell of the late Augustus), to get suspicious and intolerant in his old age: (1) because he really did become suspicious and intolerant, and *the fact* of Ovid's exile proves it? or (2) because Ovid wrote poems from exile that tell a story about that fact, fixing the way we read it by dwelling on the injustice of his plight and creating a vivid and lasting sense of Augustus' transformation into a suspicious, intolerant old man?

Here again I think that neither option tells the whole story, and that the forces of cause and effect have to be seen as running both ways. For cultural, epochal identities, such as those suggested by the terms "Augustan" and "Neronian," are never simply synonymous with "the facts" of an emperor's rule, in the sum total of decrees passed, artifacts produced, poets exiled, and so on. They emerge as identities only when those facts are rendered into stories, told as tales that "make sense" inside themselves by selecting out the clutter and chaos that characterize and confuse so much of our lived experience of the facts. Such messiness is disturbing and, in the end, intolerable, since it gives us to believe that human cultural existence, and our puny lives within that existence, really are un-orientable and spinning out of control. Epochal narratives, then, are a mode of gaining control of the mess, cosmogonic tales that place peoples, neatly defined, within a carefully ordered, meaningful space.[11] They do this by overcoming chaos, giving a clear sense of cause and effect in a cluttered, threatening space where we might never have been able to detect it. Where it may have never existed at all.[12] And thereby these cherished notions of "period" (and the same might be said of "genre"[13]), despite their being always politically and teleologically rigged from the present, give us to believe that chaos really can be controlled. And so the story, that ordered artifact we invent to suggest the existence of order, becomes itself an active means of ordering life, since by "making sense" locally, i.e. passively (as "artifact"), inside itself, it becomes the thing we take back into the world to "make sense" (actively, as "tool") of its disorienting, day-to-day clutter.[14]

Macro-musings. And perhaps more than what is required here. But the point I wish to drive home with this flight-of-fancy is that the poems of Persius are not just a knee-jerk response to a culture "out there," they are inside the cosmogonic, myth-making crucible as an active agent, contributing energy to, and drawing energy from, a number of other sense-making stories that eventually burn away and leave, if anything, the merest traces of their once impressive frames. I think it is important to see these poems working this way, making culture rather than simply reacting to it, because it means that Persius may be doing something more with them

---

[11] Kermode (1988) 121 on notions of "canon" and "period": "concepts of period not only make history manageable but inevitably involve valuation."

[12] Ricoeur (1984) vol. 1, 31, on narrative: "It goes without saying that it is I, the reader … who establishes this relationship between a lived experience where discordance rends concordance and an eminently verbal experience where concordance mends discordance." Cf. Kennedy (1997) 47, treating history "as an *effect* of narrative and the narrator's agency." "For there to be a 'shape' or 'order' to history, the 'future' (seen from whatever constitutes the narrative's 'present') must be, in some way, *known*: we are asked not only to look back to a point in the past, but also to look forward from that point to the *telos* of the here-and-now, the moment which encapsulates the interests and desires which motivate the narrative act, and which the narrative act seeks to satisfy. It is from this shuttle effect, backwards and forwards, that narratives and historical representations derive their sense of closure and fulfilment."

[13] Cf. Bakhtin–Medvedev (1985 [1928]) 133, on genre as a means of selecting and embodying what counts as real: "every significant genre is a complex system of means and methods for the conscious control and finalization of reality."

[14] Cf. Kermode (1988) 122: "once a period has got itself established we can not only argue about whether it ever existed in the way people habitually say it did, but use it very freely to scan history and make judgements of particular styles, and works, of art."

than he is commonly assumed to be doing. For one thing, seeing the poems this way may begin to explain why they met with such widespread enthusiasm (if they really did) when first published shortly after the poet's death. The writer of Persius' *Vita* tells us that when the book was first published, "immediately people were enthralled by it and scrambled to snatch it up." This most unusual response to Persius ("Persius? Popular?!!") hints that he struck a chord with a broad swath of readers in the last troubled years of Nero's reign by writing what people *already* wanted to hear, i.e. hidden digs against Nero, which certainly are there. But perhaps he is doing something else, as well, something quite unexpected. For instead of showing his audience a view of culture that they already subscribed to and had seen done up for them before, he provides them with new ways of seeing their world, flashing before them sights they never expected to see, and having them listen to sounds they never expected to hear. The culture he delivers to them is nothing like the glossy, sun-tanned version of it his audience(s) knew from the tales of Nero's promotional machine: it is sick, mottled, and broken at the seams. That is its cumulative impression, at any rate, a perspective that gets heaped together in a series of disconnected, cluttered vignettes, hard to look at and especially hard to make sense of as a carefully unified whole. And it is important that this piled-up view of culture should hold together so loosely and fail to impress us as a carefully ordered artifact, just as the poems, in themselves, often fail to impress us as cohesive "poems," and the book as "a book." For, if cultural narratives play a role in helping orient us in a scary, vertiginous space, making sense of our lives ("out there") by first making sense in themselves, then what do these poems do? What landmarks do they nail down, and what orientation do they provide?

None. None too obvious, anyway. Instead of plying us with snide political digs traded off between poet and an already-knowing few, these poems hurl us back into the abyss, shattering smugness (even *that* smugness) by leaving us there to spin in a bearing-less space. That, I think, is the net effect of their jaggedness and shocking clutter, and the necessary first act of their bigger cultural project. They leave us disoriented, with nothing at-hand to hang onto and steer ourselves by, and so they force us to find our bearings on our own, inside ourselves. Reading Persius, then, the task of patching *him* together, is a cosmogonic act and, inevitably, a study in *one's own* self-fashioning. "Spiritual exercise," as Henderson dubs it.[15] And that makes sense: the notorious brokenness of this text requires us to work through its problems and to overwhelm its chaos, just to have a sense of its being "a text," and that ordering work has tremendous potential as a means of self-diagnosis, since the solutions we use to fix Persius and render him (as best we can) seamless must necessarily derive from the personal and cultural directives that direct us from inside and push us to suture ourselves together in certain ways.[16] But the poems tell us these secrets about ourselves only when we push away from the product of our reading (that ordered artifact we render into "Persius") far enough to peer into some of its processes (our *rendering of* Persius). That is where the lesson is taught. To take just the most obvious example from the first poem: in chafing at the jaggedness and hard-joinings of this poem and striving so hard in our reading of it to smooth over its gaps and render it into a seamless and sensible whole (as we readers of Persius always do), what happens when we turn the microscope from the artifact we make to our making of it? Do we see the stunning irony of our desiring, so futilely, to make Persius into that smoothly-joined artifact he can never quite manage to be? In the act of striving we have confessed a most unsettling truth about ourselves: we are marching to Nero's beat! His cosmetic obsessions have become, to some degree, ours, and his bogus cultural directives are pulsating in us. The same realization hits us if we give up on Persius altogether and write off his work as so much precocious, second-rate nonsense. Again, in making that decision, we have located the tyrant, the only tyrant that really matters, inside ourselves. And that is what makes these poems, at times, and just as Persius warns us in his first poem, so hard to hear. By giving us nothing "out there" to rely on, no glossy, sun-tanned model to finish ourselves off by, these poems push us to look inside, to see what, if anything, we might find in there to rely on and take our directional cues from. But sometimes that is the scariest place of all to look. There, under the nicely glossed and toasted surface of our put-together selves, we sometimes find a haggard old granny

---

[15] Henderson (1992) 141.
[16] Cf. Conte (1996) 22: "The ideal reader too, by forming exactly this image of the author … takes shape in the text as a set of values in opposition to those of Encolpius."

praying silly prayers, a doddering fool, or worse, a glowering egomaniac. The Nero inside.

The choliambic Prologue of Persius starts by telling us that the
poet who speaks from the page is a hard-edged local who has
never been to Greece, not even in his dreams (P. *Prol.* 1–3):

> Nec fonte labra prolui caballino
> nec in bicipiti somniasse Parnaso
> memini, ut repente sic poeta prodirem.

I didn't wash my lips in the spring of that broken-down horse, nor do I
recall ever dreaming atop Parnassus' twin peaks to become, just like that,
a poet.

"I'm not in that tradition," he claims, no "poet" in that sense. And
he proves the point by taking such a cranky view towards the
inspired tradition to which he refers. His is a fine blend of irrever-
ence ("That broken-down inspirational 'nag,' Pegasus"), hard-
edged skepticism ("Oh sure, just drop off to sleep and, *voilà!*,
you're a poet"), and ignorance ("Poets dream on Mount Parnassus, don't they? No matter. If they didn't before, they do now!").
But it is a tradition that he has some truck with and knows at least
well enough to notice that Mount Parnassus is doubly significant
to poets, with one of its peaks sacred to Apollo, and the other to
Dionysus, both gods of poetic inspiration. The allusion is deft and
easily missed, letting us think that this speaker is perhaps smarter
than he lets on; that he may be one of us after all.

But, then, regarding that reference to a dream on Parnassus,
how confident are we that it really is just an ignorant slip? Can we
let ourselves write it off as just that without scrambling to our
libraries to find a precedent, just to make sure? That odd coupling
of programmatic dreaming with Parnassus shakes us with a shudder of doubt, so that our own control of the vilified tradition becomes the more pressing question. We ask: do we really know
where Ennius had his dream? Does he actually tell us? Better look
that one up – and the commentaries do hash through available
options *ad nauseam*. Or maybe this speaker has someone else in
mind, some little-known Parnassus-dreamer that he knows about

but we do not. Perhaps he has books tucked away in his library that we neither own nor remember ever reading. Is that what we are to think? Can we let ourselves think that this speaker is actually smarter and more deeply Callimachean than we? Or is the reference to Parnassus a deft political dig against Nero, Rome's self-proclaimed Apollo, and against the many poets who sought inspiration atop *his* Parnassus, the Palatine?[17]

That is the reverse-sting of these open-ended opening lines, just one of several ways that this Prologue has of abruptly shifting the ground beneath our feet. Immediately they toss us a problem to solve. And the way we choose to solve that problem by blaming Nero (for making the Palatine a Parnassus), or Persius (for getting *our* tradition wrong), or ourselves (for not having memory banks big enough) says much about who we are. By tumbling into this fissure we enter into ourselves, and we are made to reckon with the internal politics of our own reading. The poem starts by swearing off the overdone tradition of the poet's mountain-top experience, but in doing that, it sends us back to our books, testing our knowledge of the tradition that is, here, the very done-to-death vanity we are supposed to be so sick of. Thus the lines push us to consider just how involved with that tradition we ourselves are, and how protective of it, and of ourselves as expert keepers of that tradition, we wish to be. Just how much did we worry that the poet might have got it wrong? How urgently did we race to our commentaries, and rifle through our own memories of the tradition, to find that mysterious Parnassus-dreamer? Could we resist the urge? And how did we respond to not finding him?[18] Did we take Persius' failure to conform to the tradition he vilifies as our

---

[17] Hor. *Ep.* 2.1.216–18 makes the Palatine a quasi-Helicon (see below n. 36). Under Nero the Palatine, with its temple of Apollo and libraries, could easily be seen as a quasi-Parnassus. This is where "the god" resided and had his temple, a site to be sought out by poets thirsting for Nero's Apollinine inspiration (and all the "blessing" that went with it). On Nero as Apollo, see especially Griffin (1984) *passim*.

[18] The scholiasts of Persius are alone in putting Ennius' dream on Mount Parnassus. All other ancient sources (most notably Lucretius and Propertius) put the dream squarely on Mount Helicon. Skutsch (1985) 150 takes this discrepancy to mean that Ennius did not name the mountain in the dream sequence of *Annales* 1. I think it more likely that he did name the mountain, that it was Mount Helicon, and that Persius switches the poets' sought-after dream site to Parnassus (1) in order to send us back to our books; and (2) in order to poke fun at Nero's Apollinine self-making, central to which was the emperor's careful orchestration of Rome's literary enthusiasms from his home–temple–library complex (Rome's quasi-Parnassus) atop the Palatine hill (see previous note).

cue to vilify him? And did we detect any irony at all in our insisting that he *should* conform? Or were we perhaps more worried that
he may have gotten it right? For, as the thick burgeoning of the
commentaries on these lines prove, getting the tradition right *is*
our obsession. We are at the heart of its remarkable proliferation,
terribly convinced that getting it right, and having control of it,
matters. And the way we read and try to make sense of Persius,
begrudgingly, and with thick, tradition-obsessed commentaries in
hand, proves it. Like that *plebeia beta* ("plebeian beet") of P. 3.114,
the humble vegetable that hunts out hidden ulcers with its acidic
sting, the hard, broken edges of Persius sting us where we are most
sensitive and vulnerable. These poems find us out, and it is their
very failure to hold together and make sense ("A dreamer? On
Parnassus!?") that gives them their necessary acidic edge. Putting
Persius together, then, making sense of him, is an incriminating,
painful process. As we have seen, it stings only because we have so
much of ourselves invested in the literary and cultural obsessions
that this chiding half-rustic claims to be so deadset against.

Sequaciousness. Done-to-death repetition. These are the central
concerns of the Prologue, problems so widespread that even the
ivy-vines get in on the act, by "licking" the images of inspired
poets in a way that makes them seem *sequaces* "disposed to follow
along." The idea is echoed in the second of the poem's two broken
halves by the description of the "belly" as "a craftsman skilled
at following denied voices." And so the problem of everything
already having been done, the problem of Horace *S.* 1.1 and 2.1, is
set up as the pressing cultural vanity to be exposed and dissected
in this poem. By selecting himself out of one tradition, Persius
has located his work squarely inside another, and so we have here
the same ironic twist we saw in the poems mentioned above: by
swearing off repetition, the poet implicates himself in the doing-
to-death he condemns.

Juvenal does the same thing in the opening lines of his first
poem. And that makes me think that Persius' Prologue really does
belong here, up front, as a prologue, because that is where satirists
on both sides of him in the tradition of formal verse-satire also
start. But since P. 1, the other "first" poem of Persius, raises the
same issue again and dwells on it at even greater length, that suspicion fails to make the grade as a cogent argument. Much more
compelling is the strong tendency of poets since Hesiod to tell of

their dreams and inspired draughts right up front, in programmatic tales that seem eminently detachable from the poems that follow. At the very least, we tend to study them that way, as set-pieces that derive more of their sense vertically, from the larger tradition of mountain-top tales to which they refer, than horizontally, from the poems into which they are immediately set. The problem in Persius' case – the same problem that is always the problem in Persius' case – is that the horizonal *iunctura* ("joining") of this poem to the next is exceptionally abrupt and disorienting. It leaves us wondering whether it belongs there at all, and, if so, how.[19] And so the work of readerly suturing begins. Though it is obvious that good arguments can be made for keeping the poem up front, especially since both this poem and the first hexameter poem take aim at what they construct as dominant literary obsessions, it should be admitted that the gap between them is still unusually wide. Keeping them together requires exceptional effort. But this is necessary work, just one instance of the constant suturing we have to do to keep Persius from falling apart.

Such is the diagnostic value of the notorious detachability of this "Prologue": by not quite belonging it gets under our skin, putting us in touch with our own critical processes, and with the various, idiosyncratic ways we have of sizing up literary works and making sense of them. That inward turn tells us, if we care to look at it, just how much of that vain and awful culture "out there" we have managed to take into ourselves, and to what degree its traditions and drives have become ours. Diagnostic gaps, such as that separating the Prologue from the hexameter poems that follow, challenge us to find new, extra-traditional ways of making sense of Persius and, ultimately, of ourselves. For even if we somehow manage to decide that, yes, the choliambic set-piece belongs up front as a prologue, and that it dovetails in meaningful ways with the first hexameter poem to which it is so loosely attached, we still have to admit that our conclusions derive from unusual readerly effort, and that to make sense of the poem's belonging involves extra strain. After we have put this poem together with the rest in a way that makes tolerable sense, we are still left thinking that the result is just tolerable. And so we wonder whether we really got it

---

[19] On the question of the Prologue's belonging (and where), see Gerhard (1913). For recent considerations, see Miller (1986).

right. Some assembly is required. Clearly. But the usual ways we
have of putting together poems, and thereby poets, do not seem to
work. The result, when assembled by, and measured against tradition, always seems a bit lopsided and homely. Barely tolerable.

Perhaps the most obvious strike against the Prologue's being
thought to "belong" is its meter, choliambic. No other writer of
formal verse-satire seems to have used it. Even so, the meter has
strong associations with satire *via* Hipponax, its grumpy Greek
inventor who, tradition says, wrote so scathingly that his victims
could be spied hanging themselves from trees. So strong was his
influence on the choliambic tradition that the "limping iambic"
meter he is credited with inventing kept, almost exclusively, to
its fuming, suicide-inducing roots throughout the many centuries
of its subsequent use. All by itself, still in Persius' day, the meter is
intertextual with Hipponax, bringing with it memories of his long-
lost age of free speech, and his unique brand of searing abuse.[20]
And because these are "limping iambics" that proudly advertise
their rhythmic ugliness by awkwardly galumphing to a halt at the
end of each line, they play up the poet's stubborn failure to chime
in with the lilting sounds of poetry inspired by the sacred foun-
tain's smooth flow. Meter itself, in this case, contributes strongly to
the idea of this poet's grumpy isolation, and his failure to march
in step.[21]

But memories of Roman writers are in this meter, too.
Diomedes, a fourth-century Roman grammarian, lists the best
practitioners of *carmen maledicum* ("hostile song") in iambic meters,
the broader category to which choliambic belongs, as follows: "the
chief writers of this type of song are, among the Greeks, Archilochus and Hipponax, and among the Romans, Lucilius, Catullus,
Horace, and Bibaculus."[22] Though not all of these wrote in choliambics, writing choliambics puts Persius in their company. And
so his Prologue, the poem that seems so often not to belong when

---

[20] Cf. Plin. *Ep.* 5.10.2 *caue, ne ... illos libellos, quos tibi hendecasyllabi nostri blanditiis elicere non possunt, conuicio scazontes extorqueant.*

[21] Wehrle (1992) 6, note 4: "Of note also is P.'s choice of scazons ('limping iambics') for the prologue ... P.'s subject here is poor poesy; a 'limping' meter is therefore appropriate in describing poets who are themselves 'limp' in respect to style, production, even inspiration."

[22] *Grammatici Latini*, ed. Keil (1961) vol. 1, 485.

taken with the six hexameter poems to which it is so oddly coupled, from another, less hexametrically fixated perspective, seems
well suited to the task of putting Persius in league with Lucilius
and Horace, his principal forerunners in Latin criticism's other
branch of *carmen maledicum*, satire.

Against this it may be objected that Diomedes puts Horace on
the list not for his *Sermones*, but for his *Epodes*, and that is clearly
right. But the *Epodes* are poems that overlap with the *Sermones* not
only in their time of composition (late thirties, early twenties) but
in the sharing of many of the same themes and satiric methods, as
well as some of the same targets of abuse. Such overlap suggests
that Horace's satiric and epodic efforts are complementary, and
that they may actually have been read as such by Horace's ancient
readers, taken together as two sides of the "hostile song" coin. At
any rate, it is clear that Lucilius makes Diomedes' list as a writer
of satire and only that. Like Horace, he wrote scathing iambic
attacks, but, in his case, those efforts are credited to him as "satire."
His first two books of *Saturae*, books 26 and 27, are entirely in trochaic senarii, with books 28 and 29 mixing trochaic and iambic
meters with hexameters. Book 30 is completely in hexameters.

These five books, though perhaps published individually at first,
were eventually (re-?)packaged as a single volume, it seems, in the
author's own lifetime. But clearly we cannot think that Lucilius
numbered them books 26–30, expecting to fill in books 1–25 later.
Only after his death, sometime in the first century BCE, did editors
(likely Valerius Cato) push these first books behind the hexameters
(and perhaps behind some elegiacs in books 22–5) and number
them last, and the main criterion they had for doing this seems
to have been metrical: hexameters take precedence over elegiacs
in terms of their innate grandeur, and elegiacs rate higher than
iambo-trochaics.[23] Choliambics, if anywhere, would have to come
dead last. And that is one reason why Persius' choliambic Prologue
seems so awkwardly placed: as in the case of Lucilius' first five
books, editorial pressure, if applied, as it seems to have been, will
have pushed the choliambics from front to back, and not the other
way around. That is why we find them tacked on behind the hexameters in a few minor editions. At best, that means the problem

---

[23] See Gratwick (1982) 168.

of its not belonging becomes something we tackle last rather than first. But, in all likelihood, that is not where the "Prologue" goes. Persius put it first, and because he did that, despite the problem-solving efforts of some ancient editors, the choliambics tended to stay there, irreverent of tradition and neat metrical hierarchies, daring readers to let it stay there and to come to terms with its never quite belonging. But the point of my bringing in the precedent of Lucilius here is not to prove that Persius' Prologue belongs up front, by making it the editorially challenged counterpart to Lucilius books 26–30, though I think it both does belong there and that it is the counterpart so challenged; it is to show that it does not belong up front, even though that is right where Persius put it, weird and challenging, cracking open a nice diagnostic gap for us to stumble over and come to terms with right from the start. Racing to find helpful precedents in the satiric tradition does little, though perhaps just a little – through Horace's *Epodes* and Lucilius' first five books – to smooth over the gap.

But there are other traditions to be explored, further literary memories built into the Prologue's first lines that can help us align ourselves in our reading and get on with the suturing work that has to be done. Already we have seen that the choliambic meter, all by itself, has a strange intertextual force that comes with the mere fact of its being used, regardless of all other dictional and figurative clues: it has a built-in, Hipponactean surliness. We see just how built-in this is, for example, in the opening lines of Callimachus' *Iambs*, where the ghost of Hipponax comes back from the dead to address his audience in limping iambs, his characteristic meter. For Callimachus, it seems, the meter and the surly character of Hipponax are bound up as an inextricable pair, so that to summon one from the dead is to summon the other as well. And even though Diomedes, many centuries later, fails to include Callimachus in his list of famous iambic attackers, it is clear that the Roman satirists, especially Horace, had him on their own versions of the list, for they routinely cue us with memories of Callimachus' *Iambs* as a way of positioning their own satiric works within a larger, genre-producing matrix of texts.[24] Persius, though

---

[24] For connections between Callimachus' *Iambi* and Horace's *Sermones*, see Freudenburg (1993) 18, and 104–8.

he swears to be an enemy of overdone Callimacheanism, is no exception: he cues us to his redoing of Callimachus right from the start. Perhaps the most obvious case of an incursion from the *Iambs* is P. 1.58–60:

> o Iane, a tergo quem nulla ciconia pinsit
> nec manus auriculas imitari mobilis albas
> nec linguae quantum sitiat canis Apula tantae.

Oh for Janus, who has no stork bobbing behind his back, and no hand held up to look like floppy white ears, and no tongues big as when an Apulian dog pants with thirst!

This famously ungrammatical crux has its counterpart in the image of Callimachus' backbiting Korykaian at *Iambs* 1 fr. 191.82–3Pfeiffer:

> ὁ δ' ἐξόπισθε Κω[ρ]υκαῖος ἐγχάσκει
> τὴν γλῶσσαν †ἐλων ὡς κύων ὅταν πίνῃ

and from behind the Korykaian grins/gapes, holding his tongue like a dog when he drinks ...

Similar resonances, though not quite so distinct, can be heard playing inside the choliambic Prologue as well – right where we are metrically set to hear them. For when Hipponax comes back from the dead in *Iambs* 1, he tells us first that the target of his attacks is no longer his old enemy, Bupalus, but certain *philologoi*, whom he immediately compares to birds (κέπφοι, 6) whose feather-brained "fluting" (κα]τηύλησθ') resounds in the temples "of Dionysus ... of the Muses ... and of Apollo" (Διω]νύσου ...]τε Μουσέων ... Ἀπόλλωνος, 7–8), sites of high inspiration.[25] The *Diegesis* and other sources name these as the literati of Ptolemy's Museum.[26] In the opening lines of Callimachus' *Iambs*, then, we are introduced to a hard-edged cynic who rails in choliam-bics against an inspired, bird-like literary/philosophical jet-set of a glorious new age, taking on Ptolemy and an eager crew of poets and philosophers whom he chides for their incessant wrangling and raving obscurity. Summoned to the shrine of Sarapis to cure

---

[25] Kerkhecker (1999) 20: "the gods mentioned (Dionysus, the Muses, Apollo) suggest poets or literary scholars." The setting of Hipponax' address is not an urban temple, but an unidentified sanctuary outside the city walls; see Kerkhecker (1999) 22–3.

[26] See Clayman (1980) 11–16.

them, he comes φέρων ἴαμβον ("bearing a lampoon-song"), perhaps the counterpart to Persius' *carmen adfero* ("I bear/offer a song").[27]

Memories of Hipponax's fuming return in Callimachus *Iambs* 1, I contend, are built into Persius' Prologue, tugging at our imaginations as quickly as the poem's first lines. From the start, we are made aware of a text inside the text, in dialogue with it, and deeply textured by it, and with that intertextual dialogue comes a whole new set of ideas, symbols, institutions, and language bound up with our memories of the pre-existing poem. With these, then, come new ways of reading Persius, and of imagining what he is all about. Some first-century readers of the poem may have caught the irony of starting out this way: one voice from the dead, that of Callimachus' Hipponax, heard inside another, Persius' own (he died shortly before the poems were published). But with memories of Hipponax comes a sense that Persius, too, returns from the dead not to rail against hack-imitators generally, but to take on literary enthusiasms that are part of some bigger political scheme, as if Ptolemy and his Museum are to be factored into our reading of the poem in some modern-day counterpart.

Thus, the larger critical scene in which Callimachus worked comes to mind, and all those old lampoons levelled against Ptolemy and his well-heeled team of scholar-poets, a team that included Callimachus himself. Thus, inside Persius' attack against parrot-poets who squawk out χαῖρε for a cracker, we detect the sounds of Timon of Phlius lampooning Ptolemy's scholar-birds, the *philologoi* whom he kept caged up and nicely fed in his lavish library and Museum (*SH* 786):

> πολλοὶ μὲν βόσκονται ἐν Αἰγύπτῳ πολυφύλῳ
> βιβλιακοὶ χαρακῖται ἀπείριτα δηριόωντες
> Μουσέων ἐν ταλάρῳ.

There are plenty of book-fiends that feed in Egypt with its tribes thick as leaves. They are fenced off, wrangling incessantly inside the birdcage of the Muses.

With these old critical debates sounding in the background, Persius' Prologue, always thought to contain political digs anyway,

---

[27] On the connection, see Kissel (1990) 88, n. 54. Later in the poem Callimachus' Hipponax compares the *philologoi* to swarming flies and wasps. They are the butt of the joke again in the second poem, also in limping iambics, where the character of Aesop compares them, fable-style, to the animals they resemble individually. The list includes a parrot and a gull.

takes on a political color it never quite had before: we get a sense of the vilified imitation's being part of a well orchestrated, institutional enterprise, not just momentary enthusiasm left to run in its own direction and under its own steam.[28] Of course Nero has always been the prime suspect as the driving force behind the enterprise, and there is good reason to suspect that the joke is, at least in part, on him (as in the Parnassus problem above). Still, too often, I think, that joke is put in terms of one man's daring "exposure" of an ugly cultural "truth," Persius against the glowering monster, when it is, in fact, a case of the poet's tapping into Nero's own institutional rhetoric and turning it on its head. This is a story parodically recast, a story about a story, rather than the simple "disclosure" of an ugly, cultural "fact." For, as Sullivan and others have pointed out, Nero himself actively sought to shape his literary and artistic renaissance along the lines of the Alexandrian monarchs: "the image of the great Ptolemaic patrons of arts and letters with their libraries, court poets, and divine status proved too much of a temptation. Nero hankered after the Glory that was Greece."[29] Nero's own Alexandrian pretensions need to be factored into our reading of the Prologue. They were a featured element of his latest promotional campaign, a barrage of Ptolemaic imagery and Alexandrian songs that had *his* tunes playing in every portico and shop, *his* Golden-Age-Nero action figure stuffed into every Roman *Happy Meal.*®

And I think it is because these promotional sounds play so

---

[28] For a full reckoning of the poet as bird metaphor in Roman poetry, with emphasis heavily on mimicry, see Bellandi (1988) 64–5. For the kept philosopher as a "caged bird," cf. Plato, *Ep.* 7.348a. The Ptolemies were known as keepers of exotic birds and animals, see *FGrH* 234 F2 (= Athen. 14 654c).

[29] Sullivan (1985) 24–5. For similar Ptolemaic precedents in encouraging the arts, cf. Vitr. 7 pref. 4: *itaque Musis et Apolloni ludos dedicauit [sc. Ptolomaeus] et, quemadmodum athletarum, sic communium scriptorum uictoribus praemia et honores constituit.* Historians would later recast Nero's Alexandrian pretensions as a vainglorious attempt to "sack" Rome, or to convert the city into a foreign site. Woodman (1992) has clearly shown that Tacitus' account of Tigillinus' revels of 64 CE (*Ann.* 15.37) is based on earlier *descriptiones* of the exotic glories of Alexandria. He concludes (p. 184): "If Tacitus here at 36–7 has used similar techniques to prompt his audience to believe that Nero transformed Rome into Alexandria, the transformation is not simply a literary *jeu d'esprit* but plays a significant part in the author's presentation of the emperor. Alexandria was an essentially ambiguous city, half Greek and half Egyptian. Its Greekness not only provided a potential target for the prejudice of Tacitus' audience but also meant that the city could be represented as the object of Nero's personal enthusiasm and devotion, since his love of all things Greek was notorious."

loudly in the background that Persius can so deftly break into our memories of Hellenistic critical debates in the opening lines of his Prologue. For in the remembered barbs of Callimachus and Timon (and perhaps others) Persius has at his disposal a complete critical language designed specifically for dealing with Ptolemaic pretensions. So he begins there, with that given language, and he uses it in his Prologue to cast Nero in the role of a Ptolemy gone bad. In a very few lines he converts the slickly produced story of Rome's Alexandrian renaissance, the version that has the emperor and his chosen elite searching out Rome's new look, giving it a lilting new sound, into a scene of pathetic craveness and avidity. Retold by Persius, the story features "the Belly" on the hill, *his* inspirational hill, the Palatine, doling out crackers to a well-kept cluster of crow-poets, teaching them to repeat the sounds of his own "fat" voice.[30] Their "talent," for Persius, a mere knack for survival and nest-feathering, comes from his "largesse." He is the *ingeni largitor* ("lavisher of talent") and Rome's self-appointed *artifex* ("artiste extraordinaire"). The latter term is one of several titles Nero may well have applied to himself.[31] But here it is set in a context that plays up its built-in suggestions of "artificiality." Warped and uglified by a plethora of embedded texts, Nero's whole storied enterprise is shown up in the Prologue as an over-stuffed and pathetic fake.

But reading the Prologue this way, as a slam against Nero, corpulent "Belly" though he may have been and had, is not terribly different from the way we have always read it, with the point-of-focus set safely outside ourselves, on Nero, Rome's "one big" problem. We need to start there, I suspect, admitting up front that Nero is never far to seek in these poems, and that he is, at times, the clear target of their abuse. But the temptation to find him there, and to let him bear the brunt of our abuse, is always a game played *on us* in these poems (see esp. below on P. 4), for rarely does Persius allow us to engage in such smugness without turning that against us somewhere along the way, by challenging us to look inside ourselves to see if anything in there resembles the mon-

---

[30] Nero's increasing corpulence is not played down in contemporary portraiture; see Griffin (1984) 121.

[31] Cf. Suet. *Nero* 49.1: *"qualis artifex pereo."* For specific musical connotations of the term, see Seneca, *Ben.* 4.21.3, *Ep.* 87.14.

strous vice we have so smugly railed against in the outside world. Already we have seen that the Prologue has ways of implicating readers in the ugly moral tale it tells, giving them a sense of their own involvement in Nero's vain obsessions. We see the tables turn again at lines 5–6 where the poet tells us that he is content to leave stories of high inspiration *illis ... quorum imagines lambunt| hederae sequaces* ("to those who have follow-along ivy licking at their images"). No doubt this means the busts of famous writers, as the commentators are right to insist; all safely distant, and done up in marble at the local library.[32] But what of all those other keepers of *imagines* in Persius' audience, the nobility who advertised their own superior worth by parading the busts of their dead ancestors, dusted off and wearing leafy crowns on occasions of special importance? Are these bust-keepers automatically off the hook? Sullivan, an aggressive reader of political innuendo, turns the lines differently to give a sense of their potential second edge. He translates: "The Pierian Muses and Pegasus' fountain ... I leave *to our Roman aristocrats and court*" (my emphasis).[33]

So here, as elsewhere in the Prologue, the problem is not just the fat man in charge of cracker-distribution. If you thought it was, you have a price to pay for being so smug. Persius' satiric net takes in much more than Nero. It catches tradition-obsessed followers of all sorts, and all players in larger cultural systems where following matters and brings in handsome rewards. Rome's elite, in other words (and we, too – remember *our* desperate hunt for the Parnassus dreamer?), are implicated deeply in this ugly tale, made part of the nasty machine that keeps (Nero's) vain obsessions alive. So the belly turns out to be bigger than Nero, and its urges to reach beyond his storied desires for food, drink, and flattery. Tyrannical desires here include *our* desire to sell out to him by leaving ideals behind. They include all the compromising we do to set ourselves up nicely in one of culture's many cages, any culture's, not just his, by taking advantage of its morally unbalanced system of rich rewards. Still off the hook? Then consider that, if "the Belly," Nero, is a problem in this Prologue, it is a problem we understand first from inside ourselves, from our struggles against a nagging, irrational force that we all have in us and always, in one way or another, sell out to. He is "the Belly," the tyrant inside (an

---

[32] E.g. Harvey (1981) 11.   [33] Sullivan (1985) 93.

idea Stoic to the core). Nero is defined by us here, rather than we by him.

It seems that only the perfected soul, self-made and completely detached from culture's vain obsessions, has any chance of coming through this Prologue unscathed.[34] And how many of those were in Persius' first-century audience (no one selling out there!), and how many are in ours? But that, it seems, is the diagnostic force of Persius' gap-ridden text: it has the power to show us for what we are, miniature Neros, belly-run, he in us, and we in him, and it gives us nowhere to hide. Blaming him only seems to make our matters worse. So we are left to wonder what it takes to break free of Nero, both Nero "out there," and his more nagging counterpart inside, once and for all. How do we become independent and self-grounded, taking our cues exclusively from something meaningful inside, not from the belly, but from directives we know to be straight and true?

The Prologue puts this as a struggle to find a song we can call "our own," something truly self-made, that we can dance to and be happy with regardless of how it measures up against the pounding Neronian sounds playing all around. The task is exceptionally difficult because, Persius tells us, the fat man on the hill likes to hear his own voice repeated, and he has plenty of crow-poets, institutional judges and makers of poetic tastes, who are willing to comply. They repeat his sounds, and their repetitious squawking, in turn, becomes the stuff of pure inspiration, "Pegaseian Nectar." Other belly-driven poets pick up on it. Followers of followers, they suck it in, second-hand, and pour it out at third hand, driven by *dolosi spes nummi* ("the hope of deceitful cash"). And so the process goes on, and on, proliferating *ad infinitum*.

---

[34] Thus, built into the Prologue is a strict, Chrysippean view of the soul's perfected state (= the ideal *libertas* of P. 5); cf. Sen. *Ep.* 9.15 on Chrysippean detachment: "The supreme ideal does not call for any external aids. It is home-grown, wholly self-developed. *Once it starts looking outside itself for any part of itself* it is on the way to being dominated by fortune." Also *Ep.* 27.3: "Look around for some enduring good. And nothing answers this description except what the spirit discovers *for itself within itself*" (*nisi quod animus ex se sibi inuenit*). On these sentiments see Henderson (1999) 192: "P.'s twisted self-castigation performs (Senecan) 'introversion' (*conuersio ad se*), through which as a larger cultural mantra, the elite of the early Empire developed a (male) subjectivity in pursuit of personal absolutism on the model of, and in resistance to, the demanding centripetalism of the Imperial court. 'Take time for your self / prepare a self / withdraw into the self / become your own self / to your own self be true / free your self to be your self,' the mantra ran, and ran."

That is the literary scene painted in the Prologue. Monotonous clamour blares from start to finish, with the first half telling us what is being done to death, and the second half telling us why. But there is a momentary hush in all this self-seeking noise, in the still, small vignette of the half-rustic's offering at the *uates'* shrine. There, in that hushed middle space, the poet makes the poem's most scandalous claim: all alone, and against enormous tides of overdone, "inspired" mimicry, he has a gift to offer the inspired bards, a song that he can truly call "his own," and no one else's (Prol. 6–7):

> ipse semipaganus
> ad sacra uatum carmen adfero nostrum.

I, a half-rustic, off on my own,[35] offer to the rites of inspired poets a song that is all my own.

A lonely rustic offers his gift at the *uates'* shrine.[36] This vignette, a mere line and a half in length, is set amid, and nearly over-whelmed by, much larger scenes of droning repetition on both sides of it, five and a half lines coming before, and seven full lines coming after. And so the impression that Persius is off on his own (though smack in the middle of it all) and that his poems are, at best, barely audible amid the clamour of poets competing for Nero's attention, are ideas we are made to sense in the very physi-cal layout of the poem. Even before the first hexameter poem tells us that no one will listen, we already know that no one will listen, and we know precisely why: this poet is not talking loud enough, and his smallish voice does not make a politically astute, pre-packaged noise. A mere *semipaganus*, he is either too stubborn or too stupid to chime in with the sounds that pay off and get attended to in the city, the top ten of neo-Ptolemaic pop.

Scholars have always worried over that word, *semipaganus*. No one else seems to have used it, so what can it mean?[37] Commenta-tors routinely despair of ever "really knowing" what the word means: no precedents can be found, so we have no handy way to

---

[35] For this sense, see *OLD ipse* 7.

[36] The lines perhaps recall Hor. *Ep.* 2.1.216–18, where Augustus' Alexandrian image-making efforts are imagined as his converting the Palatine into a quasi-Helicon: *munus Apolline dignum | . . . complere libris et uatibus addere calcar, | ut studio maiore petant Helicona uirentem.*

[37] Bellandi (1988) 48–61 makes an excellent case for *semipaganus* as a variation on *subrusticus*, a slogan for the poet's natural *rusticitas* in both attitude and style.

"locate" the word's sense in the given language of tradition – as if "making" sense were ever simply a matter of "locating" it. But perhaps the futility of our rummaging through tradition here is less the problem of *semipaganus* than it is its most meaningful and salient point. That is, coming up dry is not the unfortunate dead-end of a search for meaning, but the thing itself, its meaning, inextricably bound up with the processes of our searching, and defined by all we experience in rummaging through tradition and failing.[38] For surely the word's failure to accord with, and make sense from, literary tradition is the point, and its failure to mean *the way* it means. Persius made it up, so it is a self-made word, irreverent of tradition and its (t)rusty systems of meaning and mattering. The very awkwardness of the term proves the claim it seems to make: the poet is so detached from the urban critical scene he disparages that he has no truck with and/or grasp of its critical vocabulary. Reaching for *subrusticus*, he comes up with *semipaganus*, a term with no decent cachet among critics "in the know." Thus, in its own way, the ungaugeable *semipaganus* is the perfect means for suggesting the self-made character of Persius' *carmen nostrum* ("song all my own") and, ultimately, of Persius himself.[39] In the momentary respite of lines 6–7 the poet tells us that he neither needs nor desires confirmation from his culture's traditions and driving obsessions, and he makes the point with this word! That is, *with its not belonging*, slipping it in as something he has made for himself and can truly call "his own."

But how can the poet really expect us to believe his claim? We

---

[38] Hooley (1997) 197 takes a similar approach in refusing to commit himself to any one of the word's several possible, but none too plausible, options. He sifts through the main possibilities this way (with my emphasis): "The word, a hapax legomenon meaning 'half-rustic' or 'half-clansman' is vague enough to be variously significant *depending on the interpretive assumptions one brings to it*: perhaps reflecting a connection with the country-colored satires of Horace, or some analogical relation to the Paganalia, or merely signifying a kind of poetic *rusticitas*, so that the word may have the sense of 'outsider' (to corrupt verse?) or 'novice' or 'half-poet.' Of the several possible assessments of the word, each is in its way plausible, but none fully answers to the poem. The variable suggestiveness of the coinage and *the absence of confirmatory context seems, rather, to encourage an open range of meanings*." I think he is right: nailing the term down is definitely the wrong way to go, though we have to try, and we have to fail.

[39] Oddly, if you look inside the word (where you should always look in Persius) and break it apart in an unconventional way, you can detect hints of the poet's self-making: he is not only a "half-poet," as many have suggested (from *semi* "half" and *-paganus* derived from *pangere* "fix, arrange, compose"), he is "self-made" (*se* "a self" *-mi* "for myself" *-paganus* "fix, arrange, compose," amid the general "**self**ishness" of *sequaces; ipse semipaganus*). Maybe. I will admit that this is an odd, unlikely take on an odd, unlikely word.

have already seen how deeply encrusted with poetic traditions his Prologue is, resonating with other poets' remembered voices from start to finish. And that impression of intense intertextual engagement only increases as we move from the loosely "satiric" Prologue to the full Horatian feast of Persius 1. Recently Dan Hooley has cracked open the mimetic systems of Persius' *Satires*, primarily in their relation to Horace, to show just how thick with intertextual memories these poems really are. The results are staggering. He writes regarding the first hexameter poem, P. 1: "the first poem contains a number of imitations ... ranging, according to one count, from one or two allusions to Tibullus through seven to Lucretius, eight to Propertius, twelve to Lucilius, nineteen to Vergil, to almost eighty references to the *Epistles* and *Satires* of Horace."[40] The tally, if anything, is too conservative, for Horatian incursions occur in the poem more than eighty times by my count, and the ancient *Vita* of Persius gives us to suspect that the most significant borrowings in P. 1 may, in fact, be drawn from Lucilius (especially his tenth book) rather than from Horace.[41] Almost nothing has survived from that book, so we have no way of knowing how much Lucilius we are likely to be missing, only that we are missing a lot. And who knows what other voices may be embedded in the poem, forever hidden from our view.

In the end, we can never really know the sum of Persius' intertextual forays, especially since tallies of embedded texts, however incomplete they may be in themselves, can never begin to account for all the other texts that lurk inside the embedded texts, constituting them in the first place. Tracing that out, in anything like a complete taxonomy, is impossible. But the special intertextual problem of Persius, as even a superficial tally can show, is that we are always made aware of his text's intense interactive processes, constantly made to sort through ever accumulating memories of pre-existing texts. Managing all of these memories, and making sense of them, is a monumental task and, ultimately, beyond managing. We have in Persius a text that collapses under its own intertextual weight, delivering too many memories at too quick a

---

[40] Hooley (1997) 29.
[41] See *Vita Persi* 50–9. Fiske (1909 and 1913) exaggerates the presence of Lucilius in P. 1. A more measured view is that of La Penna (1995) 283: "La portata della presenza di Lucilio non è definibile (certamente è molto inferiore a quella di Orazio), ma si tratta di presenza non trascurabile."

pace, and much too deep in themselves. Some readers give up. Others choose the ones they think matter most and put their focus there. And that is the way it has to be (and exactly the way I will proceed in the pages that follow).[42] The chance of any of his poem's being micro-managed in the same way and meaning precisely the same thing to any two given readers is, in the end, infinitesimally small. For reading Persius is a process that involves imposing limits (*fines*) at a frantic pace, aggressively stopping him from meaning too much. And that is why Persius' book, the song he brings to the shrine and calls *nostrum* "our own," meaning "his own," in another sense really is "our own." It is a book made by us, "our own" in being defined by each reader's personalized mechanisms of "defining" (lit. "setting *fines*, limits") and making sense of his unmanageable pile.

And that is how I choose to let him get away with claiming that these most crow-like of poems really are the unique, self-made artifact that he says they are. As Hooley points out, even the unruly and untraceable *semipaganus* has nothing in it that is explicitly extrapoetical.[43] In fact, the term is most maddening because it seems almost to belong, reminding us, perhaps, of another halfway poet, Ennius, a *semigraecus*,[44] or of Virgil in a rustic mode; Hesiod on Helicon (ἄγραυλος "bumpkin"), Ovid in exile; or any of more than two dozen precedents traced out in the commentaries that have been thought to qualify as possibly relevant.[45] But despite bringing with it all sorts of traditional sounds, the word never quite manages to match up and plunk in with tradition. And that is its biting irony: this most tradition-defiant word sends us racing back to our books, into the given language of tradition to

---

[42] The problem is inescapable; cf. Henderson (1992) 137: "theories of reading do but *stage* readings."

[43] Hooley (1997) 234–35.

[44] This Ennian connection, generally unnoticed, may extend from, and play upon, the allusion to Ennius' dream in the Prologue's opening lines. For Ennius as *semigraecus*, see Suet. *Gram.* 1.

[45] Ancient scholiasts posited a (strained) etymological derivation of *paganus* from Gk. πηγή ("spring"). *Pega*sus, in the poem's last line, was also (more reasonably) derived from πηγή. The connection has been generally overlooked by commentators. The "harsh joining" that occurs by placing *semipaganus* (in its watery sense) mid-way between references to the poets' inspirational spring may thus be thought to fill in some of the term's missing sense. P. is a "half-drinker," "half-inspired," neither here nor there (or is he drinking from a common country well rather than a running spring, lofty and remote?). For the ancient Latin etymologies of *paganus* and *Pegasus*, see Maltby (1991) 441 and 460.

come to terms with its being non-traditional. Tradition, in the end, is the place from which the word derives its sense, for it is only through tradition, not detached from it, that it has any chance of becoming something the poet can call "his own." So there is a stunning irony in the Prologue's one quiet moment, in that scene of the poet's offering his humble gift to the *uates'* rites. It shows that, despite all claims to being dead set against the same old thing, this poet is deeply reverent of dead poets and their ivy-encrusted images. He is, at least half-way (*semi*-paganus), one of them.[46]

FAKING IT IN NERO'S ORGASMATRON: PERSIUS I AND THE DEATH OF CRITICISM

The poet wastes no time in reaching a fever-pitch of disbelief and disgust. The first line of his first hexameter poem breaks out with: *o curas hominum! o quantum est in rebus inane* ("Good god! The things human beings obsess over! Inside all their affairs, so much nothing!" P. 1.1). No time for the usual build-up. This is an emergency! Pre-saturated, and determined to take no more, the poet cuts straight to the strains of a fuming peroration. So, for the moment, we are forced to go along with him, to take up his cause, equally pre-disgusted, without yet knowing what it is that has put us over the edge. Still, this is disgust that comes in a familiar package, in language that pushes us to frame our anger in certain, well-remembered ways. The scholiasts tell us that in the poem's first two lines, one "verse" has been lifted, perhaps word for word, from Lucilius' first book. To *quis leget haec* ("who will read these things?") in line 2 they append the following note:

hunc uersum de Lucilii primo transtulit et humanae uitae uitia increpans ab admiratione incipit.

He has brought this verse over from Lucilius' first book, and he begins by railing in amazement against vices of human life.

---

[46] Hooley (1997) 197–8: "He bears (*adfero*) given language into a new context, but as that context is this corrupt world, he must redeem it, that is, bring it back again *ad sacra vatum*. He places his words on the altar of poetry and thereby asserts that they are more than belly-prompted cawings of the moderns." *Adfero*, the bearing/offering word of line 7, is the word of choice for hosts "serving up" foods to their guests. What P. "offers" the gods, then, is his *lanx satura*, the feast (or second-rate famine) he serves to us.

They do not specify what "verse" they have in mind, since that would have been obvious to their ancient readers. But it makes sense to think they mean the whole of line 1, since that is where Persius "begins" (*incipit*) and, between the two lines in question, it is the only one that "rails against vice" as the scholiasts specify. So most scholars agree that the poem's first line either recalls, or specifically quotes, similar expressions of disgust in Lucilius' first book. That book opens with the gods meeting in consultation, the famous *concilium deorum* scene that, according to Servius, stands behind the quasi-legal consultation of the gods at *Aeneid* 10.1–117.[47] One of several fragments we have from the opening scene of Lucilius' first book is Lucil. fr. 5W: *consilium summis **hominum de rebus** habebant* ("they were holding a summit over the highest affairs of men"), so it seems likely that somewhere in close proximity to this line the initial outburst of P. 1.1 lived its earlier, Lucilian life. There one of the gods looks down from a heavenly perch and lets out with *o curas **hominum!** o quantum est **in rebus** inane!*

Knowing that these words stem from the *concilium deorum* scene of Lucilius' first book helps us make something of the surprising outburst of P. 1.1. For we recall that, in Lucilius' case, the gods' disgust has to do with Rome's second-century growing pains: enormous tides of wealth washed into the city with each new foreign conquest, and with that wealth came certain passions for exotic goods and fashions, especially for all things Greek.[48] These enthusiasms, Lucilius tells us, had Romans wearing underwear from Lydia (Lucil. fr. 12W), and racing to buy up *psilae atque amphitapi uillis ingentibus molles* ("ψιλαί [covers] and soft, deep-piled ἀμφίταποι [cushions]" Lucil. fr. 13W), gorgeous, Greek-sounding luxuries. Home-born Romans became unbearable snobs and quasi-Greeks. They took to calling *pedes lecti* ("bed-feet") κλινόποδες, and everyday *lucernae* ("lamps") λύχνοι (Lucil. frr. 15–16W). According to the poem, the chief offender in all this was L. Cornelius Lentulus Lupus, the crooked judge whose death is the cause of the gods' gathering, and whose post mortem trial, like that of Claudius in the *Apocolocyntosis*, is their first order of business. At Lucil.

---

[47] Serv. *A.* 10.104: *totus hic locus de primo Lucilii translatus est libro, ubi inducuntur dii habere concilium et agere primo de interitu Lupi cuiusdam ducis in republica, postea sententias dicere.*

[48] For the lines introducing an epic proem along the lines of Hom. *Od.* 1.32 ("Ὦ πόποι, οἷον δή νυ θεοὺς βροτοὶ αἰτιόωνται), see Marx (1904) vol. II, 6–7. For a thematic résumé of Lucilius' first book, see Krenkel (1970) vol. I, 63–4.

fr. 46W, by way of puns on *ius* ("laws/sauce") and *lupus* ("wolf-fish"), the poet suggests that the deceased has been undone by both his philhellenic obsessions and notorious crookedness: *occidunt, Lupe, saperdae te et iura siluri!* ("O Lupus/wolf-fish, those sauces/ laws of salt herring and sheatfish are the death of you!").

These broken pieces of Lucilius' first satire are the larger context of Lucilius' *o curas hominum!* and the first clue we have for coming to terms with the matching outburst of P. 1.1. So what are we to make of Persius' disgust? Do we assume, perhaps, that philhellenic obsessions and crooked judgments are again the issue to be taken up and the source of this poet's pre-saturation? That hunch, if we make it, proves not to be far off, since philhellenia, though of a very different sort, quickly emerges as the central issue in the poem. But I think there may be another point to Persius' Lucilian outburst as well. According to Harvey, who inspected the relevant manuscripts, the scholiasts' remark on the Lucilian background of Persius' first lines is attached not to line 1, where we might expect it, but to *quis leget haec* in line 2.[49] So, intending to or not, the scholiasts remind us that Lucilius started another first poem, the one that heads up his original first book (book 26, see above), with much the same question. And he put it in much the same language as Persius' *quis leget haec*, for first, or nearly first, among the numerous fragments of book 26 in all major editions of Lucilius since Marx are these lines (Lucil. frr. 632–4W):

⟨ab indoctissimis⟩
nec doctissimis ⟨legi me⟩; Man⟨ium Manil⟩ium
Persiumue **haec legere** nolo, Iunium Congum uolo.

... that I am read by the most unlettered nor by the most learned; I do not want Manius Manilius or Persius to read these things. I want Junius Congus (to read them).

Lucilius does not want Persius to read him. He means someone else, of course, an intensely learned and deep-reading C. Persius of his own day, but the irony is there to be felt all the same in *quis leget haec* of P. 1.2.[50] There we read Persius' reading of Lucilius, the proof that he did read him after all. Besides being funny, the irony may tell us something about the essentially non-Lucilian character

[49] See Harvey (1981) 13.
[50] Marx (1904) vol. II, 220–1: "Imitatus est Persius ubi aduersarius 'Quis leget haec?'"

of P.'s openly Lucilian project: Persius' readers now include the
likes of himself, the deep-reader Lucilius did not care to impress.

Perhaps that is the only audience left for satire in Persius' day.
To the Lucilian question "Who will read these things?" the answer
in line two is *nemo hercule* ("God, nobody!"). Thus, whereas Lucilius' first job was to limit his audience by locking out the extremes
of top and bottom, the oversophisticated and the idiot, Persius'
first job is to admit that he has no audience at all. No one, he
is sure, will listen. Or at best he might attract a listener or two. "A
shameful and deplorable thing" laments his interlocutor in line 3.
But the poet thinks otherwise (P. 1.3–7):

> quare?
> ne mihi Polydamas et Troiades Labeonem
> praetulerint? nugae. non, si quid turbida Roma
> eleuet, accedas examenue improbum in illa
> castiges trutina nec te quaesiueris extra.

How come? (Think I care) that all those Polydamases and Women of
Troy might put Labeo ahead of me? Piffle! If scatter-brained Rome
should weigh something up and find it too light, you shouldn't join in
(the general disdain) or attempt to adjust the balance-arm on a morally
lopsided scale like that! No, you should not look to find yourself anywhere out there!

No one will listen. Why? Rome's critical scales are out of balance,
and the latest of her addle-brained passions lies hotly with Labeo.
The scholiasts tell us that Labeo wrote word-for-word Latin translations of Homer's *Iliad* and *Odyssey*.[51] They assure us that they
were exceptionally bad, and they even quote an infelicitous line to
prove it.[52] But is that really the point Persius is making, that Labeo
is a hack-translator? Is that all we are to make of P.'s positioning
him so prominently as the first of very few named targets? Trans-
lating Homer, even ineptly, seems harmless enough. But the problem pinpointed here, I contend, goes much deeper than Rome's
adoration of one man's translations, however excellent or ridiculous they may have been – we can never really know. The problem, in this poet's view, has to do with Rome's Trojanification, her
passion for all things Iliadic that converts Roman enthusiasts into

---

[51] On Labeo, see Marx, *RE* ii.2254.45.
[52] Just how bad is it? Labeo, *Poet.* 1: *crudum manduces Priamum Priamique pisinnos.*

so many Polydamases (hinting at *poly* "many" + Dama, a common slave name?) and Trojan Women, sniping and anti-heroic critics drawn straight from the pages of Homer's *Iliad*.[53] In other words, not the deplorable state of poetry generally, but the deplorable state of criticism that is, at the same time, the deplorable state of Rome. Rampant, popular enthusiasms, in the world painted here, are passed off as the crucial standard of judgment. The critical scale is broken and beyond repair.

Rome, in the jaded view of this poet, has been utterly Trojanified. No real Romans left, only Polydamases and Trojan Women. As in Lucilius book 1, *Romanitas* is dead. But if that is the problem the poem sets for itself, Labeo, a minor player in a major trend, can hardly be held completely responsible. A quick look at the literary record of the fifties and sixties shows that his Latin translations are just a small part of a much bigger crush of enthusiasm for all things Iliadic. For example, the Latin epitome known as the *Ilias Latina* comes from this period, evincing a love of, and perhaps a burgeoning market for, not only Homer generally, but of Homer summarized and made accessible in Latin. Those truncated Iliadic sounds were playing in Rome as well. Lucan wrote an *Iliacon* in his youth, a poem that perhaps figures in the writing of Petronius' mock epic, with a (parodically) corresponding name, the *Satyricon*. The latter work includes a "Sack of Troy" parody in iambic senarii, a poem so bad within the fiction of the *Satyricon* that passersby begin hurling rocks at Eumolpus before he finishes reciting it. The poem is sometimes assumed to have Lucan as its target, but other likely candidates include Lucan's uncle, Seneca, whose tragedies often treat Trojan themes in iambic senarii, and, more obviously, Nero himself.[54]

If anyone had a driving interest in Trojan themes and ways of getting others to share those enthusiasms, it was Nero. Miriam Griffin notes that "Nero's interest in sympathetic treatment of

---

[53] Harvey (1981) 14: "*Polydamas et Troiades* represent unfavourable public opinion. The allusion is to two famous Homeric lines, *Iliad*, xxii.100 ... and 105 ... which refer to fear of public censure."

[54] Sullivan (1985) 175–6: "The *Troiae Halosis* (*Sat.* 89) calls for a similar explanation. The most likely purpose of Petronius' poem was to parody Seneca's tragic style, and vv. 406–57 of Seneca's *Agamemnon* may be recommended for comparison ... Nor should it be forgotten that Nero was especially interested in dramatic recitation and performances."

Troy goes back to his successful speech on behalf of the city in 53."[55] It predates his accession, in other words, and may have even played some necessary rhetorical role in securing it. Tacitus tells us that that advocacy of 53, permanently exempting the city of Troy from Roman taxation, Nero based not on any pressing political concern or recent injustice to the people of the region, but on the mythical tradition.[56] That, it seems, is where the injustice was felt and a case contrived. Those youthful efforts would soon be extolled in song by Calpurnius in his first Eclogue.[57] Later, both the act exempting Troy and the eclogue praising the act are searingly parodied in lines 38–41 of the first Einsiedeln Eclogue.[58] There the poet tells the personified Troy that she should be grateful for her destruction. It was completely worth the price of her agony and disgrace because it gave her *alumnus* ("protégé"), Nero, the chance to raise her from the dust.[59]

Nero's youthful speech figures in the first Einsiedeln Eclogue as a source of parody. But the more obvious target it takes aim at is his well-known *Troica* ("Trojanic Tales"), a Callimachean epic that has Homer's musician-weakling, Paris, in the role of Troy's protector and tragic champion.[60] The poem is mercilessly strafed with praise at lines 45–9 of the first Einsiedeln Eclogue, in a scene that features the unlikely poetic triad of Homer, Virgil, and Nero, imagined here as an ascending tricolon:

> ergo ut diuinis impleuit uocibus aures,
> candida flauenti discinxit tempora uitta
> Caesareumque caput merito uelauit amictu.
> haud procul Iliaco quondam non segnior ore
> stabat et ipsa suas delebat Mantua cartas.

---

[55] Griffin (1984) 151.

[56] Tac. *Ann.* 12.58.

[57] Calp. *Ecl.* 1.42–5.

[58] Sullivan (1985) 58–9 posits a strong connection between these lines and the advocacy of 53.

[59] Here *alumnus* ("protégé") perhaps pokes fun at Nero's claim to have been descended from Aeneas (Calp. *Ecl.* 1.44–5 *alma Themis posito iuuenemque beata sequuntur | saecula, maternis causam qui uicit Iulis*). Cf. Sullivan (1985) 56: "Echoes and allusions to Calpurnius' œuvre make clear the author's intention, which is to cast doubt on the propaganda themes sounded by Calpurnius, the return of the Golden Age with peace, justice, and prosperity established again on earth under Nero-Apollo."

[60] Serv. *A.* 5.370: *sane hic Paris secundum Troica Neronis fortissimus fuit, adeo ut in Troiae agonali certamine superaret omnes, ipsum etiam Hectorem.* In defeating all other contenders in the poem's athletic contests, it is easy to see how Nero's playboy-musician, Paris, will have reminded some in his audience of the emperor himself.

Therefore once [Nero] filled his ears with his divine voice, [Homer] loosened the golden wreath from his white temples and covered the head of Caesar with that well deserved covering. And close by the Mantuan [Virgil]. He, at one time, no less vivid in singing Ilium's song, stood there erasing his pages with his own hands.

Nero sings his song, and the immortals give up: Homer hands over his crown. Virgil destroys his *Aeneid*. All the great Trojan epics of the past, it seems, have now been eclipsed by Nero's *Troica*.

Absurd. Too outrageous, I think, ever to have been heard as uncomplicated, un-self-defeating praise.[61] The scene takes aim not only at Nero, the writer of the only epic story that counted anymore, but at all the unctuous effusions of poets since Calpurnius who sought to score points with him by praising his poetic skills in terms that bordered on being just as ludicrous as these. Dio informs us that Nero recited from his *Troica* at the second *Neronia* ("Festival of Nero") of 65, the year after the great fire.[62] That performance may have been judged untimely by some, depending especially on what Nero chose to read, and it may have given rise to rumours, now famous, that the emperor sang his "Capture of Troy" while watching Rome burn. Those rumours, hostile and unreliable as they are, dwell on the problem of Rome's Trojanification under Nero, his converting the city into a foreign site to be plundered and destroyed. If the Einsiedeln Eclogues do, in fact, date to late 64 or 65, as Sullivan and others have suggested, that means that rumors of Nero's fiddling were circulating almost immediately after the fire and that, despite being clearly hostile and "unreliable," they need to be taken seriously as a very real and accurate read on the kind of hostile rhetoric that flared up as a result of that disaster.[63]

But the seeds for that story seem to have been planted well before the fire: Trojanification, the central metaphor that plays in rumors of Nero's fiddling, plays already in Persius. He alerts us

---

[61] Cf. Korzeniewski (1971) 111: "Zwar ist es ein Topos der αὔξησις, einen Dichter über Vergil zu erheben; aber darf man unserem Dichter soviel an hündischer κολακεία zutrauen, dass er das in der Form *et ipsa suas delebat Mantua cartas* ausdrückt, selbst wenn man die Nachricht von des Dichters letztem Willen ... für glaubhaft hält? Wird man nicht vielmehr an den Spott des Persius (1, 96ff.) über die Leute erinnert, die die minderwertige moderne Poesie der Äneis vorziehen? Wird das Lob zu dick aufgetragen so wirkt es komisch. Hier will es so wirken."

[62] Dio 62.29.1.

[63] On the date of the *Einsiedeln Eclogues*, see Korzeniewski (1971) 4–5; and Sullivan (1985) 57.

to the problem in the opening lines of his first hexameter poem. Labeo's tight Latin translations of the *Iliad* and *Odyssey*, he tells us, are all the rage, a quick and easy Homeric fix for upwardly mobile Romans who have fallen behind in their Greek; all those "*Polydamases*" and "Trojan Women" who cannot manage their Homer in the original. For them, Labeo's work is just the thing.[64] It does not generate the frenzy, it feeds it. Labeo is a follower and a relative nobody, intent on cashing in on a hot, new trend. And so, with amazing efficiency, in the first few lines of P. 1 we have re-entered the world of the Prologue. Again we have the lonely poet, set against the driving literary obsessions of his day. And again a point is made about the need to stay out of step and to take one's cues from inside oneself rather than from anything *extra* ("out there"). For the weighing-scale used by Rome's trend-seekers to size up what counts or does not count as poetry is completely mis-aligned. It cannot be repaired or recalibrated to give anything like a true measure of what has value and what does not. That, the poet asserts, is something best determined from inside ourselves, from an internal scale of measurement that does not misread or lie. His advice *nec te quaesiueris extra* ("and don't go looking for yourself out there") repackages the Greek maxim "know thyself." Another way of saying *nec quaesiueris* **extra te** ("don't go looking for yourself **outside yourself**").

But why is the scale of popular enthusiasm so broken and utterly useless? The poet starts to tell us in line 8, only to break off in mid-sentence: *nam Romae quis non – a, si fas dicere* ("for at Rome who is not – god, if only I could say it!"). He has something scandalous to say, but he cannot bring himself to say it. Not quite, anyway. Scholars have long noted the connection between this line and the "private joke" of line 121: *auriculas asini* **quis non** *habet?* ("Who doesn't have ass's ears?"). What they have not seen is that the poet lets half his secret slip already in line 8: the breakaway phrase **a, si** *fas dicere* has in it half the ass of **asini** *quis non habet*. Read for that nuance, line 8 has a sense resembling: "for at Rome who is not an ... as(s) if I could actually say it!" But he has

---

[64] Polydamas and his supporting chorus of Trojan women have their anti-heroic desires met in Nero's telling of the tale. In Homer's *Iliad* Polydamas and the Trojan Women beg Hector to stay behind the walls of Troy and refuse to fight. In Nero's version of the tale, something like that happens, as Hector's fighting is displaced by the questionable "heroism" of Paris.

said it. The line both lets out the secret, and keeps it. For the moment, it has to be clipped back, and we know that we are being cheated. But even in cheating, Persius challenges us to read deeply, to find meaning hidden inside his words, half-expressed, less in what we read, than in the ways of our reading.

Instead of letting out his secret, the poet paints a picture of what makes him let out an irrepressible, balance-restoring laugh: seeing white-haired Romans in the role of staid, censorial critics, *cum sapimus patruos* ("when we get a taste for our chiding uncles").[65] Somehow that is at the heart of what he so desperately wants to tell us but cannot. So again the problem concerns not poetry generally, but criticism, the mechanisms of weighing and assigning value to poetry. He relates that the crucial standard of excellence is now vastness, and that the first prerequisite of successful writing is a good set of lungs (P. 1.13–14):

> scribimus inclusi, numeros ille, hic pede liber,
> grande aliquid quod pulmo animae praelargus anhelet.

Closed off [sc. "in our once open homes"] we write, this one in verse, that one in prose, something massive to keep an outsized lung panting for air.

In *scribimus inclusi* we hear the critic of Hor. *Ep.* 2.1.103–4, longing for the days long gone, when **reclusa** | *mane domo* ("with the house wide open at sunrise"), the Roman elite would receive their clients and deal with their concerns. Now, Horace says, that upright social scene is defunct. Young and old, clever and fool, all are frantically scribbling away. In the company of their fellow diners they rattle off any and all songs that happen to come into their heads: **scribimus indocti** *doctique poemata passim* ("learned and ignorant, here and there, we are all writing poems," 117).

Missing for both Horace and Persius are the deep learning and painstaking work required to produce poems of exceptional quality. The processes of good writing, they say, are in a shambles, with everyone claiming to be a poet, and every poet's poetry getting as much air time and applause as anyone else's. But whereas

---

[65] The poet's inability to contain his laughter is the first of many (often grotesque) physiological analogies for his activity as satirist. Bellandi (1988) 46 (esp. n. 47) connects the poet's "irrefrenabilità" to his natural manner of expression as *semipaganus*; cf. La Penna (1995) 285: "Il poeta è di umore tale che, anche se volesse, non potrebbe evitare di sghignazzare: è quasi una questione fisiologica."

Horace pictures his poets improvising at dinner-parties, Persius has them closed off by themselves, busy scribbling away at monster projects destined not for a smaller editorial screening, but for immediate public recitation. Thus, the editorial processes of *Ars* 385–90 are completely reversed:

> tu nihil inuita dices faciesue Minerua:
> id tibi iudicium est, ea mens. si quid tamen olim
> scripseris, in Maeci descendat iudicis aures
> et patris et nostras, nonumque prematur in annum
> membranis intus positis: delere licebit
> quod non edideris; nescit uox missa reuerti.

You will say or do nothing on your own without Minerva's help. That is your means of assessing, she your intelligence. Still, once you have finished writing something, let it sink into the ears of Maecius, the judge, and your father's ears, and my own. And keep it back, writing-skins tucked safely away, for nine years. It is easy to erase what you have not published. Once you have set it free, your voice hasn't a clue how to find its way home.

Not so the critical scene in Persius: no time for a smaller screening, let alone for Horace's nine-year moratorium. The process of editing, in his Rome, coincides with the poem's world premiere! For what poets write *inclusi* ("closed off") by themselves, neglecting the duties of an open home (*reclusa domo*), they take straight to the public: *scilicet haec* **populo** ... | *sede leges celsa* ("but of course you will read these things **in public**, perched on a lofty seat," P. 1. 15–17). The lines pay off the antithesis set up by *inclusi* ("closed off") in line 13. Even more, they answer the question of line 2, *quis* **leget haec**?, telling us that this, the stuff of everyone's frantic scribbling, is what Romans read instead of Persius: *scilicet* **haec** *populo* ... | *sede* **leges** *celsa*.

The first half of P. 1 says much less about the content of Rome's private scrawlings than it does about their performance. Put in Persius' terms, the emphasis is on **leges** *qua* critical/editorial act, rather than **haec**. Under the surface, the tenets of Horace's *Ars Poetica* and *Epistles* book 2 accumulate at a rapid pace, adding to the impression that this is a treatise on writing, Persius' Art of Poetry, as much as it is a parody of modern habits.[66] Sometimes memories of Horace are all we have to bridge our way over the

---

[66] Hooley (1997) thus studies the poem under the heading "The *Ars Poetica* of Persius."

fractured bits of Persius and hold him, awkwardly, together. For example, without those memories to help us fill in the open-ended *scribimus inclusi* ("closed off we write") we are lost, left to wonder what the drawback of writing "closed off" is, and how that problem relates to the broken bits of criticism that precede and follow. Memories of Horace tell us that this problem has to do not with the poet's being shut off from reality, or of his/her failing to get enough sun or inspirational air: it has to do with poetry's emerging in a *critical vacuum*. Poets invite no feedback, they consult no Maecius and make no revisions before staging the poem's world premiere. Through Horace, Persius holds together. As Hooley puts it: "What are we missing when we conceive of the poet, as we have, as a Stoic apologist or maker of bizarre metaphor ... of discomposed fragments of discourse, promising yet always deferring resolution, of, finally, exceedingly curious Latin? In a word, we are missing what lies between all these things. The almost invisible bridges of thought and idea – qualifications, hesitations, colorings, orientations, that provide larger continuities, the *conditions* of sense. I will contend that Persius's imitations of and allusions to Horace largely provide that continuum."[67]

Memories of the *Ars Poetica* and *Epistles* book 2, several dozen at least, bring an odd tension to P. 1. In those earlier works, the voice that speaks from the page fashions a calm, and mostly helpful critic. His message, frequently, has to do with fine-tuning popular enthusiasms and checking their extremes rather than with hurling them, one and all, into the trash. There is no overt antipathy in Horace to the idea that good poetry can, and often does, have a popular following, so he leaves the impression that his advice really can make a difference. His wry, yet hopeful, spirit is completely absent from Persius. Persius' didactic is devoid of hope. The voice he projects is that of a loner, profoundly alienated from his culture, addressing a world gone completely mad, with critical processes that do not take to minor adjustments, not even a complete overhaul. Criticism in Persius' world is completely dead. So what is the point of this remake of Horatian didactic if, as he explicitly asserts, none of it will be listened to?

Thus the tension between the speaker's despairing message and his didactic mode. The calm, confident voice of Horace,

---

[67] Hooley (1997) 22.

reconditioned by Persius, is no longer calm, and certainly not confident. Reinscribed by Persius, the voice is unstrung, cynical and dismayed. But those memories of Horace not only color our hearing of Persius, mapping out ways to make sense of him along Horatian lines (bridge-work), they also reconfigure cherished notions of Horace, coloring the way(s) we *hear him through Persius*. Heard through Persius, that once familiar and steady critical voice sounds feckless and passé, out of place in the strange new world of Persius' Rome. Horatian criticism is no longer enough. Thus, the poem's memories of Horace hover between reverent re-processing and parody, as the once sane and helpful critic is made to speak in uncharacteristic ways.

We see this, for example, in the pumped-up cynicism and gross physicality of the *scribimus inclusi* lines quoted above. Horace's problem with impromptu dinner-party musings gives way in Persius to a frantic, lung-busting obsession. We see the same transformation in the recitation scene of P. 1.15–23. These lines, though patterned after performance scenes at Hor. *Ars* 208–19 and 427–33, have none of the steadiness of the former critic's voice, nor the understated mode of his chiding. What we have instead is one of the most jarring and (metaphorically) pornographic scenes in all of Roman satire. Leading into it are these lines (P. 1.15–18):

> scilicet **haec** populo pexusque togaque recenti
> et natalicia tandem cum sardonyche albus
> sede **leges** celsa, liquido cum plasmate guttur
> mobile conlueris, patranti fractus ocello.

Sure, you will read **these things** [sc. "not mine"] in public, perched on a lofty seat, all combed and in a fresh white toga, flashing that gemstone you finally got for your birthday. Once you have given your throat a good falsetto rinse, the voice wavers, eye ejaculates.

Dan Hooley has shown that the passage draws on a comparatively bland scene at *Ars* 208–17 treating the lamentable new style of flute-playing. He points out that the emphasis there is on luxurious dress, and an increase in gestures and license.[68] Left in precisely those general terms, *licentia* ("license"), *motus* ("gesture"), and *luxuries* ("extravagance"), there is a remote quality to the lamenta-

---

[68] Hooley (1997) 40.

ble world Horace describes, and a sense of the speaker's steady control over it, that is completely absent from Persius' hard, physical remake. There the physical realities latent in Horace's abstractions are pulled out and painted in the most garish of colours. An ejaculating eye?! At *Ars* 428–30, the second passage layered into the remake, Horace stages the reaction of an *adsentator* ("flatterer") to the poetic performance of his rich friend:

> clamabit enim "pulchre, bene, recte",
> pallescet super his, etiam stillabit amicis
> ex oculis rorem, saliet, tundet pede terram.

He will cry out "Gorgeous!" "Well done!" "Yes!" He will grow faint over these things, and he will even drizzle a little dew from his friendly eyes. He will bolt upright and strike the ground with his foot.

The real actor, Horace points out, is not the performer, but the listener, a poor friend on the make. The scene bears an obvious similarity to the recitation scene of P. 1, especially to lines 19–23 where the satirist's gaze turns from the dandified reciter to the outlandish enthusiasm of his listeners. But whereas in Horace it is the grasping listener who "drizzles dew" from his eyes, pretending to be touched deeply by his friend's story, in Persius it is the reciter himself who breaks into tears in a moment of high, voice-quavering emotion.[69] The calculated feminizing of the performer's voice in that "falsetto rinse," seconded by *fractus* ("broken") in line 18, suggests that the poet has adjusted his voice to perform the part of a grief-stricken female.[70] That fits with the way poetic obsessions are cast elsewhere in the poem, since repeatedly in P. 1 the vilified theme of choice is the plight of an overwrought heroine, or of a castrated male, favorite themes of Catullus and Ovid.

But an ejaculating eye? The metaphor is so harsh and unlikely (the most extreme *iunctura acris* that I can cite) that commentators have refused even to consider it. They opt instead for the idea that the performer is winking, or casting a "lustful," even "orgasmic" glance (whatever that is), or being "broken" by someone else's. But as Kissell's thorough study of the verb *patrare* shows, the word

---

[69] Grammatically *patranti ocello* may refer to *someone else's* tears as well.

[70] On *fractus* ("broken") referring to "softened/effeminate" qualities of dress, gait, and voice, see *OLD frangere* 8, and *OLD fractus* 4; cf. Isid. *Orig.* 10.30 *inde ... blaesus, quia uerba frangit.*

refers to nothing as abstract as being generally "lustful" or "orgas-mic."[71] It refers to a sexual climax (thus the scholiasts' *rei ueneriae consummatio*). Not an orgasm generally, but an ejaculation (thus *patrare* etymologized as "fathering").[72] Thus the moment of climax in this performer's tear-jerking(-off) show, the point where he breaks into breathy, quavering tears, Persius figures as a climax of a very different kind. Horace's endearing "drizzling of dew" is remembered here, but in Persius it has been contorted and ugli-fied to express, and instil in us, an attitude of maximum disgust. Things now, for Persius, are far worse than anything Horace ever had to face. And so we are disgusted, too, not just at what we see played out before our eyes, but at Persius, for making us see it, and our steady old Horace, in that disgusting way.

Or are we turned on by this? Disgusted and turned on?[73] Commentators never opt for the notion of the ejaculating eye. Too disgusting, and terribly unlikely. But the meaning of *patrare* is not really in question, its metaphorical softening is.[74] And that is much harder to support when one considers that: (1) Horace painted a softer, but explicitly "teary" scene at *Ars* 428–30; (2) Persius was demonstrably fond of just this sort of "hard-joined" metaphor; (3) he actually carries through with the notion of "reci-tation as sexual penetration" in the lines that directly follow (no one denies this); and (4) Lucilius, in his sexually explicit eighth book, imagines the same metaphorical notion in reverse. At Lucil. fr. 335W he describes an ejaculating penis breaking into tears:

---

[71] See Kissel (1990) 137–8. Despite his own evidence, Kissel shies away from what I think is the obvious conclusion.

[72] Isid. *Orig.* 9.5.3: *pater autem dictus eo quod patratione peracta filium procreet*; cf. Porphyrion, who annotates the wet-dream sequence of Hor. *S.* 1.5.84, quite bluntly, with *super se ipsum patrasse*.

[73] Gunderson (2000) 19, on the built-in erotics of Roman oratory: "Oratory is saturated with problems of pleasure and desire felt between males. The good perfomance of the orator and the one towards which he is educated, is the enactment of the body of the good man as a socially desirable entity, an entity that gives pleasure specifically as a male and specifically to other males. . . . Rhetorical handbooks routinely inculcate an oratory that is erotic, yet in the course of so doing steer that Eros into such channels as are socially respectable. In other words, Freud's euphemised homosocial pleasures are actively pursued, and explicit homosexual ones are berated."

[74] Powell (1992) 154: "The phrase *patranti fractus ocello* hardly presents difficulty. *patrare* was the colloquial verb for sexual climax and it is unlikely that it had any other meaning in the ordinary Latin of Persius' time." But then he adds, "in Lee's phrase, the poet has an 'orgasmic eye'."

at laeua lacrimas muttoni absterget amica

But with his left-hand lover he wipes the tears from his cock.

The image does not take to being toned down. Still, I suspect, it is even more shocking in reverse, with an eye ejaculating. Persius turns up the volume even on the blaring tones of Lucilius.

Putting all this together, I maintain, not only involves Horace, it depends on him. For without memories of the *Ars Poetica* to guide our assembly, the poem's unlikely images and fractured train of thought remain just that: fractured and unlikely. Meaningless. Recently Thomas McLaughlin has argued that "the use of the figure makes us active participants in the meaning ... we have to compare the images, find the category they belong in ... and work out the analogy that makes the metaphor possible."[75] That is terrifically hard work in P.'s case because rarely do his metaphor's elements belong together in any obvious, or conventional way. The gap between them, the sheer distance that separates their semantic domains, is exceptionally large, so to find the common ground linking them is to solve the metaphor's very "hard" riddle: what is penis-like about this performer's eye? Trouble is, once we, "active participants in meaning," have located the shared category (liquid discharge), we are appalled at what we have been made to do and think. Thus, making sense of Persius is not just inordinately difficult, it is a test of one's willingness to see things in his grotesquely figured way.

What in Horace is a "clever" (*callida*) image of teary "dew," in Persius is a "harsh" (*acris*) metaphor that leaves us disgusted, but never to think of teary recitations in quite the same way. And so here we have a telling case-study in the ways of metaphors respectively "clever" and "harsh," Horatian and Persianic. Both poets

---

[75] McLaughlin (1990) 88; cf. Ricoeur (1991) 81: "the dynamics of metaphor consists in confusing the established logical boundaries for the sake of detecting new similarities which previous categorizations prevented our noticing. In other words, the power of metaphor would be to break through previous categorization and to establish new logical boundaries on the ruins of the preceding ones ... to grasp the kinship in any semantic field is the work of the metaphoric process at large." P.'s metaphors work very much "on the ruins" because they are so aggressively about the business of ruining established categories. La Penna (1995) 334–5 points out that Persius' metaphors are not terribly new in their components, but that: "audacia e novità consistono piuttosto nello spostare il termine reale di riferimento della metafora e specialmente nell'accorciare le distanza fra termine reale e immagine analogica."

have exceptional talents at putting together mismatched things, a penchant for metaphor that makes us actively imagine things in unaccustomed ways. But whereas Horace's images, at times, border on the risqué, Persius' have the potential to shake us to the core, to disorient and disgust. In Horace, his figures draw us into a metaphorical fun-house, with floors and mirrors askew to distort perspectives and make us see the world, and ourselves in that world, in curious new ways. That happens in Persius, too, with its images and objects all vaguely familiar from Horace. That familiarity tempts us to think that the game, and the point of our being here, is the same. But as we make our way through his fun-house with its wild distortions, we sense that the images around us are doubly warped, *acris* "hard" in the sense of their being exceptionally hard to make sense of. But as we peer into these images, pick them up and turn them this way and that, we soon see that they are not Horatian at all. We have been tricked. For once we actually see what it is we hold in our hands, we are startled, and our first instinct is to drop the object and run screaming from the room. This fun-house, we discover, is no fun at all. Its images, besides being "hard" to figure, are exceptionally "harsh," with tremendous power to unsettle. Nothing like Horace at all.

In the stark environs of P. 1, the teary recitation of a heroine's woes is an act of sexual penetration and climax. The *grande aliquid* ("some big thing") that the dandified performer pulls out for his birthday audience, panting all the while, is something clearly other than just his big poem.[76] And so it is no wonder that when he reaches his teary climax in line 18, the listeners respond in lines 19–21 by playing the part of the artfully screwed, acting out the pornographic role that the metaphor writes for them:

> tunc neque more probo uideas nec uoce serena
> ingentis trepidare Titos, cum carmina lumbum
> intrant et tremulo scalpuntur ubi intima uersu.

Then you can see strapping Tituses pulsate in an unseemly way, their voices unsteady, once the song sinks into their loins and their insides are stroked by (the performer's) throbbing. . . . *verse*!

The postponed *uersu* in line 21 delivers the punchline. If we dodged the metaphor in *patranti ocello* we cannot dodge it here: the

---

[76] On *anhelare* as sexual "panting," see Juv. 6.37.

poet pulls out his "big thing" (the pocket edition) and, in an amazing feat of folio-phallic dexterity, penetrates them all, artfully, and simultaneously. The unsteady shouts and quavering of the penetrated suggest that the performer is good at what he does, and that these "strapping Tituses" actually enjoy being performed on in this way. Their pleasurable writ(h)ing is the last pitiful remnant of "criticism" in Rome: according to the metaphor, this is now what it means to play the "severe old uncle" in Rome, and to give a poem its first critical hearing. The whole process amounts to so much mutually pleasurable stroking.[77]

But is it really as mutually satisfying as the audience lets on? We recall from the comparatively innocent version of the scene at Horace, *Ars* 428–30 that the eager critic in those lines is an *adsentator* ("flatterer") whose well-timed tears and cries of "Gorgeous!" are counterfeit to the core. The point is made clearly in the lines directly preceding (*Ars* 419–25):

> ut praeco, ad merces turbam qui cogit emendas
> adsentatores iubet ad lucrum ire poeta
> diues agris, diues positis in faenore nummis.
> si uero est unctum qui recte ponere possit
> et spondere leui pro paupere et eripere artis
> litibus implicitum, mirabor si sciet inter-
> noscere mendacem uerumque beatus amicum.

Like an auctioneer who coaxes a crowd to buy up merchandise, a poet who is rich in fields and has plenty of cash loaned out on interest urges flatterers to go after gain. Yet, if there is someone who knows how to spend his money aright and who pledges to pay for a man of slender means and cut him loose when he is enmeshed in a tightly knotted court case, I will be stunned if that rich fellow knows how to tell a liar from a true friend.

---

[77] For the public recitation as an editorial exercise, cf. Plin. *Ep.* 5.3.8–9 (trans. Radice, with my emphasis): "I have therefore two reasons for reading in public; the reader is made more keenly critical of his own work if he stands in some awe of his audience, and he has a kind of expert opinion to confirm his decision on any doubtful point. He receives suggestions from different members, and, failing this, *he can infer their various opinions from their expressions, glances, nods, applause, murmurs and silence*, signs which make clear the distinction between their critical judgement and polite assent." He makes clear in *Ep.* 7.17 that the public recitation comes rather late in the editorial process. First he makes his own correction, then has a small screening; he corrects, has another small screening, then *"finally I read the work to a larger audience."* For the problem of false exuberance at public recitations, cf. *Ep.* 5.12: "I invited some friends to hear me read a short speech which I am thinking of publishing, just enough of an audience to make me nervous, but not a large one, *as I wanted to hear the truth.*"

That makes us think twice about all the writhing and pleasurable moaning we see and hear in the remake of P. 1. Doubt is woven in as an intertextual question mark. Remembering Horace, we ask: do they really mean it? Or is theirs, too, a purchased, but stunningly performed, fake orgasm?[78] We note that the man who performs on the strapping elite of P. 1 resembles his Horatian counterpart in being noticeably well-heeled. That birthday sardonyx he flashes on his finger is suggestive of enormous wealth, the kind of wealth that impresses and makes panderers come out of the woodwork.[79] So do these "strapping Tituses" really enjoy getting penetrated, or are they just pretending, like the clever prostitute who assures her 2:30 appointment, "You're the best I've ever had. No, *really*, you are!"?

But that birthday ring and the performer's new, white toga may suggest something else as well, for the image has in it suggestions of this performer's "finally" coming of age (thus the mysterious *tandem* in line 16?). His *toga uirilis* is brand new (*toga recenti*, 15) making him shine noticeably white (*albus*, 16) because, sitting on stage, the performer dons it for the first time.[80] That means that the Roman elite, an established crowd of burly Tituses, are getting screwed by an upstart, and a mere ephebe. Perhaps. At the very least, this recitation is cast as having the basic trappings of a coming-of-age performance, a "first time" penetration that marks the performer as a "real man" or, more accurately, makes him into one.

But if we allow ourselves to think along these lines, and to make *that* the reason of the toga's being so new and white (and we do have to make something of its being new and white), other thoughts creep in. Once again, the background noise of Nero's image-making machine starts to be heard and to make an impact upon the way we read. For both Tacitus and Dio make Nero's coming-of-age celebration, the *Juvenalia* of late 59, a new low point in his ever plummeting moral career. Clearly, as a public-relations show, Nero intended it differently, perhaps as a first, aggressive effort to assert himself as *tandem* ("finally") his own man.

---

[78] Cf. Lucr. 4.1192 *nec mulier semper ficto suspirat amore | quae complexa uiri corpus cum corpore iungit.*

[79] On the high price of the sardonyx, see Kissel (1990) 133–4.

[80] On *albus* referring to the performer's toga, see Powell (1992) 153–4. For the wearing of one's "birthday white" in P., cf. 2.2, and esp. 5.33 *permisit sparsisse oculos iam candidus umbo.*

After five years under his mother's thumb, he makes a point of his no longer being mommy's little emperor. At last, she is out of the picture, and Nero intends in the *Juvenalia* of 59 to show a side of himself that has previously been held back, and that he will not allow to be held back any more. Seneca and Burrus try to dissuade him, the historians assert, but he carries through with the performance as planned.[81] Scandalous stories, true or not, are its lasting aftermath. And that not only in the historians, but in the hostile rhetoric of Nero's own day, the rhetoric that Persius certainly knew and may have done much to shape.

Both Tacitus and Dio put their accounts of the *Juvenalia* last among their entries for the year 59 CE. Nero's birthday was December 15, so it may be that the festival commemorating his first shaving coincided with the celebration of his twenty-second birthday.[82] But more importantly, both Tacitus and Dio tell us that the festival was a "first time" for Nero in quite another important respect: here, for the first time, Nero mounted a stage in a lyric performer's garb to play before his invited guests a piece called the "Attis" or "The Bacchantes" to the accompaniment of his lyre. That poem, under either name and sung in either voice, whether of a lamenting castrato or maenad, has plenty of room in it for falsetto histrionics, and the effeminate/feminizing nature of the song is clearly an issue for Dio in his account of its premiere performance.[83] J. P. Sullivan has argued that the poem is parodied several times in P. 1, most noticeably at 93–106, and there is good reason to suspect that he is right.[84] But, if we allow that its performance at the *Juvenalia* of 59, later a chestnut of finger-wagging historians, was already notorious in Persius' day and emerging

---

[81] According to Tac. *Ann.* 14.14, Nero defended his desire to perform in public at the *Juvenalia* of late 59 CE by claiming to follow the precedent of none other than Apollo himself: *enimuero cantus Apollini sacros, talique ornatu adstare non modo Graecis in urbibus sed Romana apud templa numen praecipuum et praescium. nec iam sisti poterat, cum Senecae ac Burro uisum ne utraque peruinceret alterum concedere.*

[82] But he explicitly did *not* don the *toga uirilis* on this occasion. That happens, for Tacitus, "prematurely" in 51 as part of Agrippina's dynastic scheme; cf. *Ann.* 12.41. Dio 62.20.1 reports that Nero donned the "outfit of a lyre-player" (τὴν κιθαρῳδικὴν σκευὴν ἐνδεδυκώς) at his inaugural performance.

[83] Dio 62.20.

[84] See Sullivan (1978). La Penna (1995) 286 is more circumspect: "Anche se interpreti insigni hanno sostenuto l'attribuzione ... e se l'ipotesi resta rispettabile, oggi, giustamente, quasi nessuno ci crede; ma certamente quegli *échantillons* rievocano l'ambiente letterario del tempo, caratterizzato da vizi che Nerone poeta e attore condivise e incoraggiò."

into the deplorable moral tale that the historians tell, then there is good reason to factor it into our reading of the recital scene that comes at the poem's beginning. Not that it has to be read there, but that, for some readers, it likely was.

Dio tells us that Nero's performance that day in late 59 CE had his entire audience of invited guests mixing laughter with tears. Burrus and Seneca, though horrified, stood by and motioned towards the audience with approving gestures. Both historians report that, to ensure success, Nero had stationed a guard of about five-thousand soldiers known as "the Augustans" in the audience hall. They had the job of extorting the desired response, so when they cheered, everyone else was expected to cheer along. Rome's "most illustrious men" (οἱ ἐπιφανεῖς), Dio says, were forced to call out during the performance, and to make a show of enthusiasm for Nero's new sounds.[85] They were heard to second the Augustans with shouts of "Hurrah for Caesar! He's Apollo! Augustus! A match for the Pythian himself! We swear by your own self, O Caesar, no one defeats you!"[86] Fed through the pipes of Persius' image-twisting machine, such sounds of breathless enthusiasm take on an unseemly, fake-orgasmic colour: "God, that was good, Caesar! No, *really*, I mean it! Best I ever had!"

Maybe. We can never really know what Persius fed into his machine to come up with the pornographic recitation of P. 1, or what historical moment, if any, he intends us to recall inside it. We can only remark that uncanny parallels exist between the scene he paints in P. 1 and the emerging story of (or "the fact of"?) Nero's coming-of-age spectacle of late 59. And we can speculate that some of Persius' first-century readers may have noticed these connections as well, especially since talk of Nero's Juvenalian "scandal," constructing it as scandal, was buzzing away already in the early sixties, when Persius drew his (version of "the"?) scene, and that such talk gained momentum with each new instalment of the emperor's Apollinine self-making. Thus, whether Persius intended them to read this way or not, some in his audience would have made the leap of seeing one story inside the other, "the fact"

---

[85] Tacitus, *Histories* 2.71 suggests that Vitellius was unusual in his admiration of Nero. Unlike the majority of "the better sort," he attended Nero's song-recitals out of admiration rather than compulsion.

[86] Dio 62.20.5.

of Nero's notorious performance inside Persius' ugly, but truth-telling, "fiction." They were ideologically ready, and generically set up (by P.'s naming these poems *Saturae*), to see it that way, "one good screw deserving another." And I doubt that Persius was the first to figure Nero's "first time" on a public stage as such.

But others, still basking in Nero's glow, will have been ideologically unprepared to see it that way, and/or to credit the figure with a knowing wink and a laugh. Still others would have rejected the connections on much more mundane, "philological" grounds, believing, perhaps, that connections noticed by themselves, rather than explicitly signalled in the text, amount to nothing when it comes to finding an author's "fixed" and "intended" meaning. And so, readers of this sort will have refused to credit these analogies as at all meaningful to their interpretive work. Thus the dynamic at work in this kind of "allusion(?!)" is much different than that of, say, the wry and openly parodic shakedown of Domitian's court in the "fish-summit" of Juvenal 4. Not a case of open parody, in other words, but of some readers, perhaps many, being unsettled by their own thoughts, rather certain that they have seen this scene played out before, but not quite sure whether they should credit their own analogical thoughts.[87] Should they really be seeing what they are seeing? Is it really "there," something "intended" and "built-in"? This is not parody *per se*, but the hint of parody, with effects that linger and probe into the politics of one's own reading and self-fashioning: what role do we play when we read? What hat do we wear? Compliant Neronian? Hermeneutical control freak and future president of the American Philological Association? Knowing insurgent? Perhaps the poet's every word "against Nero" struck a chord with us, sinking in by way of our expertly calibrated "little ears." Dare we express our wholehearted critical assent ("Yes, Persius! *Yes!!*")? Dare we give in to that (premature) desire to place Nero, and Persius, and ourselves, that smugly? As always in Persius, choosing a self is diagnostic, and the act of choosing exacts a price. The price of self-knowledge: *nec te quaesiueris extra.*

Persius puts a strange, pornographic spin on poetic recitations in the early stages of P. 1, and once that figure is in place, it is terribly hard to shake. The notions of performance as penetration,

---

[87] Martindale (1993) 14, on irony's "strictly unprovable" and unquantifiable character.

ears as loins, persist to the end of the poem, exerting an unseen force even on the famous secret of line 121: *auriculas asini quis non habet?* A dirty secret rendered dirtier by the figurative economy of the poem. If we imagine that the "ears as loins" metaphor has fallen away by this point in the poem, we should pay close attention to what gets built into these *auriculae* ("little ears") at lines 22–3, the lines that break away from the recitation scene analyzed above:

> tun, uetule, auriculis alienis colligis escas,
> auriculis quibus et dicas cute perditus "ohe"?

Are you [sc. when you debase yourself at recitations], pathetic old man, harvesting tidbits/bait[88] to plant in someone else's little-(asshole)-ears? And, what's more, the very little-(asshole)-ears to which you, now that your dick is practically worn off, should say "Hey, that's enough!"

The cantankerous *ohe* ("enough already") might also belong to the interlocutor as his way of cutting the poet off before he can let out with his scandalous secret (as above, *quis non − a si fas dicere*). In either case, the abrupt joining of this passage to the recitation scene that precedes has a decided effect on the way these "little ears" are construed: the "ears as loins" metaphor carries over, so that we hear the repeated *auriculis* of lines 22–3 not merely as a cute diminutive ("little-ears") but as a construct of *auris* ("ear") plus *culus* ("asshole").[89] This, yet another "hard-joining" that gets us to see something familiar in a new, and terribly harsh, light.[90]

---

[88] At Petr. 3.4 Agamemnon describes parasites wangling dinner from rich hosts by setting traps with "bait" (*esca*) for their patrons' ears.

[89] For *auriculis* as *auris + culus*, see Bramble (1974) 95. La Penna (1995) 286 n. 4 is extremely skeptical: "L'opera del Bramble è notevole per competenza ed acume; ma chi potrà credere, per es., che *innāta* (1, 25) alluda a *in năte* (p. 94) e *auricŭlis* (1, 23) ad *auri-cūlis* (p. 95)?"

[90] Seeing *auriculis* this way helps us make better sense of the notorious crux, *perditus cute*, of line 23. Some have thought that the *cutis* ("skin") here is the old man's "hide." And it makes some sense to think that a pathetic old man might have a worn-out hide. Vaguely funny, I suppose, but not relevant to the argument in any obvious way. But in the metaphorical language of the Priapea, satire, and epigram, *cutis* often refers to the "foreskin," and that works nicely here because that is precisely what this particular old man, a strapping Titus, regularly penetrated, might be imagined to have worn off through overuse; cf. Korzeniewski (1970) 394: "*Cutis* ist hier gleichbedeutend mit *praeputium* und somit als pars pro toto mit *penis*." For this sense of *cutis*, see *OLD recutitus*, Adams (1982) 73, and Bramble (1974) 89. Elsewhere Persius keys us to the "skin" for "writing-skin" metaphor under the terms *membrana* and *pellis*, never *cutis*. However, an early explicit reference to the metaphor in his third satire (P. 3.10 *bicolor membrana* "mottled skin") perhaps allows one to think metaphorically of his *cutis* later at P. 3.30 (*cute noui*) and 3.63 (*cutis aegra tumebit*). For the "skin" as "writing-skin" metaphor in P. 3, see Kissel (1990) 383–6, and Gowers (1994) 142–3.

THE SATIRIST-PHYSICIAN AND HIS OUT-OF-JOINT WORLD

The world of P. 1 is bloated with images of bodies in various states of distress. Parts and functions, we have seen, are harshly re-configured: eyes ejaculate, ears are penetrated sexually, even plugged with bits of "bait." As Emily Gowers, following a now "classic" article by Kenneth Reckford, has seen, "Persius' bizarre, conflated anatomizing suggests a world out of joint."[91] He takes a physician's eye-view towards his world. There he spies clear signs of imminent death. The reciter on stage has a bulging lung. His panting is out of control, and he has a terrible problem with his eye, signs of an internal disease that his gorgeous trappings cannot hide. Similarly one of the well-dressed "Sons of Romulus" in line 33, sporting the colors of Apollo's lover, Hyacinth, snorts *rancidulum quiddam* ("some rotten chunk") of lugubrious myth, the tale of some jilted Phyllis or Hypsipyle, straight from his nose.[92] How long, then, can a man in his condition be expected to live? Persius, looking past the gorgeous coverings, routinely uses his satiric arthroscope to peer straight into the muscle, veins, and heart of his society. And into himself, a Stoic physician set with healing himself, in poems that prod, and cauterize, and sting.[93] And the pre-scription he writes is gloomy and devoid of hope. By line 40 his interlocutor, awash in his barrage of cynicism and despair, accuses him of being too critical and scoffing. He insists that public ap-plause must count for something in reckoning a poem's worth. Can so many people who expect to draw at least a small modicum of pleasure from poetry, really be so hopelessly wrong?

The satirist counters by challenging the fellow to look past those pleasurable sounds of *euge!* ("Ooh, that's nice!") and *belle!* ("Gor-geous!") to the substance and middle of orgasmic criticism (49–51):

> nam "belle" hoc excute totum:
> quid non intus habet? non hic est Ilias Atti
> ebria ueratro?

Give that "gorgeous" of yours a thorough shake. What don't you find inside it? Isn't Attius' *Iliad* here, all drunk on hellebore?

---

[91] Gowers (1993a) 183, drawing on Reckford (1962).

[92] Does it matter that he should dress like Apollo's lover, in a culture that hails Nero as Rome's Apollo? Perhaps heard here again are suggestions of the elite's being happily buggered by Nero.

[93] For the background of the "philosopher as physician" analogy in Stoic thought, see Scivoletto (1956) 69.

The theme of line 1 is revisited. Human obsessions, when cracked open, spill out a great big nothing. Or the equivalent of nothing, in yet another overblown Trojan myth, still reeking of the cheap inspirational draught that inspired it. This, the poet says, is the kind of trash that gets gushed over in Rome because the hack-poet serves it up to his shivering listener with a nice bit of hot tripe, maybe tossing in a threadbare coat to help warm him to his cause. Coat and soup purchase the listener's good will, and make him disposed to react to his generous friend's song in a certain, overly enthusiastic way, prostitute fashion, with all of the requisite groans and sighs.[94] Saying what he really thinks, and what everyone knows to be the truth, is simply out of the question. *qui pote?* ("how can he?") the poet asks. He needs that coat. So the satirist steps in and says what no shivering client can say (P. 1.56–60):

> uis dicam? nugaris, cum tibi, calue,
> pinguis aqualiculus propenso sesquipede extet.
> o Iane, a tergo quem nulla ciconia pinsit
> nec manus auriculas imitari mobilis albas
> nec linguae quantum sitiat canis Apula tantae.

You want me to say it? You are a lightweight trifler, Baldy, even though your fat little water jug juts out with a foot-and-a-half droop. Oh for Janus, who has no stork bobbing behind his back, and no hand held up to look like floppy white ears, and no tongues big as when an Apulian dog pants with thirst!

This is the sound his society refuses to make: devastating, non-orgasmic, genuine. With *propenso* in line 57 he reverts to the metaphor of his culture's broken scale (above lines 6–7): what superficially seems terribly weighty, and thus valuable, by its outlandish "hang-down/propensity," in reality amounts to lightweight drivel. Behind the obese, hairless target of these lines is the panting "baldy" of Callimachus, *Iambs* 1.29.[95] His water-jug belly recalls *ampullas et sesquipedalia uerba* ("the flasks and foot-and-a-half words") of Horace, *Ars* 97. That image refers to inflated expressions and high, tragic bombast after the manner of Aristophanes' ληκύθιον ("little oil-jug"). Here, however, in another clear moment of Persius' intensification of Horace, *ampulla* becomes *aqualiculus*, perhaps to bring back the *culus* ("ass-hole") of *auriculis*,

---

[94] Bonner (1949) 79: "The adverb *belle* was extremely fashionable among declamatory audiences, both as a favourable criticism and as a delighted ejaculation."
[95] See above.

but certainly to cover the desired one and one-half (metrical) feet required of a sesquipedalian word (*a/qualicu/lus*). The image suggests that the target has taken his inspired, neoteric water-drinking a bit too far, sucking the little font dry, so that he appears just as bombastically "fat" and "bald" as any of the overblown targets of Callimachean/neoteric abuse. But no one tells him that. No one lets on that the man is a spectacular freak. Rather, his critics take to taunting him from behind, waggling their hands to resemble asses' ears.[96] Because of memories we cannot shake, his ears put the freak squarely in the orgasmatron as one of its players, a performer on its performers. Looking ahead to flop-eared Midas, remembered at the poem's end, we see that his ears figure him as a dullard critic as well, someone who loves to have his ears stroked with soft, flattering sounds rather than subjected to any hard or uneasy truth.[97]

The physician-poet has made his diagnosis: the man is sick, with tender ears, and a monstrous, foot-and-a-half bulge. But no one else tells him (P. 1.63–5):

> "quis populi sermo est?" quis enim nisi carmina molli
> nunc demum numero fluere, ut per leue seueros
> effundat iunctura unguis?

"What do the people say [about him]?" What else, but that songs now, at long last, flow smoothly, so that the joining, when tested by critical nails, spills them off over a surface perfectly smooth?

His poetic artifact, like his hairless head, is so smooth that no amount of testing can detect a gap in the *iunctura* ("joining"). The metaphor, well attested in rhetorical theories of "arrangement" (Gk. σύνθεσις = variously Lat. *compositio*, *collocatio*, or *iunctura*), comes from marble-working, the joining of one piece of a statue to another, arms to torso, neck to head, in a way that defies detection.[98] Thus, what Persius has presented to us as the broken,

---

[96] Cf. Call. *Aetia* 1.fr.1.29–32 Peiffer, where Callimachus figures the Telchines as braying asses.
[97] On *auriculae* as receptacles of flattery, cf. Hor. *S.* 2.5.32–3 *gaudent praenomine molles/auriculae*. Reckford (1962) remains a fundamental study of P.'s metaphorical imagery.
[98] As a common compositional metaphor, cf. Quint. *Inst.* 7 pr.2, and D.H. *Comp.* 25. On Stoic theory in the latter, see Freudenburg (1993) 132–5. Cf. also Hor. *Ars* 295–301 where the crazed poet's total neglect of *ars* in favor of *ingenium* is symbolized by his shaggy appearance. He refuses to trim his nails or to submit his head to a barber (thus his antitype in the *calue* "baldy" of P. 1.56?). The unkempt compositional style he embodies, is, in essence, Persius' rumpled artifact. The *Ars* itself has built into it centrally the idea of self as artifact, i.e. poetic deportment as key to social identity; see Oliensis (1998a) 206–15.

disjointed body of modern poetry, in the (fake-) orgasmic telling of the common crowd ranks as perfectly smooth. It has reached the superordinate state of glossy perfection that elsewhere belongs only to the Stoic *sapiens*. The rare *per leue* in line 64 recalls Davus' words to Horace at *S.* 2.7.83–7:[99]

"The wise man [is free] who rules over himself … is entirely within himself, smooth and round, so that nothing from outside can cling to his polished surface (*per leue*)."

Nails slide off the slippery poetic artifact like troubles off a Stoic sage. Like the cosmos itself, and the Stoic god, the sage is himself perfectly rounded, smooth, and impenetrable (not an orifice in sight). That is how perfect poetry is "now, at last" under Nero.[100] For his enamoured *populus*, all absolutely beyond criticism.

So the satirist steps in, unshaven, and with jagged, un-trimmed nails, and he criticizes, with poems that give no pleasure (except to Flaccus' knowing few) because they are an expression of himself, harshly joined, gaping, and offensive. "Pleasure" (*delectare*), as Franco Bellandi has expertly shown, is never the point of Stoic didactic.[101] Nor is it a goal to be sought by the Stoic *sapiens*. Thus, what is delivered to Persius as seamless, quasi-Stoical perfection he probes with a harsh critical nail. And where no one else has detected cracks, he finds them, both in Nero, and, more directly, in himself, a rock-hard Stoic, quasi-perfected.[102] These surfaces he pries open with his satiric toolkit to deliver the artifact back to us hideous and disjointed. In these poems, we see Nero's world as we have never seen it before. The glistening Helio-Apollo of the Palatine is mottled and flabby, sick to the core, besides sporting a ridiculous set of floppy ears. Like Persius' own (A. Persius *Flaccus*).

This is the work of P. 1: to pry into the smooth surfaces of self-assured societies and selves. To "shake out" their flattering sounds and to expose the empty and/or diseased core inside every *euge!*

---

[99] Kissel (1990) 194 is understandably stunned by the connection: "die Formulierung selbst is Hor. sat. 2,7,87 *externi ne quid valeat per leve* (an der gleichen Verstelle!) *morari* entlehnt."
[100] For *leuis* as compositional metaphor, cf. Cic. *De Orat.* 3.171 *quae* [sc. *uerborum collocatio*] *iunctam orationem efficit, quae cohaerentem, quae leuem, quae aequabiliter fluentem.*
[101] Bellandi (1988) 34–8 connects P.'s many physiological and medicinal metaphors to Stoic theories of poetry found in Cleanthes and Seneca. He has made an excellent case for the Stoics' categorical exclusion of "pleasure" (*delectare*) from poetry, and for their privileging "instruction" (*docere*) above all else.
[102] Henderson (1992) demonstrates that to see Persius as a perfected Stoic is to stick to his surface, and to miss the crucial point of his poems' self-introspective force.

and *belle!* He asks, what do they really consist of? At lines 85–91 Persius tells us that even the lawcourts have been infected. Hearing Pedio's clever antithesis a fan calls out *bellum hoc* ("That's gorgeous!"). To which the poet: *hoc bellum? an, Romule, ceues?* ("You mean "gorgeous!" Sir Romulus, or are you just enjoying getting reamed?"). That is, is "gorgeous" your heartfelt critical review, or yet another orgasmic "Yes! yes!!"?[103] The poet goes on to sample a number of modern epic's teary complaints in lines 92–106 before moving on to the poem's famous conclusion. His complaint is, by now, perfectly familiar: modern epic, he says, is awash in tears of overdone emotion, nearly drowned by the froth that comes with trying to pronounce so many easy-gliding "liquids" (l, m, n, r) in rapid succession.[104] Such an exaggerated compositional technique makes Nero's *Attis* nothing more than "spit" and insubstantial "cork."[105] Meaningless, yes. But, in his world, judged by its superficially fixated rules, defiant of critical nails.

But this is precisely what sounded so perfect and unassailable to the deluded *populus* of line 63: liquids lubricating, spilling critical nails from the surface. The interlocutor, clearly irritated, asks (P. 1.107–9): "But what's the point of rasping tender ears with biting truth? Watch out that the thresholds of the the powerful don't grow cold towards you. Heard there, the dog's snooty sn**arrrr***l*." The liquid *r* freezes into a gruff, Lucilian growl.[106] Say nothing offensive to men in power, he warns. So the poet responds with some orgasmic sarcasm of his own (P. 1.111–14):

> nil moror. euge omnes, omnes bene, mirae eritis res.
> hoc iuuat? "hic" inquis "ueto quisquam faxit oletum."
> pinge duos anguis: "pueri, sacer est locus, extra
> meiite." discedo.

---

[103] The verb *ceuere* ("to move the haunches in a lewd manner") matches movement to sound. It suggests that the hearer rhythmically writhes, as if in the heat of passion, penetrated, and enjoying it. And knowing the metaphor is there puts a fairly dirty spin on what follows in lines 88–91, esp. *me incuruasse* ("bend me over").

[104] The modernist compositional affectations of lines 99–102 also include a strong preference for patterned interlacings of nouns and adjectives, and carefully rhymed line-endings that feature repeated "booming" effects (*cornua bombis ... ablatura superbo ... flexura corymbis*).

[105] The scholiasts attribute the quoted lines (99–102) to Nero: *hi sunt uersus Neronis et huic sunt compositi*. Opinions are divided as to whether the scholiasts are right. Most recently, Sullivan (1978) 162 has argued that "the probability that they are really by Nero is higher than modern critics allow."

[106] On *r* as the dog's letter (*cacosyntheton atque canina*), see Lucilius frr. 389–92W.

OK, then: you're all "gorgeous!" "Good stroke" one and all! Is that all right? "Nobody make a stink here!" you say. Then paint two snakes: "Boys, this is a holy precinct. Piss outside!" I give up.

The message is clear: the orgasmatron is a happy place, where poets put their critical pen(i)s to its other, pleasurable use, and only that! However strong and "natural" the urge, the satirist must keep his bile to himself.[107] The injunction "piss outside" (*extra meiite*) reverses the message of line 7, *nec ... quaesiueris extra* ("don't search on the outside"). It is less an order to "write no satire at all" than to "keep to the surface of things." Do not probe within, to the inner sanctum of culture and self. Past the bubble's surface, only trouble. Penetrate there and the bubble pops. Snarling hounds are loosed.

Then what is he, a satirist, generically sworn to expose and unsettle, supposed to do? He complains (P. 1.114–19):

> secuit Lucilius urbem
> te Lupe, te Muci, et genuinum fregit in illis.
> omne uafer uitium ridenti Flaccus amico
> tangit et admissus circum praecordia ludit,
> callidus excusso populum suspendere naso.
> me muttire nefas? nec clam? nec cum scrobe? nusquam?

Lucilius lashed at the city, at you, Lupus, and you, Mucius. The targets he cracked a back tooth on were the likes of these! Flaccus applies an expert's soft "touch" to his laughing friend's every vice and, once let inside, he jibes close to the heart. He is an old hand at suspending the crowd from his well-blown nose. But, for me, the law says no mumbling? Not in private? Not even in a hole? Nowhere at all!?

In the movement from Lucilius, to Horace, to Persius, we feel the ever-tightening turn of Rome's totalitarian pipewrench. Lucilius, as this story puts it, says whatever he wants. He lashes at the entire city (*urbem*) with an inborn, "genuine" tooth, while Horace shares a laugh with a single, anonymous friend (*amico*).[108] Lucilius' targets include the likes of Lupus and Mucius, two prominent members of

---

[107] The lines express a natural "physiological" theory of satire, with the satirist's disposition a condition of his balance of "humors." See Bellandi (1988) 46, n. 47.

[108] With the singular *amico*, P. signals the importance of Horace's other *Sermones*, his *Epistles* (each poem addressed to a single, gently chided friend), to his own satiric enterprise. The forms *genuinus* ("molar" from *gena* "jaw") and *genuinus* ("inborn," "genuine") are indistinguishable.

the anti-Scipionic elite of his day.[109] They are named here because Lucilius named them *nominatim* ("by name"). Not so Horace. He "touches" vice rather than bites, and his friend, the target of his satire, laughs along at the joke. No names are mentioned, and no pain is inflicted. But even so, Persius makes clear that there is a hidden, penetrating edge to what Horace says: vices are touched, and the friend laughs. No hard tooth in that. But the joke chafes, and it gradually makes its way inside. Once "let in," the satirist's words penetrate to the heart, and that is something that Lucilian satire, however hard it may bite, cannot do.[110] His words inflict pain, like Persius' own, but they get just past the skin.[111] The tooth cracks when it hits bone. What *Flaccus* "flabby" has that Lucilius, for Persius, does not, is a technique that keeps listeners "suspended" from his nose. The metaphor derives from Horace's description of Balatro, the ironist of *S.* 2.8, whose words to Nasidienus hover between encouragement and abuse.[112] His is not an open attack. Rather, his words are "poised" and carefully "weighed" to suggest the well-intentioned chiding of friend to friend.

But where does that leave Persius? Rome now, he says, is off-limits for censure of either kind, whether hard Lucilian or flaccid Horatian. And that is not just because uttered abuse is danger-ous and restricted. That is not the problem put to us here at all. Rather, he says, Rome suffers from the grand delusion that she has

[109] On Lupus, see above chapter 1. Scholars have long been divided over the second name, most taking it to refer to P. Mucius Scaevola (praetor 136, consul 133 BCE), some to Q. Mucius Scaevola (praetor 120, consul 117). Though the former was the more promi-nent of the two, and known as a leader of an anti-Scipionic faction in the Senate (Cic. *Rep.* 1.31), the latter seems the more likely reference here because he had his legal trou-bles exposed in Lucilius' second satire. Thus Kissel (1990) 263, n. 506 concludes: "Wenn gerade Lupus und Mucius hier die Rolle von *exempla* zugedacht wird, mag dies nicht zuletzt dadurch begründet sein, dass sich die ihnen geltende Polemik gerade in den Büchern 1 und 2 und damit am Anfang der Luciliussatiren vorfand."

[110] The description of Horace's laughing "admission" into his friend's outer heart (**ridenti ... amico ... admissus** *circum praecordia*, 116–17) resembles the *suspendere naso* meta-phor of the next line not only in being fashioned by, and reminiscent of, Horace's own critical vocabulary. Specifically it recalls the critic's response to the rough-joined figures of *Ars* 1–5 (**admissi risum**, *teneatis*, **amici?** 5). But that laughter, Oliensis has shown, is undone in the *Ars* itself by the grotesque figure that frames the treatise, and for which figure these lines serve as the "head" (*humano capiti*, 1) and the last line's bloodsucking leech (*plena cruoris hirudo*, 476) the tail; see Oliensis (1998a) 215–16.

[111] Persius recuperates specific aspects of each of his predecessors' satiric programs by adapting Lucilius' painful aggression to a more penetrating, Horatian technique. See Bellandi (1988) 39–40.

[112] See above, chapter 1.

nothing to censure. She is a sacred precinct, having now achieved absolute perfection in the harmonic convergence of emperor, adoring mass, and jubilant elite. That is the bubble Persius wants to burst in the private, little joke of lines 120–3:

> hic tamen infodiam. uidi, uidi ipse, libelle:
> auriculas asini quis non habet? hoc ego opertum,
> hoc ridere meum, tam nil, nulla tibi uendo
> Iliade.

Still, I will dig my hole right here. I saw, my libellous little book, I saw it with my own eyes: is there anyone without little ass(hole) ears? I keep it covered up. The laugh is mine. So much nothing, but I won't sell it to you for any [sc. "high priced"] Iliad.

Despite his interlocutor's warning, the poet digs a latrine-hole *hic* ("right here") in the sacred space of perfected Rome. Or is it a treasure-hole? He tells his secret to the hole, to the book, to us, then covers it over, like a treasure kept safely hidden. His adjective, *opertum*, captures the crucial "covered" and "obscure" character of the book itself, the hole that holds this poet's one, small, but enormously valuable secret, a secret about everyone, especially himself. Like its prototype in the hole of Midas' barber, the book cannot keep the secret. It lets it out in a faint, sibilant whisper, like wind passing through the reeds: *auriculas asini quis non habet?*

That is the laugh the poet calls his own and refuses to trade for any story of Troy. Iliadic sounds, we have seen, are in demand, and they fetch an outlandish price, so again a point is made about the lopsided rigging of Rome's critical scales. Here the poet refuses to trade his half-line nothing for a complete set, in twenty-four books, of his culture's most valued literary commodity. His half-line, he is convinced, is heavier by far, a nugget of gold to outweigh his culture's voluminous fluff on any fairly rigged scale.[113] It is a treasure, to be buried and kept because, if nothing else, it is something he can call "his own." What that means we have already seen from the image of the half-rustic's *carmen nostrum* offered at the rites of the bards. The issue here, I contend, is the same: Trojanic tales, though invented and traded at a frantic

---

[113] Behind Persius' refusal to trade is a similar refusal in Lucilius' twenty-sixth book (Lucil. frr. 650–1W): *Publicanus uero ut Asiae fiam, ut scripturarius | pro Lucilio, id ego nolo et uno hoc non muto omnia.*

pace, can never amount to anything uniquely "one's own," since they exist only as so many versions of the same thing. In contrast, the poet of P. 1 does possess something he can call his own, *ridere meum* ("my own laugh"). It is his not only in being unique and self-made, but also in its being directed against himself, something he keeps for himself, as a guide to becoming himself, in a world of prepackaged Polydamases and Trojan Ladies. The laugh is his because he makes it, is made by it, and he is both its teller and target, healer and healed.

But we recall from the opening lines of the poem that his audience may, on a good day, number as many as two. In lines 123–5 he tells us who that second, potential listener is: "you." And this is what "your" listening entails:

> audaci quicumque adflate Cratino
> iratum Eupolidem praegrandi cum sene palles,
> aspice et haec, si forte aliquid decoctius audis.

Whoever you are, inspired by Cratinus' daring, when you [in your studies] pour over enraged Eupolis and the giant Old [Comic] Man [Aristophanes], cast a glance at *these things* too, if perchance you have an ear for anything more boiled down.

The anonymous "you" of these lines has a driving passion for the "big three" of Attic Old Comedy. The adjectives attached to them put us in touch with this reader's obsession, by pushing us to focalize through his/her eyes: Cratinus astounds with his "daring," Eupolis with his "rage." Aristophanes is Old Comedy's giant, "enormous" in the power of his language and the weightiness of his themes. Such words seem hardly to apply to the clipped, "covered over" poems of Persius. So how can this reader, "you," i.e. someone who reads *this* way, ever be turned on by Persius? But that, he insists, is exactly what these poems have inside: Old Comic daring, rage, enormity. If that is what you are after, reader, that is what you will find, but only if you have an ear for it in this poet's unique "cooked down" form. These are the ingredients in his satiric stew, the full, raging enormity of Attic Old Comedy, boiled down into the pungent, searing concoction that is Persius. It is all in there, he says. Just deeply inside.

But few can handle it. Maybe two, maybe none. Can "you"? Roman audiences, with tender, assified ears, have a terrible time putting anything so stinging into them. Still Persius refuses to stroke them (126): "Let my reader seethe with ears steaming from this [decoction]." The reader's "steaming ear," I suspect, indicates the poems' medicinal function.[114] Celsus, a near-contemporary of Persius, uses words in *decoqu-* and *decoct-* (generally rare in Latin) at least seventy-nine times in his *De Medicina* to describe medicines concentrated from various ingredients. And some of these he clearly intends for aural infusion. For example at *Med.* 6.7.1C.5 he writes the following prescription for the patient suffering from a severe inflammation of the ear:

> There should be added to the poultice half its quantity of toasted and pounded poppy-head rind, and this should be boiled down (*decoquatur*) with the rest in diluted raisin wine. It is desirable also to pour some medicament into the ear (*in aurem . . . infundere*), and this should always be made lukewarm beforehand (*ante tepefieri*, Loeb trans.).

Persius, the physician, prescribes a potent drug for his aurally diseased listener. But, lacking the bedside manner of a Celsus, he pours it in hot, leaving the patient with a steaming ear. His regimen, unlike its remembered antecedents in Lucretius and Horace, hurts like hell. Lucretius rimmed his bitter cup with honey.[115] Horace passed out cookies to recalcitrant schoolboys.[116] Persius intensifies. His patients are not suffering from slave-boy sniffles. They are ravaged from within by a fatal disease, obsessed by various swellings, oozings, and with orifices all askew. So Persius gives it to them, and to us, boiled-down, straight and hot. No "pleasurable" honey around the rim.[117]

So the question we are left to consider at the poem's end is, can "hard" Stoic poetry have any appreciable impact in the real world? Can anyone really stand to take the cure? Against the lonely, listening "you" of *audis* (line 125) he closes the poem with a list of those he specifically does not want for his readers, and thus

---

[114] The analogy is hinted at, but not explored, by Bellandi (1988) 38. There is much more boiled into the poet's *decoctius aliquid* than just medicine. For a sense of the metaphor's unfathomable density, complete with a full infusion of acidic political overtones, see Gowers (1994). The metaphor's density is surely key to the way Persius means to intensify and remake the *conuiua satur* metaphor of Hor. *S.* 1.1. In favour of privileging the metaphor's medicinal potential here is the fact that Persius specifically imagines his decoction as something infused into his listener's ear.

[115] Lucr. 1.936–50.

[116] Hor. *S.* 1.1.25–6.

[117] Bellandi (1988) 34–8 demonstrates P.'s deliberate "theoretical" rejection of Lucretius' honeyed cup.

he ends where Lucilius began, by telling us who need not
bother.[118] Among those who cannot take the cure he describes
a man who loves to poke fun at Greeks with outlandish shoes,
and another who thinks it daring to call a squint-eyed man
"Squinty."[119] Surface criticisms of superficial critics. They and
their sort, he implies, have no feel for the hard, scathing ways of
Cratinus, Eupolis, and Aristophanes. Rather, theirs is the bland,
socially useless criticism of someone trying not to offend anyone
who matters, or to say anything too critical of Nero's nail-defying
Rome. Those expecting to find criticism of this type in his poems,
he says, will not find it. So he leaves them to their delusion, pre-
scribing the inert pabulum of the sanctioned shows (134): "for
them a dose of playbill in the morning. After lunch, the *Callirhoe*."
Instead of real medicine, a placebo: the orgasmatron and its regimen of watery song. For them, he says, straight from the Academy-
Award-winning producers of the *Phyllis* and *Hypsipyle*, Studio
Nero® proudly presents the *Callirhoe*. A stunningly original tale
about a Greek girl done wrong – what else? And she, with a
liquid, mellifluous name.

SATIRE'S LEAN FEAST: FINDING A LOST "PILE" IN P. 2

The theme of P. 2 is the corruption of prayers by stupidity and
greed, a set-piece of the philosophical schools, perhaps best known
to Persius from diatribe and the Pseudo-Platonic *Alcibiades* 2.[120]
But here the theme is set inside a birthday invitation to a friend,
Macrinus, urging him to break free from his daily routine and
to "count this day on a nobler pebble" (1). Macrinus, like his principally remembered counterpart in Horace, the elusive Phidyle
of *Odes* 3.23, can be imagined as a sparing sort (Phidyle from
Gk. φειδύλη "sparing, thrifty," as Macrinus from *macer* "lean,
meager"), disinclined to lavish spending (*non prece emaci* "not
with bargain-hunting prayer" line 3, an etymological play on his

---

[118] Harvey (1981) 52: "The question *quis leget haec?* (2) is belatedly answered. P. lists the kind
of readers he wants and the kind he rejects ... the ultimate model may be Lucil. 592M.
Persium non curo legere, Laelium Decumum uolo."
[119] Sullivan (1985) 103 sees a possible connection with *Suet.* Dom. 1.1 *Clodium Pollionem prae-
torium uirum, in quem est poema Neronis quod inscribitur Luscio.* But the connection is highly
problematic; see Kissel (1990) 280.
[120] See Dessen (1968) 97–105, and Hooley (1997) 175–6.

name), and extraordinarily devoted to cipherings and sums (*numer-are* "count," *lapillus = calculus* "counting-stone," *apponere* "accrue," etc.).[121] And so he fulfills the role of many a Horatian invitee, reluctant to seize the day in company with the poet's own insouciant and uncalculating lyric self.

But just how lyrical and carefree can we allow ourselves to think this poet is, here, fresh on the heels of P. 1? How much fun, do we think, can be had *with him*, at one of *his* parties? At first glance, the searing, iambic brew of P. 1 seems to have cooled considerably in the opening lines of this poem, with the poet now showing a friendly, sociable side that we did not know he possessed. And he has even the makings of a basic social network in the person of one dear friend, with whom he wishes to "spend" the day and share a flask of birthday wine. But with that wine he wants to pass along a few ideas about prayers, and piety, and all that is wrong with the Roman world. "Let's pour some wine to your genius," he says to Macrinus in line 3. "But birthday libations call for prayers, don't they? Good wishes uttered to the splash of wine? But what to pray for, that is the question. We are not like the rest of humanity, you and I. After all, have you ever heard what people out there pray for? What prayers! Greedy, ignorant, wretched!" And so he has his start, taking nothing-in-particular as his cue to go on and on, and to tie himself in ever-tightening knots of disgust. Seventy-odd lines later we are still left holding the patera, wondering whether this birthday libation will ever get poured, and whether poor Macrinus will ever get to taste his birthday wine. The poet's sociability, briefly spied at the poem's beginning, is quickly regretted. "Brace yourself! Persius is throwing a party! A Horatian fiesta!" But when Persius throws a party, is anyone masochistic enough to attend?

Though marking a happy occasion, and remembering a series

---

[121] On the poem's general hardening and darkening of *Odes* 3.23, see Hooley (1997) 183–201, esp. 192 (treating the crone's prayer of P. 2.31–8): "At issue is not wrong intention but rather the implications of Persius' turn from the thematic commonplace that lies at the heart of Horace's ode. With fine subtlety of implication, Horace had made the case that, in the idealized world of pastoral fantasy, innocence and purity of heart were enough, were even the best one could do. Persius' setting, however, is the fallen, flawed world of contemporary Rome, and the hints of rustic coloring serve only to illustrate the crones' distance from right ... innocence has become credulity, frivolous or even destructive naïveté."

of happy invitations in Horace, the poem quickly turns into an irate diatribe, poor Macrinus' party into a dirge. Among the more prominent of allusions to specific party invitations in Horace, perhaps the most suggestive are to two invitations to Maecenas; namely, to *Odes* 3.8, where the poet invites his busy patron to take some wine and join him in paying his vows (***acerra** turis | **plena**, 2–3) on the anniversary of his encounter with the killer-tree (***hic dies anno** redeunte festus*, 9), and to *Odes* 4.11, on the occasion of Maecenas' birthday (*ex **hac | luce Maecenas** meus **adfluentis | ordinat annos***, 18–20). Strong verbal parallels in P. 2.1–5 suggest that Persius' ***Ma-cri-ne*** might well be heard as a "meagre" stand-in not just for Horace's Phidyle, but for his ***Mae-ce-nas***. In other words, whether real or simply imagined, a poet's invitation to his patron is suggested, the poem proffered as a commemoration and birthday gift. The scholiasts tell us that Macrinus may well have played this quasi-patronly role in Persius' life. They annotate P. 2.1 with: "He addresses Macrinus, a man of deep learning who loved him like a father. He taught in the house of Servilius. He [P.] purchased a small farm from him, at a price that had been reduced for him somewhat."

No Sabine villa, but an *agellum*. No outright gift, but a friendly break on the price. What we have in Macrinus is a poor man's "lean" Maecenas: deeply learned, fatherly in his devotion to the poet, but hardly a man of enormous means and a lavish spender. And so it is fitting that the gift offered to the gods at the poem's end, in a poem that is itself a proffered gift, from poet to "patron," should so closely match the character of both giver and receiver, besides looking so much like the book itself: rough-hewn, smallish, issued from the deep recesses of the giver's soul (P. 2.71–5):

> quin damus id superis, de magna quod dare lance
> non possit magni Messalae lippa propago?
> compositum ius fasque animo sanctosque recessus
> mentis et incoctum generoso pectus honesto.
> haec cedo ut admoueam templis et farre litabo.

No, why not offer the gods what the blear-eyed offspring of big Messala are unable to offer on a big offering-plate? Justice/sauce and a sense of divine right composed/blended in the soul, and holy recesses of the mind, and a heart cooked in well-bred honor. Let me bring these into the temples and with [a plate of] grain my prayer will be heard.

The pots and pans of Persius matter terribly. Always. But perhaps nowhere else more than here. The cooking puns heard in *ius*, *compositum*, and *incoctum*, coupled with suggestions of the poet's lonely gift, recall not only the programmatic culinary/medicinal language of the previous poem, but the central image of the Prologue as well, where the poet offers his homespun gift at the *uates'* shrine, amid the general bustle and noise of crow-poets clamoring for attention. Here the background noise that threatens to drown him out, and to discredit his humble offering, is provided by the offspring of "Big Messala" with their attention-getting gift, an array of foodstuffs, complex and gorgeously arranged on an outsized *lanx*. But that outwardly generous offer, Persius tells us, is made by hearts that are ignoble and mean. Thus, his own gift is theirs in reverse: outwardly mean, but from a complex, beautifully arranged, and well-seasoned soul.

With the name Messala, referring to M. Valerius Messala Corvinus, come suggestions of old nobility, rhetorical expertise, lavish patronage of the arts, and deep, personal connnections with the emperor.[122] His plate, a large sacrificial *lanx* loaded with foodstuffs, was Roman satire's most enduring etymological symbol. But the contrasting image of the poet's own small offering of grain hides a second, rival image of satire: that of the Stoic grain pile, the *soros* that was parodied, sworn off, and ultimately remade by Horace in the first "satire" of his first book.[123] Because of that poem we associate the grain pile primarily with the endless dialectical fumings of Fabius and "blear-eyed" Crispinus (*Crispini ... lippi*, *S.* 1.1.120), diatribe writers targeted by name in Horace's first poem. But here the image has been refined and significantly reduced: a mere plate (or handful) of spelt. Hardly a pile at all. And so we are left to ponder the old soritic riddle remembered from the closing lines of *Sermones* 1.1: when does a pile become a pile? When does satire become satire, and enough enough?

Memories of Horace's programmatic first satire proliferate at the end of P. 2. They tell a story about satire's remaking in the image of Persius' small gift of seeds. With that image the grain

---

[122] Kissel (1990) 361: "Dieser *magnus Messalla* war als Valerier Spross eines der ältesten und vornehmsten römischen Adelsgeshlechter und stand überdies auch persönlich in höchstem Ansehen: Als politiker war er einer der engsten Vertrauten des Augustus ... als Redner besass er ebenso einen Namen ... wie als Dichtermäzen ... und Kunstkritiker."

[123] See above, chapter 1.

pile makes a quiet return as a symbol of the satirist's own work. Horace has been taken to task, and his satire, complete with its denizens of "blear-eyed" fools with their overflowing, endless piles, remade. The signals of that remake, though subtle, are fairly regular in P. 2, with Persius' *Hunc, Macrine* recalling Horace's *Qui fit, Maecenas* from the very first line. The diatribal features of P. 2, like those of Horace's first poem, are the most pronounced in the book, and its theme, generally construed ("fools chasing after foolish things") is a good match for that of Horace's first poem. Perhaps the most obvious of precise verbal sallies into Horace's first diatribe in P. 2 comes at line 5, with ***at bona pars procerum*** *tacita libabit acerra* matching *S.* 1.1.61–2: ***at bona pars hominum*** *decepta cupidine falso |* "*nil satis est*" *inquit,* "*quia tanti quantum habeas sis*" ("But a goodly portion of men, deceived by vain lust, says, 'nothing is enough, because **you are** only as much as **you have**'").

The contrast is telling. In Horace the fool is not searched out. He simply passes our way, virtually demanding that we notice his folly by loudly announcing that he cannot get "enough." In Persius, however, the fools-of-choice are "noble" and discreet, and finding them out involves a good deal more work than simply keeping an open ear. His fool, too, is quoted in detail, but he does not parade his folly. For although he speaks just as loudly as his remembered counterpart in Horace, his prayer sounds perfectly admirable and just: "*mens bona, fama, fides,*" *haec clare et ut audiat hospes* ("'(Give me) a sound mind, a good reputation, fidelity.' These things he speaks aloud, so that his invited guest can hear them," P. 2.8). Yet, the poet says, under his breath he speaks another prayer, full of greed, envy, and murderous intent. That prayer, mumbled in a remote corner of the temple, wafts its way upwards to the gods on the smoke of a "silent incense-box."

Folly, for this satirist, is not of the street-corner variety. It has to do with what one hides deep inside one's heart, so the street-corner, where diatribists since Diogenes have waited for the world's outlandish fools to pass their way, is not the place where he sets up shop. Rather, he takes us into a temple, a place where, he says, despite the dim, flickering light, the echoes and the smoke, you can just make out the sub-lingual murmurings of Rome's glittering elite. There, not in the public streets, you can glimpse into their inmost desires, so that is where this satirist proposes to ply his satiric/diatribal trade. For his job, as he has newly defined it, is not simply to poke fun at surface folly that passes by, but to locate its matrix, the causes of the disease within the narrow *recessus mentis* ("recesses of the mind"). That is where satire's real target lurks, in the dimly lit temple of a man's own soul.

But this "Stoic shift," as every reader of Persius knows, comes at a very steep price. For if the project of this newly remade satire is to take us past surface structures into places unseen and, at times, utterly belied by a man's surface look, how does he propose to get us there, into the dark recesses of another's soul? Can satire, generically set up to do something quite different, quite public and rather less penetrating, really be made to do this? Shouldn't the satirist, because he is a satirist, be stationed outside, like a Diogenes or Lucilius, working the city's main streets and lashing at its most notorious criminals and fools? But, for Persius, foolish and criminal activities are mere epiphenomena, symptoms of a sickness within, so his many hints of writing old-fashioned diatribe are hardly in keeping with what he actually delivers. Diatribe's trappings, for Persius (much as they were for Horace), are a holdover and a tease, for it is exactly when these trappings are most prominent, as they are in this poem, that this poet shows himself the least diatribal of all satirists. For example, when he announces *ecce auia* in lines 31ff. ("look at granny over there, with her foolish lustrations and prayers"), however much he may sound like someone pointing and preaching in the streets, he cannot be imagined in anything like that standard satirist's role. After all, he is hiding behind a temple column, and we with him, keeping a low profile, with ears pricked up to catch an old woman's secretive prayer.

But that prompts a crucial question: is this sane behaviour? How much of this grim introspection can the genre, and we, its listeners, handle? Can a lonely Stoic's temple-skulking really fill out the expansive frame (diatribe satire) into which it is here, especially through regular memories of Horace *Sermones* 1.1, so obviously set? Thus again, the limits of satire, and our limits of Persius, are tested. The little grain pile's conundrum is put to us again, as it is in every smallish, obscure, silently fuming poem in the book: why such a small gift, Persius? Why not offer the gods, and us, a big heap of grain, like those expansive, hard-hitting diatribes of Crispinus and Fabius? Does this piddling handful of seeds really amount to a pile at all? When does a pile become a pile, a satire a satire, and enough enough?

TEACHING AND TAIL-WAGGING, CRITIQUE AS CRUTCH:
P. 4

If ever a poem could rate as a mouthful of horseradish, acidic, hard to palate, and utterly revealing in its power to drive us inside our smoke-filled selves, it is P. 4. The texture of this poem's dialogue, if it really is a dialogue, is so jagged and rough-joined that no two scholars can quite agree on how to hold it together.[124] The poem is a full-scale assault on both senses and sensibilities, delivering a barrage of obscenities and pornographic vignettes in its second half, the intensity of which is unmatched elsewhere in the book. This is Socrates' berating of Alcibiades, we are told in the first two lines. But this Socrates is hardly the sociable, humorous searcher we know from the dialogues of Plato.[125] He is irate, jaded, and fiercely offensive, juiced up on a "cruel gulp" (*dira sorbitio*) of poison, we are told in line 2, and so we have that bitter taste put in our mouths from the start. We feel the poison take effect in us as we proceed to mouth this man's words, to spew his venom and to regard the world before us in his grim, drug-hazed way. Not a sick man's dream, this time, but a dear sage's sickening nightmare. His last, rancid gasp.[126]

But since when does Socrates, our remembered Socrates, talk this way, even (or especially!) on his deathbed? How do we account for his hardening? We have traced this same intensification in the Horatian voices of the previous poems, so perhaps Socrates' new sound in this poem can be accounted for in much the same way; that is, told as the story of how Socratic dialogue breaks apart in the harsh transition from Plato's Athens to Persius' Rome, with the stakes of a moral education now having been raised, and a new bottom having been scraped, by the accession of Nero; how it is no longer possible and/or reasonable to think that Socrates, as we remember him, could ply his old dialogic, heuristic trade on the streets of Rome and expect even to be heard, let alone to gain a devoted following; or, in the words of this poem's most famous

---

[124] For a sampling of the possibilities, see Kissel (1990) 495–8.

[125] Hooley (1997) 126: "Persius has written a poem whose language scathes the sensibility, especially the sensibility attuned to the gentler verbal tusslings of the Platonic dialogues."

[126] Peterson (1972–3) 206: "The speaking voice in this satire is that of a bearded sage, indeed, but it is a voice which breaks into something like a raving."

line, "how no one hazards the climb down into oneself" anymore, *not even Socrates*, once the most balanced, introspective and self-doubting of all teachers, because vice is now so easily spied as the saddle-bag strapped to the back of Rome's one, most spectacular, tail-swishing ass, Nero, and thus pegged as a problem "out there," of *his* making, to be griped about and excoriated in the most spectacular of verbal attacks (like these!), but never to be looked for in the private recesses of the attacker's own soul.

Scholars have long doubted whether Nero belongs in this story at all. Iohannes Britannicus first suggested that we find him there in his 1494 edition of Persius. Ever since, commentators on P. 4 have been divided over whether the idea has merit or sense. Most credit Britannicus and his latter-day epigones, from Casaubon (1605) to Bo (1987), with hyperactive imaginations.[127] My point in raising the issue here is neither to insist that Nero really is "in" the poem as its target, thinly veiled, obvious, or otherwise. Nor, conversely, to argue that readers are wrong to find him there. Rather, I wish simply to note the persistence of a readerly habit that simply will not go away, no matter how hard the majority of Persius scholars have tried to kill it. For, whether he actually belongs here or not, Nero has a way of creeping into many a reader's imagination in this poem and getting himself noticed, if only to be told to go away because he is not really there. The glide from Alcibiades to Nero, and with that, from Socrates to Seneca, is a slippery one, but quite easily, and happily, slipped on. And it is especially tempting to find Nero here if we happen to like our Persius less introspective and philosophical, and more "traditionally" capable as a satirist, thus politically engaged and risk-taking. With Alcibiades as Nero our options broaden out nicely, into the political world of Seneca and Nero, where we "know" this satirist has plenty of work to do, but where Persius so rarely, and never obviously, takes us.

Thus, it is with extraordinary relish that some have made the leap from Alcibiades to Nero, insisting that this is no leap at all, but rather a straightforward step. The Alcibiades of P. 4, they point out, is a perfect stand-in for Nero: a shaveling who undertakes to rule before he is ready; a spoiled, sun-tanned noble who

---

[127] The most recent attempt to deny Nero's relevance to the poem, and to discredit those who argue otherwise, is Kissel (1990) 497–8.

boasts his right to rule as a family prerogative. Like Nero, he basks in the glow of his current popularity, drinking in public acclaim with "bibulous ears," swishing his "tail" (or *is* it his tail?), ass-like, before an adoring crowd.[128] What better way to suggest Nero, especially since the ass's ears of P. 1 already can be thought to belong to him? Even more, one must consider that, by this time, Seneca was so well ensconced in the Roman imagination as a "Socrates" (largely of his own making) that in the last lines of his *De Vita Beata* (58–60 CE) he must fend off the charge of having buggered (or otherwise ruined) his "Alcibiades."[129] What more evidence could one want?

The temptation to read Nero into the poem is strong, and certainly not without reason. But that is not to say that he really is "there." Rather, the point I want to make with this observation is not to prove the nay-sayers wrong, and thus to insist that the poem is really more politically engaged and scandalous than they have allowed it to seem. Rather, I want to show the price we pay in taking that attractive leap, however much the poem may set us up to take it – as I, for one, believe it does. For by following this poem's many "Neronian" leads, hand-in-hand with our own generically encoded desires for what we want it to say, we make Nero the target, and the butt of the joke. And thus, the joke is on us. We have allowed ourselves to hear the poem's insults hurled *at him*, thus locating the saddle-bag strapped to *his* back, without considering the load that weighs heavily on our own. This is a problem that dogs every attempt to find Nero in Persius, no matter where we happen to find him.

This diagnostic turning of the tables we have seen before. But here, I believe, the trick does more than simply expose the reader's personal motives in passing judgment and his/her maneuvers of self-protection. Instead, dodging criticism here gets at a very real cultural problem of the early sixties CE, a pathology rampant in Persius' Rome that he, as a writer of satire, understood perhaps better than most: the temptation, in some circles (most likely his own), to see Nero everywhere, as Rome's one big problem. The

---

[128] Kissel (1990) 518 follows Casaubon and Némethy in taking *caudam iactare* (15) to refer to a peacock's tail. I see it as Persius' lending an ass the peacock's signature vanity.

[129] Sen. *De Vita Beata* 27.5: *mihi ipsi Alcibiadem et Phaedrum obiectate, euasuri maxime felices, cum primum uobis imitari uitia nostra contigerit!*

mammoth, tail-swishing ass on the Palatine. And thus to avoid the
required "descent into self" by hiding behind a smokescreen of
externally-targeted abuse. We are treated to a sampling of that
abuse in the two conversations reported in lines 25–41. In the first
of these, we listen in as the mere mention of a rich, but sparing,
landowner brings on a torrent of colorful nastiness (P. 4.27–32):

> "**hunc** ais, **hunc** dis iratis genioque sinistro,
> qui, quandoque iugum pertusa ad compita figit,
> seriolae ueterem metuens deradere limum
> ingemit 'hoc bene sit' tunicatum cum sale mordens
> cepe et farratam pueris plaudentibus ollam
> pannosam faecem morientis sorbet aceti?"

"You mean **that man, that god-forsaken man**, hated by his own
spirit, who every time he nails a plow to that broken-down shrine of his
balks at shaving off his wine-jug's hoary grime? Instead he proposes a
toast with a groan, "Let's live it up," nibbling on an onion with salt,
tunic and all. His slaves burst into applause for a pot of spelt. He gulps
down the ragged dregs of vinegar that's near dead."

The repeated pointers, **hunc** ... **hunc** in line 27, point away from
the speaker, and thus they pound home the truth of line 23, even
as they echo its refrain, *nemo in sese temptat descendere,* **nemo** ("no
one hazards the climb down into oneself, no one"). The gossip-
monger treats us to a colorful, if outlandish, vignette: "Talk about
a tightwad! The very spirit inside that man resents having to keep
him alive! And what an old prude! Hell, this man won't even
munch on an onion if it's undressed! Mr. Cato himself. Even his
wine jug could use a shave!" And so on.

From accusations of prudish over-dressing, and nibbling Stoical
onions, we turn immediately to the problem of over-exposure, in
a scene much too well exposed by the foul-mouthed "spit" (*acre
despuat,* 34–5) of a second "nobody" (*ignotus,* 34) who happens to
have caught us sun-bathing (P. 4.35–41):

> "**hi** mores! penemque arcanaque lumbi
> runcantem populo marcentis pandere uuluas.
> tum, cum maxillis balanatum gausape pectas,
> inguinibus quare detonsus gurgulio extat?
> quinque palaestritae licet haec plantaria uellant
> elixasque nates labefactent forcipe adunca,
> non tamen ista filix ullo mansuescit aratro."

"What morals **these**! Pulling weeds from your dick and spreading out your crotch's dark secrets and your shrivelled-up bags for all to see! You keep a balsamed patch of felt on your jaws, nicely combed. Then why shave the windpipe that juts out of your crotch? Even with five wrestlers yanking out the seedlings, boiling your asshole, then making it all slippery-smooth with hooked tweezers, that fern-patch of yours still refuses to be tamed by any plow."

Wincing as we laugh – if we laugh – we are treated to a finger-painting of exceptional obscenity. Was it ever politically judicious to be seen laughing at this, to be thought to think it funny? But, for all its bravado, the scene's exposure is scarcely even skin-deep. In both vignettes, surfaces and coverings are the only focus of abuse: a wine-jug's "beard" of grime, and an onion's "tunic." At best we reach skin-level with "the crotch's dark secrets," but nothing beyond. Thus, not only do these finger-pointers fail to "descend into themselves," as the introductory aphorism requires, they do not even get inside their targets in any significant way.

Flanking the second, and nastier, of the two finger-displays is the poem's second most memorable aphorism, *caedimus inque uicem praebemus crura sagittis* ("we strike, and, in turn, we expose our legs to arrows," 42), making clear that the habits chided in the previous lines (sun-bathing, onion-munching, etc.) are not the point of focus, rather the chiding itself. This is satire's criticism of criticism. But that raises a potentially damaging irony. As Dan Hooley has argued, "It is difficult, at least problematic, for a satirist to satirize a gossip who exercises the customary language and topics of satire."[130] The difficulty is doubled when the gossip-mongers happen to sound so much like Persius himself.[131]

But why make the gossip-mongers resonate with satire's standard sounds and sound so quasi-Persianic, even in chiding them for being so glib and extreme? The irony is telling, and somewhat disorienting, for it blurs that crucial, but hard to fix, line that we normally maintain in separating "satire/dialogue" (*OLD sermo* 1b) from "common gossip" (*OLD sermo* 4). And thus we are made to judge our own judging of *this* "Socratic dialogue," such as it is, and of Persius generally, as either one or the other. Or worse, a

---

[130] Hooley (1997) 131.
[131] E.g. both gossip-mongers favor Persius' favourite "nailing" metaphor (*figere*).

bit of both. Furthermore, this blurring of perspectives captures a problem not only of our reading of Persius, our choosing to regard him in one way or the other, but it captures a problem of satiric writing as well, an enormous angst felt in deigning to criticize at all in *Nero's* Rome of the late fifties and early sixties CE. For, as I have argued already, the urge to pack all of Rome's woes into one enormous saddle-bag and load it on Nero's back must have been enormous at this time, at least in certain ideological sectors. How much superficial gossip might that bag contain, especially if those loading it full subscribed to strong, anti-imperial sentiments, based on philosophy, family-connections, or whatever? Nero, given that he was such a showman, and so enamoured of public adoration, could easily be cartoonified and ritually beaten in street-corner gossip. But the problem that that manner of criticism raises for Persius' own work is that his satires can easily be read in much the same way; that is, as a collecton of so many outlandish and, at times, hideously hilarious cartoons ("Remember the one about the ejaculating eye?!") that take aim at problems "out there" in Nero's world – Persius' own laughable, judgmental tail-swishing, *his* "nailing a theta to vice," before an enamoured few with "drinking ears" – rather than aimed at anything deeply inside himself, let alone in us. "The filthy rich land-baron who makes such a show of his being detached from worldly things, a beard-wearing Stoic right down to his wine jug and onions, that was Seneca, right? And the sun-bathing exhibitionist of lines 35–41, that must be Nero! Or at least someone basking in his bag-shrivelling glow? Good shot, Persius!"

These are not bad instincts, we have seen. But, once we have used Persius this way and decided that this is what he is about, we have slipped into the role of the poem's two gossiping fools: ***hunc ais***, ***hunc*** ("you mean **that** man, **that** man"), ***hi*** *mores* ("what morals, **these**!"). And thus we have loaded the pack on Nero, to painstakingly avoid the required "descent into self." The same thing happens if we insist that Persius tells on himself in these lines, by letting us sample the ways he was bound to be heard. Isn't *he* the rag-wearing Stoic in this story, the poor little rich boy whose idea of "living it up" in satire (another harvest feast, that!) finds him serving plates of grain and acidic vegetables to us, starveling slaves who applaud his every move? And what of the sun-drenched exhibitionist who performs his pornographic "self-improvement regime" in broad daylight for all to see, helped along by an army of Greeks. He has the look of Persius, too, right down to the Stoic beard on his balsamed chin. For aren't Persius' pages his exhibitionist regime for "getting inside himself" and surgically weeding out what doesn't belong? Why should he think that anyone would want to watch him perform a procedure so utterly private and, at times, disgusting – or is our desire to watch and be disgusted something that tells on us?

Placing Persius in the story of his two gossip-mongers is a step we are set up to take. But choosing a role *for him* in that story once again finds us in the role of its superficial critics. Persius' criticism has served the function of a smokescreen, a welcome critical noise we make to drown out the telltale rattling in our own chests.[132]

LEFT FOR BROKE: SATIRE AS LEGACY IN P. 6

We begin on a cozy Horatian note, with a Sabine hearth-fire warming Caesius Bassus on both sides, blocking a winter's chill that the thin wall of a weak caesura just barely holds back: *admouit iam bruma^foco te, Basse, **Sabino**?* Wrapped snug by his Sabine hearth, Persius says, Bassus plays tunes on a lyre that run the gamut from gloomy, ancient, and manly, to playful songs of love. He himself, on the other hand, enjoys a much milder, less active, winter, set back, mid-line, from a lukewarm Ligurian *ora* "shore/margin" at the line's margin (6–7):

> **mihi** nunc Ligus *ora*
> intepet hibernatque **meum mare** ...

Liguria's shore now lessens its chill for me, and in its winter harbor the sea is mine alone.

Perched atop a shoreline crag, the poet peers down, as do we, at a private sea directly below him, a "manly noise" (***atque marem strepitum***, 4) faintly heard in its wintry waves (*hibern**atque** meum **mare**, 7) as they wash back among the bay's craggy recesses. This is a place worth exploring, the poet says in lines 9–14:

[132] The writer(s) of Persius' *Vita* display keen sense in describing the inward focus of Persius' criticism. Their rank-ordering of his satire's targets makes clear that Nero, while often there as an implied target, is never targeted first: *cuius libri principium imitatus est,* (1) **sibi primo**, (2) **mox omnibus** *detrectaturus cum tanta recentium poetarum et oratorum insectatione, ut* (3) **etiam Neronem** *illius temporis principem inculpauerit.*

"Lunai portum, est operae, cognoscite, ciues."
cor iubet hoc Enni, postquam destertuit esse
Maeonides Quintus pauone ex Pythagoreo.
hic ego securus uolgi et quid praeparet auster
infelix pecori, securus et angulus ille
uicini nostro quia pinguior.

"Learn of Luna's port, citizens. It is worth the trouble." That is what Ennius' heart advises after he snores off his drunken dream of being Homer-Number-Five out of Pythagoras' peacock. I don't worry about the crowd here, or about what an ill-omened south wind has in store for my sheep. And I don't care that my neighbor's corner lot is fatter than mine.

Two men wait out winter's chill, each in his own way, and in his own uniquely fitting place. One stays near Rome, high in the Sabine hills. The other is far off to the North, not caring what a strafing south wind (from Rome?) might blow his way. Bassus' place bustles with activity, sometimes intense (*intendisse*), sometimes playful (*lusisse*), and it resonates with voices both young and old (*ueterum ... uocum ... iuuenes ... iocos*). Persius, on the other hand, keeps to himself, quieting himself (*securus ... securus*).

Scholars have long seen that this contrast of estates and their activities has in it a second contrast between rival poetic enterprises, figured here by the estates themselves, and the powerful memories they cue. Hooley summarizes: "As Bassus is to the lyric Horace, so is Persius to the satiric Ennius."[133] Bassus, writer of a Latin treatise *De Metris*, and thus, by necessity, a scholar of Horace, also wrote lyric poems that Quintilian regarded as well-wrought, putting him, and only him, in Horace's league (though a distant second), so it is no wonder that he should be pictured here in a Sabine retreat, playing songs now manly and austere, plucked by a "stern quill," then, tossing the quill aside, strumming softer tunes with his thumb.[134] Hard quills, we are to assume, make harsh sounds. Thumbs, because tipped with flesh, strum lighter themes in softer tones. A way of suggesting the full, polymetric variety contained in Bassus' two (or more) books of lyric song.[135]

---

[133] Hooley (1997) 161.
[134] Quint. *Inst.* 10.1.96.
[135] I see the antithesis, treated by White (1972) as an irreconcilable dissonance, rather as a way of expressing the full range of Bassus' Horatian project. For Horace as a lyric poet defined by exactly these antithetical extremes (manly/martial/civic versus nugatory and playful) see Lowrie (1997).

Persius, in contrast, occupies a space high in Luna's crags, a place once described by Ennius as worth seeing, but, Persius adds, only after he had "snored off" his *Annales'* drunken binge. That is, when he undertook to write *Saturae*, the presumed source of the quoted line.[136] But Lucilius, too, on at least several occasions, but more likely many, poked fun at Ennius for his higher, inspired pursuits, much as Persius does here.[137] On one of those occasions he refers to him as *alter Homerus* ("a second/another Homer"), perhaps to poke fun at Ennius' dream in the *Annales* prologue, where he tells of learning from Homer himself that he was the *fifth* and latest stop, thus **Quintus** *Ennius*, on the transmigrational tour of Homer's soul. Thus, not only do clear memories of Ennius, satire's *auctor*, issue from these lines, but memories of Lucilius, the genre's *inuentor*, recalling his jesting demotion of Ennius from Homer-Number-Five to yet "another" second-hand Homer.[138]

But the remainder of the passage quoted is thick with memories of quite another Quintus, the one we expect Persius to interweave with a darker thread, as his preferred intertextual resource, *Quintus Horatius Flaccus*. In particular, lines 12–14 recall Horace's proud description of *his* villa, and the new life he leads there, in *Sermones* 2.6. The strongest of the lines' several cues we hear in *securus et* **angulus ille**|**uicini** *nostro quia pinguior* (13–14), recalling *o si* **angulus ille**|**proximus** *accedat* (*S.* 2.6.8–9). And that, in turn, brings memories of Horace's programmatic first satire, where Horace warns against envying someone else's goat, only to be caught spying Virgil's goat (see above, chapter 1). Here the *angulus* ostensibly not envied turns out to be Horace's corner lot, and at the same corner spot in the line. His is a richer generic niche spied by neighbor Persius, the next satirist down the road, on the borders of his own craggy, less exuberant field. Thus, inside the contrast of Bassus and Persius occupying opposite generic spaces, and pursuing opposite pursuits, one hot-and-cold, hard-and-soft,

---

[136] Thus here, as in P. 3.3, snoring is figured as a poetic sound, i.e. the grand, rumbling tones of epic treated as Ennius' wide-mouthed way of working off an inspirational buzz. For the derivation of line 9 from Ennius' *Saturae* rather than from his *Annales*, see Skutsch (1985) 750–1.

[137] See above, chapter 1.

[138] If that was, in fact, the point of the joke. For the *alter Homerus* remark in Lucilius, see Brink (1982) on Hor. *Epistles* 2.1.50. Jerome's note, preserving the remark, throws significant doubt on the idea, commonly taken for granted, that the designation expresses Lucilius' admiration for Ennius: *sed et poeta sublimis – non Homerus alter, ut Lucilius de Ennio suspicatur, sed primus Homerus apud Latinos.*

young-and-old, etc., the other temperate, distant, and craggy, we hear a second contrast of two men pursuing rival *Horatian* projects, defining themselves, and their space, and what takes place in that space, by their relation to him.

Though close friends, Bassus and Persius are clear opposites, drawn to the same poet, but in remarkably different ways – one much closer to his model, the other more distant and saltily rumbling.[139] Like the twins told of in lines 18–22, they happen to share the same *horoscope* (punning Horace-scope?), but they are driven in different ways.[140] They have inherited estates deliberately marked as having been handed down from the same literary father, Horace, and, in Persius' particular case, from grandfather Lucilius and great-grandfather Ennius. Thus, their rival projects are figured as quasi-heritable "fields" of endeavour, laid out and plowed by other pioneering souls who went before. This matters considerably for what follows, for the remainder of the poem's subsequent "ethical" discourse concerns Persius' own inheritance, and the legacy he is determined to leave behind. Thus, there is good reason to believe that the "personal" address of the poem's opening lines is anything but a detached and casual lead-in to what follows. It sets up the central metaphor of "satire as estate."

That was true of the previous poem as well. There, too, we began on an apparently "detached" personal note, telling us that Persius and Cornutus are cut from the same cloth, and that the same astral force (among several posited) guides their concordant aspirations and destinies. Here, in P. 6, an opposite tale is told, that of a single horoscope producing twins of "divergent spirit/ talent" (*uaro genio*, 18–19). One rifles through his inheritance, diminishing its substance, while the other takes care to leave it intact. But, with Bassus and Persius figured into that mix, one is left to wonder "Who is the lavish spender here, and who the tightwad?" At first glance, given the description of Bassus as a playful old man, one might be tempted to peg him as the spendthrift, especially since, as Hooley points out, the phrase *lusisse senex* contains suggestions of "delicate dispraise" by "explicitly echoing and drawing in as commentary Horace's *et tempestiuum pueris concedere*

---

[139] Hooley (1997) 162 sees here a contrast between the more complex mimetic technique of Persius, and "the simpler, more directly mimetic Horatianism of Caesius Bassus." My argument owes a great deal to this crucial observation.

[140] The pun, peculiar and stretched, if there at all, is apparently Horace's own invention. See Reckford (1997) 604–5.

ludum."[141] Set atop Luna's crags, Persius is easily taken as the more frugal of the two. Yet, in lines 22–6, he talks as if he is the one who stands accused of spending too freely:

> utar ego, utar,
> nec rhombos ideo libertis ponere lautus
> nec tenuis sollers turdarum nosse saliuas.
> messe tenus propria uiue et granaria (fas est)
> emole. quid metuas? occa et seges altera in herba est.

I will use [my goods] myself, I will use them, but that does not mean that I lavishly lay out flatfish for my freed slaves, or that I'm an expert at distinguishing the savory nuances of thrushes. Live as far as your own harvest takes you, and grind out the grain you have stored away – it's allowed! What are you afraid of? Hoe your soil and a second crop sprouts up.

Persius explains that spending his substance, in his case, is hardly a matter of laying out sumptuous and showy banquets. He lives off what he has harvested, his own pile of grain, and he does not worry about keeping extra grain in his bin. That resource, he explains, is inexhaustible, because it can be renewed by a subsequent planting.

Such grain-talk hints at the Stoic *soros*, Persius' preferred model for his book since the end of P. 2, in several obvious ways. But it suggests the pile image in a rather fine way as well, hiding it in the intertextual fold of *utar ego, utar* ("I will use, I will use"). For behind these words stand Horace's response to *his* disappointed heir at *Epistles* 2.2.190–1, claiming to draw from a "modest pile":

> utar, et **ex modico** quantum res poscet **aceruo**
> tollam, nec metuam quid de me iudicet heres.

I will use [my goods], and I will remove as much as circumstances demand from my modest pile. Nor will I fear what judgment my heir will pass on me.

Points of contact between the passages are many and obvious. For example, just as in Persius, the lines preceding the "I will use" claim feature twin brothers who, though guided by the same constellation, pursue opposite ways of life, one spending lavishly, the other tending his fields, actively expanding the plot he inherited. Further, and again just as in Persius, Horace turns immediately to the demands of a greedy heir. Thus, points of imitation between

---

[141] Hooley (1997) 158 and 159. The line quoted is Hor. *Epistles* 2.2.142.

this section of P. 6 and lines 183–99 of Horace's *Epistle to Florus* are some of the most obvious, extensive, and involved in the entire book. Others have seen this before. But the rather different point I wish to make about that imitation here is one I base on the figure with which the poem begins; namely, that when Persius says "I will use, I will use," and so on, in such obvious and extended imitation of Horace, he is not just talking *about* using his inheritance, he is using it. He is drawing on Horace, freely spending what he left him, not in the form of a "modest pile," but a grain-field to be hoed and replanted, and thus fully capable of producing a pile that Persius can call his own.

Throughout the poem, Persius both tells of and *enacts* his living off the grain harvested from an inherited field. On the surface, his expenditures seem neither lavish, nor self-indulgent – e.g. his Horatian *mensa tenuis* ("thin table") is now so thin it sounds like *messe tenus* (25). At lines 26–33 he tells of breaking off a piece of that inherited "living turf" for an unfortunate friend who has lost all he had in a shipwreck. And because of this his greedy heir rages at him for "lopping/castrating" the estate (*rem curtaueris*, 34). He has not considered that the turf broken off will grow back, so he is determined to skimp on the dead poet's funeral dinner, on the incense, and the ossuary (or is it his book-case?). At line 37 he lets out, *tune bona incolumis minuas* ("What! You thought you could dice up your goods and get away with it?"). The poet then compares this heir of his, always wanting more by expecting Persius to spend less, to a certain Bestius, once mentioned by Horace (*Epistles* 1.15.37) as a spendthrift who reformed his ways and took to raging against spending (P. 6.37–40):

> et Bestius urguet
> doctores Graios: "ita fit; postquam sapere urbi
> cum pipere et palmis uenit nostrum hoc maris expers,
> fenisecae crasso uitiarunt unguine pultes."

And Bestius rails at his Greek teachers: "That's the way it goes! After this pansified sharp-tastes/wisdom of ours came to the city with pepper and palms, our hay-cutters have ruined their grits with fat oil."

The real problem, Persius' Bestial heir says, is the Greek *sapere* ("to-be-wise/to-have-sharp-tastes") that washed into the city on the pepper boats, and taught good, simple Romans to grease their grits. Feeding those finicky tastes he regards as an exotic expense, totally unnecessary, and the unfortunate ruin of what he had hoped would be a full and rich inheritance.

Though serving no flatfish to his freed slaves, and though grinding his own grain, Persius is found to be a lavish spender. He spends freely on shipwrecked friends, and on Greek teachers whose exotic "wisdom" costs plenty. His heir regrets Persius' having ever acquired such expensive "tastes," and his being altruistic with goods that he counts as his by right of inheritance. He accuses Persius of leaving his estate "lopped" (*curtaueris*, 34) and "lessened" (*minuas*, 37), and that lets us see Persius in an unusual light, as a lavish spender determined to "use" what is his. That heir's-eye-view hardly fits with the idea of Persius as a lean, uncompromising Stoic, but it is a view that has found plenty of support in scholarly criticism of Persius over many centuries, in demanding critical attitudes towards what he has left us, his latter-day heirs, to deal with. Too often these attitudes amount to what Quintilian said of Bassus. In sum, "He tries, but he is no Horace." As if on his cue, scholars take up the cause of this poem's rapacious heir, commonly expressing regret over what Persius did to the rich Horatian field he was left, as if simply being Horace, an *alter Horatius*, was what he was after in his poems, but obviously failed to achieve. "Why chop that estate into such small bits, Persius, leaving us so little to read, and so difficult, and so full of exotic, philosophical obsessions? Why not make me laugh, the way Horace did, softly, ironically, instead of scouring my ears and stuffing them with seeds in a smug attempt to save my shipwrecked soul?"

Persius, it seems, has a good sense of how he will be received, and he writes a preemptive response, not just to a greedy heir remembered from Horace, but to us, his heirs further down the line, and, more immediately, to Caesius Bassus, the literary executor who would soon be left the task of editing his messy pile – just as Florus, Bassus' remembered counterpart in Horace, *Epistles* 2.2, was left to deal with Horace as *his* literary executor. Thus Persius draws us aside, all of us, and he quietly lets us know why he spends so freely on the things that we, his many heirs, generally do not value (41–52):

> at tu, meus heres
> quisquis eris, paulum a turba seductior audi.
> o bone, num ignoras? missa est a Caesare laurus

insignem ob cladem Germanae pubis et aris
frigidus excutitur cinis ac iam postibus arma,
iam chlamydas regum, iam lutea gausapa captis
essedaque ingentesque locat Caesonia Rhenos.
dis igitur genioque ducis centum paria ob res
egregie gestas induco. quis uetat? aude.
uae, nisi coniues. oleum artocreasque popello
largior. an prohibes? dic clare. "non adeo" inquis
"exossatus ager iuxta est."

But you, my heir, whoever you may be, step back from the crowd a bit
and listen! Oh, friend, you're not unaware are you? The victory laurel
has been sent by Caesar because of his glorious slaughter of German
youth. Cold ashes are being shaken off the altars, and already Caesonia
is renting arms for the gates, already kings' robes, already golden cloaks,
and wagons, and mighty Rhines. Therefore, to gods and to our leader's
spirit, I am staging a show of one hundred pairs of gladiators on account
of his brilliant achievements in the field. Who stops me? I dare you! But
be careful if you don't go along. I'll lavish oil and meaty lunches on
the crowd. Or do you object? Speak [your objection] clearly. "I do not
inherit," you say. "The field is near about deboned."

Persius objects to his heir by saying "Look, friend, you want me to
stop spending my inheritance on broken-down souls and Greek-
style *sapere*, the stuff that makes my satiric field look so craggy and
spent? Then how about I shift into a more popular mode and
contribute lavish sums to the emperor's sham triumphal show, a
sham so obvious that Caesonia has to rent the arms and outfits
that her 'victorious' husband, Caligula, failed to capture? One
hundred gladiator pairs and free oil and meat for the crowds!"[142]
That means devastation for the tidy sum the heir already counts as
his, so we expect him to stand up for himself and make a vocifer-
ous objection. But, surprisingly, he does nothing of the sort. Invited to state his objection clearly and openly, the befuddled heir
manages only to bumble out some nonsense about the field's being
"deboned," whatever that means – is the field like a slab of
chicken or fish, mere *pulpa*?[143]

That is one way of construing his mysterious response. Scholars
have long troubled over these difficult lines, never quite sure

---

[142] For an account of Caligula's sham triumph over the Germans after his northern campaigns of 39–40 CE, see Kissel (1990) 824–5.
[143] For *exossatus* meaning "deboned" (its most common use), cf. Pl. *Ps.* 382 *exossabo ego illum
... ut murenam coquos*; and Petr. 65.2 *exossatas esse gallinas*.

whether to take *adeo* as an adverb ("not so completely deboned"), or as a verb ("I do not inherit"). The latter option, I believe, makes slightly better sense, since the poet proceeds in the lines that follow to look for another heir to inherit his plot.[144] But that is not to say that there is anything readily apparent in the heir's response. Quite to the contrary, perhaps the most meaningful thing in his response is not what it eventually, after the weaker options have been sized up and weeded out, says, but the work that goes into determining that it says it. For the poet has issued a challenge to his heir, inviting him to state his objection clearly and for all to hear (*dic clare*, 51). But the response he gets is one of the murkiest *cruces* in all of Persius. And that may be the point! Persius asks his heir to play his role for a moment; or better, the role that his heir, always expecting "more" of him, expects him to play, namely, that of politically engaged and openly critical satirist. But, handed the satirist's microphone, the man has nothing clear to say, even though drawn off from the crowd by being featured in one of Persius' crowd-hating poems. In the end, given his shot at speaking openly, he sounds just like Persius at his most figuratively adventurous (a filleted field?!) and hard to figure.

But his answer *seems* to be "Forget it! I refuse to inherit such a boneless, i.e. worthless, pulpy, lacking-hard-substance (as praise of Caligula's boneless, boneheaded northern campaign must have seemed) field, so Persius threatens to find another heir in lines 52–60. But his heir persists in complaining that "something is missing from the sum" (*dest aliquid summae*, 64). He thinks that the poet should have expanded his net worth and left his estate bigger and richer than when he inherited it from Lucilius and Horace. Persius objects (66–74):

> neu dicta, "pone paterna,
> fenoris accedat merces, hinc exime sumptus,
> quid relicum est?" relicum? nunc nunc inpensius ungue,
> ungue, puer, caules. mihi festa luce coquatur
> urtica et fissa fumosum sinciput aure,
> ut tuus iste nepos olim satur anseris extis,
> cum morosa uago singultiet inguine uena,
> patriciae inmeiat uoluae? mihi trama figurae
> sit reliqua, ast illi tremat omento popa uenter?

---

[144] For various solutions to the *exossatus ager* crux, see especially Hooley (1991).

Stop telling me "Register what you inherited, add in the income from interest, subtract your expenses, and what's left?" Left?! Now, boy, right now, splash oil on my salad without stinting. Am I to cook stinging nettles and smoked jowls, split-eared, for my holiday feast, so that, one day, that playboy-descendant of yours might stuff himself on goose guts, and then, when that finicky vein starts to throb/sob on his roving crotch, he might jack his wad into a well-bred bag? Am I to be left a thread-thin figure while that man's belly, fed on the choicest sacrificial cuts, jiggles with fat?

So much for the warm, personal note sounded at the start, heard in memories of Horace's letter to Tibullus (*Ep.* 1.4), the sixth satire of his second book, and so on, as if to show Persius, at long last, and after so much fractured seething, comfortably ensconced in his inherited Horatian digs, the heir of *that* gentle fortune. From the start, right to the point where the poem's end is coming into view, Persius persists in sounding just a bit "off" for Persius: too mellow, too easy in his ways, talking about how he will spend on himself, as Horace once did, without working himself into one of his gnarly, uncompromising fits. But, right before ending the book, he lets us hear, one last time, just how wildly different he and Horace, whose legacy he readily draws on throughout, really are. Determined not to seem a thread-thin "figure," he proves the point by firing off some of the coarsest, and most intertextually resonant metaphors (*figurae*) in the book.[145] Most telling of all is the fastidious "vein" that throbs on the fat wastrel's roving crotch. The verb chosen, *singultire* ("heave/sob") refers normally not to pulsating motions, but to spasmodic sounds emitted from the throat and chest. Most commonly it refers to the act of catching one's breath in sobs, i.e. uncontrolled weeping, and only here (and only by a great stretch of the imagination) does it seem to mean "throb." Taken at face value, with *singultire* meaning what it always means, this playboy's penis is not just bobbing, it is heaving with sobs, so we *hear* it catch its breath as it wags about – if such can actually be imagined (and you just imagined it)!

The metaphor is outrageous and hard to construe, but certainly not without precedent in Persius. A *iunctura acris*, "hard" to figure (if I may) and, once figured, hard to stomach and/or forget, it has his signature, rasping design. But the metaphor has a strong

---

[145] La Penna (1982) 63: "*Sat.* 6, 72–73 sono, e non senza ragione, fra i versi più tormentati del tormentato Persio."

Horatian stamp as well, for it is reminiscent of Horace's talking cock in his sexually explicit second satire, especially since there Horace has his *animus muttonis* boast of never being finicky about the status of the woman in question (*S.* 1.2.69–70): "I never demand from you a cunt sprung from a mighty consul, do I?" But here the "vein" *is* finicky about status, releasing its teary load into a *patriciae uuluae* ("patrician womb"). Rather than chiding, it is heaving with sobs. That takes us back past Horace to the remembered source of Horace's chatty member in the crying *mutto* of Lucilius' book (quoted above), clearly the least finicky of all personified penises in Roman satire in being content with a left hand (not even a right one!) for a lover.[146] But, in addition, and perhaps most significantly, we recall the figure's reverse-image in the ejaculating eye of P. 1.18. There the ephebe-singer's outsized songs penetrate the loins not of no-one-in-particular, but of the Roman elite, "huge Tituses" who cannot hide their (fake?) enthusiasm for what is being put to them.

By now it is clear that what is left to Persius here, and thus, what he intends to leave to us as his satiric legacy (*mihi . . . sit reliqua*, 73–4, drawing on *quid relicum est*, 68) is anything but a "thin thread of a figure," just as he says. It is a figure bloated with the coarsest intertextual memories in all of Latin literature, featuring Lucilius at his most Lucilian, Horace at his least Horatian, and Persius tying their threads together with one of his own, in a gnarled knot, showing himself at his most figuratively adventurous, difficult, and, in the end, Persianic. Just as before in lines 41–52, where he refused to apologize for the costs of *sapere* when the only other option available to him was to spend his entire worth on Caligula's sham triumph, here he tells of spending on himself than saving sums to be wasted by *tuus iste nepos*, whose finicky, jiggling belly, "stuffed" with goose-livers, is the perfect match for his finicky, waggling cock. The thought of spending his worth that way, *on him* – and, by now, we have ideas about who *he* might be – makes Persius call for more oil to be doused on his cabbage greens.

His urgent *nunc nunc* **inpensius ungue | ungue**, **puer**, **caules**.

---

[146] Porphyrion sees Lucilius' "weeping" member behind Horace's "chiding" *animus muttonis*. He remarks at *S.* 1.2.68–9: *muttonem pro uirili membro dixit, Lucilium imitatus. ille etenim in VIII sic ait: a laeua lacrimas muttoni absterget amica.* For the relevance of both passages to the "sobbing vein" of P. 6.72, see La Penna (1982) 68.

mihi ... recalls not only the Stoic financial lesson of Horace, *S.* 2.3.124–5 (*quantulum enim summae curtabit quisque dierum,* | ***unguere si caulis*** *oleo* ***meliore?***), but Catullus' call for stronger cups at Cat. 27.1–2, ***puer ... mi calices amariores***. That call comes right before the *Pisonis comites* abuse of poem 28, Catullus at his most aggressive and acidic, a tone maintained against Mamurra in poem 29. With those stronger cups, he achieves a drunken high, out of control, and openly political. Persius, in his turn, keeps to his philosopher's cabbage, but the effects of his dousing it with more oil are clearly felt in what follows. He calls to Catullus' slave-boy to signal the fattening of the belly-talk that follows, his stuffing it full of all the intertextual, politically charged nastiness that he can muster. But Persius does not just talk of spending lavishly here, he spends lavishly, drawing on an inheritance that is clearly much bigger and deeper than the field Horace left him. In *ungue ungue* we hear him delivering on the threat of *utar ...* , *utar* "I will use, I will use," spending from his Catullan larder, then rifling through his Lucilian goods, then tossing off some Horace, and so on, as if to show, just as Horace showed us at the end of his first satire (*conuiua satur ... satis*), just how much inexhaustible thickness hides inside his starving thread (*nepos ... satur ... trama figurae*).

But we are still left to wonder, is Persius poorer for spending so wildly? Have his lavish habits of loading things so thickly, as he does here, and stuffing them so full, and into such a tiny space, "deboned" the field he inherited? The last lines do not give the answer, but put the question, to us (P. 6.75–80):

> uende animam lucro, mercare atque excute sollers
> omne latus mundi, ne sit praestantior alter
> Cappadocas rigida pinguis plausisse catasta.
> rem duplica. "feci; iam triplex, iam mihi quarto,
> iam decies redit in rugam. depunge ubi sistam,
> inuentus, Chrysippe, tui finitor acerui."

Sell your soul for cash. Trade, and shake out the world's every flank, so that no one outdo you in slapping fat Cappadocian meat on a hard slave-block. Double your estate! "I've done it. Already tripled it. Already quadrupled it. Already returned a tenfold profit into my fold/pocket. Put a point/period where I should stop, and there he is, Chrysippus, the man who puts an end/limit to your pile."

Two speakers speak. But which is Persius? The transition is abrupt, as most commentaries admit, but the "Sell your soul" advice is normally thought to be spoken by Persius to his heir, whom he now gives up on and regards as irredeemable.[147] The heir then boasts of having made a tenfold fortune that still does not satisfy his boundless greed, its lack of limit symbolized by Chrysippus' limitless pile. This is a fitting ending, generally judged "right" in giving Persius his book's final say. But an equally good case can be made for the roles being reversed in these lines, thus leaving us to choose what ending we want, according to what Persius we want. And that readerly work of sifting through options and choosing the best in the lot finds us doing exactly what the lines talk about: fixing limits to Persius, striving desperately to "finish" his unruly pile and keep it from meaning too much. For the heir has been pushing hard since line 33 for Persius, his quasi-father, to expand the estate he hopes to inherit, or at least keep it intact, rather than reduce it by lavish spending. Here, according to ending number 2, he persists in making that demand, telling Persius to "double the estate," only to be told of the poet's having done that already, and actually much better. He has put ten times what he inherited into his pocket/fold, exactly where riches hide in Persius. Exactly where the greedy reader-heir cannot see it: in the hidden folds and intertextual threads of his verse, tucked under the surface where the vastness of his cloth is hard to see, belied by its being crumpled and gnarled.[148] So he tells the fool who challenges him: "Put a point where I should stop," that is "Find the bottom to my bottomless work, and do your best to keep me from meaning more!" "Do that," he says, "and the joke is on you! For you will have done what Chrysippus proved could not be done, saying 'It's a pile now, *period*!' – as if it could ever be as simple as that" (and we know it cannot).

But that is exactly what readers are forced to do with Persius' poems, and with his book's last ga(s)p. The last word Persius writes is "pile." Then, in all modern editions, comes a *punctus*, a period to mark the pile's end, to *make* it end. But the period may not have been there for Persius' first readers, since writers of a more archaic, orthographical bent, even in Persius' day, often chose to

---

[147] See Kissell (1990) 857–8. The scholiasts themselves, though they consider only one option, thought the interchange sufficiently confusing to merit a note naming the heir as the first speaker.

[148] For the proliferation of "fold" imagery in these lines, see Harvey (1981) 203–4.

leave their texts unmarked.[149] In such cases, marking the text *would* be the reader's job. Thus, without knowing what Persius' last page looked like, whether it was marked or not, we are left not knowing whether he himself was "found" (*inuentus*) to be the pile's limiter in these lines, the one who put a period on the page to tell us where to stop, or whether that job fell to the anonymous "you" whom he tells to *depunge* ("put a period") where *he/she* thinks he should stop. That "you," in the most obvious case, is his heir, the greedy fool who has baited him since line 33. But it may also include Bassus, the "you" he addresses at the poem's beginning, his literary executor, to whom he would soon leave the chore of editing his unruly pile and "pointing" the way for us. Or perhaps this final "you" really means "me," his befuddled reader-heir, stuck with *making* sense of the poet where he himself seems to mean too much, or nothing at all, by imposing limits that are, by necessity, an extension of myself, and an expression of my own exasperated "enough!" Thus, my Persius is a product of my reading and only that, an utter pretense that tells on the pretender. Set with limiting Persius, each reader thus becomes the genre's *inuentor*, making him mean one thing and not the other (or the other, or the other, *ad infinitum*). We end up finding limits, just as Persius says, just not the limits we expected to find: not those in Persius, but in ourselves, the narrow, controlling stuff of our own self-making.

---

[149] Only in the early empire was punctuation (ranging from minimal to baroque) regularly employed in Latin books, and often in long inscriptions. See Wingo (1972).

CHAPTER 3

Juvenal

A LOST VOICE FOUND: JUVENAL AND THE POETICS OF TOO MUCH, TOO LATE

The opening lines of Juvenal 1 picture for us a moment of liberation, the precise point where the satirist, for whatever reason, has decided that he has had enough of listening. It has all been too much, and too awful. A kind of cruel and relentless punishment that has kept him pinned to his seat, braced against an unending assault of meaningless blather, and nervously wrestling with a smile to contain his rage (Juv. 1.1–21):

> Semper ego auditor tantum? numquamne reponam
> uexatus totiens rauci Theseide Cordi?
> inpune ergo mihi recitauerit ille togatas,
> hic elegos? inpune diem consumpserit ingens
> Telephus aut summi plena iam margine libri
> scriptus et in tergo necdum finitus Orestes?
> nota magis nulli domus est sua quam mihi lucus
> Martis et Aeoliis uicinum rupibus antrum
> Vulcani; quid agant uenti, quas torqueat umbras
> Aeacus, unde alius furtiuae deuehat aurum
> pelliculae, quantas iaculetur Monychus ornos,
> Frontonis platani conuolsaque marmora clamant
> semper et adsiduo ruptae lectore columnae.
> expectes eadem a summo minimoque poeta.
> et nos ergo manum ferulae subduximus, et nos
> consilium dedimus Sullae, priuatus ut altum
> dormiret. stulta est clementia, cum tot ubique
> uatibus occurras, periturae parcere chartae.
> cur tamen hoc potius libeat decurrere campo,
> per quem magnus equos Auruncae flexit alumnus,
> si uacat ac placidi rationem admittitis, edam.

Am I always to be *just* a listener? Am I never to pay back the likes of Cordus for pummeling me so often with that gut-busting *Theseid* of his?[1] That man over there, shall he go unpunished for reciting his comedies to me, and this one here his elegies? And what of that oversized Telephus? Shall he go unpunished for swallowing my entire day? Or what about Orestes? When his book's last margins were crammed full, he was scrawled across its back and still wasn't finished! Nobody knows his own house as well as I know the grove of Mars, and that cave of Vulcan, one door down from Aeolus' crags. Fronto's plane-trees, his overturned statues, and those pillars of his, smashed by one of his too-eager readers, they all continue to clamor with the noise of what the winds are stirring, what ghosts Aeacus has in his dungeon, what place what's-his-name left behind when he carted off the gold of his stolen fleece, and those mammoth ash-trees that Monychus hurled like spears. From top poet to bottom, it's always the same stuff! Sure, I went to school, too, and I gave Sulla the standard advice about his sleeping better by retiring from public life. But, now that everyone you run into anywhere happens to be "blessed" with god's own epic "gift," it's stupid of me to follow that "Take no revenge" advice and to spare pages that are sure to be trashed anyway. But, even so, why should I prefer to race over the same literary plane that mighty Lucilius steered his horses across? If you have a minute, and listen calmly to my reasoning, I will tell you.

How is it that recitations here constitute such an extreme form of torture? Could the poetry of Cordus really have been that bad? We have no way of knowing, unfortunately. Cordus is just a name to us, so commentators on these lines have generally let Juvenal have his way: Cordus, they concede, was a disastrous poet. That is good enough for Cordus, whoever he may have been, but what about the bigger target of lines 7 and following? The grove of Mars, the crags of Aeolus next to Vulcan's cave, the golden fleece, and Monychus hurling tree-sized javelins: these point not to anyone as irrelevant as Cordus, but to Valerius Flaccus, and they do so, as John Henderson has recently shown, in a way that parades Juvenal's deep and impressive intimacy with the very projects that he has set up as the foil to his work.[2] He writes: "*this* disclaimer undertakes to show that he knows poetry and poetics so expertly that he can present a telling skeleton-parody of its grandest genre. And to produce a bad take-off on purpose is to know how a good

---

[1] A certain "Theseid" is marked as an inept epic already by Aristotle at *Poetics* 1451a20.
[2] Henderson (1999) 266: "the Argonautic association of 'Mars' Grove', 'Vulcan's Cave cheek-by-jowl with Aeolus' cliffs', with 'what the Winds get up to', stems specifically from reading Valerius rather than any other Latin epic."

model worked."[3] So we ask, does the satirist-critic get his way here too? Is Valerius an exemplary hack? Does his *Argonautica* rank among the worst, most ill-starred attempts at epic of all time? Clearly, this is a road we may not want to go down. Too many pitfalls. Too many chances that the joke may be on "us" instead of "them."

Valerius is not, by any standard reckoning, a "bad" poet. Nor is that necessarily Juvenal's point in alluding to him here, so perhaps the better question to ask of his mistreatment in Juv. 1 is not "Was Valerius, or Cordus, or whoever, a bad poet?" – a question we cannot really answer anyway. Rather, "What makes his poetry so bad *here*, in Juv. 1, where overstatements and bigotry color and unhinge critical judgments at every turn?" Put this way, the question takes a different turn. For within the figurative economy of this poem, epic poetry rates as a type of disengaged, self-indulgent, and above all, "safe" literary enterprise. It is non-satire, or anti-satire, a noise made to keep the disgruntled poet silent and seething. For him, it is the hole one can speak into without saying anything, and a place to hide from the totalitarian monster. "Write about Tigillinus" the interlocutor warns at line 155, "and you'll go up in flames, a human torch with a nail right through your throat." "It is safe and sanctioned (*securus licet*)" he adds at line 162, "to send Aeneas into battle against savage Turnus. And nobody gets upset when Achilles gets shot down, or when the search party goes looking for Hylas once he has tumbled in after his jug." The point is clear. The only ones who get hurt in epic are the heroes of the story: Achilles with an arrow in his foot, and Hylas at the bottom of the pool.[4]

And yet, listening to epic is far from carefree. It is purchased, this poet says, at a fairly large and painful price. For, to listen to epic is, at the same time, to listen to yourself not speak; to listen to

---

[3] Henderson (1999) 258.

[4] The Hylas story is mentioned as an overdone epic theme already by Virgil at *G.* 3.6: *cui non dictus Hylas puer?* For Juvenal's processing of the proem to *G.* book 3 in his first satire, see Henderson (1999) 256–7 and 271. According to Suetonius, even the most distant of "innocent" mythological themes could be construed as subversive by Domitian. For example, at *Dom.* 10.4 he asserts that Helvidius Priscus (the Younger) was put to death for having written a farcical version of the tale of Paris and Oenone, subsequently taken by the emperor to refer to the affair between Paris, the actor, and his wife, Domitia, in the early days of Domitian's reign. But the assertion that literature was the cause of Helvidius' death merits due suspicion (see below).

yourself not do satire, and to be reminded, again and again, of just how irrelevant and docile poetry has become. And so epic, no matter how "good" it is, even if it is the stunning finale of Virgil's *Aeneid*, let alone the worst abuses of Cordus' *Theseid*, begins to grate on the nerves and to sound like so much irritating blather. So much of the same old, self-indulgent, "safe" noise. Thus, the question of line 1, "Am I always to be *just* a listener?," is not, as it is usually taken, simply the complaint of a disgruntled poet-client, dragged off to an afternoon, or two, or three, of bad recitations. Rather, it is figured as the complaint *of a satirist*, or better, of satire herself, who has for so many months, years, even decades, been forced to sit on her hands and keep silent while listening to (what she hears as) the meaningless, toadying sounds of sanctioned verse. The time has come, Juvenal announces, for satire to find her voice again, and in the first line of his first poem he pictures the decisive moment. The next selection on today's epic program, he says, has been canceled. The droning epic perfomer has been kicked from the podium, and someone we have not heard from before has pushed his way forward. Juvenal, saturated with frustration, makes his way to center-stage and, for the first time in anyone's memory, he finally begins to speak.

The tirade begins. And as it proceeds, we slowly come to sense just how long this satirist has been sitting on his hands. Valerius was awful, he tells us. No matter that Valerius has been dead for some time now. Perhaps ten years. Perhaps much longer.[5] Still, this is the first time that this poet has had the chance to say just how awful he thinks Valerius was. And saying it out loud, after so much long-suffering silence, obviously feels very good. And so he goes on (and on). He finds it hard to hold back: *difficile est saturam non scribere* ("it is a hard thing not writing satire") he says in line 30. He should know, for *not* writing satire is exactly what he and everyone else active in the recitation scene he tells of belonging to had been doing for decades. Satire has been in hiding since Persius! The point here, I think, is not just that he finds it difficult

---

[5] Quint. *Inst.* 10.1.90 (c. 95 CE) remarks on the "recent" death of Valerius Flaccus. Feeney (*OCD*[3] (1996) s.v. Valerius, p. 1578) points out that "since Quintilian can use 'recent' of Caesius Bassus' death in AD 79 (10.1.96), the conventional dating of Valerius' death to the early 90s is without foundation."

to keep silent, and therefore he writes – though that is precisely the way this, Juvenal's most famous programmatic line, is normally taken. Rather, it is that "*not* writing" is an excruciating reality he knows all too well.

The point is well made by the strong Domitianic coloring of the lines that directly precede and follow the claim, lines that draw us into a past that is Juvenal's present tense (1.22–36):

> cum tener uxorem ducat spado, Meuia Tuscum
> figat aprum et nuda teneat uenabula mamma,
> patricios omnis opibus cum prouocet unus
> quo tondente grauis iuueni mihi barba sonabat,
> cum pars Niliacae plebis, cum uerna Canopi
> Crispinus Tyrias umero reuocante lacernas
> uentilet aestiuum digitis sudantibus aurum
> nec sufferre queat maioris pondera gemmae,
> difficile est saturam non scribere. nam quis iniquae
> tam patiens Vrbis, tam ferreus, ut teneat se,
> causidici noua cum ueniat lectica Mathonis
> plena ipso, post hunc magni delator amici
> et cito rapturus de nobilitate comesa
> quod superest, quem Massa timet, quem munere palpat
> Carus et a trepido Thymele summissa Latino.

When a eunuch, lacking "hardware," takes a wife, and Mevia stabs a Tuscan boar, bare-breasted and a spear in each hand, and when one man, all by himself, the very man who used to clip my beard when I was young, provokes with his wealth all of Rome's oldest families, and when some piece of Nile-river dregs, a home-born slave of Canopus by the name of Crispinus, drapes Tyrian purple off his shoulders and, now that it's summer, fans a ring of solid gold on sweaty fingers – unable, you understand, to sustain the weight of his "heavier" jewelry – it's hard to not write satire. For who is so long-suffering towards this lopsided city, who is so iron-hard that he can hold himself back when that brand new litter of Matho, the prosecutor, comes along, stuffed with the man himself, and right behind him follows the man who informed on his influential friend and is about to make off quickly with what's left of Rome's half-eaten nobility, a man whom Massa fears, whom Carus strokes with presents, and whom Thymele goes to "visit" in secret, sent by her leadingman, Latinus.

Bartsch, following Townend, notes that the names listed are of prominent figures from the previous two decades: "The satirist has located himself with some consistency in a Domitianic context, and 'Mevia, Crispinus, Matho are all Flavian figures from Martial, as Massa and Carus are informers from Domitian's last years.'[6] Therein lies a crucial problem: the issue of Juvenal's timing. When Crispinus waves a gold ring in your face, *that*, the poet tells us, is when it is hard to not write satire. But that is exactly what Juvenal, and all other would-be satirists of his day, did when Crispinus waved the gold ring in his face, now fifteen (or so) years before: *not* write satire. How painful that was, he says; *difficile est saturam **non** scribere*.

Crispinus, in retrospect, one of the most hated members of Domitian's court and, according to Juvenal, a man bloated with vice and ripe for satire, never got what was coming to him when he was alive. Along with that bigger monster, Domitian himself, he managed somehow to slip off into the night unsatirized. Baebius Massa and Mettius Carus in lines 35–6 were notorious informers under Domitian. Latinus was Domitian's favorite actor, possibly a member of his court, and Thymele was Latinus' leading lady. While most of these figures received favorable mention, even praise, in the *Epigrams* of Martial and in Statius' *Siluae*, none made the pages of satire while Domitian was alive. They were his favorites, and satire of a Lucilian stamp was nowhere to be seen then.[7] So Juvenal, now that the terror has passed, seizes the moment. He flies at them in a foaming rage, as if they were still out there, right before his eyes. Never mind that they are no longer alive, or no longer a factor in Roman politics, or both. It is payback time, he says: *reponam* (line 1), *impune* (lines 3 and 4), and so on. Juvenal is not about to let this opportunity pass. Domitian's reign, still so vivid in everyone's memory, is simply too rich in the stuff of satire, too stuffed with vanity and vice, to let slip away without his first having at it with satire's punishing cudgel.

And so it is no wonder that this satirist has so much to say, too much, we often complain, and in such fulsome, aggressive tones. This is satire in a time-warp, making up for all the satires never

[6] Bartsch (1994) 92, quoting Townend (1973) 149.
[7] Of the three satirists thought to have been active during the Flavian period (Manilius Vopiscus, Silius, and Turnus) only Turnus was remembered as a satirist of some small note by writers of late antiquity. The two-line fragment that survives of his work (*Frg. Poet. Lat.*, p. 134, Morel) suggests that his satires looked back to the cruel follies of Nero's court rather than to the persons and activities of the contemporary Roman scene. This may explain why Turnus, though of humble birth, was held in high esteem by the emperors Titus and Domitian. For these issues, see Coffey (1976) 119.

written in the last twenty years or more. Actually the project is much bigger than even that. For as the satirist proceeds with his vendetta in the course of book 1, he consistently reaches back beyond the cruel follies of Domitian's court, to Nero, to Claudius, Sejanus, and Tiberius, and to all the notorious criminals and imperial favorites of the first century CE. This poet, it turns out, has an exceptionally large memory, an enormous vendetta, with an equally expansive, browbeating style, that is just the right vehicle to carry his vendetta off.

REMEMBERED MONSTERS: TIME WARP AND MARTYR TALES IN TRAJAN'S ROME

Seen in these terms, Juvenal's project looks rather familiar. It bears an uncanny resemblance to several of the most famous literary productions of the Trajanic age, especially to Tacitus' *Agricola*, and to his *Histories* and *Annales*. Although these works belong to genres that claim to be above giving in to wrath and partisanship, as Juvenal so unabashedly does in his first satire, Tacitus (and slightly later, Suetonius) is clearly about the business of remembering these same monsters and cutting them down to size. His memory, like that of Juvenal, is powerfully engaged by the emperors from Tiberius to Domitian. Augustus interests him not quite as much, and least of all does he have anything to say about the "better" times of Nerva and Trajan, the period in which he wrote all of the works that he is known to have published. For Tacitus, history reaches its acme with Domitian, whose reign he featured in the last books of the *Histories*, now lost. After that there is simply not much left to say, and so he does not – even though he specifically promises that he will.[8]

Strangely, the letters of Pliny show these same tendencies. Though they all date from the decade-and-a-half immediately

---

[8] At *Histories* 1.1 Tacitus makes a promise that he ultimately fails to deliver: *quod si uita suppeditet, principatum diui Neruae et imperium Traiani, uberiorem securioremque materiam, senectuti seposui.* After finishing his *Histories*, instead of moving ahead to treat the reigns of Nerva and Trajan, Tacitus goes back to cover the period from Augustus to Nero in his *Annales*. As I hope to demonstrate in the pages that follow, the demand for books condemning the Julio-Claudians, especially Nero, was especially intense in the first fifteen years or so of the second century CE. This demand fueled the success of Tacitus' monster-hating *Histories*. It was likely a factor in keeping him fixed on the past, rather than moving ahead to the present, in his *Annales*.

following the death of Domitian, the very period of Juvenal book
1, Pliny's letters repeatedly turn from the day-to-day affairs of a
consular senator in early second-century Rome to the world of the
Julio-Claudians and the Flavians. Often they introduce matters of
topical relevance only as a handy means of referring us back to
the recent "traumatic" past, to dwell on that trauma in luscious
detail. Emperors are painted as monsters, cruel and insatiable.
Tragic heroes are immortalized in clean little narratives, miniature epics that show them standing up to the beast, only to be cru-
elly slaughtered. The eleventh letter of Pliny's fourth book, one
example of the type, tells the story of Valerius Licinianus, once a
famous senator and advocate, now a mere schoolmaster in Sicily.
"Would you like to know how that transformation came about?"
he asks his addressee, Cornelius Minicianus. And so quickly the
topic turns to Domitian, the monster behind Licinianus' demise.

Domitian, the story goes, charged Licinianus with violating
Cornelia, a Vestal Virgin. As Chief Priest, Domitian took his
tyrant's cruelty to new heights, declaring Cornelia guilty without a
hearing, and reviving the ancient custom of live burial to make
hers a stunning and exemplary punishment.[9] And this from the
man who as Chief Priest, Pliny reminds us, impregnated his own
niece and forced her to undergo an abortion that took her life.
Juvenal tells an exceptionally grotesque version of that story at
Satires 2.29–33. Suetonius closes his *Life of Domitian* with the same
story, and there can be little doubt that Tacitus worked it up in
some detail in the final pages of his *Histories*.[10] Each writer, it
seems, needs to tell that story, to establish a clear relation to those
events through narrative. Pliny, in his version of the tale, goes on
to describe Cornelia's death march; how she remained defiant to
the end, refusing under pressure to grovel at the emperor's feet or
to admit that she was, in any way, responsible for her untimely
fall. "Like Polyxena," Pliny adds, "she took great care to fall in

[9] The trial of the Vestal Cornelia is commonly dated to the middle of Domitian's reign.
Gsell (1894) 80–1, n. 9 puts it between March 87 and March 90. Jones (1992) 102 points
out that "it was perfectly clear that they were guilty and no criticism should be levelled at
Domitian on that score. What apparently horrified Pliny was the thought that someone
of his status should have to face the same penalty as any other malefactor."
[10] At *Hist.* 1.2 Tacitus indicates that, among the many topics to be covered by his work
are *pollutae caerimoniae, magna adulteria*. According to *Hist.* 1.3, he also intends to describe
numerous noble and horrific death scenes, to which category Cornelia's death certainly
belongs: *ipsa necessitas fortiter tolerata et laudatis antiquorum mortibus pares exitus.*

decent fashion." Licinianus, on the other hand, managed to stay alive. He confessed to the affair with Cornelia, and begged for mercy. Pliny cautions us against believing his confession. It too conveniently let Domitian off the hook for convicting and executing Cornelia without a trial. Domitian was so pleased with the confession that he gave Licinianus easy conditions of exile as his reward. And thus was the senator reconstituted as a schoolteacher in Sicily. End of story.

Stories of this type are common in the major authors of the Trajanic age. That is obvious enough. But it is only in reading the letters of Pliny that the mantra-like quality of these stories, and the obsessive, competitive nature of their telling, shows itself not just as a hallmark of early second-century literature, but as an urgent cultural obsession that keeps writers of that age nailed to the past, researching famous deaths, writing about them, and finding ever new, grander ways to tell the same dead-men's tales. These letters indicate that, when it comes to telling stories of Rome's first-century trauma, Pliny was just as much in the thick of that urgent cultural enterprise as were his friends, Tacitus and Suetonius. The works of all three writers happen to have survived from the period, and little else. But Pliny's letters themselves indicate that these works, seen for their shared obsession with re-membering, and remarking on, the same "traumatic" past, were by no means without precedent in their own day. They are just the tip of the iceberg, and Pliny's letters help us imagine just how large that iceberg was.

For example, at *Ep.* 5.5 Pliny tells of his grief over the recent death of Gaius Fannius.[11] "This is hard but not unbearable," he says. "Much more serious is the fact that he has left his finest work unfinished . . . he was bringing out a history of the various fates of the people put to death or banished by Nero." Pliny goes on to tell us that Fannius had already finished three volumes of that work, and he still had much more to say. "He was all the more anxious to complete the series," Pliny adds, "when he saw how eagerly the first books were read by a large public." Nero's victims, it seems, were the stuff of best-sellers, and the reading public Pliny has in mind just couldn't get enough of it.

---

[11] Unless otherwise marked, translations of Pliny's *Letters* are from Radice's Penguin edition.

Such stories of defiant heroes standing up to tyrants, and suffering for it, took many forms in Trajan's Rome. We know these
tales, most famously, from the last two books of Tacitus' *Annales*,
where he relates the bloodletting that followed the exposure of the
so-called "Pisonian Conspiracy."[12] Similar martyr tales, he tells us
at *Hist.* 1.3, were written into the later books of his *Histories* as
well, so his practice in writing these stories extends to at least
twenty years. Given the foreboding with which he describes
Baebius Massa at *Hist.* 4.50 as "the deadly enemy of good men,
and a character destined to figure more than once in our story
among the causes of the sufferings we were later to endure," we
can be sure that the noble deaths of Massa's victims in the bloodletting of autumn 93 CE down to the last days of Domitian's reign
were a prominent feature of his *Histories*' last book, just as the
Pisonian suicides would subsequently be featured in the last extant
books of his *Annales*. These bloodbaths, followed by the deaths of
Nero and Domitian, are the respective *tele* of these works, and
they may thus be thought to have exercised some influence upon
one another.[13] Still, despite our now associating these martyr tales
primarily with Tacitus, it is likely that Tacitus worked them into
his historical narratives not in an effort to make obscure tales
known, but in a calculated response to their already burgeoning
popularity in Rome. For stories of the same type, as Fannius'
eager readership for his "Victims of Nero" books shows, were
widespread in the Trajanic age. They could take on many forms
and reside comfortably in genres as far-flung as eulogy, rhetorical
controuersiae, and anonymous pamphlets.[14] Already we have seen
that these stories are not foreign to the letters of Pliny, a selected
sampling of business letters and private correspondence where
they would not necessarily seem to matter, or even "belong." In
fact, they occur with enough frequency in Pliny's letters to suggest

---

[12] These books may date from as late as the first years of Hadrian's reign. See Syme (1958)
vol. II, 471–4.

[13] For example, Nero's behavior might be thought to foreshadow, perhaps to comment upon
by analogy, or even be shaped by, popular stories of Domitian's cruel last days, stories
frantically traded in Trajan's Rome. The reverse may also be true. For Domitian as a Nero
type (e.g. later taunted by Juvenal as a "bald Nero"), see Bartsch (1994) 93, esp. n. 66.

[14] On the existence of a vast martyr literature already in Nero's day, works known
generally as the *exitus illustrium uirorum*, see Conte (1994) 542. The writer(s) of Persius' *Vita*
record the satirist's youthful endeavor in this vein (*Vita* 44–7): *scripserat in pueritia Flaccus
... paucos [sororum Thraseae] in Arriam matrem uersus, quae se ante uirum occiderat.*

that they are anything but incidental to his personal, political, and cultural aims in publishing this, his so-called "private" correspondence. At the very least, they play some role in shaping an idea of Pliny as an author always on the right side of a bloody ideological rift, on good terms with, and properly impressed by, those who stood up to Domitian and suffered for it. For example, at *Ep.* 7.19 Pliny tells the story of Fannia's defiance towards Domitian and his favorite prosecutor, Mettius Carus, in 93 CE, and letter 3.16 relates a number of her grandmother Arria's acts of bravery and defiance towards Claudius, tales less well known than her famous suicide ("It does not hurt, Paetus"), Pliny tells us, but told to him, personally, and exclusively, in the course of one of his many visits with Fannia herself. That is the important point. He has a better Arria story to tell, something that the other Arria tellers of his day have missed, because he is that tight with the noble Arria's tyrant-defying family.[15]

Although martyr literature of the "freedom-fighting noble versus glowering tyrant" variety seems to have gained new life in the immediate aftermath of Domitian's death, stories of this type had been circulating in Rome, and raising imperial eyebrows, according to Tacitus, for the better part of a century. The first instance of the type he cites is the eulogizing histories of Aulus Cremutius Cordus. At *Ann.* 4.34–5 he relates that, under Tiberius, Cremutius Cordus was tried and condemned on what Tacitus describes as "a new and previously unheard-of charge: praise of Brutus in his *History*, and the description of Cassius as 'the last of the Romans.'" Tacitus goes on to relate Cordus' speech in his own defense, closing the speech with these words (*Ann.* 4.35):

num enim armatis Cassio et Bruto ac Philippensis campos optinentibus belli ciuilis causa populum per contiones incendo? an illi quidem septuagesimum ante annum perempti, quo modo imaginibus suis noscuntur, quas ne uictor quidem aboleuit, sic partem memoriae apud scriptores retinent? suum cuique decus posteritas rependit; nec deerunt, si damnatio ingruit, qui non modo Cassii et Bruti set etiam mei meminerint.

---

[15] But cf. Syme (1958) vol. i, 92: "Pliny's relations with the circle of Helvidius Priscus were not perhaps as close and continuous as his professions imply." These "professions" are frequent in his letters, often hiding in such "innocent" forms as a letter to Junius Mauricus (2.18), exiled brother of Arulenus Rusticus, agreeing to find a tutor for his dead brother's children. Why should Pliny think we need to know this? What he clearly gains by publishing such a letter (among other things) is a subtle means of advertising his close connections with Helvidius' relatives.

Are Cassius and Brutus armed for battle, positioned in the plains of Philippi? Am I at the head of an assembly, inciting the people to civil war? Those very men, dead now for seventy years – how is it that they are recognized by the images that belonged to them, which even their conqueror did not efface, and that they are still remembered this way among writers? Posterity gives to each the glory that was his. If I am condemned, there will there be no lack of those who will remember not just Cassius and Brutus, but me as well.

Tacitus makes a prophet of the condemned Cordus. For, by recording his story, he has established the truth of the condemned historian's final words, remembering him in his *Annales*, just as Cordus said he would be remembered, not merely as someone who wrote a history that happened to praise two famous tyrannicides, but as someone classed in their same league; someone who took similar risks, and was destined to suffer an equally undeserved fate under a dangerous tyrant, Tiberius.[16]

Death, Tacitus would have us believe, was a common result of telling a freedom-fighter's story in the first century CE. In his *Annales*, *Dialogus*, and *Agricola*, he relates numerous cases where the telling of stories *about* freedom-fighters itself plays a significant role in securing the story-teller's demise. In other words, the making of martyrs *in stories*, according to Tacitus, in the first century CE became a sure and regular means for the making of new martyrs *in fact*. Those who tell such stories are put to death, and their deaths, in turn, become the source of new martyr tales, equally dangerous, and so on, and so on. An air of risk is thereby attached to Tacitus' own telling of martyr-tales in his several published works. But in his case, given when he wrote, there is good reason to suspect that the risk he hints at is all air, and no risk.

Among later examples of martyr tales making martyrs (if Tacitus can be believed, see below) is the case of Arulenus Rusticus, consul in 92 and a member of the Stoic opposition of 93. Rusticus was put to death on the charge of having written "eulogies" (*laudes*) of Thrasea Paetus and Helvidius Priscus.[17] The former had

---

[16] Cordus' *Histories* somehow survived to be re-published under Gaius. See Griffin (1976) 33.
[17] See Suet. *Dom.* 10.3 and Tac. *Ag.* 2.1. On the inconsistency of the ancient sources in their treatment of the events of 93, see Jones (1992) 123; cf. Mart. 1.8 addressing a certain Decianus who is commended for following the teachings of Thrasea and Cato without being drawn into their suicidal fanaticism.

been put to death under Nero, the latter under Vespasian. In telling their stories, Suetonius says, Rusticus "had called them the holiest of men" (*appellassetque eos sanctissimos uiros*).[18] Thrasea, one of the "saints" in Rusticus' story, had himself, nearly three decades earlier, written a life of Cato of Utica, the archetype of a Stoic freedom-fighter, and this is generally thought to have contributed to his own demise. Maternus, the central "defiant" figure in Tacitus' *Dialogus*, wrote a historical tragedy known as the *Cato* under Vespasian. As the parties in the dialogue frequently assert, this put him at significant risk, and scholars have thus generally assumed that his writing this play and refusing to emend it secured his untimely demise.[19] A second "martyr" of 93 CE, Herennius Senecio, Tacitus questionably maintains, was put to death for having written a laudatory biography of Helvidius Priscus, who had been put to death under Vespasian.[20] According to the *Histories*, Helvidius Priscus was a leader of the Stoic opposition, known to have "classed himself with Cato, Brutus, and their like." He was the husband of Fannia (Pliny's Fannia, above) and grandfather of the Helvidius who headed the foiled conspiracy of 93.[21]

At the beginning of his *Agricola*, Tacitus posits a connection between the story that he is about to relate and the eulogies of the Stoic martyrs written by Arulenus Rusticus and Herennius Senecio in 93 CE, stories that, he would have us believe, secured their authors' deaths. The primary difference between himself and them, he asserts, is one of timing: they wrote then, under Domitian, when praise of virtuous men was a capital offence (*capitale fuisse*). He writes now, under Nerva and Trajan, when tales of "the works and ways of famous men" (*clarorum uirorum facta moresque*, *Ag.* 1.1) are no longer suspect. At *Ag.* 3.1 he says:

---

[18] See Suet. *Dom.* 10.3.
[19] See esp. Bartsch (1994) 104–7.
[20] In contrast, Plin. *Ep.* 7.33.4ff. urges that the real cause of Senecio's demise was his prosecution of Baebius Massa on behalf of the province of Baetica. Thus, both Tacitus and Pliny explain Senecio's demise in terms that happen to give them, individually, some claim to his defiance, Tacitus as a fellow writer of a risk-taking "martyr's" eulogy, the *Agricola*, and Pliny as a fellow prosecutor with Senecio against Massa. Pliny's explanation, though it perhaps seems the more plausible, is hardly untainted by his own self-interest. Dio 67.13.2 gives the cause of Senecio's demise as his biography of Helvidius Priscus, and his refusing to stand for any office beyond the quaestorship.
[21] For Helvidius Priscus' being classed with Cato and Brutus, see Tac. *Hist.* 4.8. On his downfall in 74 or 75 CE, see Dio 65.12.2–3, and Suet. *Vesp.* 15.

Nunc demum redit animus; et quamquam primo statim beatissimi sae-
culi ortu Nerua Caesar res olim dissociabiles miscuerit, principatum ac
libertatem, augeatque cotidie felicitatem temporum Nerua Traianus ...
natura tamen infirmitatis humanae tardiora sunt remedia quam mala.

Now at last our courage/morale is returning. And although from the
very first moment of this most blessed age, Nerva Caesar has combined
things that were once incompatible, the principate and freedom / free
speech, and Trajan is daily increasing the happiness of the times ...
because of the nature of our human weakness, the cure is slower than
the disease.

A moment of liberation is staged. The "disease" that ravaged
Rome, Tacitus says, has abated, though its effects still linger. A
long-lost will to speak has been recovered. At *Ag.* 3.1–3 Tacitus
goes on to say that he, too, spent fifteen years "in silence" (*per
silentium*), infected by the widespread "lack of spirit" (*inertia*) and
"inactivity" (*desidia*) that Domitian's "savagery" (*saeuitia*) inflicted
upon Rome. Referring to his *Histories*, apparently soon to be
begun, he promises to write an account of those fifteeen silent
years that will constitute a "record of our past enslavement, and a
testimony to our current blessings."[22] The past as he will write
it, Tacitus admits, is very much about the present. Meanwhile,
he says, "this book, written to honor my father-in-law, Agricola,
will be either praised or excused by its profession of filial duty"
(*professione pietatis*).

The eulogy proper commences in the next paragraph. Tacitus'
first order of business is to set out Agricola's family background.
His account could well have included many figures from the near
and distant past. And it could have been shaped in many different
ways. Tacitus, however, aggressively trims Agricola's family tree
in order to make two basic points about what kind of inherited
familial stuff went into the making of Agricola: (1) from his
father's side he derived a penchant for running afoul of tyrants
and refusing to do their dirty work.[23] And (2) from his mother's
side he learned to keep a cool head and check his high-flying,
philosophical ideals.[24] These two traits, taken together, are the

[22] For this as a reference to his forthcoming *Histories*, see Syme (1958) vol. I, 19.

[23] *Ag.* 4.1: *Pater illi Iulius Graecinus senatorii ordinis, studio eloquentiae sapientiaeque notus, iisque ipsis
uirtutibus iram Gai Caesaris meritus: namque M. Silanum accusare iussus et, quia abnuerat, interfectus est.*

[24] *Ag.* 4.3: *memoria teneo solitum ipsum narrare se prima in iuuenta studium philosophiae acrius, ultra
quam concessum Romano ac senatori, hausisse, ni prudentia matris incensum ac flagrantem animum
coercuisset.*

ironic and unlikely sum of Agricola, and the unrelenting mantra
of his son-in-law's eulogy from beginning to end. Agricola, Tacitus
says, was a man of high principles, driven to stand up for what is
good and right, no matter what the consequences. Still, he had an
uncanny knack for surviving these ideological encounters, and for
keeping on the good side of even the worst of emperors. Because
of this, his high ideals did not result in his "timely" demise.

But that is the most difficult obstacle Tacitus faces in telling
Agricola's story, and having us believe that the man he praises here,
now three or more years after his death, really was a freedom-
fighter in anything like the same way that Senecio and Rusticus
were. Their stories were much purer versions of the martyr's
tale, clean narratives with lots of showy defiance and blood. These
men stood up to the monster and were destroyed for it. Agricola,
on the other hand, seems to have repeatedly dodged any direct
conflict with Domitian. In fact, he seems to have done quite well
for himself not just under Domitian, but because of him. In that
he resembles Tacitus himself, who is both teller and subject of this
tale of high principles, moderation, and good sense.[25] But that
Agricola prospered under Domitian is only the way things look
from the outside, Tacitus would have us believe. For, throughout his
eulogy he assures us that Domitian was not just suspicious of Agricola, but passionately hated him for his illustrious successes in the
field of battle. Near the end of the work he even hints that Agricola
may have been poisoned by one of Domitian's agents – a charge
so insubstantial that even Tacitus must balk at embracing it.[26]

Still, despite these vigorous protests of unseen enmity between
Domitian and Agricola, Agricola, taken as the sum of his illustrious achievements – including a consulship, triumphal ornaments,
and the amassing of a reasonable fortune[27] – retains the look of
someone who prospered under Domitian rather than suffered
under him. And that is a problem that Tacitus himself shares in
full with his father-in-law, giving one to suspect that this is his
story as much as it is Agricola's. From the best evidence we have,
Agricola died a natural death on August 23 of 93 CE, just weeks

---

[25] For Tacitus' political career under Domitian, see Syme (1958) vol. i, 59–74.
[26] *Ag.* 43.2: *augebat miserationem constans rumor ueneno interceptum:* **nobis nihil comperti
adfirmare ausim**. In contrast, Dio takes a much more aggressive line, insisting that
Agricola was poverty-stricken, "disgraced" and "murdered" by Domitian; see Dio 66.20.3.
[27] See *Ag.* 44.3–4.

before the bloodletting began, so his story, despite Tacitus' skillful telling of it, can never quite have the bold and noble look of the martyr tales that were being frantically traded in Trajan's Rome, such as the stories of Senecio, Rusticus, and Thrasea. His is a much more problematic case. His freedom-fighting cannot be demonstrated from any obvious facts of his career, such as a famous tirade inveighing against the emperor, or an attempt on Domitian's life, or a trial, or condemnation, or suicide. Thus, Tacitus is forced to find other ways, well off the beaten path, to fashion Agricola's story as a version of the freedom-fighter's tale, that noblest of eulogies so worth having in Trajan's Rome. But, despite these efforts, near the end of his tribute to Agricola, Tacitus lets us know that not everyone in his audience is likely to credit his version of the tale.[28] He writes (*Ag.* 42.3–4):

Domitiani uero natura praeceps in iram, et quo obscurior, eo irreuocabilior, moderatione tamen prudentiaque Agricolae leniebatur, quia non contumacia neque inani iactatione libertatis famam fatumque prouocabat. sciant, quibus moris est illicita mirari, posse etiam sub malis principibus magnos uiros esse, obsequiumque ac modestiam, si industria ac uigor adsint, eo laudis excedere, quo plerique per abrupta sed in nullum rei publicae usum ambitiosa morte inclaruerunt.

Indeed Domitian was by nature quick to anger, and all the more secretive in what he was determined. Still, he was calmed by Agricola's moderation and foresight, because Agricola did not provoke renown and ruin by being stubborn and making a pointless show of his independence. For let them know, those who are in the habit of admiring forbidden acts, that good men can exist even under bad leaders, and that submission and modesty, if coupled with hard work and energy, exceed the height of praise that some reach by a steeper course. But their fame is achieved by a popularity-garnering death that is of no use to the state.

Some martyrs may have showier tales told of them, Tacitus says, but they are wrongly admired. Their deaths he figures as a kind of political pandering, more in the business of gaining popularity from the masses (*ambitiosa morte*), like a politician canvassing for votes, than about benefiting the state in any measurable way. Thus, he says, even though his story is not as flashy and hotly

---

[28] Syme (1958) vol. i, 25 comments on the unexpected outburst (the emphasis is mine): "Tacitus proclaims his scorn for the brave enemies of dead tyrants, the noisy advocates of the heroes and the martyrs. They had not confined their reprobation to evil men, the willing agents of despotism, but had gone much further ... Attacking those who admired the martyrs unduly, Tacitus defends his father-in-law – *and shields his own conduct under the tyranny of Domitian.*"

traded as those eulogies of the Stoic martyrs who died violently in the same year, Agricola can be credited with making a difference in Rome when it really mattered. His moderation and foresight kept Domitian's wrath in check. After his death, the outright defiance of the Helvidian idealists baited the beast, and a "bloodbath" (much exaggerated by the historians) ensued.[29] This is an attractive line to take in the early days after Domitian's death, perhaps the only tack Tacitus had available to him given the compromising facts of Agricola's long and successful political career. But clearly this story is not of the standard "Stoic martyr" variety that traded so deliriously in the streets and salons. Thus, as Tacitus himself admits near the end of his work, it is not so easily sold to those who like their monster narratives straight, bold, and bloody.

Venues for praising freedom-fighters were many and varied in Tacitus' day. At *Ep.* 1.17 Pliny praises the recent efforts of a certain Titinius Capito in obtaining permission from the emperor to set up a statue in the forum to Lucius Silanus, one of Nero's victims in 65 CE.[30] This request, at an earlier time, might have been construed as an act of defiance. Historians of the first century CE record several instances of men put to death by suspicious emperors for displaying the statues of martyrs and/or tyrannicides in their homes.[31] Thus, setting up a statue to Silanus in the early days of Trajan's reign, just as writing a martyr's eulogy, had a distinct air of risk-taking connnected to it, even though the risk that these activities once suggested had substantially disappeared with the accession of Nerva. Here again, we get a sense of just how frenetic

---

[29] Though Pliny and Tacitus would have us believe that Domitian's wrath knew no bounds, the reprisals of autumn 93 CE seem to have been much more limited in scale than those of his counterpart, Nero, in 65–6 CE. Those put to death in the autumn of 93 were Helvidius Priscus (the younger), Arulenus Rusticus, and Herennius Senecio. Junius Mauricus, Rusticus' brother, was sent into exile along with certain women of his family. Soon after, the professional philosophers were banished from Rome. Dio 67.13.3 asserts that "others" perished at this time under the charge of philosophizing, but he gives no names. For the limited scope of these reprisals, see Jones (1992) 119–25; cf. the class-coded bloodbath that befell Sejanus' supporters after his demise. Griffin (1976) 49: "Everyone had courted Sejanus when he was in favour, but it was the little men – obscure knights and *novi homines* – who perished when he fell. Even the noblest of his relatives survived."

[30] For the details of Silanus' demise, see Tac. *Ann.* 16.9.

[31] For example, Dio 62.27.1–2 records that Nero put to death an anonymous "conspirator" on the grounds that he possessed an image of Cassius, one of the slayers of Julius Caesar. At *Ann.* 3.76 Tacitus notes that, at the funeral of Junia Tertulla, niece of Cato, wife of Cassius and sister of Brutus, sixty-three years after Philippi, the effigies of Cassius and Brutus, which one might expect to head the procession, were conspicuous for their absence. Cf. *Ann.* 11.35 where Narcissus stirs up Claudius' indignation against Gaius Silius by opening his home and pointing to a statue of Silius' condemned father.

and repetitive this trade in the (first century's) symbols of defiance was in Pliny's day. Standing up to tyrants and memorializing their victims, were themes writ large in this man Capito's life. Later in the same letter Pliny tells us that he kept the family busts of Brutus, Cassius, and Cato on display in his own home, and that he celebrated their lives in what, Pliny assures us, was "excellent verse." Especially telling is the last line of Pliny's letter, where Capito's own stake in all of this is made patently clear: in recognizing Lucius Silanus with a statue, now almost fifty years after his death(!), Pliny writes, "Capito has won immortality for himself as well, for to erect a statue in the forum of Rome *is as great an honour as having one's own statue there.*"

Like the made-to-order hero-stories of Pliny, Tacitus, and so many others, Capito's statue-work is instrumental not only in defining Lucius Silanus, whom the statue portrays, as a hero who dared to stand up to Nero. More importantly, it says something about who Capito is, what he values and, most importantly, how he relates to the events of Rome's recent, traumatic past. He takes a "risk," such as it is, in approaching the emperor with his request. By erecting the statue, and putting his name on it, he claims some small share in Silanus' defiance. Pliny, like the last link on a perilously long chain, gets in on this defiance by publishing the letter. His aggressive approval of Capito's act writes him into the story in a small, but important, supporting role.

We hear of Capito again at Plin. *Ep.* 8.12.1–2 where the topic turns from statues to Capito's recent literary enterprises, activities that are an uncanny match for his statue-work. Pliny begins by telling his addressee, Cornelius Minicianus (same as above), that he plans to take the entire day off from work in order to attend a recitation at Capito's house. Capito, he says, is an ardent promoter of literary pursuits. "He cultivates literary studies, and he patronizes, encourages and promotes men of letters. To many writers, he is a safe harbor and a haven, as well as an example to them all. In short, he is the restorer and refashioner of literature itself that has recently been in decline" (*ipsarum denique litterarum iam senescentium reductor ac reformator*).[32] Corroborating evidence for this claim can be derived from an earlier letter to Capito, *Ep.* 5.8, where Pliny indicates that Capito has for some time been trying to convince him to refocus his literary talents from oratory to the

---

[32] My translation.

writing of Roman history. No indication is given of what kind of history Capito has in mind for Pliny, nor the period he wishes him to cover, but that can perhaps be surmised from the last lines of his letter to Minicianus. There Pliny tells his addressee why he feels obliged to take an entire day off to attend Capito's recitation (Plin. *Ep.* 8.12.4–5):

quod si illi nullam uicem nulla quasi mutua officia deberem, sollicitarer tamen uel ingenio hominis pulcherrimo et maximo et in summa seueritate dulcissimo, uel honestate materiae. scribit exitus inlustrium uirorum, in his quorundam mihi carissimorum. uideor ergo fungi pio munere, quorumque exsequias celebrare non licuit, horum quasi funebribus laudationibus seris quidem sed tanto magis ueris interesse. uale.

But even if I didn't owe the man any return, no services, as it were, proffered in exchange, still I would be pressured (to attend) either by his talent, which is most attractive, and both greatest and sweetest in the utmost seriousness, or by the honorable nature of his material. He is writing the deaths of famous men, some of whom were very dear to me. And so I seem to be paying them the tribute they are owed, and to be present at what amounts to the funeral orations of men whose funerals it was illegal to celebrate, orations that are late in coming, but all the more sincere. Farewell.[33]

"Late but sincere/unbiased." This is not just a catchy rhyme (*seris ... sed ... ueris*) but the mantra of Capito's backwards-looking life, and of the age in which he lives and writes. Better as a catch-phrase than as a means of logical debate, the antithesis does not bear up well under serious scrutiny. Can funeral orations delivered fifteen years too late really be thought to rate as sincere and "true"? By whose reckoning are these speeches the real thing, a *professio pietatis*, as Tacitus calls his woefully late eulogy of Agricola?[34] Or are they perhaps more about redeeming the living than honoring the dead? Always more about Pliny, Tacitus, and Capito, their tellers, than about Helvidius, and Agricola, etc., their incidental subjects?

Capito's eulogies, we see, are an uncanny match for his statue-work, and for the poems of "excellent verse" described in *Ep.* 1.17. Taken together, the evidence from Pliny's letters strongly suggests

---

[33] My translation.
[34] At *Ann.* 16.16 Tacitus will again use the metaphor of history as funerary monument to describe his accounts of the deaths of famous aristocrats under Nero: *detur hoc inlustrium uirorum posteritati, ut quo modo exequiis a promisca sepultura separantur, ita in traditione supremorum accipiant habeantque propriam memoriam.* For the proliferation of the "text as epitaph" metaphor under Nero, see Connors (1994).

that Capito was an active promoter of literature and the arts, "the
Maecenas of Trajan's Rome," Syme calls him, but with a very
narrow focus and political purpose to all the works he is known to
have both written and promoted.[35] A man of deep Republican
sentiments, it seems, he vigorously exploited every means at his
disposal to make his disapproval of bloodthirsty emperors known
to the general public. But that picture, however attractive and
elaborately fashioned it may be, falls apart with the chance survival of an inscription recording Capito's earlier career under
Domitian. *ILS* 1448 names him (Cn. Octavius Titinius Capito) as
a man whose military service under Domitian merited not only
military decorations from the emperor, but a new career as well,
as Domitian's confidential secretary *ab epistulis*.[36] That office as-
sumes a fairly high degree of intimacy and trust shared between
Domitian and Capito, so his holding it hardly fits the portrait of
the freedom-fighter that he was later so anxious to paint for himself. That earlier success as a man of "letters," *Domitian's* letters, is
conveniently left unmentioned by Pliny. The inscription further
relates that Capito went on to hold the same office under Nerva,
then a third time under Trajan, thus proving that he, much like
Nerva himself, was remarkably adept at shifting with the changing
political winds of the late first century CE. And thus, despite treating his friends, and even the emperor Trajan himself, to so many
elaborately performed gestures of his sharing in the old Republican cause and of his deeply regretting the reprisals of the "tyrant"
in the autumn of 93 CE, there is good reason to believe that Capito
himself was anything but the freedom-fighter that his symbolic
gestures make him out to be. Noting the striking incongruity
between the public record and Capito's later Republican protestations, Syme concludes, "no suspicion of Republican sentiments incriminates the life of Titinius Capito, nor does any link of
propinquity with the aristocratic houses explain or extentuate his
behaviour. Not a noble, not even a senator, but merely a Roman
knight, Titinius is a document of social mimicry."[37]

---

[35] For the comparison with Maecenas, see Syme (1958) vol. I, 93.
[36] Dessau notes in his commentary on *ILS* 1448 that Domitian's name has been deliberately
  suppressed. The inscription reads: Cn. Octavius Titinius Capito | praef. cohortis, trib.
  milit., donat. | hasta pura corona vallari, proc. ab | epistulis et a patrimonio, iterum
  ab | epistulis divi Nervae, eodem auctore | ex s. c. praetoriis ornamentis, ab epistul. | tertio
  imp. Nervae Caesar. Traiani Aug. Ger., | praef. vigilum, Volcano d. d.
[37] Syme (1958) vol. I, 92.

How do you relate to Rome's traumatic past? Where were you when Domitian was assassinated? What role did you play in bringing him down? Though never stated in such blunt, and potentially embarrassing terms, these questions dog poor Capito's every move, just as they haunt the pages of Pliny's correspondence at every turn. These letters, it should by now be clear, do much more than simply provide information *about* Roman social and political history of the period. They are themselves active agents *in* that history. They represent Pliny at his most intense and competitive, struggling to contain the damage, and to define himself as a certain kind of highly valued subject within a world of competing, and sometimes potentially damaging, selves. Making villains and heroes; accessing the stories that everyone else is telling; reacting to them, and telling them again: all are major parts of this project.

Just where *was* Pliny when Domitian went down? What role, if any, did he play in bringing him down? Although his letters clearly and consistently urge us to believe that Pliny was an active member of the opposition, and that he took many risks in making his antagonism known, in the end, they can never tell us anything other than the story that Pliny wants us to hear. That is, the story that he urgently *needs* his second-century audience to hear in order to protect his political career after Domitian's fall. All of his letters were written conveniently after the fact, when the winners and losers of the last century's struggle were irrevocably set. It would be all too easy, in retrospect, to write oneself in on the winning side. Thus, we are left with no reliable means of checking whether these letters exaggerate Pliny's past antagonism towards Domitian or even tell outright lies. Still, it can be noted that Pliny did manage to do quite well for himself under Domitian, and this despite his well-known claim to have been held back by him.[38] Especially surprising is his singular advancement in the immediate aftermath

---

[38] At *Pan.* 95.3 Pliny writes: *uos modo fauete huic proposito et credite, si cursu quodam prouectus ab illo insidiosissimo principe, ante quam profiteretur odium bonorum, postquam professus est substiti, cum uiderem quae ad honores compendia paterent longius iter malui.* Regarding the claim Syme (1958) vol. I, 82 writes: "The chance survival of authentic evidence, disclosing the prefecture of the *aerarium militare*, blows away the orator's assertion that he called a halt in his career. No more tangible is the notion that Pliny would infallibly have been prosecuted but for the providential assassination of the tyrant, even though he supports it by alleging that a notorious 'delator' had laid an information." At *Ep.* 4.24.4–5 Pliny summarizes the ups and downs of his career as an advocate this way: *studiis processimus, studiis periclitati sumus, rursusque processimus: profuerunt nobis bonorum amicitiae, bonorum obfuerunt iterumque prosunt.*

of the prosecutions of the autumn of 93, events in which he repeatedly claims to have run significant risks. In fact, he advanced
up every major rung of the *cursus honorum*, except for the consulship, with remarkable speed. And there is no reason to suspect
that he would not have attained that office too under Domitian,
had Domitian managed to stay alive.[39] Perhaps the most questionable post occupied by Pliny in his earlier career was the quaestorship he held in the late eighties. Coloring in a few of the missing
details, Syme notes, "he was one of the two quaestors attached to
the Emperor with the duty of reading out the ruler's communica-
tions to the high assembly ... when the quaestor recited the imperial dispatches to the sad submissive senators, they endured the
hollow phrases of deference, the dishonest asseveration of their
collective loyalty and patriotism; and they heard the authentic
language of anger, of irony, of exultation. Pliny has not chosen to
tell how he fared during his uncomfortable apprenticeship in the
arts and hypocrisies of public life. It was no bad training for one
who hoped in due course to compose and deliver his own speech
of thanksgiving to Caesar."[40] Would Pliny have written a panegyric for Domitian upon taking up his consulship just as he did
later for Trajan? Strange that all correspondence from that earlier
period, the one place we might expect to find an answer to the
question, should have disappeared so completely. Are we to believe that Pliny wrote no letters at all in the early years of his
career?

It is at this point, perhaps, that we should rehearse our regret
for having lost Tacitus' account of Domitian's reign. At *Hist.* 1.1
Tacitus admits that Domitian played a direct and decisive role in
forwarding his political career, and at *Ag.* 45.1, Syme indicates, he
"goes out of his way to make a passionate confession of collective
guilt ... Tacitus puts himself among the majority that witnessed

---

[39] Syme (1958) vol. I, 77 notes the incongruity of Pliny's published hatred of Domitian, and
his remarkable advancement under him: "Pliny is not reticent about his own courage –
and his own peril. All around him fell the thunderbolts, striking down his friends. Yet
Pliny was serene and unscathed. In fact, he prospered. With scarcely any delay, Pliny is
discovered in possession of a fresh office, as one of the three prefects in charge of
the *aerarium militare* (not a word about this anywhere in his letters) ... In the last years
of Domitian Pliny bounded forward in his official career." Later Syme notes (p. 83) that
if any emperor can be thought to have held Pliny back or slowed his career, it is Trajan
rather than Domitian.

[40] Syme (1958) vol. I, 75–6.

and condoned the worst acts of tyranny."[41] Thus, his approach to relating a general impression of his political success under Domitian, even a sense of his own shared complicity in some of Domitian's worst abuses, is remarkably more direct than the "always the tyrant's worst enemy" line taken by Pliny. So perhaps we should assume that the lost pages of Tacitus' *Histories* were the place to track the day-to-day dealings of Tacitus, Pliny, Capito, and so many others who outlasted the "monster" under whom they once prospered.

I rather doubt it. At *Ep.* 7.33 Pliny actually suggests to Tacitus, his close friend, that he write him into his histories as a kind of undersung freedom-fighter; namely, as the man who prosecuted Baebius Massa (the same Massa we saw in Juvenal 1) and made his conviction stick. The story, told this way, would make Pliny a champion of the Senate, someone who dared to stand up to Domitian when it really counted. Whether or not Tacitus actually complied with this request is unknown. Still, the letter gives clear indication of the tremendous personal and social pressures put upon the historian to write his histories in a certain way, and of just how terribly relevant his stories were thought to be (and certainly were) in the making of identities for the elite of post-Domitianic Rome.[42]

One last letter of Pliny before I return to Juvenal. *Ep.* 9.13 is the letter that, I think, best captures the mood of urgency that surrounds Rome's early-second-century obsession with continually rehearsing, and thereby defining itself against, its traumatic first-century past. Ummidius Quadratus has written to Pliny asking him to provide a historical introduction to the speeches he recently published in vindication of Helvidius Priscus (the younger), executed by Domitian in 93. Although Helvidius has been dead now for at least fifteen years, his story is still being pored over and retold. Pliny's speeches vindicating him are making the rounds, and further details are in demand. Here again I think of Capito,

---

[41] Syme (1958) vol. I, 25.

[42] On this letter, see especially Woodman (1988) 158: "Pliny evidently takes it for granted that Tacitus will share his own estimation of his role (namely, that it was 'honourable') ... both Cicero and Pliny leave no doubt that when they speak of 'truth' they mean 'impartiality'; the likelihood that their friends' rhetorical narratives would scarcely accord with the recollections of other contemporaries does not seem to have been an issue. This is some measure of how different classical historiography is from its modern counterpart, and how different the expectations of its readers."

the statue-man, and his vigorous attempts to write tyrant-killing into his own life. Pliny's speeches vindicating Helvidius can be seen in much the same way. They arise from the same cultural obsession, and they compete for the same prize.

Quadratus wants the details, so Pliny obliges. He writes (*Ep.* 9.13.2): "Once Domitian was dead, I decided on reflection that this was a truly splendid opportunity for attacking the guilty, avenging the injured, and making oneself known." *Occiso Domitiano*, "once Domitian was dead." That was the decisive moment. That, Pliny indicates, was what sent him racing to his study to find his lost paper and pen. The race was on to "make oneself known" (*se proferendi*), to invent yourself as a subject after the fall, to define yourself as part of the solution rather than as part of the problem. And the way you did this, Pliny indicates, was to mark off a clear distance between yourself and the enemy: to "attack the guilty" and to "avenge the injured." His speeches directed against Publicius Certus, the praetorian senator who prosecuted Helvidius in the autumn of 93, are part of this project. And we may note with some slight discomfort that they are written not "in defense of" Helvidius, but "to vindicate" him (*de Heluidi ultione*).[43] Pliny, when it really mattered, three years before when he could have "defended" the man, said nothing. But now that Domitian has died, when it really matters to him, he has plenty to say. It is payback time. Time to start writing those speeches that have welled up inside him for the past fifteen years or more, the ones he found so very difficult to *not write*. It all sounds terribly familiar.

But the actual attack against Certus lagged well behind Pliny's initial decision to act, a decision made, Pliny says, in the immediate aftermath of Domitian's death.[44] At *Ep.* 9.13.4 he explains the delay as a matter of sober judgment: "I myself thought it a more

---

[43] Pliny was fully aware of the problem of publishing speeches too "conveniently" long after the fact. Earlier in the same book, at *Ep.* 9.1, he urges a friend (Novius Maximus?) to publish immediately the speeches he made in his own defense against Pompeius Planta, lest he be thought to have waited for Planta's death to publish them. A side-effect (and perhaps a hidden purpose) of the letter's identity work is to mark Pliny as someone who knows better, and thus to establish his own suspiciously late speeches as politically un-suspicious and well-timed.

[44] Syme (1958) vol. I, 77 notes that "[Pliny] did not go into action until some months had elapsed. It would be valuable to know the reasons for the delay, what turn of events now made Certus seem vulnerable. Pliny was not a rash man."

moderate and steadier course to attack a most brutal defendant not with the general hatred of the times, but with a specific criminal charge, after the initial outburst had died down, and rage, which was daily subsiding, had returned to justice." The immediate flurry of reprisals to which Pliny refers targeted only minor officials, freedmen, and slaves rather than men of high standing.[45] As if by prior agreement, no member of the Senate is known to have incurred the Senate's elaborately performed wrath. And thus, the attack Pliny intended to level against Certus was of a different kind, against a much more "ferocious" and influential opponent (*immanissimum reum*). Certus was a praetorian senator whose treasury position as prefect of the *aerarium Saturni* put him next in line for the consulship. But, by the time Pliny gets around to making his charge against him in the Senate, the time for reprisals has largely slipped away.

The Senate's willingness to punish its own members was never there to begin with, so one may reasonably question what Pliny thought he could achieve by accusing Certus. Because Nerva wished to slow down the pace of reprisals against Domitian's henchmen rather than stir them up, Pliny's attack against Certus, sometime in 97, resulted in no formal motion against him.[46] No conviction or punishment followed – so why carry through with publishing the speeches against him? Still, Pliny asserts that it was because he dared speak up against him that Certus was subsequently removed from his treasury post, a post to which Pliny himself was then appointed, thus putting him in line for the consulship of 100. But Pliny's own personal windfall from these events is wisely left out of the letter. Instead he claims that the real beneficiary was the Senate, now given new resolve to take action against its own members. In closing the long letter describing these events, at *Ep.* 19.13.24–5 Pliny says that Certus fell ill a few days after the speech and died, harried by an image that floated

---

[45] For these reprisals, see especially Dio 68.1.2–3. Syme (1958) vol. 1, 7: "Of the agents of despotism, only minor officials perished or men of low degree. The more important were saved by wealth and influence, by protection alertly contrived against any change of fortune."

[46] Dio 68.1.3 relates that after Domitian's death there was an "uproar ... that came of everyone's accusing everyone else." Nerva put a halt to that furor at the urging of the consul, Fronto, i.e. *Juvenal's* Fronto (above).

before his eyes, of Pliny attacking him with a sword. Thus the letter ends. And thus Pliny's vindication of Helvidius is rendered unassailable and complete. The tyrant's lackey is dead, killed off by a sword-wielding hero. Pliny himself.

GHOST-ASSAULT IN JUV. I

By now it is clear that the time-warp problem of Juvenal's first book is something much bigger than one man's private literary game, an illusion that he and only he creates and neatly controls within the margins of a book. It is, rather, a central cultural obsession that bears upon and colors not just this poetry, but every significant literary enterprise of the Trajanic and early Hadrianic periods. What makes Juvenal's version of the time-warp so unique and challenging in book 1 of his *Satires* is that he handles it with nothing like the finesse of a Pliny or a Tacitus. With them, obsessing over the past makes a certain generic sense. Tacitus, after all, writes histories and eulogies, so he is generically set up to dwell in the past and to say little, if anything, about the present in which he lives.[47] As a result, his readers, like those of Pliny and Suetonius, are inclined to refrain from asking embarrassing questions about his sometimes-too-tidy narratives, such as "Where were you when it mattered?" With Juvenal, on the other hand, the cracks in the stated program are simply too wide to gloss over or ignore. What happens when he, a satirist, tries to play the same game? Is there really such a thing as retroactive satire? Can a satirist play the same retroactive game, writing years after the fact, and still expect to qualify as a satirist?

Generic expectations get in the way here, making Juvenal's program a problematic, if not absurd proposition. And yet this is precisely the problem he tosses our way at the end of his first satire. There the interlocutor warns the satirist (Juv. 1.168–70): "Consider this privately to yourself before the trumpet sounds: once your helmet is on it is too late to have second thoughts about

---

[47] Still, there are certain features of his historical works, such as the heavy infusion of formulaic, eulogistic death-scenes, which cannot be explained in terms of generic expectations. These, I believe, are much better handled as the result of certain politically "urgent" (read "correct") demands being applied pan-generically to literature (and to various other symbolic media, e.g. Capito's statues) in the Trajanic age.

the war" (*galeatum sero duelli paenitet*). And so he backs off in lines 170–1: "I'll see what I can get away with against the dead who lie beneath the Flaminian and Latin roads." Domitian himself was buried along the Flaminian Way. Paris, once his favorite actor, was buried along the Latin Way.[48] That is where the poem ends: satire, stuck in the graveyard, outside the city walls rather than taken to its bustling streets, where the poet had boldly announced he would take it.

What do we make of the contradiction? How do we react to being told that the satirist will reclaim that Old Republican freedom to attack his enemies only to be told a moment later that the would-be Lucilius has changed his mind and decided to play it safe? It is, by all accounts, a troubling moment. Why bring in all of these high-flying generic expectations only to defeat yourself, and to show how your satire does not really measure up? Scholars commenting on the lines have often taken this as their cue to rescue Juvenal; to show how, from a certain angle, he really *does* measure up. For example, some have insisted that Juvenal is drawn into the past either because the past has produced the worst of Rome's contemporary evils, or because the biggest threat to Rome in the early days of Trajan's reign is that the past should repeat itself by not having been thoroughly beaten to death.[49] Thus his satire qualifies as relevant and socially useful. Even crucial.

Perhaps a more profitable line to take would be to see Juvenal as a risk-taker along the lines of the programmatic *apologia* of Tac. *Ann.* 4.33; that is, as one whose abuse of the long-dead brings with it the danger of offending relatives who are still alive. That excuse

---

[48] See Anderson (1982) 207.
[49] For these options, see especially Anderson (1982) 207–8. To Highet's suggestion that the past, for Juvenal, figures as the source of current evils, Anderson adds that "the past, to a certain extent, promises objectivity on the part of the satirist." Courtney (1980) 82, attempts a biographical explanation: "We must infer that the grim past had so ingrained itself in Juvenal's mind that to some extent he failed to recognise contemporary realities." Most recently Braund (1996) and Bartsch (1994) have been less anxious to rescue Juvenal from himself, even ready to let the contradiction stand and "mean." For Braund (pp. 119–21) the contradiction is explained in terms of the author's persona, taken as further evidence that Juvenal is an extreme and addled critic who cannot be taken at face value. Bartsch (pp. 91–7) argues that Juvenal's disclaimer at the end of *Satires* 1 is, by design, self-defeating, a hallmark of double-speak, thus spurring readers to suspect that the past is really, by analogy, about the present.

is face-saving, but by no means indisputable, especially in Tacitus' own case. Tacitus gains much by making it.[50] But this is a strategy that Juvenal does not even bother to hint at. And even if this "solution," externally supplied, is true, it hardly makes the gap between generic expectations and the delivered product any less obvious or troubling. For even with apologies in place, we feel strongly that barricades are being set up around these last lines, like yellow tape around a crime scene. Standing outside the scene, commentators predictably attempt to hurry us along with "Nothing to see here, folks – just keep moving." But these helpful disclaimers do not really convince us that there is nothing to see. Quite the opposite. The presence of hermeneutical SWAT-teams and the blaring of their sirens makes us all the more curious and convinced that there really *is* a problem behind the tape.

My point here is not to insist that scholars are deluded in their attempts to make sense of these last lines, or that in solving the problem they have always got it wrong – as if I actually believed that, or could convince my readers of it. Rather, I contend that their attempts to get it right are both necessary and meaningful, perhaps even more meaningful than any of the individual solutions they have posited. Put in another way, the problem we face at the end of Juvenal 1 is not just an obstacle we grapple with and do our best to dislodge in order to dicover what the poem finally means – as if its meaning were some fixed and stable thing "out there" just waiting to be located. Instead, the act of dislodging that obstacle (and we do have to try!) is itself central to the experience of reading and the *very stuff of meaning*. Barbara Johnson put it well: "The poem is not *about* something *separate* from the activity required to decipher it."[51]

---

[50] The claim merits strong suspicion, especially given the cachet it adds to the writing of the *Annales* by intimating that Tacitus himself runs a significant risk in daring to pass judgment on Rome's first-century past. It serves Tacitus' programmatic aims, even his political purposes, in a fashion that seems terribly convenient, and much too highly crafted, to merit uncritical acceptance. Because the *apologia* is set immediately ahead of the account of Cremutius Cordus' demise (see above), one cannot help reading Cordus' story as somehow analogous to that of Tacitus himself, and vice versa. Both are described as victims of potential misreadings, running similar risks, even death-defying risks, in the writing of their respective histories. By means of this clever, ostensibly casual *iunctura*, Tacitus adds to his own work a needed air of defiance, figuring himself as a risk-taker along the lines of the much lionized Cordus. That, we have seen, carries huge social value in Trajanic Rome.

[51] Johnson (1985) 144. I owe the observation (and citation) to Henderson (1992) 137.

The problem with Juvenal's first book of satires, I have argued, is that these poems come too late.[52] They make a deliberate point of their coming too late. They bluster on about being relevant and risk-taking when, in fact, they are all too flaunting of their failure to address the present. That failure is felt most keenly at the end of the first satire, and no amount of scholarly patchwork has been able to fill the cracks completely. Thus, maybe the better question to ask of these lines is not "How do we keep Juvenal from defeating himself?," but "What do we make of his defeating himself?" Why *does* he defeat himself, and do it so decisively, opening cracks that are too big for us to plaster over? Cast this way, the problem of Juvenal's "hypocrisy" is not an obstacle to meaning, but a meaningful obstacle. Making up for lost time *in satire* is an unlikely, if not irredeemable, notion. No one has ever used satire to do this before. The genre is not set up to work that way. Satire is a genre that must engage with the present, and any attempt to make it seem that it can work as a kind of retroactive payback has got to come off as just a little absurd. Why, then, should Juvenal so openly dwell on his late-coming? Wouldn't he have been better off covering that up? Couldn't he have been more like Pliny and kept us from noticing?

But maybe that is the point. Maybe it is precisely where Juvenal's "failure" spills off his page and contrasts the parallel "success" of, say, a Tacitus, or a Pliny, or a Capito, or whomever, that his hypocritical late-coming finally ceases to be just *his* problem, a problem we seek to solve to understand Juvenal, and becomes a problem of general cultural relevance, with an active potential to offend (something that readers of satire generally demand of the genre). For it is clear by now that Juvenal's fixation with Rome's first-century past is not just his problem. The retroactive game that he plays in his first book is precisely the same game that so many members of his society were engaged in and made such a grand show of playing in the early years after Domitian's death. Tacitus, Pliny, Titinius Capito, Gaius Fannius, we have seen, were driven by the same impulse in their histories, statues, correspondence, and so on, to invent themselves after-the-fall, and to say what they conveniently managed to *not say* a decade or two before. Though very much alive, they are buried in the Domitianic past

---

[52] The same problem is easily traced in books 2 and 3 as well. See Bartsch (1994) 130.

with the likes of Domitian and Paris, deep under the Flaminian
and Latin Ways. All are drawn into the same traumatic past in
an attempt to make up for lost time. At the end of his first satire,
Juvenal tries his hand at the same game and gets it wrong. And in
getting it wrong, he lets us see some of the cracks that threaten to
bring down one of the main cultural enterprises of his day: the
race to "make oneself known" after the fall.

This I take as a kind of "diagnostic" parody; parody that presents extreme challenges to readers by riding the edge of respectability and almost working as the genuine article. For Juvenal has
the basic trappings of someone who suffered under Domitian:
"pummeled" (*uexatus*, 2) and disgraced in Fronto's torture chamber,
he saw a rag-wearing Telephus sent into exile, and poor Orestes
with letters scrawled across his back (*scriptus et in tergo*, 6). Then, as
if in exile himself, Juvenal tells of his deep, personal knowledge
of Aeolus' cave, a prison-house of the winds, and of the agonies
meted out in Aeacus' torture chamber. The man orchestrating this
ghastly "punishment," he says, was Fronto, no obscure man of
letters, but suffect consul with Nerva in 96, perhaps appointed
to that post by Domitian himself.[53] Thus, Juvenal would have
us believe that he, too, suffered under the tyrant and his lackeys,
but his account is clearly off-base and overdone. His "tortures"
in Fronto's recitation hall, though done up in the trappings of
freedom-fighting respectability, are comical. They can never rate
as the genuine article.

But if this is parody, what is it a parody of? The story of Juvenal's
finding a long-lost voice, staged in the first poem of his first book,
is an uncanny match for Tacitus' *nunc redit animus*, Pliny's *occiso
Domitiano*, and Capito's *seris ... sed ... ueris*. His story runs parallel
to the epic-styled "tyrant versus hero" stories that rang out so
loudly in the recitation halls of early second-century Rome, but
Juvenal has turned up the volume so loud on his particular version

---

[53] Most significantly, Fronto is known to have played an active role in slowing reprisals
against Domitian's favorites after the emperor's death (see above n. 46). In that role, he
is best known as the co-defendant, with Salvius Liberalis, in the case of Marius Priscus,
the wine-sipping exile of Juv. 1.49–50. As Juvenal's comments on Marius' exile indicate,
not everyone was pleased with the outcome of this trial in which the Senate undertook to
punish one of its own. The prosecutors assigned to the case were none other than Pliny
and Tacitus, and Pliny goes to great lengths in *Ep.* 2.11, one of his longest letters, to
demonstrate that he had argued for a harsher punishment than the one that Marius
eventually received.

of the abuse-and-liberation tale that the sounds of that tale have become comically distorted and disorienting. We are left to wonder whether what we hear in Juvenal's first poem are the sounds of honorable indignation, the genuine article, or a parodic shakedown of the whole indignation industry. That is, the raging against past abuses that was the hallmark of literature in the Trajanic age, sounds playing in every bookshop, portico, and pub.

But that is where Juvenal leaves us at the end of his first satire, wondering where we stand, and not quite sure how to hear what he has to say. He tosses us a live grenade and promptly exits the scene. What we are to do with it he leaves entirely to us. But deal with it we must. And so, what we usually think of as his problem, in the end, becomes our problem. Our hermeneutical crisis. And the way we choose to deal with that crisis says an awful lot about who we are as readers, what we put up with, the hoops we are willing to jump through in order to make sense of Juvenal and "rescue" his fractured, retroactive programme.

How do we come to terms with the poet's inconsistencies? Do we even admit that they are there? If so, do we try to rescue Juvenal and to insist that, despite initial impressions, his program really does make sense? And how do we feel about having to save him? Do we resent all the work that has gone into preventing his self-destruction? If so, does that resentment spill over into the way we read his contemporaries, Tacitus or Pliny? Did we allow ourselves to think of them along the way? Or maybe we just decided that Juvenal is beyond redemption, that his inconsistencies make him a second-rate poet, not up to the task he has set for himself. Several scholars have gone in that direction, content to insist that Juvenal is mere silver to Lucilius' gold. Still, that decision itself requires that we turn a blind eye to any possible analogies with Pliny or Tacitus. Otherwise, disparaging Juvenal brings with it the uncomfortable side-effect of implicating them as well. Or is it precisely because we are anxious to distance Pliny and Tacitus from any hint of hypocrisy that we are so quick to draw a hard, black line between their "success" and his more obvious "failure"?

These are the kinds of questions that the poet's diagnostic work poses. The principal diagnosis, in the end, is not on Juvenal, his society, or the literary personalities of his day, but on us, readers centrally engaged in the experience of making sense of those personalities and of this difficult, pushy, and extreme author. In reading Juvenal, this sense-making work is a full-time struggle, for his failure to address his own age is just one of many hard-to-reconcile ironies that threaten to sabotage his stated programme. Among the more famous of these threatening ironies is the poet's clear failure to extricate his *Satires* from the very tragic and epic modes of thought and expression that they so aggressively despise. He begins his work by telling us of the long abuse he suffered listening to Cordus (oddly, a man with a freedom-fighter's famous name) ramble on about Theseus, the Minotaur, the hero's sad return to Athens, and so on. Valerius, it seems, was just as bad, maybe worse: Lapiths fighting centaurs, tree-sized javelins, and so on. And yet, when he finally gets his chance to break free and say something new and relevant, Juvenal ends up bombarding us with the same stuff. He is just as much a part of the myth-making industry, just as fixated on a distant, heavily mythologized past as Valerius was. One of the more ironic and challenging features of lines 22–9, the book's first catalogue of vice, is that the villains they attack are all imagined in the colors and motifs of epic: there is Mevia, the spear-wielding amazon, in line 22; line 23 features a great boar-hunt; *prouocet unus* in 24 sounds like a hero's challenge to single combat. And Crispinus, in lines 27–9, works up a terrible sweat by hoisting a giant stone. Epic, it seems, is built into the poet's imagination. It shapes the way he sees the world.

And yet, if listening to epic is that extreme form of torture that he describes in the book's opening lines, then what do we imagine he is doing *to us* when he subjects us to the same stuff? How do we justify his racing straight back to those same inane fantasies to formulate his satiric vision? The whole project threatens to collapse from the start as the speaker's criticism turns on itself and gets figured into the very mess he is trying to purge away. Thus, the urge to toss Juvenal aside, once again, is very strong. But as before, I think the problem is less an obstacle to meaning than it is the point. It probes the way we read and make sense of Juvenal. And that activity, the *experience* of removing the obstacle, is his satire's diagnostic work, inseparable from what it means.

Semper ego auditor tantum? ("Am I always to be just a listener?") If you read that first line aloud, as most Romans probably did, you have answered the question by asking it. You have ceased to be just a listener and begun, finally, to speak. If you read it silently, though, you remain a listener and, according to this poem, a victim. The torture, in this case, is not meted out by Cordus or Valerius, but by Juvenal, their counterpart in satire. Now it is his turn to abuse us. In keeping silent, we listen dutifully as he rambles on in grand epic tones, not about Theseus or Jason this time, but about the various monsters and sadistic villains that stalked the Roman landscape of the first century CE.

That is the bind we are put in by the poem's first lines. We are given a dubious choice between silent resentment, on the one hand, and letting the satirist's scripted *ego* become ours on the other. The trouble with that is that his *ego* is so notoriously pushy, loud, and self-defeating. Is it really the *ego* we would choose to speak for us in our moment of liberation, and to represent our experience of finally having the chance to speak? Does being set free after such a long silence really mean we have to talk like *that*? But maybe that is the point. Maybe the resentment we feel in being given such meager options is a central function of this poem's getting us inside ourselves. Being set free to speak should mean something else. And yet here we are forced to see that freedom as a version of the same old slavish abuse: the freedom to keep silent, or to say only what someone else is saying; to follow his script, and in the same, overdone epic mode.

That insight, I suspect, may have been especially troubling to certain members of Juvenal's second-century audience, some of whom may have felt a similar resentment towards their newfound, much-vaunted "freedom." After the fall, the race was on to come to terms with the past and to retell the story of Rome's first-century "trauma," i.e. by constructing it *as* trauma. But as I hope by now to have shown, the choices available in that so-called "free-speaking" enterprise were actually quite limited: you could either keep quiet about the emperors, by damning their memory altogether, or you could write them up as monsters, absurd, easy-to-read, and extreme. Treating them as complex, human characters, or with anything other than outright scorn, does not seem to have been an option. Not one you would want to explore too far, anyway. For, whatever you said about them would be closely scrutinized, so the pressure was on to watch what everyone else was doing, and to say what everyone else was saying, no matter how overdone and unreal that might seem.

With Juvenal it all seems especially unreal. That is the problem he presents to us, and to the various audiences that he addressed in his own day. He takes a sledgehammer to what others have handled with discretion, refined generic sensibilities, and a very fine brush. That kind of clumsiness and bluster is funny, of course, and we are certainly right to laugh at it. But, I suspect, there is an uncomfortable edge to that laughter as well. For, if I am right in drawing some of the analogies I have drawn in this chapter, Juvenal's flawed, hypocritical program touches on one of the main cultural enterprises of his day. His is a louder, sleazier version of that enterprise: the panic-driven search for monsters, and for an easy narrative-fix, one "box" at a time, on an impossibly complicated past. Setting Juvenal's project beside that one has some potentially disturbing effects. Yet it is precisely there, I think, in the poetry's potential to disturb and to perform its diagnostic work, that it finally emerges as the one thing we never quite imagined that Juvenal's *Satires* could be: satire. The real thing. Satire that measures up, needing no apologies, because it is really not as late and irrelevant as it seems. It has in it a very real potential to disrupt, offend, and tear into the most deeply-felt anxieties of the Trajanic age.

THE POOR MAN'S LUCILIUS

Juvenal has precious little to say against specific, named members of the social and political elite of his day, and he keeps the precise details of his private life to himself.[54] Thus, despite his elaborate protestations to the contrary, he can never be counted as the *Lucilius redux* he claims to be. Nor does he resemble Horace, a friendly ironist, in any obvious way, or Persius, a riddling Stoic ideologue. Instead, scholars have long seen that Juvenal's hallmark, and his chief contribution to modern expectations of the genre, is anger.[55] His *indignatio* "moral outrage" is so all-encompassing that it leaves no room for the genre's more understated registers of ironic play, introspection, and philosophical calm. His preferred mode in books 1 and 2 is a grand-style, declamatory rage. The satirists who went before him all had their moments in that register. Juvenal apparently knows no other.

---

[54] Though he tells of general frustrations in abundance.
[55] Rudd–Barr (1991) ix: "there is no surviving Roman satirist whose approach more nearly matches readers' expectations of the genre."

In his first poem, we have seen, Juvenal figures his work as an outburst of rage, pent up by decades of pressurized seething. His pen he compares to a long neglected Lucilian sword that he wields against the vicious and the vain. But that Lucilian act quickly falters when he comes to consider the price he may be forced to pay for freely speaking his mind. A worried friend steps in at line 150 to remind him that the "frankness" he intends to use is a throwback to another age (*illa* **priorum** ... *simplicitas*, 151–3), and that such high ideals are no longer safely pursued. But Juvenal makes a strong Lucilian objection to his interlocutor's warning at Juv. 1.153–7:

> "cuius non audeo dicere nomen?
> quid refert dictis ignoscat Mucius an non?"
> "pone Tigillinum, taeda lucebis in illa
> qua stantes ardent qui fixo gutture fumant,
> et latum media sulcum deducit harena."

Whose name am I not daring enough to mention? What difference to me if Mucius overlooks my words or not? "Write about Tigillinus and you will blaze on the same torch that burns men alive, leaving them to smoulder with a nail through their throats. He/it [sc. when dragged away] draws a broad trough from the middle of the sand."

The sword-wielding *Lucilius ardens* (165) becomes just that in these lines, a non-metaphor, a "burning Lucilius." Tigillinus likes such metaphorical bravado, the poet's friend warns him, because he can make the would-be Lucilius' every figurative pretension come literally true, even driving a pen-like weapon straight through the satirist's voicebox to show him wielding his vaunted "sword of free speech." Juvenal's stated program will become the script for his torturer's satire-killing show.

But there is a second, less obvious side to this retort that makes it much more than a general warning about the dangers of free speech in first-century Rome. For the abrupt change of satiric targets from the poet's Mucius to the cautious friend's Tigillinus brings with it a strong sense of the passing of time, and of Juvenal's being hopelessly out of date and naïve. He is trying to revive satiric ideals that are a throwback to an age long past, when Mucius and his like were still interesting as satire's principal targets, and when they could be counted as any satirist's most fearsome threat. Juvenal refers to P. Mucius Scaevola, the same Mucius that Persius works into his "shutting down" of the genre as a free-speaking enterprise at P. 1.115.[56] This Mucius was an eminent politician of the second century BCE whose impeccable pedigree, high political connections, and illustrious official career made him someone not to be taunted. And yet Lucilius taunted him. That is the point. That is how fearless Lucilius was, how powerful *that* satirist's own high birth, his enormous wealth, and the security of his having powerful friends, made him. He could boast of having nothing to fear from Mucius. And what an impressive boast that was!

But no longer. His wary advisor is not impressed. For Juvenal has naïvely assumed that Mucius and his like still matter in Rome, that they are still the ones whom satirists need to target and to fear, the ones from whom severe reprisals must be expected. Mucius' reputation as a threatening figure not to be taunted harks back to a different age, when power actually belonged to senators of noble birth in Rome, when membership in the Senate, especially for a former tribune of the plebs and consul, as Mucius was, brought with it real, menacing power. But the mere mention of Tigillinus, set within a two-line sample of the power he wields, hurls the Lucilian throwback into a (past) present tense that he can by no means understand.

Tigillinus, in clear contrast to Mucius, was a man of remarkably low birth, and yet he attained a degree of power and political influence over Nero that no Republican senator, not even the most powerful enemy of the Scipios, could match.[57] Tacitus relates that Tigillinus attained his inordinate power by catering to Nero's every cruel whim, and by his stylish innovations in the fields of feasting, whoring, and torture – often innovating by combining all three. Thus, whereas Lucilius used his old Roman nobility and political influence to attack vice, Tigillinus is said to have used vice to attain political influence and to attack the old Roman nobility. The world of Lucilius, the world his would-be imitator understands and intends to work within, has been turned completely upside down by the likes of Tigillinus and Nero. And that is what makes Juvenal's reprise of Lucilius so utterly unthinkable in a first-century, totalitarian context.

But the particular brand of torture described in these lines speaks not just to a change in times that Juvenal has failed to take

---

[56] See above, chapter 2.
[57] For Tigillinus' low birth, see Tac. *Hist.* 1.72 and the Scholiasts on Juv. 1.155.

into account, it is a subtle but firm reminder of Juvenal's dubious standing within the elaborate hierarchy of Roman *Herkunft*. For the punishment his interlocutor describes to him would never have been suffered by any real Lucilius, not even one who happened to hurl insults, live, and die an unnatural death in Tigillinus' day. It was reserved for the slaves and urban poor of Rome, having been tailor-made, it seems, for those who professed to being Christians under Nero. Tac. *Ann.* 15.44 tells us that the making of human lamps to light up the emperor's late-night orgies was a cruel innovation for which Tigillinus may well have been responsible. It has his signature (i.e. "demetaphorizing") design, making Christ's low-life "lights (lit. "lamps") of the world" into the lamps they boasted to be.

Nobles, on the other hand, were not normally subjected to this kind of extreme punishment, degrading by design. Their recalcitrance might be punished by exile or an enforced suicide, punishment leisurely pursued, often elaborately orchestrated by the victim himself/herself as a final show of defiance and free agency, and performed with a distinct and ennobling stylistic flair, *the victim's own* personalized design. But no such attractive and ennobling punishments could be expected by the likes of Juvenal. His death, his interlocutor reminds him, would be a spectacle of his powerlessness and his utter disgrace. For whereas Rome's first-century "monsters" were wont to leave traces of the noble heroes they consumed, in hero tales that lived beyond the grave, common folk and fake heroes they consumed completely. The only trace they left of themselves, literary or otherwise, was a signature line drawn in the arena sand, a charred trough for the grounds-keepers to rake smooth before "processing" the next batch of nameless condemned.[58] Such is the "menace" posed by a second-rate, poor man's Lucilius in Tigillinus' Rome. Like a second-tier hero in epic, he takes up a fallen hero's weapons and tries to wield them as his own. But the principal threat he poses in using them is to himself. Lucilius' pen-sword in hand, Juvenal will end up impaling himself right through the throat.

---

[58] The literary dimension of the victim's "broad trench" is suggested by *deducere*, the word of choice among poets who wished to identify their writing as refined both in and by the Callimachean tradition. For *deducere* referring to the removal of corpses from the arena, cf. Tert. *Apol.* 15.5 *uidimus et Iouis fratrem gladiatorum cadauera cum malleo deducentem.*

Juvenal brandishes an impressive epic sword once owned by Lucilius, but he cannot use it as its former owner so famously did. So he wields it against the long dead, and against living targets of no account. The sphere in which these targets operate and offend, he tells us, and thus the place where Juvenal routinely takes us to see them, is not the Senate house, nor the Palatine hill, nor a noble friend's well appointed villa, but the bustling crossroads of downtown Rome, the *quadriuium* (the "four roads"), an intersection that rates as one notch more trivial than the *triuium* (the "three roads"). At Juv. 1.63–8 he says:

> nonne libet medio ceras inplere capaces
> quadriuio, cum iam sexta ceruice feratur
> hinc atque inde patens ac nuda paena cathedra
> et multum referens de Maecenate supino
> signator falsi, qui se lautum atque beatum
> exiguis tabulis et gemma fecerit uda?

Wouldn't you like to fill large notebooks at/with the intersection of the four-roads whenever some forger sweeps past in a litter that's wide open, carried by six slaves, looking just like some lounging Maecenas now that he has made himself elegant and rich by means of his niggling codicils and ever-ready sealing ring?

Here we are treated to a sample of the highways to be traveled along, and the sights to be seen in these poems. For named targets of any real political and social significance he takes us outside the city walls, to the attractive graveyards of the Flaminian and Latin Roads. Live targets, such as the one described here, and others in the lines that follow, will be spied along the dusty *quadriuium*, by a would-be horseman who cannot afford a horse.

Despite this lowering of perspective and locale, the grand proportions of this man's rage are not reduced. The point is well made by the enormity of the wax tablets he tells of filling in these lines, tablets crammed so full, he says, that they contain the entire *quadriuium*, as if the pages he writes on were as wide and full as the four converging roads they describe. Impossible. But that is what he intends to deliver, a bustling scene of scrappings and goings-about, the poor man's eye-view of *his* Rome, the city at its seediest and least elegant. This view, he makes clear, is observed by someone travelling on foot, at street-level, specifically not from a sedan chair high above the bustle, or from a quiet, suburban hillside overlooking the scene. What happens in those higher places, he admits, is generally hidden from his view, blocked off by crowds of gawkers and retainers and screens that keep him from getting a clear view of the city's power brokers and their negotiations of high import. And thus our view of these same higher matters is blocked off as well, screened by the poet's failure to rate as the Lucilius he aimed to be, and severely skewed by his jaundiced and outraged way of seeing his world, a world that he can neither rise above nor master. Still, at lines 85–8 he makes grand, comprehensive claims for his work that his limited eye-view can never manage to deliver:

> quidquid agunt homines, uotum, timor, ira, uoluptas,
> gaudia, discursus, nostri farrago libelli est.
> et quando uberior uitiorum copia? quando
> maior auaritiae patuit sinus?

Whatever people do, their desires, fears, wrath, pleasure, passions, and runnings-about, that is the fodder of my little book. And when has the harvest of vice ever been more abundant? When has Greed's pocket ever gaped wider?

The enterprise is massive, beyond all bounds, impossible. No less than *quidquid agunt homines* ("whatever people do"). In the lines that follow he gives yet another sample of the places he will take us, and of how he will paint the scenes he sees, telling of "what huge battles you will see" (*proelia quanta . . . uidebis*, 91) in the gaming parlors of Rome. The metaphor is typical of Juvenal, and telling: for this satirist, the squabbles of greedy gamblers are on a par with the grandest battles of Roman epic. The one scene, no matter how seedy and trivial, and no matter where it is spied, he can only conceive through the other. And that is the way he intends to tell it to us: "Sing, Muse, the wrath of Corax, when he lost ten thousand to the scar-faced juggler of Scuffle Street."

That is the ironic sum of Juvenal's stated program. He fixes his eyes on what happens at street-level in Rome, in the brothels, taverns and alleyways where no satirist has taken us before, and he describes what he sees there in the fulsome tones and tropes of Rome's grandest poetic enterprise, as if the two could really be made to work together. He enters these places armed in Lucilian battle gear, failing to notice how overdressed he is, and paying no mind to the snickers rising above the beer. There he puts up a spectacular, Quixotic fight against the denizens of his daily routine, railing against all the various nobodies and the long dead who have shown him no respect and, as he tells it, made his life a series of labors to rival any epic hero's worst travails. His railing is constant. Overdone. Self-defeating.

Perhaps the most obvious problem he faces in getting us to take him seriously is his chosen rhetorical mode, a high-flying declamatory rage. Roman theorists of rhetoric had long insisted that such a showy display was precarious and had to be used with great care, sparingly fitted to certain parts of a well made speech, and worked up to in certain well defined ways. The grand show of *indignatio* in Roman oratory was heavily restricted by those who knew its self-destructive potentials, but Juvenal does not seem to have learned the rules of compositional theory restricting its use, especially the rule of "variation" (*uariatio*). His first poem he begins in a full-blown rage, and he stays in that mode with little variation throughout his first three books. Steady, reasoned arguments are momentary and few in Juvenal, displaced by a barrage of grand-style devices, commonly considered the mechanisms of a good speech, not the thing itself.

Special effects overshadow argument, leaving us to wonder what to make of the poet's stated moral and punitive aims. Are they completely undermined by rhetorical incompetence? Can anything he says be taken seriously as the truth about the way things are? His show of self-defeat makes for a good, comic gag, an ancient version of a standup comic's "I don't get no respect" routine. But does it rate as satire? That is, does it deliver on any significant generic expectations as received from Lucilius and remade by Horace and Persius? Most importantly, what of the genre's well advertised penchant for telling *the truth* with a smile, whether delivering that as raw Lucilian mockery, or hiding the bitter inside the sweet, by "cooking it down" in schoolboy cookies, or in plebeian beets and plates of grain that nourish, annoy, expose, and teach? Does Juvenal's low-grade *farrago* ("horse-feed," contrasting Persius' pious "grain-pile") have any nutritional value at all? Or is our laughter his only point?

LIFE ON THE EDGE: FROM EXAGGERATION TO
SELF-DEFEAT

Juvenal's second and third poems tell of vice so widespread and overwhelming that it pushes the last of the city's "real Romans," such as the poet and his alter-ego, Umbricius, claim to be, clear off the map of Rome's ever expanding world, to the frozen Sea of Azov in the far north, and to the Sibyl's gateway to hell in the south. That is how far one has to run from Rome to escape her rampant depravity. That is how far this satirist is forced to go to describe it to us: off the map of commonplace and carefully delimited modes of censure, into the frigid, uncharted realms of grand, Asianist hyperbole. Just how wild and overdone that exaggeration can be he demonstrates in all the poems of books 1 and 2, neatly fitting the mode to the vice these poems decry, with *descriptio* pushed to reality's edge, defying belief, in order to demonstrate just how monstrous and extreme Roman moral habits have become. These habits, like a disease, have spread to the farthest reaches of an empire that is now, under Trajan, as huge and unwieldy as it will ever become. With a Rome so big and preternaturally extreme, the satire that claims to censure it must be equally vast and unbounded.

Thus we hear outlandish tales in these poems, of vice always expanding and ever reaching new, record-setting extremes, like the empire itself, only to be outdone by new extremes in the descriptions that immediately follow. The second poem begins with a description of Cleanthean sodomites, moral censors who screw one another amid the trappings of their high moral ideals. Later in the same poem we hear of drag-queen statesmen who celebrate the rites of "The Great Goddess," in a *Bona Dea* scandal several degrees more scandalous than Cicero's. His tales are so outlandish that they constantly invite the suspicion of informed listeners who might otherwise, given the stated moral aims of satire and the speaker's own self-assured earnestness, be tempted to take them, and him, seriously. That suspicion regularly extends to unbelief, and elicits a knowing laugh.

And yet, these tall tales do more than simply entertain with their outlandishness. For they resemble certain other moral/didactic shows that played in Juvenal's Rome, and that sounded, at times, nearly as extreme and comically grim as his own. Thus, the laughter that these tales elicit has a catch, a hidden "satiric" barb that lingers and chafes long after the show has closed and the laughter faded. For this show has the potential to take in others as well, and to drag them down in Juvenal's own, brilliantly idiotic self-defeat.

Near the beginning of his second poem, Juvenal cues us to the existence of rival performances of moral censure that played in higher places in Rome, and that traded among those who claimed to be much more philosophically directed and informed. These moralists, not effeminates, transvestites, and homosexuals *per se*, but those who made a grand, philosophical show of berating them, only to bugger one another right in front of the philosopher's busts that peered out at them from the couch's rear shelf, are the targets of this poem's shabby but colorful attack. Their stern efforts *de moribus*, Juvenal insinuates, were employed as a means of sexual arousal, a peep show in the guise of serious moral philosophy. His counter-tirade, in turn, is itself explicit and titillating. Its ability to arouse is thus one of the problems it presents, a hidden triggering device for its own self-defeat.

Juvenal would have us believe that such hypocritical shows of moral outrage played in very high places in Rome. In the time-warped vignette of lines 29–35, where the poet's *nuper* ("recently") means "at least fifteen years ago, if not more," the moral reforms of Domitian himself are addressed:

> qualis erat nuper tragico pollutus adulter
> concubitu, qui tunc leges reuocabat amaras
> omnibus atque ipsis Veneri Martique timendas,
> cum tot abortiuis fecundam Iulia uuluam
> solueret et patruo similes effunderet offas.
> nonne igitur iure ac merito uitia ultima fictos
> contemnunt Scauros et castigata remordent?

And so it was, recently, when that adulterer, stained by an affair of a "tragic" kind, set about to revive stern adultery laws to be feared by all, even Mars and Venus. But while he was doing this, Julia would wash her fertile womb with one abortive-rinse after another, discharging hunks that looked like her uncle. Given all this, isn't it right and deserved for even the most depraved to despise these fake preachers, and to bite them back when they chide?

From the Late Republican figures of the Gracchi, Verres, Milo, Clodius, and Catiline in the lines immediately preceding, all popular type-villains of Roman declamation, the poet makes a precipitous plunge into the (relatively) "recent" remembered past. But in making that move he has not left his suasorial, declamatory imagination behind. Domitian's notorious affair with his niece, Julia, he colors as a titillating and disgusting "tragic" scene, blurring the line between history and myth by making us see one through the other. The adultery laws revived by Domitian, he says, were bitter enough to send a shudder of fear through the gods themselves, Venus and Mars, the most famous adulterous lovers of Greek and Roman myth. The hyperbole is thick. The fictionalizing of fact is obvious, even though that is precisely the danger that the lines themselves urge us to be wary of. Those hideous, "look-alike hunks" of Julia's aborted fetuses are just the most obvious detail of the poet's paint-by-numbers routine, his following rhetoric's rules for *descriptio* that is tailor-made to disgust and enrage.[59]

This is Juvenal's revenge, he claims, the punishment he metes out for having been forced to sit and watch a scene of such outlandish, even "tragic" hypocrisy, with an incestuous emperor acting the part of an outraged Cato in charge of Rome's moral improvement. But the punishment he delivers gets lost in its own unreality and late-coming, and thus it threatens to punish the punisher himself. For Juvenal's tortures, in the end, are every bit as wild and spectacular as those invented by Tigillinus, torturer extraordinaire under Nero, and thus they can be seen as rebounding against the satirist-torturer himself. His "extreme depravities" (*uitia ultima*) bite back, just as he said they would. But this rebounding of the blows he inflicts can be taken in several ways, most obviously as a sign of the poet's ineptitude, intended or not, or of his putting on an act that is more clownish than Catonian, i.e. mistakenly, and hilariously, set on a tragic stage, but with nothing terribly serious to say. Perhaps this is the inevitable price one pays for waiting too long, and letting the pressure to revenge oneself build too high. If, in fact, that is what he is really about. Given the long gap that separates crime from punishment in these poems, the poet is bound to overplay his part, and to appear, if not a hypocrite, a buffoon. At best, a "lovable" buffoon.

And that is precisely where his performance catches others as well. Juvenal's abuse is outrageous, but he is not alone in his outrage. He begins his second poem by complaining that displays of moral severity cannot be trusted, especially when dressed in philosophical garb. But he then gives us every reason not to trust his own moral show, certainly not as a true account of "the way things were" under Domitian. But that may be the point. His own

---

[59] On rhetorical *descriptiones* in Juvenal, see especially Braund (1988) 1–23.

rage, outrageous as it is, is set up in this poem as the unsophisti-
cated foil to another, more philosophically informed and astute
philosophical enterprise. Juvenal, as we have seen, wrote in an age
that styled itself "post-traumatic." Its literature was dominated
by symbolic performances of moral censure in many forms, many
of which performances could easily be judged expedient, if not
openly hypocritical. That self-assured, moral-talking-head industry, targeting the Julio-Claudian and Flavian emperors, is thus
swept into the offense of this poem's failure to stay within bounds,
taken down, if only a notch, by the poet's overdoing of what many
had done extremely well.

But one moral censor stands out in Juv. 2 as its unlikely hero
and lone teller of the truth. Laronia, the inset speaker of lines 38–
63, is given sole credit for speaking up against Domitian's hypocritical moral reforms when they were first being promoted by his
supporters. One reformer, wearing a dour expression on his face,
calls out "where are you sleeping, O Julian Law?" (*ubi nunc, lex
Iulia, dormis?*) in line 37. We have just been given a clear idea of
where Julia, the law's latter-day namesake, was sleeping, so it is
easy to see why Laronia takes this man's hypocritical expostulation
as her point of departure, the precise point where she can hold
back no more. Her response is scornful, but carefully fitted to its
historical setting by being understated, ironic, and thick with figurative double-meanings. Such defiance, however indirectly turned,
is impressive, especially for a woman who has perhaps been accused of adultery herself. Here she takes up the satirist's role. For
a time, she becomes Rome's unlikely moral censor, the real censor
that Domitian could never be, and the censor-satirist that Juvenal,
under Domitian, never was, but perhaps wishes he had been. She
actually said something when it counted!

But impressions are false in this poem, just as the poet has
warned from the start: *frontis nulla fides* ("appearances are not to
be trusted," 8). That applies to Laronia as well, for as Susanna
Braund has clearly shown, Laronia cannot completely hide the
fact that she is herself a *ficta Scaura*, Juvenal's invention, a Diotima
to his Socrates, and his like-minded and highly stylized mirror image.[60] And that poses a problem for our assenting to what she has
to say, especially given the larger moral tale in which she is made

---

[60] See Braund (1995).

to speak. For she, allegedly the poem's only non-hypocrite, is exposed as none other than Juvenal himself, the censor-satirist, in drag! Ferreted out by us, readers who already know this poet too well, Juvenal is thus centrally implicated in his own self-defeat. We have found him parading in Laronia's clothes, engaging in rites of free speech, right before Domitian's face, where no satirist can claim to have spoken the truth she speaks, openly, ironically, or otherwise. Juvenal took no such risk. He never said anything of the sort. And yet, here, (s)he does. Thus, he is exposed as a fraud, yet another dour-faced moralist in a frilly dress, posing in front of a mirror. In the end, the chiding, rhetorical dress he sports is as showy, tartish, and see-through as that of the rhetor Creticus, the "harsh and indomitable teacher of free speech" he lampoons for dressing so provocatively in the lines that directly follow (65–81).

Perhaps the most obvious sign of Juvenal's turning tricks in Laronia's dress is the figuring of her response as a categorical matter of women versus men, *nos* ("us") versus *uos* ("you"). Instead of demonstrating that the accused are free from blame, she simply claims that men, as a group, are worse, and she proffers several *exempla*, thick with innuendo, to prove her point. Such a grand sweep of disgust, targeting an entire gender, has its most obvious parallel in the sweeping, mock-Catonian attack of Juv. 6, an apotreptic against marriage that quickly turns into a categorical disparagement of women. That poem begins with a mock anthropology in the spirit of Hor. *S.* 1.3.99–112, telling of a time far back in the reign of Saturn when a chaste wife, however shaggy, could still be found. But that was terribly long ago, he says, in an age of myth that this speaker regards as perfectly real. His addressee he thus aptly names Postumus ("Born After"), a man who seems to want a good wife, but is, regrettably, too late.

The poet cites dozens of instances of feminine immorality, mythical, historical, and contemporary, in the course of Juv. 6. None of these is clearly detached from the exemplary scandals of Roman declamation, historical myth, epic, and tragedy, through which they are figured. After more than 600 lines of fuming, the poet recalls the murderous intrigues of the Julio-Claudian women, and that leads him to lose his bearings completely. The poem ends with the poet's free fall into the world of myth. We watch him rail against the husband-killers and child-killers he claims to see on every Roman street, women far worse than the

Danaids, Procnes, and Clytemnestras known from the Greek tragic stage. He urgently wants us to believe that they are really there, right before our eyes, chopping children for their husbands' stew. Just look anywhere, he says, and you will see them. Don't you see them?

But we don't. What we are looking at, at this point, is Juvenal himself, the madman satirist. He is the show. We watch as he loses control, at last swept into the world of myth so completely that he himself becomes the principal spectacle of uncontrolled *ira* (647) and *rabies* (648) that he claims to deplore in "this sex" (*hunc sexum*, 648). And there, in that complete loss of control, he again becomes his satire's chief target. For the failure to distinguish myth from reality has been earmarked by him as a deplorable feminine vice since early on in this poem. The most memorable scene both deploring this loss of control, and showing its effects on the poet himself, we see at lines 60–6, Juvenal's version of the orgasmic recitation scene of P. 1.15–21. The poet asks Postumus:

> porticibusne tibi monstratur femina uoto
> digna tuo? cuneis an habent spectacula totis
> quod securus ames quodque inde excerpere possis?
> chironomon Ledam molli saltante Bathyllo
> Tuccia uesicae non imperat, Apula gannit,
> sicut in amplexu, subito et miserabile longum.
> attendit Thymele: Thymele tunc rustica discit.

Is there any woman you can point to in the arcades who lives up to your wish? Or do the spectacles/seats in the theater's every tier offer anything for you to pluck out and love free from care? Bathyllus nimbly dances the part of a gesturing Leda. Tuccia loses control of her bladder. Apula lets out a sudden and sustained yelp, as if she is the one being embraced [by the swan]. Thymele pays close attention. She is still a country girl, so she is taking notes.

Here the real spectacle, as in the orgasmatron of P. 1, is the critical reaction playing in the seats. Watching Bathyllus dance the part of Leda, at a point of high emotion in the play – presumably at the point where "the swan," Zeus, gets amorous – the women in the audience lose control. The boundary separating the "show" (*OLD spectaculum* 2) from the "seats" (*OLD spectaculum* 3) is completely erased. Thus, the spectators become the players, the show itself, in an exuberant, overdone, and utterly unbelievable loss of control. And that is where they seem most like Juvenal himself. Like them, he watches. He reacts. Failing to separate myth from lived experience, he loses control.

Outlandish pictures, often said to represent vice at its worst, are Juvenal's specialty. But scenes even more garish routinely follow. New vicious extremes are continuously being reached. At Juv. 2.83 the poet claims that "no on has become filthiest of the foul in an instant" (*nemo repente fuit turpissimus*), and yet that is exactly the way he presents vice, "filthiest of the foul," to us, in an instant, precipitous, downward slide, with each successive *descriptio* purporting to reach a new low. He follows his taunting of Creticus' rhetorical peep show, described in the lines immediately preceding this claim, with a description of male transvestites profaning the rites of the Bona Dea, a festival from which men were normally excluded. This festival, like that of the goddess Cybele, described later in lines 110–16, was marked by a loosening of certain moral restrictions normally observed by the sect's devotees, such as limits on heavy drinking and free speech, the hand-in-glove symbols of satire herself.[61] Juvenal's pumped-up version of Cicero's most famous and spectacular scandal is thus suitably unbounded. It features not just a single male infiltrator who tries to keep his identity a secret, but an entire sorority of noble Roman "pathics," each trying to outdo one another in modish dress-up and debauchery. One applies eye-liner to his brows and eyes with a pin. Another fellates a glass Priapus, while yet another primps in front of a mirror wearing a golden hair-net and paper-thin garments of yellow and sky blue. Creticus' see-through business suit seems chaste by comparison.

This is Juvenal's outdoing of Cicero, and of himself, precisely where, one might have thought, neither could be credibly outdone. And they cannot. The performance is grand and incredible, reminiscent in tone and detail of one of Greek Old Comedy's most shocking plays, the *Baptae* of Eupolis.[62] And, like the Old Comic play it resembles, the scene hides a striking, satiric sting in its tail. For at the end of the description of an all-male Bona Dea, Juvenal adds (Juv. 2.99–103):

---

[61] For the loosening of social restrictions at these festivals, see Braund (1992) 73 with notes.
[62] For strong connections with Eupolis' *Baptae,* see Braund (1996) 148.

ille tenet speculum, pathici gestamen Othonis,
Actoris Aurunci spolium, quo se ille uidebat
armatum, cum iam tolli uexilla iuberet.
res memoranda nouis annalibus atque recenti
historia, speculum ciuilis sarcina belli.

That man there is holding a mirror, the battle-gear of Otho the pathic, "stripped from Actor who hails from Aurunca." In it he [Otho] used to look at himself dressed for battle, even as he was issuing orders for an attack. Here is a theme worth recalling in annals of recent events and in history that is fresh: a mirror inside a civil war battle kit!

Otho died nearly four decades before these lines were published, in the civil conflict of 69 CE. Still he is described here as the subject of history that is emphatically "new" and "recent." But perhaps the point of the emphasis is less the relative temporal proximity of the events described, i.e. "annals of recent history as opposed to ancient," than it is what it takes for historical narratives, in Juvenal's day, or in his unique reckoning, to rate as "modern" and "up-to-date." Thus the basic sense may be: "If you don't believe me" (and, of course, how can we!) "you can consult Otho's tale as it is told in any of the historical annals that are just now hitting the shelves, the hottest tales on the market today. There you will see the truth of what I am saying. After all, histories are unbiased by design. They never exaggerate. Just consult one of them and you will see for yourself: Otho was a primping, mirror-packing pathic."

Given the close coupling of *annales* with *historia* in lines 102–3, scholars have generally taken the line as a reference to Tacitus' *Histories* which, as Courtney notes, "record the instruments of luxury brought by some of Otho's army" without mentioning the mirror *per se*.[63] Thus, Juvenal can be seen in these lines in the act of applying a dab of glossy eye-liner to Tacitus' account of Otho's reign soon after the *Histories* were first published, with *res memoranda* referring to a "topic that should have been recalled" by Tacitus, but was not. Either that, or he is providing an editorial suggestion for their final improvement: "a topic that *should be* recalled." But if the reference is to some work already published and circulating in its final form, a work in which Otho actually does look into his mirror before entering battle, then the reference

---

[63] Courtney (1980) 139.

must be to some version of Rome's civil wars of 69 CE now lost to us, and about which we can know nothing other than that it featured an emperor primping before battle.

In whatever scenario we imagine the reference working, its damaging effects on the historical-moral work it refers to are clear to see. For, much as Juvenal may (pretend to) want to flatter the historian(s) he has in mind, he is not capable of doing that without involving them in his own self-defeat. Is this poet the sort of critic that any serious historian would seek the approval of? Would any writer of history in Juvenal's day really want his reliability taken for granted, in writing, and seconded by him? Even if the reference is not to Tacitus, it involves him, for it sends his readers, both ancient and modern, back to their *Histories* in a vain search for Otho's missing mirror. They will not find it there, but they will find plenty of other descriptive touches that resemble it in their power to drag history-telling down to the level of mirrors and mushrooms and descriptive props. That mirror, for Juvenal, is an accoutrement of civil war when the telling of that war rates, in his tabloid imagination, as "modern" and "fresh." In other words, it is not just something that "pathic Otho" pulled from his bag in someone's telling of his tale, whether he really did anything of the sort or not. It is something that the history writer himself pulls from his civil war writing kit, a descriptive touch tailor-made to insult Roman sensibilities and to enrage, like that needle-sharp pen Domitian is said, by several historians, to have used to stab flies at his Alban estate; a pen that Dio, nearly a century later, must apologize for pulling out, even openly admitting that the detail is perhaps beneath his history's dignity. But he insists that it is useful, all the same, for sketching Domitian's "true character."[64] Thus, that pen, like Otho's mirror, is less important as a demonstrable "fact" of history, than it is as a tool of history writing. And that leaves us to wonder who the real hypocrite is in this scene: is it Otho, primping before his mirror? Or is it the history writer who pulls that mirror from his bag of history writing tricks, a kit normally packed with the instruments of war?

Juvenal looks at the "mythically" troubled world that surrounds him, and he reacts to what he sees by gesturing wildly, and with little evident control, like the orgasmic women he spies in the

---

[64] See Dio 65.9.4; cf. Suet. *Dom.* 3.1.

audience of a pantomime show. His reaction is outlandish, even titillating, far more interesting than anything that takes place in Rome, the stage on which his eyes are fixed. Thus, his reaction is a terrible gauge for determining "what actually happened" in Rome in his day, in the lived experience he claims to respond to. But that is perhaps the scandal of his hailing contemporary moral writers and historians into his cause, if only to favor his own work over theirs, or to claim that he actually likes what they have to say. For, in doing that, he invites us to compare his work to theirs. And so we imagine, if only for a moment, that they really may have something to do with one another, as if part of the same cultural, restorative project, and stemming from the same desire to say what needed to be said after "the trauma" had passed. Juvenal does not hide the rage and the desire for revenge that drive him to write. They do. And thus, he cannot avoid the inevitable self-defeat that goes with shouting so loudly. Even so, he gives us to believe that his performance is really not so different from theirs. It is simply louder and more direct. The joke is on Juvenal, that is clear enough. But others, his rivals in what seems to have been a much larger industry of contemporary moral criticism, are implicated as well.

BEATING A DEAD FISH: THE EMPEROR-SATIRIST OF JUV. 4

The fourth satire tells of a time not long ago (*nuper*, 9) when Rome was brooded over by an outsized beast that "mangled the world when it was already half-dead" (37). No one dared raise a finger, let alone a thunderbolt, to stop him. The tale features an epic prelude with no hard-fighting payoff: muses are hailed, forces rallied and catalogued, a summit held on high, and a divine weapon is crafted. But no battle ensues. Instead, Domitian, the titan in this story, is left to brood over the world he tortures, and to smother it, like an enormous flatfish on a plate, attended by his minions in miniature, the shrimp-monsters that swim in his sauce. No noble hero arrives on the scene to do battle against the beast, and thus, set up for a titanic "clash," we are given no battle, no cosmoscrator, no epic satisfaction. Instead, the best Rome can muster in this poem is a skittish, late-coming "cash-laborer" (*cerdo*, 153), an embezzler in Domitian's palace who kills the emperor because he fears being caught with his hand in the till.

The final complaint of this poor man's titanomachy is that the monster robbed the city of her most illustrious souls "without being punished, and with no one attempting to avenge them" (*inpune et uindice nullo*, 152). But that is precisely where Juvenal himself steps in to fill the gap, with this poem, a late-arriving thunderbolt. Punitive work, after all, is his declared programmatic aim. But the end result leaves us to wonder how he, as a self-declared agent of punishment, figures in his own story. Does he resemble the skittish palace servant, an underclassed hero who at last delivers the blow that no noble Roman was willing to attempt? Or is he more in line with the titan himself, Domitian, torturing a world that he keeps well stocked with monsters now that it is "half alive," and serving up monster-fish that he expects us, his readerly minions, to stand in awe of and scramble to make a plate for, a satiric *lanx* big enough to hold this man's overblown notion of "satire," and his fish stories that defy both generic confines and all good sense?

The first big fish in the story is Crispinus, "a monster of vice without a redeeming virtue" (2–3).[65] Juvenal explains that this creature had a taste for illicit sex that was both extreme and discriminating, so much so that he made a rule of "spurning" unmarried girls, as if chastely bound and committed to sex within (someone else's) marriage. But he once made an exception to his "no virgins" rule for a Vestal Virgin, the most illicit sexual target of all in Rome. That affair was subsequently found out, and the Vestal was punished by a stern, Catonian censor and chief priest, Domitian, by being buried alive. Crispinus, the seducer, went unpunished.

To further pique our disgust and desire for revenge, Juvenal adds the descriptive brushstroke that the two slept together while the Vestal was "wearing her ribbons" (*vittata*, 9). In her nun's habit, as it were. Crispinus had a fetish for dress-up that was both criminal and sacrilegious. Her sacred ribbons turned him on. Hard to believe. Surely he exaggerates(?). "Did she really wear her sacred ribbons to bed, and nothing else?" Imagine it (you just did!). Now who is being turned on? Who is becoming Crispinus? This is revenge with a reverse sting.[66]

---

[65] The translation of Rudd–Barr.

[66] Braund (1996) 168, quoting Henderson, comments on the moral crusading of *Satire* 2: "his language [is] full of the marks of indignation … and too suspiciouly 'lurid and lip-smacking' to sustain his pose of moralistic preaching."

Juvenal asks (14–15): "What do you do when the person [on trial] is dreadful and more obscene than any criminal charge?" His next word is *mullum* "mullet," in what seems to be a shift of topic from greater crimes to lesser, and from punishment to fish. He writes (Juv. 4.15–17):

> mullum sex milibus emit,
> aequantem sane paribus sestertia libris,
> ut perhibent qui de magnis maiora locuntur.

He bought a red mullet for six thousand, actually paying out one thousand sesterces per pound. Those who tell of big things in even bigger tales insist that it's true.

By the satirist's own admission, the fish defies belief. His authorities exaggerate, Juvenal says, but their exaggeration simply becomes what he leaves us to take for granted in his telling of the tale: one thousand sesterces per pound. That is the exact selling price of mullet in this story, for those who are buying it (are we?). Take it or leave it. That is the image he leaves us to seethe over. Again, this is a case of an unpunished crime. Such prodigality was a criminal offense in Rome, deserving the censor's *nota* and the disgrace that went with it. But the censor at this time was Domitian, Crispinus' promoter, defender, and friend. Thus, the unspoken question inside the question of lines 14–15 is: "What do you do when the censor himself has a taste for monster fish, and for little monsters, like Crispinus?" Answer: "Nothing."

But the fish is not just the crime in this story, it is the punishment. For the (apparently) rhetorical question of lines 14–15, "What do you do with a monster like this?" really does have an answer, and it happens to be the very answer that follows the question in the text: *mullum* "The mullet." At Juv. 10.316–17, Juvenal describes the punishments that await adulterers caught in the act: "this man cuts him down with a knife, that one with bloody lashes of the whip. And still others get a mullet inside." Courtney annotates *mugilis* ("grey mullet") with the following: "This was a fish with a large head tapering into a small tail ... It was inserted in the adulterer's anus as a substitute for humiliating him by homosexual rape ... and also to inflict pain with its spines."[67] Crispinus was a monster of vice, Juvenal says. His

---

[67] Courtney (1980) 484.

crimes earned him no ordinary mullet. The one he bought, a
record-setting six pounder, the biggest on ancient record, is the
perfect fish to both fit, and punish, the crime. Juvenal lets him
have it, the fish he so ostentatiously bought, returned as the one he
never got. The crime is the fish. The fish the punishment. The
punishment the poem.[68]

But not only do fish and fiend deserve one another in this poem,
they resemble one another in very specific ways.[69] By the time
Juvenal finishes his "fish-insertion" of Crispinus, the lines separating man and fish, criminal and punishment, have been substantially erased: in line 24 we see Crispinus wrapped in paper, like a
fish sold at market, a phenomenon expressed in the very layout of
the line (**succinctus** ... *Crispine,* **papyro**). In line 33 he is berated
as a seller of Nile-river *siluri* ("catfish"), small fry that are said
to be his *municipes* ("fellow townsmen"). Domitian himself will be
similarly fish-figured later in the poem, shown taking bait, sporting
fin-like crests, and smothering his world like a monstrous, overfed
rhombus ("turbot") on a plate.[70]

That is where this story has been leading: to Domitian, and his
big fish; that is, to the big, overstuffed monster that, Juvenal insists, he was. At the transition point of lines 28–33, Juvenal insists
that Crispinus' fish, huge as it was, counts as little more than a
side dish served up "on the margins of a modest feast" (*modicae ...
de margine cenae,* 30) at Domitian's regal table. And so Crispinus and
his fish become just that in the poem: an introductory, "marginal"
footnote to the bigger fish story he is about to tell.

For that story Juvenal needs a full measure of inspiration. At
lines 34–6 he calls on the muses of epic:

> incipe Calliope. licet et considere: non est
> cantandum, res uera agitur. narrate, puellae
> Pierides, prosit mihi uos dixisse puellas.

---

[68] The idea may derive from the "gourding" of Claudius that is the *Apocolocyntosis*; cf.
Coffey (1976) 167–8: "A very different view has been accepted by a number of modern
critics, that in form and meaning ἀποκολοκύντωσις is based on ἀποραφανίδωσις, the
Greek punishment for adultery in which a horseradish was thrust into the adulterer's body *per anum* and that, as the gourd is the largest of vegetables and the shape
of some species suited to the action, the title is an indecent joke depending on comic
exaggeration."

[69] As the empty-headed Claudius resembles his punitive gourd.

[70] For the resemblance of Domitian to the turbot, see Gowers (1993a) 207–8, and Deroux
(1983).

Begin, Calliope. And feel free to sit down. No singing needed. The case
we are considering is true! Relate the story, maidens of Pieria. And may
it help me to have called you "maidens."

Juvenal hints that his muses are not as young and pure as they
would like us to believe. Like all the other "once-chaste" women
in this poem, they have been seduced by Domitian and/or his
fellow monsters. That defilement is both told of in the poem, and
punished by it. For, in the fish summit that follows, Juvenal treats
us to a parodic version of one of the epic muses' most notorious
love affairs under Domitian, the *De Bello Germanico* of Statius, a
panegyric epic on the emperor's military campaigns against the
Chatti in 89 CE.[71] They allowed themselves to be seduced in that
work, Juvenal insinuates. Statius, their pimp, was rewarded handsomely for getting "maidens" so noble and chaste to turn tricks in
the emperor's bed.[72] Not to be outdone by Crispinus, Domitian
had a fetish for sacrilege as well.

Four lines of the *De Bello Germanico* survive. They describe
the summoning of a council of war at a precarious moment in
the campaign. The list of those summoned is partial, broken at the
front and back, but it mentions Crispus, Veiento, Acilius, and, less
certainly, Catullus, all of whom are summoned to the fish summit
of Juv. 4. Thus, scholars generally concede that the parodic direction of Juvenal's attack is evident. Not surprisingly, Statius won a
prize at Domitian's Alban games of 90 CE, presumably for his *De
Bello Germanico*.[73] Here, in Juv. 4, he gets the satirist's booby prize.
He has his glorious panegyric handed back to him holding something it did not hold before: a gigantic fish. His poem has become
Juvenal's fish-wrap, and thus it has suffered the common fate of
bad, voluminous writing since Volusius' "shitty sheets."[74]

The bigger the crime in this poem, the bigger the fish. Ac-
cordingly, the fish netted for Domitian's *Apomullosis* is a beast of
primordial girth, perfectly suited to this *Flauius ultimus* ("the last /

---

[71] On the influence of Statius' *De Bello Germanico* on Juv. 4, see Braund (1996) 271–2.

[72] Statius is specifically named only once in Juvenal, at 7.82–7, where he is described as a
once-popular poet who hits on hard times and is thus forced to pimp one of his poem-
girls for cash, selling his "virgin Agave" (*intactam ... Agauen*, 87) to Domitian's favorite
pantomime actor, Paris.

[73] See Courtney (1980) 195.

[74] For references to the "poetry as fish-wrap" metaphor, and a discussion of the metaphor's
relevance to Juv. 4, see Gowers (1993a) 205, with n. 332.

most extreme of the Flavians," 37–8). Gowers notes the incredible size of the beast: "The fish swims into view with its astonishing bulk (*spatium admirabile rhombi*, 39), prize specimen of the world that is Domitian's personal safari-park (*uiuaria*, 51) ... the ambiguous words *impleuit sinus* (41), literally "it filled the fold," begin the fishy distortion of scales in the poem. The fish either filled the fisherman's net, or it filled an entire gulf: we can magnify or telescope it at will, tell our own tall story."[75]

Given the size of the fish, fully as big as we make it, the summit's principal agenda is to find a dish large enough to hold it. That search, Gowers has argued, is the perfect symbol for the satirist's own struggle to contain Domitian's enormity on satire's relatively small *lanx*, especially since that plate has been radically scaled down by his immediate, more "philosophical," predecessors, Horace and Persius. A huge, new plate is called for, one specially made to take in the enormity that is Domitian, Juvenal's big fish. Gowers writes: "The search for a container big enough for the fish, *sed derat pisci patinae mensura* (72), rephrases Juvenal's rhetorical question in *Satire* I: *unde | ingenium par materiae?* ... Juvenal needs to rise to the occasion. But he also wants to suggest that Domitian's monstrosity is out of his range ... Juvenal "fills out" this satire with epic bombast."[76]

Juvenal stretches his plate to fit the beast. His satire is more enraged and effusive than satire has ever been before. Clear enough. But just how hungry does he imagine we are? How large a fish can he reasonably expect us to swallow, especially when a six-pound red mullet is, by his own admission, a red herring, done up by those given to telling tall tales? His Domitianic turbot, by comparison, is the biggest fish story of all time, and terribly hard to take seriously. Can any emperor's "reign of terror" really have been that bad, horrid enough to deserve a punitive fish of that size, shoved so far up the offender's anus so long after his death? Or did the fish Juvenal "remembers" in this poem just get bigger with time, as fish, when they slip off the hook, tend to get, all the while that he sat brooding over the punishment that he intended to mete out?

The answers to these questions will depend, in large part, on the listener's own appetite for revenge, credibility always being a con-

[75] Gowers (1993a) 206–7.   [76] Gowers (1993a) 210.

dition of desire. That, ultimately, is what will determine whether we swallow this dish whole, impossible as that may seem, or whether we simply brush it aside as a fish story and only that, i.e. not revenge *per se*, but an overdone, unbelievable gorging on revenge.

But there exists a third way of hearing this tale, not simply as one or the other, but as a "revenge-performance" that straddles the poles of credible and incredible, thus leaving us poised, uncomfortably, in between. Taken this way, the fish story of Juv. 4 invites circumspection as its way of getting us inside ourselves, forcing us to consider some of the more overdone, hypocritical, and laughable extremes not just of Rome's post-traumatic feeding frenzy in the years just after Domitian's death, but of our own desire for those extremes. Appetites for revenge, at that time, we have seen, were generally quite large. Juvenal's appetite, seen in the measure of the rage he doles out to us, is the most voracious of them all. Thus, his primordial fish is not simply a dish once served up to a tyrant, if it ever really was. It is something that he, as satirist and dealer in plates and paper-wrapped fish, serves up to us, inviting us to "open wide," and thus to test the measure of our own desire for revenge, especially our desire to believe that Rome's "recent" past was really as recent, horrid, monstrous, and simple as so many in Rome were actively, and impossibly, claiming it was. Juvenal, with this poem, is out to find that point *in us* where revenge becomes tyrannical. Where we become Domitian, with an appetite (for *his* fish) that huge.

SATIRES 3 AND 5: THE POOR MAN'S LUNCH OF UMBRICIUS AND TREBIUS

Juvenal's fifth poem, the last in the book, lets us experience a rich man's feast to the book's bitter end, with no hasty, Horatian exit to save us, this time, from the host's sadistic abuse. For our dinner, a rotten apple and sewer-fed fish, all reeking of Canidia's cookshop. Still, we force it down with a grimace on our face, teeth tightly clenched, struggling to maintain our composure in the hopes of someday being considered "worthy" (*dignus*) of the real thing. The feast is described from the perspective of a tag-along client, the lowest man on the low couch. He is free-born, we are told, but poor, jaded, and tattered, barely "in" this feast at all.

If the feast-story is told from a higher perspective, he disappears altogether. Still, he clings to that last "free" seat as his last, desperate hold on freedom itself. It is his one last chance to count as a "free man" (*liber homo*, 161) in Rome, even though that seat entitles him to nothing more than bad food and abuse, along with the expectation that he play the comic, simian role that he has been invited to play. For his is the seat of parasites and buffoons, those washed-out Romans of free birth who were left to gossip, wheedle and jest for their evening meal.[77] Their gruff, tall tales of life in the streets, the stories behind their tattered clothes, black eyes, and ruptured shoes, become the evening's entertainment. The loser sings the blues. His sorrow, another man's comic show, earns him a crust of rock-hard bread, and a full portion of disgrace.

That is the main course at this feast. Not foods that entice and satisfy, but shame. The guest leaves the book a pale, poor man's shade of Horace's "stuffed dinner-guest" (*conuiua satur*), i.e. stuffed, but not satisfied, up to his eyes with rage and bile. "Still hungry?" the poet asks Trebius in this poem. "That bile welling up inside you any good?" But Trebius is not the expert on parasitism here. Juvenal is. He speaks to him as teacher to novice, telling him what it is like to have lived the life he knows so well, the very life that he has performed for us so entertainingly in the course of his first book. In the first poem we watched him take the top seat at Lucilius' grand, satiric feast, only to be told to move down two spaces, to the low seat on the low couch. He is not entitled to the same seat Lucilius had.[78] He is not the host at this feast, nor a guest of any distinction. He is a last-minute tag-along, here to keep things lively and entertaining, but not terribly meaningful. Like Trebius in Juv. 5, the poet himself hungers for the full, rich fare of satire, but he is not entitled to it. Thus, he cannot provide it to us. Instead, he is stuck with leavings and scraps that are a pale, parodic "shade" of satire's rich Lucilian feast. That, at least, is the scenario he paints, and the source of his famous *indignatio*.

---

[77] In contrast, Hor. *S.* 2.8 is told from the perspective not of the host's lowly client, but a friend of the guest of honor. Juvenal tells his story from the perspective of a Porcius or Nomentanus rather than a Fundanius.

[78] Henderson (1999) 270–1: "he will show why he must and, for the same reasons that he must, dare *not* attempt to play the Italian-Warrior-Hero-Staunch-Republican-Absolutely-Free-Blazing-Swash-Buckling-Sword-Wielding *Lucilius rediuiuus*. Yet *that* was the act he tried to conjure up for himself. How over-ambitious could you get?"

Thus he seethes, and his indignation becomes the show, the scraps of satire he leaves to us.

Scraps? Or are these poems the real feast, as full, rich, and meaningful as Roman satire ever got? Answer the question too quickly, or too decisively, and you will have stripped Juvenal's *Satires* of much of their power to question, trouble, and satirize. For it is a question that the poems themselves ask repeatedly without giving much purchase on a single, credible solution. That puts the onus on us. We answer the question. And our answers, inevitably, tell on us. Most obviously, they reveal the place we presume to take at the feast of Juvenal's *Satires*, and the seat cushion we set aside for Juvenal himself as satire's "host," "parasite," or "man in the middle" (e.g. "noble guest," or "ignoble host"). That activity of embedding ourselves, and Juvenal, into the feast he serves ultimately determines how we rate his satiric fare as either sumptuous, sickening, or just so-so.

The poems repeatedly pose the question of their own value, but they make us pay a price for answering it. For they let us see just how highly conditional, artificial, and unstable, the answers we give to it are, always uncannily "right" from one perspective, and "dead wrong" from another. For the fare served in Juvenal's first book, just as in the feast that concludes it, changes drastically from one seat to the next, ranging from "a poor man's hilarious griping" seen from the top seat, to "honest rage" seen from the bottom. We have all been invited to this feast. Question is, where do we presume to sit?

The question of the "feast or famine" of these poems is one that the poet leaves us to consider as we depart his first book. The questions he puts to Trebius ("Aren't you ashamed yet?" "Still haven't had enough?") might well be asked of us, his scrap-fed readers; or put, by us, to him. For these are questions that we have been forced to ask ourselves all along in reading his book, a work of dead serious rage that borders on idiotic bluster. Sometimes Juvenal even invites us to sample ways of seeing his performance and judging it, by embedding scenes that picture audiences looking upon and judging inset performances of the poor man's plight in Rome. And thus we are given one pauper's show inside another. The poor man's epic ecphrasis.

The most obvious case of this, outside of the fifth poem, comes at the midway point of Umbricius' tirade in Juv. 3, the middle poem of the book. This poem, whether centerpiece, or main course (as you like it), is the most elaborate performance of the poor man's woes in all of Juvenal. Thus, it is commonly regarded as his signature piece, "a classic and archetype."[79] Umbricius takes center stage in the poem. His name suggests both native, Italian rusticity (Umbria) and tag-along status (*umbra*), so he has the nominal look of someone who tried to make it in the big city, but failed. And that is exactly the story he tells of his washed-out life in the poem, making him the perfect stand-in for the poet himself.

Umbricius seethes over the scrappy life he has been forced to live in Rome. He claims to have been squeezed out onto the margins of a "free" existence by a massive influx of Greek freedmen and slaves. In his grand, epic imagination, Rome, like Priam's Troy, has been raided and plundered by an army of nefarious Greeks. He is a refugee of war, a poor man's Aeneas, setting off to find a new home for gods and family. Fittingly, his destination is Cumae, gateway to the underworld and home of Aeneas' Sibyl. Thus, the scenario he paints for his life is familiar, a parody of Rome's most patriotic myth.[80] But the emphasis here is not on the haggard warrior's trip to the south, his *Odyssey*, but on the battle he fought, and lost before setting out, his *Iliad*.

In Rome, he says in lines 147–51, the poor man's woes, evident in his stained toga, and shoes, split and stitched, are the "cause and substance of jokes" (*materiam ... causasque iocorum*, 147). The pauper is a comic spectacle, not that he ever intended to become an actor or play for laughs. And that, he says, is the harshest aspect of his life in the city (Juv. 3.152–3):

---

[79] Braund (1996) 230.

[80] The poem is also set up as a parody of Virgil's first Eclogue, where one friend is displaced from his rustic home, and another stays behind. On the poem as an urban eclogue, see Witke (1970) 128–34; and Braund (1996) 235–6. Cf. Calpurnius, *Eclogues* 4, for which Sullivan (1985) 52 provides the following précis: "Calpurnius begins by complaining that the Muses had been niggardly toward him and he had been about to emigrate (or return) to Spain when he had attracted the notice of 'Meliboeus' ... Whoever he was, 'Meliboeus' had helped him, and perhaps got him an official job in Rome." No Meliboeus steps in in Umbricius' case. Does that perhaps says something about imperial stinginess (the lack of the expected "Meliboeus," an Augustus or Nero) in the early days of Trajan's reign?

> nil habet infelix paupertas durius in se
> quam quod ridiculos homines facit.

There is nothing in luckless poverty harder to bear than that it makes men into buffoons.

Not only does the poor man suffer. His sufferings are ridiculed! Cruel and wrong as he makes that seem, we should be wary of placing blame with him, where he places it, too quickly. For that is what we have been doing all along in these poems: laughing at the loser. His failures and frustrations have been staged throughout the first book as a comic show playing on a tragic stage. The performance is extreme and parodic. But that "performance," he says, is his life. That is the way that he, a pauper, "plays" in downtown Rome: a hopeless parody of a "real Roman." He is someone who strives to become the real thing, but cannot, a spectacle of "poverty on the make" (*ambitiosa|paupertate*, 182–3).

    The man kicked from the theater's best seats in lines 154–8 thus symbolizes life for Umbricius in Rome. Like him, he has presumed to take a seat, and "belong" there, in Rome, only to be told that he is in the wrong spot, sitting in a seat of honor to which he is not entitled. Thus, he is summarily removed, shoved off to Cumae, as it were, and his red-faced removal becomes the show, the poem. That embarrassing little scuffle in the stands, Umbricius indicates, is where Rome's real drama plays, tragedy to the victim, but a comedy to everyone watching in the stands, especially to heartless snobs (like us).

    But there are other places, Umbricius continues, where the same poor man's show plays very differently, not as an uproarious parody of a "real life," but as the thing itself, and a serious show of frugality, contentment, and shared equality (Juv. 3.168–78):

> fictilibus cenare pudet, quod turpe negabis
> translatus subito ad Marsos mensamque Sabellam
> contentusque illic ueneto duroque cucullo.
> pars magna Italiae est, si uerum admittimus, in qua
> nemo togam sumit nisi mortuus. ipsa dierum
> festorum herboso colitur si quando theatro
> maiestas tandemque redit ad pulpita notum
> exodium, cum personae pallentis hiatum
> in gremio matris formidat rusticus infans,
> aequales habitus illic similesque uidebis
> orchestram et populum.

Feasting from clay dishes is embarrassing [in Rome]. But you will deny that it's shameful if suddenly transported among the Marsians or to a Sabine table. There you will be happy in a dark-blue hood. Truth be told, there is a huge part of Italy in which no one dons a toga unless he is dead. Even if a holiday's pomp is being observed in a grassy theater, and a well-known farce at last returns to the stage, when the peasant baby cowers in its mother's lap, afraid of the white mask's gaping mouth, you will notice that there everyone's dress is of the same status and alike, from front to back.

As in the feast of Juv. 5, here the value one assigns to the performance (again, less on the stage than it is in the stands) is a condition of the quality of one's seat. From the distant, cheap seats of the Italian countryside, the poor man's show looks admirable and pure. His dark-blue, hooded cloak, as Braund notes, was the outfit of a poor man on the Roman comic stage.[81] Thus, transported to the Italian countryside, he is all dressed up for pratfalls and laughs. But no one is laughing. This time no one notices "the show" in the seats. For this is a place where no one has money and everyone is poor and dresses alike, even on the most ceremonial of rustic holidays, when country folk crowd into the theater, taking whatever grassy seat they can find, in order to watch some hackneyed Italian farce. This is where Umbricius is headed: to his Shangri-la, a dreamworld that he is not likely to find. The Rome he runs from is equally extreme and unreal, the product of an enraged imagination.

But, if a note of cruelty is sounded by the urban spectator's laughter in taking the poor man's tragedy for comedy, a note of gullibility is sounded by the rustic audience's packing the theater for the most outmoded and hackneyed of slapstick routines, the local Italian farce, featuring Manducus, with his huge, clattering jaws.[82] The babe in arms watches the show and blanches with fear. For this, the most naïve member of the speaker's utopian audience, where everyone belongs and is eligible for whatever seat they can find (even young mothers and their children!), the reaction to slapstick is horror. Comedy is taken for tragedy.

Where do we place ourselves in these scenes? That is, how do we see ourselves watching *in* them, with one poor man's show, that

---

[81] Braund (1996) 203.

[82] On the *exodium* of line 175 referring to an Atellan farce, see Courtney (1980) 178–9.

of rustic farmers, playing inside another, Juvenal's own, the one
we have been watching all along? Do we laugh at his failures and
frustrations in the first book as if viewing a comic show, making
his pain into our entertainment? Dare we take such a cruel, comical view of the poor man's plight in Rome, and thus risk being
caught reclining in Virro's high seat, hosting his sadistic feast? Or
do we see his show as tragic and true, an honest man's honest
complaint about the way things "really are" in Juvenal's Rome?
That puts us in the cheap seats, back with the speaker himself,
dressed in his bumpkin blue, and sporting his ruptured shoes.
Dare we let ourselves slip that far down the social scale and
become, ourselves, that comically low and naïve?

In either case we, Juvenal's spectators, become the show. His
embedded scenes of spectation push us to consider our watching
of him. But these inset, diagnostic tools do not solve the problem
of who he is for us, or how we "should" react to him. They simply
put the question again, the same nagging question that we have
been forced to ask ourselves all along. And they invite us to embed
ourselves as either one kind of watcher or another, and thus both
to see and feel the drawbacks of choosing too glibly. For Juvenal's *Satires* show the ugly extremes of the several most obvious
roles (cultural icons/caricatures, discursively encoded) that "we
Romans" are most likely to play in reading these poems, whether
with him, by making him a tragic Cato and one of "us," or against
him, a comic parasite and the butt of our joke.

But the question that the fifth poem seems to ask more force-
fully, and problematically, than the third is not where do we place
ourselves at this culturally encoded feast, but where do we place
Juvenal, the second half of the same question. Is he really as
abused and indignant as he lets on? Or has he perhaps taken us
for fools by slipping into the high seat at this feast, that of the
cruel host whose greatest pleasure comes from watching *us* seethe
over the miserable dishes he serves to us in this, his five-course,
poor man's satire? The steady series of resemblances that connect
the poor man's fare in Juv. 5 to what Juvenal himself has served to
us in the poems that precede (and all that follow in books 2–3) are
uncanny enough (if we choose to take such things seriously) to
cause us to reconsider our place at his feast.

Trouble lurks, for example, in the wine that Trebius complains
of receiving as the feast commences. For that wine, we are told,

has a strange, transfigurative quality, the power to turn dinner guests into fanatics and figures of myth (*de conuiua Corybanta*, 25). The drunken haze it "inspires" blurs the lines between myth and reality, making the world look not just any way, but exactly the way *we* have been made to see it in the first book, through Juvenal's fanatical haze. Fittingly, this low-grade wine inspires a mock epic battle in lines 26–9. Meanwhile, Virro drinks deeply of a fine vintage from a far corner of his cellar, wine such as that drunk by the freedom-fighters, Thrasea and Helvidius on the respective birthdays of their tyrant-killing heroes, the Brutuses and Cassius. This is wine to inspire uncompromised, republican "freedom," and thus a very different kind of fight. But Juvenal is not entitled to it. He tells of desiring it, satire's pure nectar, but not being allowed to drink it. So he seethes, indignant. He deserves better. But, perhaps, so do we.

Symbols for satire, both teasing and obvious, are abundant in the poem. The most prominent and suggestive of these include the bejewelled cup from which Juvenal would love to drink, and perhaps to steal an epic stone or two (hasn't he been doing just that throughout the book?) in lines 37–45; the reference to his "riding" through the tombs of the Latin Way, thus matching his journey to our dead-man's tour in his out-of-date poems, in line 55; and the stale, rock-hard crusts of lines 67–9 that keep the complainer's Lucilian "molar" (*genuinus*) busy, without allowing any genuine "bite" (*quae genuinum agitent, non admittentia morsum*, 69).[83] All mouth-work, no bite. Is that just Juvenal's complaint? Or are we not perhaps justified to make the same complaint concerning our experience of reading him?

But the most potent symbol of *our* being served a substandard feast in these poems lurks in the rival fish courses of lines 80–106. The giant "lobster" (*squilla*) of line 81 is served on a large, ceremonial *lanx*, satire's most prominent symbol in the ancient world. Held aloft in the hands of Virro's fish-ministers, it looks down on the rest of the crowd, snubbing them with a swish of its glorious tail, more peacock than fish (*qua despiciat conuiua cauda*, 82). Desired from below, it is simply too glorious, costly, and noble to be eaten

---

[83] Besides remembering the cynic beggar of line 11 (*sordes farris mordere canini*), the image recalls programmatic descriptions of Lucilius as an "attacking dog" at P. 1.114–15 and Hor. *S.* 2.1.68–9. Here the image is used to symbolize not ferocity, but vain frustration. The poet's gnawing keeps his mouth busy, but he is unable to bite.

by the likes of the satirist. Seen from his angle, the fish is utterly
unattainable, "walled off on all sides" (*undique saepta*, 81) by a veritable palisade of asparagus. That is the way it looks from his
low seat, the seat he forces us to share with him: luscious, hotly
desired, unattainable. The speaker cannot have the full plate he
desires, so he seethes, indignant. To compound the insult, he is
served a "crayfish" (*cammarus*) squeezed onto a dish with half an
egg, "a funeral feast served on a puny plate" (*ponitur exigua feralis
cena patella*, 85). His plate is crammed full, in other words, but
miniscule, holding a second-rate, dead man's feast that is, by design,
a deliberate parody of the rich man's impressive *lanx*.

This last set of images poses the question of what we ourselves
presume to have been served in these poems. Have we been given
satire's full, rich plate, or a lowly, crammed saucer, a pale, parodic shadow of what our Lucilian desires demand? Are these poems
fit for the living, or for the dead, a late-arriving "funeral feast" to
complement Capito's self-serving eulogies, *seris sed ueris*? Here
again, what we think we have been served by these poems depends
on the seat we have presumed to take, the culturally encoded
space from which we view the scene. Which fish is ours? Virro's
lobster? Or the low complainer's crayfish? Did we desire the big
plate in these poems and not receive it? Or did we get it? Like
the expandable fish of Juv. 4, the book itself is fully as big, or as
pathetically small, as we make it. We get exactly what we deserve.

The meal's final fish course, third for Virro, second for his
low guest, is equally suggestive of the poet's cruelty *to us*. Virro is
served a magnificent "moray eel" (*muraena*), reminding us again
that this parting feast is, in fact, remade from Horace's final satire,
S. 2.8, the dinner party of Nasidienus which featured the same
epic fish. Virro's moray, like his jewel-encrusted cup in lines 37–
45, and the boar of lines 115–116, has an epic pedigree. A giant
"from Sicily's whirlpool" (*gurgite de Siculo*, 100), it was caught by an
adventurous fisherman who sailed straight into "the middle of
Charybdis" (*mediam ... Charybdim*, 102). The low guest, in his turn,
is served an eel more viper than fish, or a blotched Tiber river
bass, "home-bred slave of the river banks, fed fat on the city's
gushing sewer, and accustomed to go as far as the vault underneath the middle of the Subura" (105–6).

The guest desires the impressive, epic fish. His filthy bass parodies it, mocking that desire. Both feed in swirling waters, one in

epic Charybdis (*mediam ... Charybdim*), the other under the streets of Rome's **lowest** district (*mediae ... Suburae*), and thus a very low feeder. As Gowers points out, its foraging takes this fish not just anywhere, but to "a favourite seedy haunt of Roman satire," under the very streets where the satirist himself forages for vice.[84] It is thus an apt symbol for the book itself, a work fed fat on crime and urban corruption. Thus, the fish that the satirist complains of being served at the feast is a clever match for what he has served us all along. Unless, of course, we consider this book the real thing and not its pale, parodic shade, a noble, epic fish worthy of its plate, straight from the waters of Charybdis.

Braund notes at lines 107–13 that "The speaker interrupts the menu to attack the patron with increasing directness and rising indignation."[85] Just as in the dinner party of Nasidienus, the client's bile level rises as the feast nears its conclusion.[86] By line 159 it spills from his eyeballs – thus another "wrong humor" issuing from the eyes, this time in reference to the poet's own critical performance, his satire's "teary bile." With the pressure rising, we expect something to give. But it does not. In lines 120–4, Petronius' "carver" (*structor*) arrives to cut up Horace's fury-inducing "hares" (*lepores*).[87] His swashbuckling performance is the client's last straw, a spectacle orchestrated on his behalf "lest any cause of rage be lacking" (*ne qua indignatio desit*, 120). That *indignatio*, the anger that comes from his being treated "unworthily," is the energy behind the poet's voice, his muse. It makes him break out in a rage, he says in his first poem, but that is not what happens here at Virro's feast, and right at the point of highest pressure where we most expect it. For he follows his description of the "indignity" of the carver's show with a cautionary note to Trebius concerning his need to keep silent and not say what he wants so desperately to say (Juv. 5.125–31):

> duceris planta uelut ictus ab Hercule Cacus
> et ponere foris, si quid temptaueris umquam
> hiscere tamquam habeas tria nomina ...
>   ... plurima sunt quae
> non audent homines pertusa dicere laena.

---

[84] Gowers (1993a) 215 and 219.   [85] Braund (1996) 293.
[86] See above, chapter 1.   [87] See Petr. 36.2, and Hor. *S.* 2.8.89.

You'll be dragged by the heel and set outside, like Cacus after Hercules clubbed him, if you ever attempt to open wide like someone with three names ... there are plenty of things that men in moth-eaten cloaks dare not say.

Poor men in rags dare not "open wide" (*hiscere*) either to eat or to talk. Their meager food does not require it for eating. A nibble will do. Their low status does not allow it for speaking. Clearly, food and speech figure one another in these lines. The poet tells Trebius, "You are what you eat. You speak, and eat, whatever you are." It is a nasty, frustrating cycle, but one he is wrapped tightly inside as well, just as we are, because of him.

In good Roman fashion, apples end the feast. Virro's are suitably magnificent and pedigreed, like those grown in Homer's Phaeacia, or stolen from the Hesperides as Hercules' twelfth and final labor. But this is Juvenal's final labor as well, the last of his twelve epic dishes served to Virro in the course of the poem.[88] But the party is not over for the client. His apple is not to be taken home. It is to be consumed on-site as the last scene of the evening's comic show (Juv. 5.153–60):

> tu scabie frueris mali, quod in aggere rodit
> qui tegitur parma et galea metuensque flagelli
> discit ab hirsuta iaculum torquere capella.
> forsitan inpensae Virronem parcere credas.
> hoc agit, ut doleas; nam quae comoedia, mimus
> quis melior plorante gula? ergo omnia fiunt,
> si nescis, ut per lacrimas effundere bilem
> cogaris pressoque diu stridere molari.

You "enjoy" a blighted bit of apple like that gnawed atop a waste-pile by some creature in a shield and helmet, learning through fear of the whip to hurl a spear from a goat's hairy back. Perhaps you believe that Virro is holding back on his expenses. No, he does it to make you suffer! For what comedy or mime is better than your whining gullet? Therefore, just so you know, the whole thing has been set up to make bile gush from your tear-filled eyes, and to keep you clenching your teeth, and loudly seething.

Trebius' dessert is a rotted bit of trash, an apple fit for a performing monkey. That monkey, like the fish served as Trebius' main

---

[88] The count is that of Braund (1996) 307. Another note of finality is sounded in the same line with the phrase *sororibus Afris* (152), recalling the last line of Hor. *S.* 2.8 *serpentibus Afris*. As Gowers (1993a) 216 notes, Virro's fine dishes are thus (intertextually) "tainted under the surface."

course, forages for trash, and thus it bears a certain figurative resemblance to the satirist himself. But, more importantly, like the homunculus who shares its apple, the monkey is all dressed for a fight, a sideshow parody of a real warrior and knight, such as Lucilius. Without a horse to carry him into battle, he hurls insignificant sticks from a goat's shaggy back.

But, bad as that apple is, the client eats it. He is the performing monkey in this story, dressed up to play the part of someone he can never be: a real Roman. His tears and indignant rage, like the monkey's fake warfare, are a hilarious show of feckless rage, better than any mime act. Instead of letting out a menacing snarl, or lashing out with Lucilius' free-born *genuinus* ("molar"), the abused client swallows his rage "with molar clenched tight" (*presso . . . molari*, 160). He grinds his teeth, in other words. Even his tooth, a *molaris* (from *mola*, "grinding stone") is a parody of the real thing: instead of using it to express rage and "bite," he uses it (like Varius' laughter-stifling napkin at Hor. *S.* 2.8.63) to hold it all in.

Juvenal's tooth-grinding has been this book's entertainment all along, so it is easy enough to see him in these lines, seething with indignation for us one last time. But the last lines of the book throw significant doubt on who exactly has been duped by the feast, given to expect something grand, only to be served scraps. The speaker says (Juv. 5.166–173):

> spes bene cenandi uos decipit . . .
>   . . . inde parato
> intactoque omnes et stricto pane tacetis.
> ille sapit, qui te sic utitur. omnia ferre
> si potes, et debes. pulsandum uertice raso
> praebebis quandoque caput nec dura timebis
> flagra pati, his epulis et tali dignus amico.

You are deceived by hopes of a grand feast . . . and that is why all of you remain silent, with your bread poised and ready, untouched and unsheathed. That man who uses you this way is wise. If you are able to put up with it all, you deserve it. And someday you will offer him your head for slapping, shaved at the top, and you won't flinch at suffering even worse abuses. For you deserve feasts like this and that kind of friend.

Who is the deluded fool in these lines, and who the sadistic host? Surely he means Trebius! Or is the mysterious plural *omnes* ("all of you") of line 169 really big enough to include "me," his long-suffering reader, or anyone else who happens still to be reading at this point, dead set on sticking this book out to its bitter, teeth-clenching end? For, if we came to these poems expecting a veritable feast of open, uncompromised, "noble" Lucilian rage, generously apportioned on satire's stuffed plate, then we really were duped, deceived by our own high hopes. Those hopes were fed fat in Juv. 1, only to be deflated by the poem's end. And yet here we are, still holding our breadsticks at the ready, unsheathed, as if still expecting the main course, the big plate, to be passed our way. But the feast is over. The apples have been handed out. Our bread-swords, a pathetic parody of the sword wielded by "burning" Lucilius at Juv. 1.165 (*ense ... **stricto** Lucilius ardens*) remain "untouched," that is, "unbloodied."[89] The fight is over before it started, and those who came expecting that fight, with bread-swords drawn to indulge in that kind of noble feast, have seen their gravy trains pass them by. They are left to seethe in silence.

Now who resembles a monkey on a goat? Our wanting Juvenal to play Lucilius for us, waiting for him to deliver the goods, turns out to say as much about us as it does about him. Treated to the best he could manage, a sideshow routine, we end up looking like monkeys ourselves, compliant parasites on the bottom couch, still waiting for some real food to sink our teeth into. Why are we still here? Why did we allow ourselves to be treated this way? Dare we let this book, now that it is over, count as "satire," the full, rich feast, so as to leave contented, and full? Or do we admit that we are still hungry, and not at all pleased, enraged at what Juvenal has fobbed off on us in the course(s) of this sham-epic book and deigned to name "satire." Now who is indignant, and ready to burst out? Now who is *becoming Juvenal*?!

Whatever our reaction to the feast just served, Juvenal is quite sure that "someday" (*quandoque*) we will return for more of the same. And in coming back for more, we will have shown that we fully "deserve" the friend who treats us so shabbily (*tali **dignus** amico*, 173). The phrasing is ironic, deprogramming the book's signature *indignatio* in its very last line. For here, for the first and only time in the book, we are told that, despite our being abused so flagrantly, we have no just cause for feeling indignant. We are

---

[89] Braund (1996) 303 comments: "'bread' is the surprise final word where 'sword' (e.g. *ensis*) might be expected, after the three participles. *Intacto* is especially witty: a sword would be "untouched", i.e. unbloodied, before the fighting commenced; the bread is "untouched" because the clients have no gravy into which to dip it. The clients are like soldiers waiting to fight: this *cena* is a battle-field."

complicit in our own abuse, thus deserving what we get, as maso-chists to sadist. Thus, our seething must stop. And so it does. The book is over. Like it or not, "feast or famine," we have been per-fectly matched to the friend, and the book, we deserve. For if we leave this feast feeling indignant, quite sure that "we Romans" deserve better from our satire than this, something up-to-date, Lucilian, and expressive of *his* uncompromised freedom, then we have a soul-mate in Juvenal, a companion in our frustration. We seethe at him for serving us scraps. If, however, we feel that his monkey-on-a-goat routine is damn funny and good enough to count for satire, fully up to the level of *libertas* that suits us; or, even worse, if we somehow failed to notice that the fighter in Lucilius' battle gear was a monkey and not a real knight, and that his "noble steed" had stubby horns and a beard, then we got what we deserved. We have no dignity left to insult. No cause for *indignatio*. In either case, we get precisely the Juvenal we deserve. And he is right. We will return for more *of him*, just as he says, in book 2.

Works Cited

Adams, J. N. (1982) *The Latin Sexual Vocabulary*. Baltimore
Anderson, William S. (1963) "Pompey, His Friends, and the Literature of the First Century BC," University of California Publications in Classical Philology 19: 1–88
  (1982) *Essays in Roman Satire*. Princeton
Allen and Greenough (1888, repr. 1988) = J. B. Greenough, G. L. Kittredge, A. A. Howard, Benj. L. D'Oooge, eds. *New Latin Grammar* (Aristide D. Caratzas: New Rochelle, N.Y., 1988)
Armstrong, David (1986) "*Horatius Eques et Scriba: Satires* 1.7 and 2.7," *Transactions of the American Philological Association* 116: 255–88
Badian, Ernst (1972) "Ennius and His Friends," in O. Skutsch, ed. *Ennius*. Entretiens sur l'antiquité classique 17. Geneva: 149–99
Bakhtin, M. M. and Medvedev, P. N. (1985 [1928]) *The Formal Method in Literary Scholarship*, trans. A. Wehrle. Cambridge, Mass. and London
Barchiesi, Alessandro (1997) "Otto punti su una mappa dei naufragi," *MD* 39: 209–26
Barr, W. and Lee, G. (1987) *The Satires of Persius*. Liverpool
Bartsch, Shadi (1994) *Actors in the Audience*. Cambridge, Mass.
Bellandi, Franco (1980) *Etica diatribica e protesta sociale nelle Satire di Giovenale*. Bologna
  (1988) *Persio: Dai "Verba Togae" al solipsismo stilistico*. Bologna
Bentley, Richard (1869) *Q. Horatius Flaccus ex Recensione et cum Notis*. Berlin
Bernstein. M. A. (1987) "*O Totiens Seruus:* Saturnalia and Servitude in Augustan Rome," *Critical Inquiry* 13: 450–74
Bettini, Maurizio (1979) *Studi e note su Ennio*. Pisa
Bonner, S. F. (1949) *Roman Declamation in the Late Republic and Early Empire*. Liverpool
Bramble, J. C. (1974) *Persius and the Programmatic Satire*. Cambridge
Braund, S. (1988) *Beyond Anger: A Study of Juvenal's Third Book of Satires*. Cambridge
  (1992) "Juvenal – Misogynist or Misogamist?" *Journal of Roman Studies* 82: 71–86

(1995) "A Woman's Voice? – Laronia's Role in Juvenal Satire 2," in B. Levick and R. Hawley. eds. *Women in Antiquity*. London: 207–19

(1996) *Juvenal Satires Book I*. Cambridge

Brink, C. O. (1963) *Horace on Poetry: Prolegomena to the Literary Epistles*. Cambridge

(1982) *Horace on Poetry: Epistles Book II*. Cambridge

Brown, P. M. (1993) *Horace Satires I*. Warminster

Burton, R. W. B. (1962) *Pindar's Pythian Odes*. Oxford

Casaubon, Isaac (1605) *Auli Persii Flacci Satirarum Liber*, edited with additional commentary by Friedrich Duebner (1833). Leipzig

Christes, J. (1989) "Der frühe Lucilius und Horaz: Eine Entgegnung," *Hermes* 117: 321–6

Clayman, Dee (1980) *Callimachus' Iambi*. *Mnemosyne* Supplement 59. Leiden

Coffey, Michael (1976) *Roman Satire*. London

Connors, Catherine (1994) "Famous Last Words: Authorship and Death in the *Satyricon* and Neronian Rome," in Elsner–Masters (1994): 225–35

Conte, Gian Biagio (1994) *Latin Literature: A History*, trans. Joseph B. Solodow. Baltimore

(1996) *The Hidden Author*, trans. E. Fantham. Berkeley

Courtney, Edward (1980) *A Commentary on the Satires of Juvenal*. London

(1993) *The Fragmentary Latin Poets*. Oxford

Crook (1967) *The Law and Life of Rome*. London

Deremetz, Alain (1995) *Le Miroir des Muses: Poétiques de la Réflexivité à Rome*. Villeneuve d'Ascq (France)

Deroux, C. (1983) "Domitian, the King Fish and the Prodigies: A Reading of Juvenal's Fourth Satire," in C. Deroux, ed. *Studies in Latin Literature and Roman History*. Collection Latomus. Brussels: 283–98

Dessen, Cynthia (1968) *Iunctura Callidus Acri: A Study of Persius' Satires*. Illinois Studies in Language and Literature 59. Urbana

Desy, P. (1988) "La traversée de l'Apennin par Horace," *Latomus* 47: 620–5

DeWitt, Norman (1939) "Epicurean Doctrine in Horace," *Classical Philology* 34: 127–34

Dryden, John (1693) "Discourse Concerning the Original and Progress of Satire," in *Works* (1974), vol. 4, 3–90. Berkeley

Eden, P. T. (1984) *Seneca Apocolocyntosis*. Cambridge

Ehlers, W. (1985) "Das Iter Brundisinum des Horaz (Serm. 1, 5)," *Hermes* 113: 69–83

Elsner, Jas, and Masters, Jamie, eds. (1994) *Reflections of Nero*. London

Fedeli, Paolo (1994) *Q. Orazio Flacco: Le Opere II, Le Satire*. Rome

Fiske, George Converse (1909) "Lucilius and Persius," *Transactions of the American Philological Association* 40: 121–50

(1913) "Lucilius, the *Ars Poetica* of Horace, and Persius," *Harvard Studies in Classical Philology* 24: 1–36

(1920) *Lucilius and Horace: A Study in the Classical Theory of Imitation.* Madison

Fitzgerald, William (2000) *Slavery and the Roman Literary Imagination.* Cambridge

Fowler, Don (1990) "Deviant Focalisation in Virgil's *Aeneid,*" *Proceedings of the Cambridge Philological Society* 36: 42–63

(1997) "On the Shoulders of Giants: Intertextuality and Classical Studies," *MD* 39: 13–34

Fraenkel, Eduard (1957) *Horace.* Oxford

Freudenburg, Kirk (1993) *The Walking Muse: Horace on the Theory of Satire.* Princeton

(1995) "Canidia at the Feast of Nasidienus," *Transactions of the American Philological Association* 125: 215–19

(1996) "Verse-Technique and Moral Extremism in Two Satires of Horace (2.3 and 2.4)," *Classical Quarterly* n.s. 46.1: 196–206

Fugmann, Joachim (1992) "Nero oder Severus Alexander? Zur Datierung der Eklogen des Calpurnius Siculus," *Philologus* 136: 202–7

Gale, Monica (1994) *Myth and Poetry in Lucretius.* Cambridge

Gerhard, G. A. (1913) "Der Prolog des Persius," *Philologus* 72: 484–91

Giordano Rampioni, A. (1983) "Seneca tragico in Persio," *Orpheus* 4: 104–7

Glazewski, J. (1971) "*Plenus Vitae Conviva:* A Lucretian Concept in Horace's *Satires,*" *Classical Bulletin* 47: 85–8

Gold, Barbara (1987) *Literary Patronage in Greece and Rome.* Chapel Hill

Gowers, Emily (1993a) *The Loaded Table: Representations of Food in Roman Literature.* Oxford

(1993b) "Horace, *Satires* 1.5: An Inconsequential Journey," *Proceedings of the Cambridge Philological Society* 39: 48–66

(1994) "Persius and the Decoction of Nero," in Elsner–Masters (1994): 131–50

Gratwick, A. S. (1982) *The Cambridge History of Classical Literature,* Vol. II, Part 1: *The Early Republic.* Cambridge

Griffin, Miriam (1976) *Seneca, A Philosopher in Politics.* Oxford

(1984) *Nero: The End of a Dynasty.* London

Gruen, Eric (1992) *Culture and National Identity in Republican Rome.* Ithaca, N.Y.

Gsell, S. (1894) *Essai sur le règne de l'empereur Domitien.* Paris

Gunderson, Erik (2000) *Staging Masculinity: The Rhetoric of Performance in the Roman World.* Ann Arbor

Gurval, Robert (1995) *Actium and Augustus: The Politics and Emotions of Civil War.* Ann Arbor

Harvey, R. A. (1981) *A Commentary on Persius.* Leiden

Henderson, John (1992) "Persius' Didactic Satire: The Pupil as Teacher," *Ramus* 20: 123–48

(1993) "Be Alert (Your Country Needs Lerts): Horace, *Satires* 1.9," *Proceedings of the Cambridge Philological Society* 39: 67–93

(1994) "On Getting Rid of Kings: Horace, *Satire* 1.7," *CQ* 44: 146–70

(1995) "Pump up the Volume: Juvenal, *Satires* 1.1–21," *Proceedings of the Cambridge Philological Society* 41: 101–37

(1999) *Writing Down Rome: Satire, Comedy, and Other Offences in Latin Poetry.* Oxford

Hinds, Stephen (1998) *Allusion and Intertext: Dynamics of Appropriation in Roman Poetry.* Cambridge

Hooley, Dan (1991) "A Vexed Passage in Persius (6.51–52)," *Classical Journal* 87: 15–26

(1997) *The Knotted Thong.* Ann Arbor

Hopkinson, Neil (1988) *A Hellenistic Anthology.* Cambridge

Horsfall, Nicholas (1997) "Criteria for the Dating of Calpurnius Siculus," *Rivista di Filologia e di Istruzione Classica* 125: 166–96

Iser, Wolfgang (1978) *The Act of Reading. A Theory of Aesthetic Response.* Baltimore and London

Johnson, Barbara (1985) "Teaching Deconstructively," in G. D. Adkins and M. L. Johnson, eds. *Writing and Reading Differently: Deconstruction and the Teaching of Composition and Literature.* Lawrence, Kansas

Jones, Brian W. (1992) *The Emperor Domitian.* London and New York

Kennedy, Duncan (1989) review of Peter Knox, *Ovid's Metamorphoses and the Traditions of Augustan Poetry* (Cambridge 1986) and S. Hinds, *The Metamorphosis of Persephone* (Cambridge 1987), *Journal of Roman Studies* 79: 209–10

(1997) "Modern Receptions and their Interpretative Implications," in Martindale (1997): 38–55

Kerkhecker, Arnd (1999) *Callimachus' Book of Iambi.* Oxford

Kermode, Frank (1988) *History and Value.* Oxford

Kiessling, Adolf, and Heinze, Richard (1961) *Q. Horatius Flaccus, zweiter Teil: Satiren.* Berlin

Kinstrand, J. (1976) *Bion of Borysthenes.* Studia Graeca Upsaliensia 11. Uppsala

Kissel, W. (1990) *Aules Persius Flaccus Satiren.* Heidelberg

Knoche, Ulrich (1974) *Roman Satire* trans. E. Ramage. Bloomington and London

Korzeniewski, D. (1970) "Die erste Satire des Persius," in D. Korzeniewski, ed. *Die römische Satire*, 384–438. Darmstadt

(1971) *Hirtengedichte aus neronischer Zeit.* Darmstadt

Krenkel, Werner (1970) *Lucilius Satiren* (2 vols.). Leiden

La Penna, A. (1982) "Amplessi a singhiozzo interpretazione di Persio, *Sat.* 6, 72–73," *Maia* 34: 63–8

(1995) *Da Lucrezio a Persio.* Florence

Leeman, A. D. (1983) "Die Konsultierung des Trebatius: Statuslehre in

Horaz, *Serm.* 2.1," in P. Handel and W. Meid, eds. *Festschrift für Robert Muth*, 209–15. Innsbruck

Lejay, Paul (1966) *Œuvres d'Horace*. Paris

Lowrie, Michele (1997) *Horace's Narrative Odes*. Oxford

Macleane, George (1857) *Juvenalis et Persii Satirae*. London

Maltby, Robert (1991) *A Lexicon of Ancient Latin Etymologies*. Leeds

Martindale, Charles (1993) volume introduction in David Hopkins and Charles Martindale, eds. *Horace Made New*, 1–26. Cambridge

(1997) "The Classic of All Europe," in C. Martindale, ed. *The Cambridge Companion to Virgil*, 1–18. Cambridge

Marx, Friedrich (1904) *Lucilii Carminum Reliquiae* (2 vols.). Leipzig

Mazurek, Tadeusz (1997) "Self-Parody and the Law in Horace's *Satires* 1.9," *The Classical Journal* 93: 1–17

Mazzarino, S. (1968) "Aspetti di storia dell'Appia antica," *Helikon* 8: 174–96

McLaughlin, Thomas (1990) "Figurative Language" in Frank Lentricchia and Thomas McLaughlin, eds. *Critical Terms for Literary Study*. Chicago

Miller, John (1986) "Disclaiming Divine Inspiration: A Programmatic Pattern," *Wiener Studien* 99: 151–64

Morford, Mark (1984) *Persius*. Boston

Muecke, Frances (1993) *Horace Satires II*. Warminster

Mueller, Lucian (1891) *Q. Horati Flacci Sermonum et Epistularum Libri*. Vienna

Musurillo, H. (1954–55) "Horace's Journey to Brundisium – Fact or Fiction?," *Classical World* 48: 159–62

Nehamas, Alexander, and Woodruff, Paul (1989) *Plato: Symposium*. Indianapolis and Cambridge

Newman, John K. (1990) *Roman Catullus and the Modification of the Alexandrian Sensibility*. Hildesheim

Nilsson, Nils-Ola (1952) *Metrische Stildifferenzen in den Satiren des Horaz*. Uppsala

Oliensis, Ellen (1998a) *Horace and the Rhetoric of Authority*. Cambridge

(1998b) *"Ut arte emendaturus fortunam:* Horace, Nasidienus, and the Art of Satire," in T. Habinek and A. Schiesaro, eds. *The Roman Cultural Revolution*, 90–104. Cambridge

Palmer, Arthur (1955) *The Satires of Horace*. London

Pasoli, E. (1964) "Spunti di critica letteraria nella satira oraziana," *Convivium* 32: 449–78

Peterson, R. G. (1972–3) "The Unknown Self in the Fourth Satire of Persius," *Classical Journal* 68: 205–9

Powell, J. G. F. (1992) "Persius' First Satire: A Re-examination," in Tony Woodman and Jonathan Powell, eds. *Author and Audience in Latin Literature*. Cambridge: 150–72

Putnam, Michael (1995) "Pastoral Satire," *Arion*, Fall 1995 / Winter 1996: 303–16

Radke, G. (1989) "Topographische Betrachtungen zum Iter Brundisinum des Horaz," *RhM* 132: 54–72

Reckford, Kenneth (1962) "Studies in Persius," *Hermes* 90: 476–504
  (1997) "Horatius: the Man and the Hour," *American Journal of Philology* 118: 583–612
  (1998) "Reading the Sick Body: Decomposition and Morality in Persius' Third Satire," *Arethusa* 31: 337–54

Ricoeur, Paul (1984) *Time and Narrative*, trans. Kathleen McLaughlin and David Pellauer. Chicago
  (1991) *A Ricoeur Reader: Reflection and Imagination*, ed. M. J. Valdes. New York and London

Rudd, Niall (1966) *The Satires of Horace*. Cambridge
  (1986) *Themes in Roman Satire*. London
  (1989) *Horace Epistles Book II and the Epistle to the Pisones*. Cambridge

Rudd, Niall and Barr, William (1991) *Juvenal: The Satires*. Oxford

Rudich, Vasily (1993) *Political Dissidence Under Nero: The Price of Dissimulation*. London and New York

Sallmann, K. (1974) "Die seltsame Reise nach Brundisium. Aufbau und Deutung der Horazsatire 1, 5," in U. Reinhardt and K. Sallmann, eds. *Musa Iocosa: Arbeiten über Humor und Witz Komik und Komödie der Antike*, 179–206. Hildesheim

Schmidt, M. (1937) "Mitteilungen zu Hor. *Sat*. 2.8," *Philologisches Wochenschrift* 37/38: 1071–2

Scholz, U. (1986) "Der frühe Lucilius und Horaz," *Hermes* 114: 335–65

Schütz, H. (1881) *Q. Horatius Flaccus. Satiren*. Berlin

Scivoletto, Nino (1956) *Auli Persi Flacci Saturae*. Florence

Skutsch, Otto (1985) *The Annals of Q. Ennius*. Oxford

Steiner, G. (1992) *After Babel: Aspects of Language and Translation*, 2nd edn. London and New York

Sullivan, J. P. (1978) "Ass's Ears and *Attises*: Persius and Nero," *American Journal of Philology* 99: 159–70
  (1985) *Literature and Politics in the Age of Nero*. Ithaca, N.Y.

Syme, Ronald (1958) *Tacitus* (2 vols.). Oxford

Thomas, Richard (1988) *Virgil Georgics*, Vol. 2: *Books III–IV*. Cambridge

Townend, Gavin B. (1973) "The Literary Substrata to Juvenal's Satires," *Journal of Roman Studies* 63: 148–60

Turpin, William (1998) "The Epicurean Parasite: Horace, Satires 1.1–3," *Ramus* 27: 127–40

Van Rooy, C. A. (1965) *Studies in Classical Satire and Related Literary Theory*. Leiden
  (1973) "*Imitatio* of Vergil, *Eclogues* in Horace, *Satires* Book 1," *AClass* 16: 69–88

Warmington, B. H. (1969) *Nero, Reality and Legend*. London

Wehrle, W. T. (1992) *The Satiric Voice: Program, Form and Meaning in Persius and Juvenal*. Altertumswissenschaftliche Texte und Studien 23. Hildesheim

White, Peter (1972) Review of *Kommentar zur VI. Satire des A. Persius Flaccus*, by H. Beikircher. *Classical Philology* 67: 61

  (1978) "*Amicitia* and the Profession of Poetry in Early Imperial Rome," *Journal of Roman Studies* 68: 74–92

  (1993) *Promised Verse: Poets in the Society of Augustan Rome*. Cambridge, Mass., and London

Wilkinson, L. P. (1963) *Golden Latin Artistry*. Cambridge

Willcock, M. M. (1995) *Pindar, Victory Odes*. Cambridge

Wills, Jeffrey (1996) *Repetition in Latin Poetry: Figures of Allusion*. Oxford

Wimmel, Walter (1960) *Kallimachos im Rom. Hermes* Einzelschriften 16. Wiesbaden

Wingo, E. Otha (1972) *Latin Punctuation in the Classical Age*. Janua Linguarum, Series Practica 133. Paris

Wiseman, T. P. (1982) "Calpurnius Siculus and the Claudian Civil War," *Journal of Roman Studies* 72: 57–67

Witke, Charles (1970) *Latin Satire*. Leiden

Woodman, Tony (1988) "Contemporary History in the Classical World," in A. Seldon, ed. *Contemporary History: Practice and Method*. Oxford (Blackwell)

  (1992) "Nero's Alien Capital: Tacitus as Paradoxographer (*Annals* 15.36–7)," in Tony Woodman and Jonathan Powell, eds. *Author and Audience in Latin Literature*, 173–88. Cambridge

General index

Actium, battle of, 8, 75–7, 82–7, 98, 109
Agricola, *see* Tacitus
Agrippina, 128
Alcibiades, 189–91
allusion
  and genre, 34–40, 79–81,
  and irony, 94
  as taunt, 92 n. 120
  in Persius, 149–50, 159–62, 183–7, 199–
    200
ambitio, in Horace, 60–3, 68–71
Apollo, 173; *see also* Nero; Golden Age myth
Apollodorus, 55
Apulia, 38, 54, 60, 61 n. 77
Archilochus, 116–17, 138
Aristius, *see* Fuscus Aristius
Aristophanes, 18, 181
Aristotle, 6
Arria, 219
Atellan farce, 269
Augustus, 6, 8, 54, 75–7, 82–7, 96–8; and
    Ovid, 130; *see also* Nero
Aurulenus Rusticus, 220–3

Bacchus, 28 n. 18, 48
Baebius Massa, 214, 218, 231
Bakhtin, Mikhail, 131 n. 13
Balatro, 120–1, 122 n. 24, 179
Bartsch, S., 213–14
Bellandi, Franco, 11, 147 n. 37, 176
Bentley, Richard, 110
Bestius, 200
bile, and satire, 123, 273, 275; *see also* satire,
    "natural" theories of
Bion of Borysthenes, 16, 19, 23–4, 39
birds, symbolism of, 142–3
Bona Dea, 255
Bramble, J., 59 n. 73
Braund, S., 252, 259 n. 66, 267, 269, 273,
    274 n. 88, 276 n. 89
Brindisi, 24; "Peace of," 53, 56–7

Britannicus, Iohannes, 190
Brown, P. M., 71 n. 88
Brutus, 24, 219

Caesius Bassus, 128, 195–8
Caligula, 202
callida iunctura, 32, 128, 165
Callimachus
  and Horace, 4, 7, 37–40, 43, 44, 45, 46,
    52, 79
  and Nero, 156
  and Persius, 140–1, 174–5
Calpurnius Siculus, 156, 267 n. 80; date of,
    128 n. 10
Canidia, 8, 101
Capito, *see* Titinius Capito
carmen, 8–9, 114; *see also deductum carmen*;
    Horace, *Odes*; *mala carmina*
Cato the Censor, 18, 91
Cato the Younger, 221
Catullus
  and Horace, 26–7, 67 n. 85
  and iambic, 138
  and Persius, 206
Caudium, 55–6
Celsus, 182
censor, 20; as satiric metaphor, 17; *see also*
    Cato the Censor; Domitian, censorship
    of
Ceres, *see* harvest festival
Certus, 232–3
chariot-race, as compositional metaphor,
    42, 78–9
Choerilus of Samos, 42
choliambics, *see* Hipponax
Chrysippus, 29–30, 40, 207
Cicero, 50 n. 52, 249
city, the, and satire, 61–3, 246
Claudius, 128, 152, 219
Cleanthes, 9
Cleopatra, 86

cooking, symbolism of, 182; *see also* feast
comedy: New, 39, 116–17; Old, 17–18, 39, 49, 116–17, 181
compositio, 30–2, 175–6
conuictor, 103–4
conuiua satur, 33–4, 47, 118, 265
Conte, G. B., 33 n. 28
Cordus, 209–10, 212
Cornelia, 216–17
Courtney, E., 256, 260
Cratinus, 17, 20, 181
Cremutius Cordus, 219–20, 236 n. 50
Crispinus (A), in Horace, 20, 31, 40, 186
Crispinus (B), in Juvenal, 214, 259–61
Cucchiarelli, A., 52 n. 57, 54 n. 63, 59 n. 75
cynics/cynicism, *see* Bion of Borysthenes

Damasippus, 113–16
decoction, *see* medicine
deductum carmen, 37 n. 33, 245 n. 58
Demetrius, 69
Democritus, 11
Deremetz, A., 37 n. 33
diatribe, 7, 15–23, 33, 187–8; *see also* Bion of Borysthenes; Lucretius
dinner-guest, metaphor of, *see conuiua satur*
Diomedes, 138–9
Domitian, 13, ch. 3 *passim*
    and Agricola, 224
    censorship, 216, 252, 259
    death and aftermath of, 233 nn. 45–6, 237–8, 264
    literature under, 214
    reprisals of, 225 n. 29
drunkenness, and satire, 28 n. 18, 118, 270–1

ear, symbolism of, 171–2, 175 n. 97, 180–2
Ehlers, W., 53
Einsiedeln Eclogues, 156–7
Ennius, 1; and Horace, 25, 43, 87–92; and Persius, 150
epic: in Juvenal, 209–12, 240, 253–4, 261–2, 272–3; parodies of, 118, 211 n. 4, 261–2, 276
epicureanism, in Horace, 16–17, 22–3, 47, 53–4, 64–6, 68, 117, 120–1
epinician, *see* Pindar; panegyric
eques, 51, 59–60, 64
Erichthonius, 77–8
eulogy, *see* martyrs; Agricola
Eupolis, 17, 20, 116–17, 181, 255
eye, as metaphor, 163–5

Fabius, 32, 186
Fannia, 219, 221

Fannius (A), 20
Fannius (B), Gaius, 217
fautores Lucili, 18, 24, 44, 46, 104 n. 137; *see also* Crispinus; Demetrius; Fabius; Fannius; Hermogenes Tigellius; Pantilius; Valerius Cato
feast, as symbol of satire, 44–7, 265–6; *see also* harvest festival; *lanx satura*
Fedeli, P., 53 n. 60
Feeney, D. C., 212 n. 5
fines, 27, 30–1, 34, 46, 48, 51, 57–8
fish: as punishment, 260–1; as poetry, 258–64, 271–2
Fiske, G., 38 n. 34
Flaccus, 48, 66, 93–4, 96–7, 176, 179
Flavian emperors, 13; satire under, 214 n. 7
Florus, 201
Fowler, D., 33 n. 28, 43 n. 46
Fraenkel, E., 73 n. 89, 109
Fronto, 209–10, 238 n. 53
Fundanius, 117–18
Fuscus Aristius, 65, 66

Gallus, Cornelius, 36, 40
genus, 24, 48–9
genre: and memory, 32–3, 33 n. 28, 34–44, 129; and status, 58–62; the politics of, 74
Gibbon, Edward, 53 n. 60
goats, as poetic symbol, 41 n. 41
Golden Age myth, under Nero, 9–10, 143
Gowers, E., 54 n. 65, 55, 56 n. 69, 173, 263, 273
Griffin, M., 128 n. 9, 155–6
Gruen, E., 48 n. 51, 96 n. 123
Gsell, S., 216 n. 9
Gunderson, E., 164 n. 73

Hadrian, 11
harvest festival, as symbol of satire, 28 n. 18, 45
Helvidii, the, 211 n. 4, 220–1, 232–3, 271
Henderson, J., 6, 41 n. 41, 42, 78, 133, 146 n. 34, 176 n. 102, 210, 265 n. 78
Hercules, 274
Hermogenes Tigellius, 20, 69
Herennius Senecio, 221–3
Hipponax, 138
historiography, 256–7
Homer, *see* Trojan myth
Hooley, D., 148 n. 38, 150, 151 n. 46, 162, 184 n. 121, 189 n. 125, 196, 198–9
Horace
    "discretion", 109
    Epodes, 139
    friends, 67–70, 103–4

Odes, 38, 39, 114, 128, 196
Sermones, 1–8, ch. 1 *passim*
status, 48–51
see also Flaccus; irony; Persius
horses, as epic metaphor, 59–61, 64, 96–7;
   see also eques

Ilias Latina, 155
incessus, 61–2
indignation, *see* Juvenal
intertextuality, *see* allusion
irony, 121–2, 179
Iser, W., 6
iunctura acris, 128, 137, 163–6, 175–6, 203–5;
   see also compositio

Johnson, B., 236
Julia, 252
Julio-Claudian emperors, 13
Juvenal, 1, 4, 5, 6, 10–14, 42–3, 48, 59,
   ch. 3 *passim*
   hyperbole in, 242, 248–52
   indignation of, 214, 242, 265–6, 275–7
   revenge in, 214
   time warp in, 212–15, 234–42
   see also epic

Kennedy, D., 131 n. 12
Kermode, F., 131 n. 14
Kiessling, A. and Heinze, R., 51 n. 53
Kissel, W., 186 n. 122, 190 n. 127
Korzeniewski, D., 157 n. 61

Labeo, 154–5, 158
Laelius, 102
land-confiscations, 54, 98–9
lanx satura, 1, 28, 45, 124, 263
La Penna, A., 149 n. 41, 165 n. 75, 169 n.
   84, 172 n. 89
Laronia, 252–3
Latinus, 214
Leeman, A. D., 74 n. 91
Lejay, P., 51 n. 54
libellus, 26–7, 67 n. 85
Liber, *see* Bacchus
libertas, 3–4, 28 n. 18, 48, 49, 50, 51
Licinianus, 216–17
limits, *see fines*
liquids (phonetic), 6, 177, 183
Lucan, 128, 155
Lucilius, Gaius
   and Ennius, 89–92
   and Horace, ch. 1 *passim*, 23–7, 49–52,
      59–63, 75–6, 100
   and iambic poetry, 138–40
   and Juvenal, 243–6, 265, 275–6

and Persius, 149, 151–2, 164–5, 177
influence, 1–11
friends, 19–20, 101–2
enemies, 20, 101–2, 178–9, 243–4
Lucius Silanus, 225
Lucretius, 9, 16–17, 27, 33–4, 38, 40, 42, 54
   nn. 61 and 65
Lupus, 20, 152, 179 n. 109

Macrinus, 183–4
Macrobius, 89
Maecenas, 7, 8, ch. 1 *passim*, 119–20; and
   Macrinus, 185
mala carmina, 104–5, 138–9
Marius Priscus, 238 n. 53
Martial, 214
Martindale, C., 43 n. 47
martyrs: criminal charges against, 211 n. 4,
   220–2; eulogies of, 215–34
Massa, *see* Baebius Massa
Mazurek, T., 66 n. 82
McLaughlin, T., 165
medicine, and didactic, 182
Menander, 116
Messalla, 67, 68, 70, 186
metaphor, 5
   and torture, 245
   in Persius, 163–6, 203–5
   in Juvenal, 247
metrics, problems of, 90 nn. 115–16, 91 n.
   19, 98 nn. 128–9
Mettius Carus, 214, 219
Midas, 175, 180
mime, 66, 70, 71 n. 88
Morford, M., 128 n. 8
Mucius, 179 n. 109, 243–4
Muecke, F., 51 n. 54, 87, 94
mules, symbolism of, 58–9, 64, 96–7

narrative, problems of: in Horace 22, 72–3,
   110–13; in Persius, 125–31
Nasidienus, 117–22, 179, 272
neotericism, *see* Callimachus
New Criticism, 6
Nero, 9–10
   and Domitian, 218 n. 13
   and Golden Age myth, 126–7, 143–4,
      170
   and Troy, 154–8
   as target of satire, 126, 145–6, 169–71,
      177, 190–5
   Augustanism, 128–9
   lyric performances of, 157, 168–72, 177
   victims, 217–18
nota, 17
nugae, 26, 64

Octavian, *see* Augustus
Octavius, 67
Oliensis, E., 21, 41 n. 39, 94 n. 121, 179 n. 110
orgasm, 163–5, 254–5
Otho, 256–7
Oxford Latin Dictionary, 49

Palatine, 9; as Parnassus, 135 nn. 17–18, 147 n. 36
panegyric, 78, 87–92, 97–8
Pantilius, 69
pantomime, 254–5
parabasis, 17
parasites, 6–7, 22–3, 47–8
Parnassus, 134–6; Palatine as, 135 nn. 17–18
Parthians, 82–7
penis: talking, 19 n. 4, 205 n. 146; weeping, 164–5, 203–5
Persius, 1, 4, 5, 9–10, 51, ch. 2 *passim*
   and Callimachus, 140–1, 174
   and Horace, 149–50, 159–62, 163–6, 174–6, 179 n. 110, 183–7, 196, 199–200
   difficulty, 131–2
   readership, 132, 153–4
   see also iunctura acris; metaphor; Nero; Stoicism
persona, 22
Petronius, 155
philhellenism, 152–3
pile
   as Hellenistic title, 25
   as metaphor for satire, 150, 186–8, 199, 207–8
   as Stoic paradox, 28–9, 42, 43, 199, 207–8
Pindar, 9, 43, 79, 97–8
Pisonian Conspiracy, 218
Plato, influence of: in Horace, 24, 110–13, 117–18; in Persius, 183, 189
Pliny the Younger, 13, 215–34 *passim*
   and Tacitus, 221 n. 20
   his defense of Helvidius, 232–3
   Letters, 216–19
   political career, 229–30
Pollio, 67, 68, 70
Polydamas, 154–5, 158 n. 64, 181
Porphyrion, 51, 93
Posidippus, 29
Powell, J., 164 n. 74
Priapus, 24
princeps senatus, 20
Propertius, 86
Ptolemies, and Nero, 143 n. 29

Pseudacron, 102–3
Putnam, M., 35–6, 38, 40, 41

quadriuium, 246

Reckford, K., 173
recitation, 167 n. 77, 168–72
Ricoeur, P., 131 n. 12, 165 n. 75
river, as compositional metaphor, 31, 45–6
Rudd, N., 74 n. 90
Rusticus, *see* Aurulenus Rusticus

satire: etymology of, 1, 15–16, 25, 28 n. 18; "natural" theories of, 46 n. 49, 47, 159 n. 65
satis, 15–16, 27, 30, 32, 36, 42
satur, 30, 32, 36, 42, 47, 119; *see also conuiua satur*; *lanx satura*
Saturnalia, 114
satyrs, as symbol of satire, 28 n. 18
Scipio (Africanus the Elder), 87, 91, 92–3
Scipio (Africanus the Younger), 19, 87, 92–3, 102 n. 135
Sejanus, 12
semipaganus, 147–8, 150 n. 45
Seneca, 128
   and Persius, 190
   and Trojan myth, 155
   Apocolocyntosis, 152, 261 n. 68
Senecio, *see* Herennius Senecio
sermo, 2, 7, 24, 112, 115, 193
Servius, 88–9, 152 n. 47, 156 n. 60
ships, as epic metaphor, 59 nn. 73–5
Silanus, *see* Lucius Silanus
skeptics/skepticism, 29
skin, symbolism of, 172 n. 90
Socrates: in Horace, 110–12; in Persius, 189–91
sorites paradox, *see* pile
Statius, 214; *De Bello Germanico*, 262
Steiner, G., 42 n. 47
Stoicism
   and poetic theory, 176 n. 101
   in Horace, 16, 18, 46 n. 49, 119
   in Persius, 4, 10, 29–31, 146 n. 34, 173, 176, 186–8
   under Domitian, 220–1
   see also suicide
Suetonius, 221
suicide, 218; and Stoicism, 220 n. 17, 225
Sullivan, J. P., 126 n. 3, 155 n. 54, 156 n. 59, 157, 169, 267 n. 80
Syme, R., 219 n. 15, 229 n. 38, 230
sword, as symbol of satire, 11, 243, 276

Tacitus, 13, 215–34 *passim*
  Agricola, 221–5
  and Pliny, 221 n. 20
  Annals, 215 n. 8, 220
  Histories, 215 n. 8, 216 n. 10, 222
  in Juvenal, 256–7
  political career, 230–1
Tantalus, 7
Tarentum, 60, "Peace of," 53 n. 59, 56–7
teeth, symbolism of, 109–10, 179, 271, 275
Thomas, R., 79, 82 n. 104
Thrasea Paetus, 220–1, 271
Tiberius, 12, 219–20
Tigellius, *see* Hermogenes Tigellius
Tigillinus, 244–5
time warp, *see* Juvenal
Timon of Phlius, 142
Titinius Capito, 225–8, 237, 272
Trajan, 11, ch. 3 *passim*; literature under, 267 n. 80
Trebatius, 8, 50–87 *passim*, 105–6
Trebius, 265–6, 273–5

Trojan myth, 154–7, 173–4, 180–1
Turpin, W., 22
Twelve Tables, 106–7

ubertas, 41 n. 42, 42
umbra, 120
Umbricius, 267–8

Valerius Cato, 67
Valerius Flaccus, 210–12
Varius, 63, 67, 120
Venusia, 54
Vestal Virgins, 216–17, 259
Virgil, 8; in Horace's *Sermones*, 27, 35–8, 40–2, 68–9, 77–82; in Juvenal, 267 n. 80
Virro, 270–2

wet-dream, 24, 54 n. 65, 164 n. 72
White, P., 196 n. 135
Woodman, A. J., 143 n. 29, 231 n. 42